ALIEN TO CITIZEN

ALIEN TO CITIZEN

Settling migrants in Australia, 1945–75

Ann-Mari Jordens

Allen & Unwin
published in association with
the Australian Archives

To my newest Australians, Ruby, Rosalee, Clare and Joshua who were all born after this book was conceived.

Copyright © Ann-Mari Jordens 1997

Published in association with the Australian Archives

All rights reserved. No part of this book may be reproduced or transmitted in any form or by any means, electronic or mechanical, including photocopying, recording or by any information storage and retrieval system, without prior permission in writing from the publisher.

First published in 1997 by
Allen & Unwin
9 Atchison Street
St Leonards NSW 2065
Australia
Phone: (61 2) 9901 4088
Fax: (61 2) 9906 2218
E-mail: frontdesk@allen-unwin.com.au
URL: http://www.allen-unwin.com.au

National Library of Australia
Cataloguing-in-Publication entry:

Jordens, Ann-Mari, 1945– .
  Alien to citizen: settling migrants in Australia, 1945–75.

  Bibliography.
  Includes index.
  ISBN 1 86448 422 5.

  1. Australia. Dept. of Immigration. 2. Immigrants—Services for—Australia—History. 3. Immigrants—Government policy—Australia—History—20th century. I. Australian Archives. II. Title.

362.840086910994

Set in 10/12 pt Trump Mediaeval by DOCUPRO, Sydney
Printed and bound by Ligare Pty Ltd, Sydney

10 9 8 7 6 5 4 3 2 1

Foreword

IMMIGRATION and concepts of multiculturalism have been perennial issues of discussion in Australia. They generate considerable debate because of their powerful ability to influence the cultural shape of the place we call home.

In *Alien to Citizen*, Ann-Mari Jordens uses the immigration records held by the Australian Archives to meticulously document one of our greatest achievements this century—the harmonious assimilation into our population of over three million migrants and their families from a diverse range of cultures.

It is appropriate that *Alien to Citizen* is being published in 1997, the fiftieth anniversary of the signing of Australia's agreement with the International Refugee Organisation, and the arrival from Europe's post-war refugee camps of large numbers of non-British migrants.

Through Ann-Mari's book, we can begin to understand the previously unexplored story of the successes and failures of the Department of Immigration. She refutes the view that governments from 1947 to 1975 did little or nothing to assist non-British migrants to settle in Australia and reveals evidence of the department's vital role in the process.

That these records of a crucial period in Australia's history survived for us to interpret today is testament to the work of our first Commonwealth archivists. People like Ian Maclean who battled the post-war 'slash and burn' mentality of many government departments have left us a legacy of national importance.

Australian Archives is pleased to have been involved both in providing raw material to the author and working again with publisher Allen & Unwin.

George Nichols
Director-General, Australian Archives

Contents

Foreword v
Acknowledgements x
Abbreviations xiii

1 The role of the Department of Immigration in migrant settlement 1945–75   1
   Constructing trust and obtaining compliance   5
   The historical context of settlement planning   8
   Academic writings on the Department of Immigration's role in migrant settlement 1966–95   20

2 The two faces of the Department of Immigration: social workers and selectors   31
   The formation and role of the Social Welfare Section 1948–52   32
   Discrimination against southern Europeans by Departmental selectors   48

3 Non-compliant women in Holding Centres   60
   Married women   62
   Unmarried mothers and widows   64
   Towards a structural solution   66

4 Marginalised migrants: the mentally ill and aliens in
   rural areas   73
   Mentally ill aliens 1950–72   74
   Aliens in rural areas 1947–56   80

5 Communicating with migrants: teaching English to
   adults and children   95
   The cultural context   96
   The Adult Migrant Education Scheme   98
   The debate about advanced English: needs vs *costs*   103
   The diversification of the Adult Migrant
      Education Scheme 1960–75   107
   Cultural change and political embarrassment   112
   English-language training for migrant children   115

6 Towards access and equity: interpreting and
   translating services   123
   The Department of Immigration's interpreting
      services   124
   Interpreting and the provision of information in
      translation by other agencies   126
   Pressure for interpreting services for migrants   126
   The Department of Immigration's translation
      functions   128
   Interpreting and translating under Labor 1973–75   138

7 From assimilation to integration   147
   The Department of Immigration's role in
      assimilation   148
   The declining role of Departmental social
      workers 1959–67   151
   Integrating national groups 1964–72   152
   The revival of Departmental social and welfare
      workers 1968   160
   The National Groups Liaison Unit   162
   The decline of the Good Neighbour Movement   165

8 Promoting Australian citizenship   171
   Administrative responses to alien
      non-compliance 1952–73   175
   Disseminating information and promoting
      citizenship   180
   Reduced incentives to take up citizenship from
      1965   185
   The Immigration (Education) Act 1971   187

9 Towards a more equal citizenship 'bargain'   189
   British migrants and Australian citizenship 1949–73   *191*
   Removing the unassimilable 1950–69   *194*
   Awareness of, and responses to, the improved bargaining position of aliens from 1965   *203*

10 The role of the Department of Immigration in eroding the 'white Australia policy'   209
   Internal and external pressure for reform   *210*
   'Mixed-race' migration 1964   *215*
   The admission of skilled non-Europeans 1966   *216*
   'White Australia' and the Labor Party 1971–75   *221*

11 The Department of Immigration under Labor 1972–75   226
   Cultural change: redefining Australian national identity   *227*
   Legislative change: removing discrimination   *228*
   Administrative change: enlisting ethnic communities   *229*
   Devolution of migrant services 1973–74   *230*
   Disseminating the vision to Australians   *233*
   The dismemberment of the Department of Immigration 1974   *238*

12 Immigration, citizenship and settlement: goals, achievements, and unintended consequences 1945–75   242
   Immigration   *242*
   Citizenship   *244*
   Settlement   *245*

Appendix: Australian Archives records of post-war immigration   249
Notes   254
Bibliography   292
Index   301

Acknowledgements

THIS book demonstrates the immense value of the archives of the Department of Immigration to historians of social, cultural and administrative change in post-war Australia. The archival research on which it is largely based was made possible by the grant of a research fellowship by the Australian National University's Research School of Social Sciences, over a fifteen-month period in 1992–93. I benefited greatly from participation in the School's Administration, Compliance and Governability Program under Professor Patrick Troy, Director of the Urban Research Program, and I am most grateful for his support and encouragement. I also wish to thank Margaret Levi, Professor of Political Science at the University of Washington, Seattle, an influential participant in the Program's annual workshops, whose writings on compliance and citizenship gave my work its focus. I was greatly assisted in my research into archival and parliamentary sources by Janine Bush, on whose accuracy, meticulous attention to detail and sheer staying power I could always rely.

I am also grateful for the support of the Department of Immigration and Multicultural Affairs, particularly for granting me special access under the *Archives Act* to its files to 1975. The insight I gained into the processes of bureaucratic decision-making during the period 1989–96, when I worked as an administrator in that Department, helped me considerably in my other role as historian. I wish to thank the many colleagues who showed interest in this work and offered helpful suggestions. Marisa Vearing, Director of the Department's library, and her staff always provided cheerful assistance. Most of the illustrations in this book are from that library's extensive collection of photographs. I hope that my book will help to increase awareness, both within and outside that Department, of the important role it played in settling migrants during the first 30 years of the post-war migration program and of the need to preserve its archives.

One of the most enjoyable tasks I undertook in researching this book was to interview former officers of the Department and others who had played an important role in migrant settlement during this period. They generously gave me their time and their comments on relevant draft chapters. I am greatly indebted to former social workers Nancy Anderson, Stephanie Charlesworth (née Armstrong), Pauline Griffin, Sylvia Lyons, Peter Rice, Nora Sebesfi (née Brack) and John Tarbath; Stan Flaherty, formerly of the Citizenship Section, and Andy Kyburz who is still there; James Houston, founder of the National Groups Survey; George Pridannikoff, who established the Telephone Interpreter Service in Brisbane; and G.C. Watson and Harold Grant, whose careers in the Department spanned the period I researched. Arthur Marshman, former Director of the State Migration Office, Queensland, added to my understanding of Commonwealth–State collaboration in settling migrants. I also wish to thank Professor Charles Price of the Australian National University, whose demographic research has assisted the Department since its inception, for his comments on early draft material, and Dr James Jupp, head of that university's Centre for Immigration and Multicultural Studies, for his views on chapter 1. I cannot thank enough my husband Jos——my very own post-war alien—for his help in every possible way, but particularly for his proofreading skills in what is, in fact, his third language.

I thank Australian Archives for co-publishing this book: Helen Nosworthy, its National Director of Public Programs; Maggie Shapley, its Publications Manager; Emma Mulcahy, and the unfailingly helpful staff in its reading room. I hope this book will encourage others to further explore the goldmine for researchers of Australia's migration history which the Archives guards and preserves. While my research used only the records of the Department of Immigration's Central Office, held in the

Australian Capital Territory repository of Australian Archives, I feel that research into the material it holds in other States would add greater complexity to the picture presented here, by showing how the experiences of migrants and of those responsible for helping them settle varied throughout Australia.

Abbreviations

AA	Australian Archives
ABC	Australian Broadcasting Commission
ACFOA	Australian Council for Overseas Aid
ACOSS	Australian Council of Social Services
ACT	Australian Capital Territory
AGPS	Australian Government Publishing Service
ALP	Australian Labor Party
AMES	Adult Migrant Education Scheme
CES	Commonwealth Employment Service
CMO	Commonwealth Migration Officer
COPQ	Committee on Overseas Professional Qualifications
CP	Country Party
CPDHR	Commonwealth Parliamentary Debates, House of Representatives
CPDS	Commonwealth Parliamentary Debates, Senate
CWA	Country Women's Association
DES	Department of Education and Science
DIMA	Department of Immigration and Multicultural Affairs
DLI	Department of Labor and Immigration
DLNS	Department of Labour and National Service
DSS	Department of Social Security
EEC	European Economic Community

ESL	English as a Second Language
ETIS	Emergency Telephone Interpreter Service
IAC	Immigration Advisory Council
ICEM	Intergovernmental Committee on European Migration
ILO	International Labour Organisation
IRO	International Refugee Organisation
NCSW	National Commission on Social Welfare
NSW	New South Wales
PICMME	Provisional Intergovernmental Committee for the Movement of Migrants from Europe
QLD	Queensland
RSSAILA	Returned Soldiers', Sailors' and Airmen's Imperial League of Australia
SA	South Australia
SEATO	South-East Asia Treaty Organisation
SMH	*Sydney Morning Herald*
TAS	Tasmania
TIS	Telephone Interpreter Service
UNESCO	United Nations Educational, Scientific and Cultural Organisation
VIC	Victoria
WA	Western Australia
YWCA	Young Women's Christian Association

CHAPTER 1

The role of the Department of Immigration in migrant settlement 1945–75

THIS book focuses on the intervention of the Australian government in the post-arrival experiences of immigrants, assessing the changing responses of the Department of Immigration to the settlement needs of migrants during the first 30 years of its existence. It is an account of cultural change in response to cultural diversity within the government agency which, for most of this period, was seen to be solely responsible for the social and economic absorption of migrants.

It takes up the challenge extended in 1972 by the demographer W.D. Borrie, chairman of the National Population Inquiry, to the sociologist Jean Martin, who was asked to 'attempt an overview of the response of Australian institutions to changes in the population brought about by the immigration programme pursued since the end of the Second World War'. While Martin examined in admirable detail the institutional responses of State governments to the needs of migrants in the areas of education and health, and of the non-government area in relation to the response of the unions, she gave scant attention to the role of the Commonwealth government. Nevertheless, she damned its response to the migrant presence in general as being characterised by 'abysmal indifference and neglect', and described the efforts of the Department of Immigration in the areas for which she believed it was responsible—migrant education and welfare—as 'limited and tardy'.¹

There are good reasons why the responses of the Department of Immigration to the settlement needs of migrants were largely invisible to Martin and to the small group of academics who worked with her. The most important source of information on its activities since its foundation in 1945—its files—were inaccessible to researchers under the rule restricting access to government archives until 30 years after their creation. Although a diligent researcher could have gleaned considerable information on the Department's settlement role from its quarterly statistical bulletins and annual reports to Parliament, it did not make such information easily accessible to the public until 1976, when it published its first annual report. (As chapter 11 indicates, the Department took little interest in its own history.)

From the perspective of more than 50 years, a close examination of the policy files of the Department of Immigration to 1975, in which its responses to a wide range of settlement needs are recorded, reveals that its ability to assist was undoubtedly extremely limited. No single government department could have met the many needs of such a large and culturally diverse migrant intake. Given the lack of support it received from other Commonwealth agencies, from State and local governments and from most non-government institutions, however, its responses were far from 'tardy' and in some areas were astonishingly innovative.

The decision to initiate a program of mass immigration was announced in Parliament by the first Minister for Immigration, Arthur Calwell, on 2 August 1945, and the Department of Immigration was established on 13 July that year. It was given three distinct functions. It became responsible for administering the Commonwealth's power under the Constitution [s. 51(xxviii)] over immigration and emigration, and also its power [s. 51(xix)] over the processes by which an alien becomes an Australian national. The former became legislation as the *Migration Act* in 1958, the latter as the *Nationality and Citizenship Act* in 1948. The third responsibility of the Department of Immigration—that for the reception of migrants in Australia and their absorption into the community—did not have a legislative base but clearly flowed from the intention of all governments during this period that migrants be absorbed into the Australian community and become citizens as quickly as possible. As chapter 8 indicates, for most of this period the acceptance of

Australian citizenship by aliens was seen as the only quantifiable indicator of the government's success in settling migrants—as the endpoint of the settlement process. The settlement role of the Department of Immigration was first spelled out at a meeting of the Permanent Heads of the Departments of Immigration and Labour and National Service at a meeting on 5 July 1951, during which they defined their departments' respective roles in relation to migrants.[2]

Until 1964 the Department of Immigration used the term 'assimilation' to refer to this process of social absorption. This term not only reflected the government's desire to retain migrants as permanent settlers—it reflected its perception of the homogeneity of Australia as a nation of essentially British culture and ethnicity. On arrival, migrants were expected to adopt the language and culture of mainstream Australia and abandon their own. The activities of all three areas of the Department—migration, citizenship and settlement—were influenced by this culturally determined imperative. Migrants considered to be unassimilable into the imagined community of Australians, notably non-Europeans, were effectively excluded by means of a dictation test under what was generally known as the 'white Australia policy'. As chapter 2 indicates, these racist attitudes also affected the selection of southern European migrants. While some non-Europeans were admitted at the discretion of the Minister before the 'white Australia policy' was effectively abandoned in 1966, they were until 1956 ineligible to apply for Australian citizenship. After that, they needed to have lived fifteen years in Australia (instead of the usual five) in order to be eligible to apply for citizenship. Indigenous Australians, who were neither British in culture nor ethnicity, became Australian citizens in 1949 like all other British subjects in Australia. The Australian Constitution [s.51(xxvi)], however, effectively deprived them of the rights and responsibilities normally accorded by the Commonwealth government to its citizens, by empowering the Commonwealth to make laws in respect of 'the people of any race, other than the aboriginal race in any State for whom it is deemed necessary to make special laws'. By the 1960s forces were at work, within both the Australian community and sections of the Commonwealth bureaucracy, to have these racist policies changed. Chapter 10 discusses the role played by the Department of Immigration in eroding the 'white Australia policy'.[3]

The officers of the Department of Immigration responsible

for its three distinctly different functions developed different ways of thinking about their clients and, as chapter 2 suggests, almost different cultures. Although those whose task it was to manage the selection and entry of migrants were more numerous and more powerful within the hierarchy of the Department, it was those responsible for dealing with the wide range of issues relating to the difficulties that non-English speaking migrants encountered in attempting to settle in Australia's monolingual and monocultural society who became agents of change.

From the late 1940s these officers tried to devise practical strategies to facilitate the economic and social absorption of non-English speaking aliens. Some of these strategies involved direct service provision. They developed an innovative scheme of English-language training (discussed in chapter 5). Departmental social workers in all States of Australia assisted thousands of migrants with their personal problems, helping them to find employment, appropriate health care, or to comply with the many laws and regulations of a society whose institutions both reflected and sustained the perceived cultural and ethnic 'homogeneity' of Australians (see chapters 2, 3 and 4). In the 1960s they developed funding arrangements designed to facilitate the delivery of welfare services to migrants by ethnic organisations (chapter 7), and in the early 1970s initiated what was probably the world's first telephone interpreter service (chapter 6). The efficacy of these services as bridges over which alien migrants could cross into the host community varied.

The bureaucrats and service-providers in areas of the Department responsible for the social integration of an increasingly diverse migrant intake quickly came to see the need for enormous structural changes and worked hard to achieve them. They conducted research, devised solutions, and pushed for change internally in areas that came under their Department's responsibilities. More commonly, they became advocates for change with those Commonwealth or State agencies with portfolio responsibility for the legislation which they saw needed to be changed, or with non-government bodies which they believed needed to restructure their services to accommodate the needs of migrants. Although the advocacy role played by the Department of Immigration in relation to migrant settlement met with varied degrees of success (and not infrequently none at all), it eventually resulted in a profound cultural change in the way the Australian government regarded and delivered services to its clients. By the end of the 1960s it was clear to those working in the settlement areas of the Department of Immigration that no one government department could meet all the settlement needs of migrants. They began to push for the devolution of responsibility for migrant settlement services to other agencies. This became government policy after Labor came to power in 1972 (see chapter 11), and was developed in the 1980s into a policy designed to ensure the equitable access of all Australians to the services of all government agencies.[4]

CONSTRUCTING TRUST AND OBTAINING COMPLIANCE

This book, and its predecessor *Redefining Australians*, are products of the Australian National University Research School of Social Sciences' Administration, Compliance and Governability Program. Coordinated by Professor Patrick Troy of the Urban Research Program, this was a multidisciplinary exercise which, between 1989 and 1996, explored and developed compliance theory in a wide range of Australian administrative contexts. Scholars from Australia, Britain and America in the fields of law, political science, economics, social psychology and history researched, in the context of Australian institutions, the conditions necessary to obtain the degree of compliance necessary for good government in a democracy. The realms of compliance studied and written about were many, and included social security, affirmative action, community participation in urban redevelopment, immigration, environmental regulations, the management of nursing homes, taxation, occupational health and safety, and trade practices. This Program influenced both the sources sought, and the questions asked of them, in my search to identify the causes of administrative and cultural change within the Department of Immigration in relation to migrant settlement.

The primary role of bureaucrats in a democracy is to assist the elected government to govern. Each government agency is responsible for ensuring that the legislation for which it is responsible is complied with. The operation of the modern state depends critically on the ability of government administrations to detect non-compliance, to enforce compliance with rules and regulations, and to encourage citizens (and proto-citizens, such as permanently resident non-citizens and children) to behave in accordance with them. Non-compliant behaviour reduces the authority of government and hence reduces its power to govern; it also increases the costs of government and reduces its income.

While the main focus of the Department of Immigration was directed at ensuring that people entered and departed Australia in compliance with the *Migration Act 1958* and earlier immigration legislation, another area monitored compliance with the *Nationality and Citizenship Act 1948*. Those who dealt with migrant settlement also had an important but broader and less clearly defined compliance role. The entry to Australia of large numbers of people, who brought with them a wide range of social values and cultural norms, posed a challenge to good government. Immediately on arrival, all migrants were subject to the range of legislative and administrative requirements which regulated the everyday life of Australian citizens, but which were neither known nor understood by most non-British migrants. This frustrated the government's intention that migrants assimilate into mainstream society and threatened to undermine the political acceptability of the migration program. All government agencies looked to the Department of Immigration to communicate information about their requirements to migrants. From the rules of the road in each State to the need to comply with the building regulations of local governments or to have their babies immunised—the expectations were immense and the resources provided to fulfil them inadequate.

Migrants came with varying expectations of the state. Refugees and many central Europeans deeply mistrusted it. Southern Europeans, particularly those from rural areas expected little of it, relying instead on family or religious and community networks for information and support. British migrants expected much of the state, particularly in the areas of social welfare and public housing, and Dutch and Scandinavian migrants expected even more. The expectations of bureaucrats concerning migrants was initially unrealistic, shaped by ignorance of both their histories and cultures and the effects on them of the migration experience. Through the reports of Department of Immigration social workers from the late 1940s, and as a result of the research and analysis conducted within the Survey and Integration Sections of the Department during the 1960s and early 1970s (see chapter 7), the level of understanding both of ethnic diversity and the effects of migration improved within the bureaucracy.

Immigration bureaucrats working within settlement areas were quickly confronted with the problem of constructing conditions favourable to compliance by migrants. Some of their non-compliance was involuntary. As chapter 2, which describes the non-compliance with their obligation to work of refugee supporting mothers in Departmental Holding Centres, illustrates, involuntary non-compliance by individuals (often referred to as 'the weapon of the weak') can be an effective spur to changes in policy and institutional arrangements. Some forms of non-compliance, the bureaucrats found, were a result of laws and regulations that were structured in ways which deterred compliance. This became evident to those responsible for promoting the uptake of Australian citizenship by aliens. They responded by simplifying the requirements and making them less costly for the migrant to comply with (see chapter 8).

Compliance is encouraged by mutual trust, engendered by perceptions of procedural fairness. When a government is obviously discriminatory, implementing and enforcing rules that favour one group and disadvantage another, the perception of an unequal bargain this generates acts as a deterrent to compliance. Discrimination between British and non-British migrants was entrenched in a wide range of legislation and institutions during most of the period to 1975. Because such discrimination acted as a deterrent to compliance by migrants and actively impeded their social and economic absorption, Department of Immigration bureaucrats responsible for migrant settlement sought to have these discriminatory provisions removed. By 1975 most discrimination on the grounds of nationality—which had, for example, prevented aliens from accessing certain social welfare benefits, from holding land or engaging in certain occupations—had been purged from State and Commonwealth legislation. Also, legislation such as that relating to the acquisition of citizenship and the exercise of the civil, social and political rights normally associated with citizenship, which had favoured British migrants in Australia, had largely been removed. These changes were not solely attributable to the bureaucratic drive to construct the trust in the state necessary to compliance; they were also responses to changes in the bargaining position of European migrants during the 1960s created by the economic recovery under the European Economic Community. They also owed a great deal to the ideology of the Labor government that came to power in December 1972 (see chapter 9).[5]

The ultimate goal of bureaucrats is not to obtain mere compliance of the governed but to obtain their consent to being governed. This consent is contingent on their perception that what is demanded of them is both consistent with their social values and in their individual interests. It is also contingent on their perception that the commitment of the government to its side of the bargain is credible, and that the procedures are fair and do not make unequal demands on different sections of society—that the government is impartial and that others are doing their fair share. As Margaret Levi points out, 'the creation and maintenance of contingent consent is often a difficult, fragile and expensive process. It is, if you will, the price of democracy'. Conversely, trust in the state can easily be undermined and disengagement and non-compliance encouraged by government policies which are contrary to the values and the interests of the governed, which are poorly administered, based on inadequate two-way communication, or which rely on inflexible compliance measures.[6]

The Historical Context of Settlement Planning

During the 30 years under consideration, decision-making within the Department of Immigration was greatly influenced by both international and domestic events, and by the changing cultural context of the community from which its bureaucrats were recruited. The international event that provided the opportunity for the program of mass migration, and which shaped its initial planning, was the 1939–45 war.

1945–52

While the rhetoric with which the program of mass migration was presented on 2 August 1945 by the first Minister for Immigration, Arthur Calwell, to a somewhat apprehensive Australian electorate very sensibly stressed its importance to the defence of Australia, its principal purposes were to produce full employment in Australia without inflation, and to increase a population in which fertility had fallen below replacement level. In 1944, a National Health and Medical Research Council inquiry concluded that it was unlikely that Australia's population of approximately 7.3 million would ever reach 9 million, even with net immigration at the level of 40 000 a year. It was also clear to all political parties, and to employer and employee organisations, that because of the fall in the number of births during the 1930s there would be insufficient workers to meet the expected high demand for consumer goods and to overcome the lags in capital stock expected after the war. Without population growth there would be neither growth in the market nor any economic development. This would discourage investors and create unemployment—the spectre that haunted those planning Australia's post-war reconstruction.

The blueprint for the Labor government's vision of a prosperous Australia without unemployment was provided in a White Paper, *Full Employment in Australia*, tabled in Parliament on 30 May 1945. It was prepared with considerable input from both the Prime Minister John Curtin and his successor, the then Treasurer J.B. Chifley. It proposed to build on the industrial development that had taken place during the war to create a diversified economy no longer vulnerable to the substantial pre-war fluctuations in levels of demand overseas for Australia's limited range of primary products.[7]

To gain community support for its economic transformation of Australia through migration, the government enlisted powerful community bodies to assist in its planning. The Immigration Advisory Council, which from 17 February 1947 to 12 June 1974 advised the Minister for Immigration on the migration and the social absorption of non-British migrants, comprised representatives of peak groups in industry such as the Australian Council of Employers' Federations, the National Farmers' Union, the Associated Chamber of Manufactures of Australia as well as the Australian Council of Trade Unions, the Australian Workers' Union and the NSW Trades and Labour Council. It also drew on mainstream ex-service and women's groups and the Australian Council of Local Government Associations.

In October 1949 the government created the Immigration Planning Council, which had a more economic focus. It had twelve members and thirteen associate members, who did not represent organisations but were 'outstanding individuals' who could speak with special knowledge on industrial matters as well as 'impartially representing community views'. They were drawn from leaders of industry (both trade unionists and employers) and the universities, and called on expert advisers when necessary. Officers of the Department of Immigration prepared research papers, agendas and notes for meetings of these bodies and their subcommittees, took minutes, and were responsible for any executive action. The Department also enlisted the support of a wide range of mainstream community organisations in encouraging migrant settlement by establishing and funding the Good Neighbour Movement and annual Citizenship Conventions from 1950.⁸

The electorate expected, and was reassured by the Minister for Immigration, that migrants would come predominantly from Britain (one alien in every eleven migrants was the figure quoted by Calwell in November 1946). It is, however, doubtful whether the government actually believed this was possible. In 1939 the British government, alarmed by its own declining net reproduction rate, had warned the Dominions that they should seek their migrants from non-British sources. Although Britain signed a free and assisted passage scheme on 31 March 1947 which brought 23 314 British migrants to Australia that year, until special hostels were built to house them only those British migrants were accepted who had friends, relatives or employers who were prepared to find them work and accommodate them. British migrants formed a minority of the intake until 1958. They were found by immigration planners to be not as economical as assisted aliens, because as well as requiring specially built hostels they could not be directed into employment and were accompanied by more unproductive dependants.⁹

The greatest obstacle to obtaining migrants immediately after the war was the scarcity of shipping. Australia was persuaded in 1947 by the International Refugee Organisation (IRO) to accept large numbers of people displaced by the war and unable to be resettled in their countries of origin because of the Cold War division of Europe. Given ships by the USA, the IRO was able to transport these refugees free of cost to whatever countries would accept them. Australia paid £10 a head to the IRO for each refugee. By the time this resettlement scheme ended in 1954 the Australian government had sponsored 170 700 'displaced persons' who had signed an agreement to work for two years in any industry into which the government directed them. Another 11 512 IRO refugees arrived independently of the Australian government, largely Jewish refugees assisted by Jewish agencies. Government-assisted aliens were accommodated in on-site work camps. Their wives and children were housed separately in Department of Immigration Holding Centres—generally former army camps.¹⁰

Australia also assisted aliens who were not officially classified as refugees. Immediately after the war and before the ratification of the peace treaties, Australia had obtained German scientists who were exempted from the wartime ban on the entry of enemy aliens, to work for various government or private sponsoring bodies under contract with the Employment of Scientific and Technical Enemy Aliens Committee. The post-war division of Europe created an estimated 12 million refugees in addition to the estimated 11 million survivors of German death and slave-labour camps. The new homeless, generally referred to as *Volksdeutsche*, were not the responsibility of the IRO, and there was no international body responsible for their welfare. Most were of German ethnicity, had lived for generations in Eastern European countries, and had been expelled, often with considerable cruelty, from those countries in the anti-German backlash that followed the war. The majority (56 per cent) were women, and one in four was under the age of fifteen. The largest occupational group among those expelled comprised highly skilled industrial workers and industrialists with experience in production and trade, the second largest group comprised former workers in agriculture who were now landless. They were not wanted in the war-devastated US and British zones of Germany, where they had a much greater unemployment rate than the rest of the population and were placing unbearable stresses on housing and the food supply. Their value to the Australian economy was obvious to migration officials both in Europe and in Australia, many of whom were ex-servicemen who had served in Europe and who were highly informed about and sympathetic to the plight of those made homeless by the war.[11]

The response of the Department of Immigration in Canberra to the settlement needs of refugees was far from tardy. As chapter 5 indicates, on 3 March 1946, when there were only a little over 8000 non-English speaking migrants in Australia, the Minister for Immigration announced the establishment of English-language training facilities for refugees. The service was extended to all aliens by a decision of Cabinet on 6 December 1948. As chapter 2 details, in 1949, after a survey of the settlement needs of refugees and other alien migrants in the Department's Reception and Holding Centres by a social worker engaged by the Department of Immigration, it established a Social Welfare Section with 39 positions for professionally qualified social workers Australia-wide to assist refugees and other non-English speaking migrants with their personal problems. At this time few government departments employed members of this relatively new and female-dominated profession. Unlike the USA, which would accept only those with family in the USA, and Canada, which selected refugees in accordance with strict occupational criteria, Australia offered re-settlement in Australia to inmates of the bleak post-war European camps who had no contacts in Australia, and took all, regardless of qualifications, who would accept a two-year work contract. It did not assess the qualifications of refugees and other humanitarian entrants, and was therefore unable to offer them employment in jobs in which they were qualified or experienced. The Commonwealth did not have the power to recognise most qualifications, as this was largely controlled by State legislation.[12]

Even the strong economic growth Australia was experiencing by the end of the 1940s, stimulated by full employment and export demand, was not enough to keep the Labor government in power. The Australian people were tired of wartime restrictions that had been carried on after the war by the Labor government. In 1949 coalminers, wharf labourers and others in low-paid and dangerous industries went out on strike in protest against the lack of investment in safety and job creation and against the maintenance of wartime wage controls in their industries. The Labor government's response made it appear irresolute to those on the Right and illiberal to those on the Left. Owners of private cars and small business vehicles, irked by continued petrol rationing, voted for the Liberal–Country Party coalition, led by Prime Minister Robert Menzies, which promised to end it. Later in 1950 the newly elected government ended rationing on the last two commodities—tea and butter.[13]

In 1950 the Department of Immigration, now under Harold Holt as Minister, carefully prepared the ground for the migration of Germans to Australia. Because, on the election of a conservative government, the USA immediately ended the ban it had placed on the Labor government's access to security information, the Menzies government was able to send influential executives of the most powerful group opposing German migration—the Returned Soldiers', Sailors' and Airmen's Imperial League of Australia (RSSAILA)—on a tour of security establishments in Germany. They returned convinced that the screening of migrants from Germany would be sufficiently effective to exclude former Nazis. On 23 August 1950 the Federal Executive of the RSSAILA recommended German migration to Australia.[14]

Until a migration treaty was signed with Germany in 1952, Australia obtained 5000 highly skilled German workers without cost under the 'Special Project Workers' scheme. They came under contract to work for two years for a range of private firms or government instrumentalities, which deducted their passage costs from their wages. As chapter 4 of this book reveals, they were possibly the most disadvantaged migrants in Australia at this time, and Department of Immigration social workers could do little to help them.

Also in 1952 the Department obtained 1000 skilled German workers at a per capita cost of only £10, through the newly formed Geneva-based Provisional Intergovernmental Committee for the Movement of Migrants from Europe (PICMME), which later that year was renamed the Intergovernmental Committee for European Migration (ICEM). Greek, Austrian and Italian workers were also carefully selected according to predetermined criteria by Australian teams, and shipped to Australia by the ICEM. That organisation itself drew on the experience and knowledge of Australian migration officers who had been involved in selecting refugees and other migrants in Western Europe after the war. Harold Grant, for example, a migration officer based in West Germany from 1949 to 1953, was seconded to the ICEM in 1953. He wrote a lengthy paper for that body on the refugee problem in Berlin in which he recommended emigration as a solution.[15]

1952–59

The Korean War, which had pushed up the export prices for Australian metals and wool, had contributed to inflation. The boom it created was over by September 1951. The US demand for wool ended and prices fell. The September 1951 Budget was deflationary but reinforced recession. For the first time since the 1930s Australia experienced unemployment. Although only approximately 2 per cent of the workforce was unemployed by November 1952, the government responded by severely cutting both assisted and unassisted immigration for 1953 to 75 000, from a planned 150 000. Government expenditure on migration was reduced and three migrant Reception Centres closed. For the first time migrants were unable to obtain jobs and the government denied that it had any legal obligation to provide employment to those under a two-year contract to work. Unskilled migrants, women, and those with poor English suffered the most. Two thousand unemployed Italians in the Bonegilla Reception Centre demonstrated in late 1952 because they wanted work, and soldiers and tanks at the nearby Bandiana stores depot were placed on alert. Departmental social workers reported severe distress among migrants, particularly in Sydney, where shelters for the homeless were unable to cope and hundreds of non-British migrants were sleeping in parks. They did their best to help those unemployed, but their role expanded and their numbers Australia-wide were cut from an establishment of 39 to 24.

While the recession was over quickly it affected the employment prospects of some categories of migrants for a number of years. Helping non-British migrants with their employment problems occupied 40 per cent of Departmental social workers' workload to 1957. While refugees still arrived during the 1950s from Czechoslovakia, Hungary (following the uprisings of October 1956), and Russians from China, they were vastly outnumbered by the generally skilled tradesmen brought in through treaties with European countries prepared to subsidise the emigration of their surplus populations. Migration treaties were negotiated in 1951 with the Netherlands and Italy, and with Germany and Greece in 1952.[16]

By October 1956, when Harold Holt was replaced as Minister for Immigration by Athol Townley, the outgoing Minister was able to report that migration had achieved much of Curtin's, Calwell's and Chifley's hopes. The population had grown since 1945 by 21 per cent, manufacturing output had more than doubled in volume since 1939, steel production had increased 83 per cent, Australia now had efficient motor vehicle and oil-refining industries, and the housing shortage had almost disappeared in most States. In its economic relations with the rest of the world, however, Australia had not lived up to earlier expectations. Australia's trading pattern at the end of the 1950s still looked more like its past than its future. Wool still made up 37 per cent of exports and minerals only 10 per cent, Britain still supplied three times the value of goods supplied by the next country (the USA) and consumed 2.5 times the value of Australian products. Although two-thirds of the migrant intake by the end of this decade was non-British, the enthusiasm the Department of Immigration had earlier shown to help them settle had waned considerably. The welcoming face its social workers had presented to thousands of distressed aliens faded like that of the Cheshire Cat in 1959 as the Department's fourth Minister, Alexander Downer, announced that he would further reduce their numbers Australia-wide to fifteen.[17]

1960–72

The 1960s was a time of momentous cultural and economic change internationally, nationally, and within the Department of Immigration. The seeds of international economic change were planted in 1957 with the establishment of the European Economic Community (EEC). The prosperity, employment and improved social welfare conditions it created within Europe stimulated internal migration from the poorer south to the more prosperous north. Far-away Australia became a less attractive place to settle. To assuage concern about possible decline in migrant numbers from Europe the Department of Immigration adopted a stronger advocacy role with the Department of Social Services to improve migrants' access to social welfare benefits. It also intensified its recruiting efforts in Britain (which had not yet joined the EEC), and looked much further afield for migrants. This contributed to the policy changes outlined in chapter 10, which in 1966 allowed for the admission of skilled non-Europeans, thus undermining the 'white Australia policy'. In 1967, after a migration agreement with Turkey, substantial numbers of non-Christians were admitted to Australia for the first time.

The earlier cultural and racial construct of Australian citizenship was also being eroded by the pressure for equal citizenship rights and responsibilities for Aboriginal Australians which intensified during the 1960s. Some political activities against racism were inspired by the American civil rights movement, notably the group of white and Aboriginal students whose 'freedom ride' publicised the racial segregation prevalent in some towns in rural NSW. Other activities, such as the June 1966 'walk-off' of the Gurindji tribe from the British firm Vestey's Wave Hill Station in the Northern Territory which began the Aboriginal land rights movement, were locally inspired.

The introduction of conscription in November 1964, which prepared Australia to commit troops to the American war in Vietnam the following year, drew attention to the citizenship status of Australian Aborigines. Although they had become Australian citizens in 1949, they were excluded from the rights and responsibilities normally accorded to citizens of the Commonwealth of Australia by the Australian Constitution [s. 51(xxvi)], which empowered the Commonwealth Parliament to make laws in respect of 'the people of any race, other than the aboriginal race . . . '. They were, therefore, subject to State, not Commonwealth law. The Commonwealth *National Service Act*, which regulated conscription in the 1960s, specifically excluded Aboriginal Australians from conscription. By 1962, however, most States had removed the bar that had prevented them from voting in State elections, and consequently they were eligible to vote also in Commonwealth elections. Although no great efforts were made to ensure that they register to vote, some conservative organisations, such as the Returned Services League, the Country Women's Association and sections of the Country Party, argued that as Aborigines now enjoyed the rights of citizenship they should be required to fulfil its duties and be subject to conscription. Aboriginal political groups, such as the Aboriginal Advancement Council of Western Australia and the Federal Council for the Advancement of Aborigines and Torres Strait Islanders, also advocated the conscription of Aborigines, arguing that their exclusion implied their inferiority to white Australians as citizens. Although almost 90 per cent of mainstream Australians voted in a referendum held in 1967 to remove the discriminatory references to Aboriginals from the Constitution, the *National Service Act* was not amended before conscription was abandoned by the newly elected Whitlam government in late 1972. Mainstream demands from 1964 for the conscription of non-citizen migrants served to shift the focus of thinking about citizenship in Australia during this decade, particularly among those on the Left, from ethnicity to rights and responsibilities.[18]

Australia's growing concern to play an active role in Asia was another factor in creating popular and bureaucratic embarrassment about the 'white Australia policy'. Since 1951 Australian university students and others had come into contact with Asian, African and Pacific students awarded places in Australian universities under the Colombo Plan who challenged conventional stereotypes about non-Europeans. More than one student in ten at the University of Sydney at the end of the 1950s was from these regions, and by 1960 Melbourne University had become a hotbed of agitation against the 'white Australia policy'. In 1962, 36 of its staff and postgraduate students, calling themselves the 'immigration reform group', published an influential attack against the policy entitled 'Immigration—control or colour bar?'. Australians were becoming more interested in learning about Asia. In 1960 both the Universities of Sydney and Melbourne established departments of Indonesian studies, and the following year a department of Indian studies was added at Melbourne University. In 1962 Canada removed most of its immigration restrictions based on race and country of origin.

However, the most important factors in eroding the 'white Australia policy' were local. In 1961 a new Secretary was appointed to the Department of Immigration (its second since the Department was created in 1945). Peter Heydon had been a career diplomat in the Department of External Affairs—a department which by that time was very aware of the handicap Australia's racist migration policy had become to relations with Asian countries, particularly in such fora as the United Nations, the British Commonwealth and the South-East Asia Treaty Organisation. Heydon's last position before joining the Department of Immigration had been as High Commissioner to India. He skilfully worked to undermine the 'white Australia policy', and was largely successful in 1966 when he supervised the introduction of a new immigration policy which allowed for the admission for permanent residence of skilled non-Europeans with qualifications in demand in Australia, who were judged likely to integrate into Australian society.[19]

The 1960s was a decade of strong growth and increased foreign investment. Despite the fears of migrants leaving Australia, immigration intakes remained consistently high and migrants contributed about 41 per cent of the population growth. The demand for housing, roads, hospitals, schools and other services which they created resulted in an unemployment rate that averaged less than 2 per cent, and secondary industry came to rely on migrant labour. Real economic growth rose from 4.73 per cent in the previous decade to 5.36 per cent between 1960 and 1970, and there was relatively low inflation. Foreign investment inflow doubled in the second half of the decade as a result of Australia's stable economy and the mineral boom. Minerals swelled the volume and value of exports so Australia could afford a larger volume of imported goods.[20]

There was considerable cultural change in the settlement areas of the Department of Immigration during the 1960s, and more money was again invested in the provision of settlement staff and services. Central Office in Canberra developed administrative structures that enabled it to understand and work with the cultural diversity of the migrant population and to develop settlement policies. As chapter 7 details, from 1964 the Department dropped from official usage the term 'assimilation' and replaced it by 'integration'. It later substituted the description 'ethnic organisations' for the earlier and more negatively conceived term 'national groups'. Throughout the 1960s and early 1970s the Integration Section was responsible for originating the Grant-in-Aid scheme, which helped ethnic organisations more effectively meet the settlement needs of their communities, dealt with the Department's translating and interpreting services, and initiated and developed an innovative telephone interpreter service. It also devised a computerised processing system to enable data on migrant settlement problems supplied by Departmental social workers to be thoroughly analysed, and arranged for the repatriation of migrants with serious settlement problems. It upgraded the Department's settlement staff, arguing successfully for an increase in the number of Departmental social workers and recruiting ethnic welfare officers. Both the Integration and Survey Sections developed administrative structures which enabled their Department to monitor migrant groups directly, thus making it less dependent on information supplied through Citizenship Conventions and the Good Neighbour Movement.

In 1968 the National Groups Liaison Unit enabled the Department to communicate directly with ethnic organisations in order better to understand both their role and the way the Department could help them. From this developed a directory of ethnic organisations in Australia. Politicians from both major political parties during this decade became aware of the growing political power of migrants, supporting the provision of settlement services to their constituents and advocating with the Department on their behalf.

1970–75

Despite Australia's economic prosperity, the Coalition government was losing support and credibility by the early 1970s. A major factor contributing to its declining popularity was its persistent, if decreasing, support for the US war in Vietnam and the increasing harshness it showed in dealing with the growing non-compliance with the *National Service Act* under which military conscription was administered. In the election of December 1972 the Labor Party returned to power for the first time in 22 years, under Gough Whitlam as Prime Minister. Whitlam formally abolished Australia's discriminatory immigration policy, substituting a points system applicable to all migrants regardless of race or country of origin, as Canada had done in 1967.

Conditions in the world economy had brought about a startling reversal of the terms of trade in 1972/73 to Australia's benefit. The price of wool rose 150 per cent on that of the previous year and the prices and receipts for most other main categories of exports rose. The average price of imports fell, and

Australia posted its first surplus on the current account for many years. The growth in the money supply this generated greatly overheated the economy; to counteract this, the newly elected Labor government revalued the currency by about 7 per cent in December 1972. The following year it cut tariffs by 25 per cent and revalued the currency again. Imports soared by over 50 per cent and, as the government intended, capital inflow was checked. The growing inflation was blamed on migration. Total permanent and long-term arrivals had reached an all-time high of over 253 000 in 1970/71 and, as its predecessors had done in response to past financial problems, the government cut migration savagely. The first Labor Minister for Immigration since Arthur Calwell, A.J. Grassby, reduced the annual target from 140 000 to 110 000 in December 1972, to 80 000 in late 1974, and to 50 000 in late 1975. The numbers of assisted migrants declined from 82 000 in 1971/72 to 36 000 in 1974/75. Despite the government's abolition of the 'white Australia policy' and its initiation of non-discriminatory selection procedures, the racial composition of the intake did not alter radically, as the number of non-Europeans admitted under Labor was small. For political reasons Whitlam was slow to respond to the refugee crisis created by the fall of the US-backed government in Saigon on 30 April 1975.[21]

The reduction in migration produced an unexpected wage push, as migrants had filled vacancies in unattractive workplaces such as steel mills and car plants, and the national wage-setting system took the metal workers' award as a benchmark. In response to the reduction in migrant numbers, major manufacturers in these industries raised wages to attract labour; this flowed on to awards in other industries. The government also responded to pressure from workers for increased wages, fuelled by the drift upwards in the cost of living. Price rises were exacerbated by the worldwide rise in the cost of oil from December 1973. Food prices escalated from 7.5 per cent in 1972/73 to 18.9 per cent in 1973/74, and housing costs rose in the cities. There was an average rise of about 35 per cent in earnings in 1974. That year marked the end of the long boom which had characterised Australia's economic history since 1942 and had fostered conditions conducive to economic and social progress.[22]

The government's decision to dismember the Department of Immigration in 1974 and to transfer its settlement services to other departments was, on the whole, a disaster. As chapter 11 explains, the Department of Social Security, which was suddenly given responsibility for migrant welfare, was ill-prepared to deal with its new role, and the quality of services offered to migrants rapidly declined. On 22 December 1975, after the dismissal of the Labor government by the Governor General, the Coalition government regained power, and by 1977 it had returned most but not all settlement functions to the Department of Immigration and Ethnic Affairs. While most of Labor's administrative restructuring was reversed by its successor, the effects of the changes it had implemented to eliminate the legislative and administrative underpinnings of discrimination on the grounds of race and ethnicity in Australian society were irreversible. Its 1973 redefinition of Australia as a multicultural society was endorsed and developed into multicultural policies by all succeeding governments. Its efforts to involve other Commonwealth departments and ethnic communities in facilitating migrant settlement were built on in the next decade.

Academic Writings on the Department of Immigration's Role in Migrant Settlement 1966–95

The cultural and administrative changes that occurred within the Department of Immigration during the 30 years to 1975 have remained largely invisible to academic writers on migrant settlement. The picture they present of the Department's role in assisting migrants to settle in Australia during the three decades before multicultural policies were developed is blank, sketchy, erroneous or unrelievedly black.

1960s

Probably the first to describe the settlement of migrants in Australia was James Jupp, a Melbourne political scientist who migrated from Britain to Australia nine years before he wrote *Arrivals and Departures* in 1966. He presented a thoughtful and perceptive analysis of migrant attitudes towards life in Australia based on interviews with 142 British, Dutch, Italian and Greek migrants conducted in Melbourne between 1965 and 1966. While giving largely the migrants' account of their settlement experiences, he did not ignore the settlement role of the Department of Immigration. He saw most areas of importance to migrant settlement as lying outside the control of the Department of

Immigration, and seemed not to have been aware of its role as advocate on behalf of migrants with other agencies on such issues as social welfare benefits and skills recognition. Nor did he refer to its responsibility for migrant language teaching or for migrant accommodation. He was better informed about the changes that were occurring in the Department in the early 1960s than he was of its role in the previous decades. He knew of the work of the recently formed Survey Section and of its 'grossly overworked and under-staffed' Social Welfare Section, and his assessment of the Department's settlement role, although based on limited information, was fair. He observed that:[23]

> Its social workers, its education research officers and its field survey unit all indicate that it is at least interested in looking after migrants on arrival and in finding out what they are doing and thinking . . . The trouble is that this side of the Department's work is only a small part of its activities . . . Were all migrants needing assistance to turn to it, its limited absorption work would collapse altogether.

He believed that the Department's 'expert knowledge and understanding' was an important factor in the success of Australia's migration program, and praised its independence of popular pressure, particularly of sections of society wishing to restrict or exclude southern Europeans. He also praised its flexible structure and approach to change under its new Secretary, Peter Heydon. He condemned politicians' 'old fashioned notions of total assimilation which their advisors have dropped years ago', but believed the Department was falling down in its responsibility to foster the social absorption of migrants.

1970s

Probably the most influential and scholarly analyses of migrant settlement were those published in the 1970s by Australian National University sociologist Jean Martin. They have been drawn on as sources by, and have shaped the perceptions of, most subsequent writers on migrant settlement. Her *Decade of Migrant Settlement* (1976) was the first comprehensive study of migrants' experiences in Australia. Prepared by the Social Studies Committee of the Australian Population and Immigration Council and intended to form the basis of an intensive review of immigration policies and programs, it was presented to the Minister for Immigration in February 1976. The report was based on a survey conducted in 1973 at the request of the Department of Immigration by the Australian Bureau of Statistics: 7700 families whose heads had arrived in Australia within the previous ten years were selected from 360 100 households in five Australian capital cities. Its main focus was on the absorption of migrants into the workforce, although it looked at related areas such as the recognition of their qualifications, their accommodation, their fluency in English and their use of available English-language services. It made no reference to the role played by the Department of Immigration in any of these areas. Its only comment on the Department was a criticism of the accuracy of the information about employment in Australia its officers provided to intending migrants. It related the failure of those who had not greatly improved their mastery of English since arriving not to poor English-language teaching, but to their inability or unwillingness to attend available classes and the low level of formal education and qualifications they had acquired in their countries of origin.[24]

Martin's next major work, *The Migrant Presence—Australian Responses 1947–1977*, was written as a research report for the National Population Inquiry and published in 1978. Although prepared with assistance from the Department of Immigration, it again dealt largely with areas outside the portfolio responsibilities of the Department, such as health, the education of migrant children, and the unions. Although it gave little attention to the Department's role in migrant settlement, it was critical of this. Martin observed that the Department was 'oriented overwhelmingly towards migrant recruitment rather than settlement—was not well-informed about migrant experiences in Australia. It employed very few multilinguals . . . had little research capacity; [and] the inquiries it did conduct were limited in scope and rarely made public'. While she found the Department's response in the areas of migrant education and welfare 'limited and tardy', she admitted that it had contributed to the debate new knowledge and new structures, and was an exception to the 'abysmal indifference and neglect' that characterised the response of other Commonwealth departments to the migrant presence. Like Jupp she was unaware of the Department's advocacy role, wrongly assumed that the Department of Immigration was responsible for the education of migrant children, and attributed initial responsibility for the Adult Migrant Education Scheme to the Commonwealth Office of Education. She also gave credit for the creation of the Telephone Interpreter Service largely to Labor.[25]

David Cox, a social worker with International Social Service in Melbourne who later became an academic at the University of Melbourne's Department of Social Studies, coedited with Jean Martin a publication commissioned by the Australian government's Commission of Inquiry into Poverty in 1975, entitled *The Welfare of Migrants*. He was also a member of the Australian Population and Immigration Council's Social Studies Committee, which she chaired. This book adopted a broad focus, examining the response of the total social welfare structure, including both statutory and voluntary agencies, and gave little attention to the role of the Department of Immigration. Where it did mention areas of Department responsibility, such as adult language training or telephone interpreting facilities, it criticised the former for its low enrolments and the latter for being 'extremely slow in developing'. While it commented that 'The Immigration Department's services are widely available', it gave little detail about them. This lack of focus on the settlement role of the Department of Immigration characterised Cox's later publications.[26]

1980s

In his 1983 article 'Welfare services in a multicultural society', Cox presented a blanket condemnation of settlement services in the assimilationist period, making no acknowledgement of the services provided by the Department of Immigration. Ignoring the activities of the Department's professional social workers, he argued that assimilationist ideology regarded the provision of separate welfare structures for migrants as inappropriate, and that 'until the late 1960s the model was one of inactivity'. He briefly mentioned later Departmental welfare initiatives such as the establishment of the Grant-in-Aid scheme and the Telephone Interpreter Service, criticising current policy developments in relation to the former.[27]

Cox's 1987 work, *Migration and Welfare: An Australian Perspective*, provided a valuable critique of the post-1975 multicultural phase of settlement services but showed little understanding of Department of Immigration settlement services before this time. It ignored the efforts of Departmental social workers to meet the needs of both assisted and full-fare-paying migrants and to refer them to community agencies. In relation to the provision of English-language training for migrants, it erroneously asserted that 'The need for and advantages of the great majority of Immigrants mastering English was not accepted until well into the 1970s'. Cox's criticism of the settlement role of the Department is oddly ambivalent. On the one hand he states: 'the general conclusion that must be reached is that Australia has failed to accept responsibility at a government level for the immediate post-arrival needs of non-government nominated immigrants. Clearly the initial philosophy was that the onus was on immigrants themselves to find their way, making immediate use of the services available in the general community as best they could'. This sits somewhat oddly with his criticism of the Department for *providing* post-arrival services (which he nowhere detailed), arguing that 'It is likely that the Department's role throughout the years has inhibited, rather than encouraged, the type of broadly based services for immigrants [that] are seemingly most appropriate, despite its valuable contribution'. Cox also ignored the organisational adaptation that occurred within the Department in the period before 1975 in his 1989 book, *Welfare Practice in a Multicultural Society*.[28]

In 1984 what was probably the first account of post-war migrant settlement by professional historians was published. Drawing largely on oral and secondary sources, Janis Wilton and Richard Bosworth's *Old Worlds and New Australia: The Postwar Migrant Experience* painted a generally grim picture of the 'complex and terrible migrant experience' of non-British migrants in particular. Not surprisingly given their sources, the authors assumed that there were no government settlement services for such migrants before the end of the 1960s, when 'Immigrants were no longer expected to adjust to living in Australia all on their own. They could obtain assistance from bureaucrats, social workers and even from fellow migrants'. Without an understanding of the various Commonwealth and State responsibilities for migrant services which had developed by the mid-1970s, the authors complained of the different roles carried out by various government agencies providing services to migrants in government hostels by that time. 'Progress and humanity shattered against the barricades built by demarcation disputes, bureaucratic buck-passing or procrastination', they alleged. Also, in the absence of an understanding either of the history of settlement services provided for aliens by the Department of Immigration or of its advocacy on their behalf from the late 1940s, the authors were unable to account for the administrative changes that occurred within the Department over time. The abolition of discriminatory policies and practices, and the transition from assimilation to integration, were attributed to changes in fashion and rhetoric and to 'the expansion of Australia's universities'. Somewhat passively, 'integrationism shaded into multiculturalism' without government intervention. The concept of integration was borrowed, they claimed, from the USA. Seeing assimilation purely as cultural imperialism, the authors viewed the Department of Immigration solely as a generous sponsor of the Good Neighbour Movement, a body which, 'by constantly reiterating the superiority of Australian ways, had aimed to detach migrants from their old cultures'.[29]

Jock Collins, an economist, brought a Marxist perspective to his analysis of post-war migration in *Migrant Hands in a Distant Land* (1988). His focus on social class and class relations in a capitalist society did not encourage him to examine in any detail the provision of settlement services by the Department of Immigration. His statement that 'the Adult Migrant Education Program *[sic]* was introduced in 1968 to provide English-language instruction to professionally qualified migrants over an eight week period' was historically incorrect, and he made few other references to state-provided settlement services.[30]

Andrew Jakubowicz, another prolific writer on migration issues in the 1970s and 1980s, was (like Cox) commissioned by the Australian government's Commission of Inquiry into Poverty in 1975. He also wrote from a Marxist perspective, seeing assimilation, integration and multicultural policies as representing 'successive stages of reconstructing Australian class relations to maintaining hegemony and class domination'. For Jakubowicz, the role of the state and its bureaucracy was to maintain 'those conditions of social reproduction which benefit the bourgeoisie and minimise the transformational potential of class analysis and class struggle'. As with Collins, this perspective was not conducive to analysis of the provision of settlement services by the state.[31]

This is evidenced in Jakubowicz' contribution on welfare provision to James Jupp's 1988 reference book on migration, *The Australian People*. The entry did not acknowledge the existence of any Commonwealth welfare services for migrants before 1960, and assumed that welfare personnel were first appointed to the Department of Immigration after 1971 as a result of the success of Grant-in-Aid welfare officers working with migrant organisations. Jakubowicz incorrectly stated that aliens were initially ineligible for unemployment benefits, and confused the residency requirements for pensions with discrimination on the ground of nationality (removed as a result of Department of Immigration advocacy in 1966). He attributed policy changes in the 1960s entirely to the government's response to pressures from the leadership of emerging community associations, and asserted that, except occasionally in some courts, 'Professional interpreters were non-existent within government services'. Most of these factual errors were repeated in Jakubowicz' 1989 article, 'The state and welfare of immigrants in Australia'. He had by then discovered that the Department had established 39 positions for social workers in 1949, but assumed, quite incorrectly, that these were provided primarily to assist British migrants.[32]

Frank Lewins' contribution on assimilation and integration to Jupp's 1988 reference work *The Australian People* asserted that the bureaucracy lagged behind academics in not replacing the term 'assimilation' by 'integration' until the early 1970s. (In fact, 'assimilation' was officially abandoned for 'integration' by the Department in 1964, which by the mid-1960s had established an Integration Section.) Whereas this change in terminology among academics may, as Lewins described, be attributed largely to the influence of American social scientists, there is no archival or oral evidence that bureaucrats in the Department's Integration and Education Section during the 1960s were influenced by academic analyses. Lewins also incorrectly claimed that the 'assimilation' was 'mainly employed in reference to the more "look alike" migrants and less often to indigenous Aborigines or migrants with "obvious" physical differences'. 'Assimilation' was widely employed in relation to Aborigines, although by the mid-1960s the term was being replaced by 'integration' in areas of the bureaucracy dealing with Aboriginal affairs.

Readers of the chapter 'Assimilation to integration 1945–1972' in Castles et al.'s *Mistaken Identity: Multiculturalism and the Demise of Nationalism in Australia* (1988) were presented with a view of government intervention in the immigration program which was 'a result of elite (as opposed to popular) consensus'. The authors viewed assimilation not as policy, designed primarily to achieve the social absorption of migrants, but as 'essentially an ideological construct facilitating the acceptance of the immigration programme by a largely xenophobic population'. Policy changes, including the shift from assimilation to integration in the 1960s, were attributed not so much to changes in the attitudes of the elite towards questions of race, ethnicity and national identity, and 'Still less [to] changes in wider public attitudes', but to 'Australia's shifting industrial structure and international economic position'. Although the chapter purported to concentrate on 'politicians and bureaucrats', it did not mention any government settlement services developed and administered in either the assimilation or integration periods.[33]

1990s

Writing about the Department of Immigration's role in migrant settlement in the 1990s has been uneven. James Jupp's chapter 'Immigrant settlement policy in Australia', in *Nations of Immigrants: Australia, the United States, and International Migration*, presented a general overview of the various settlement services provided by the Australian government from 1947. Before detailing the legacy of problems resulting from past policies, he commented that 'while no immigrant settlement programme can be altogether successful', Australia had succeeded in achieving a 'relatively benign state of ethnic relationships and immigrant settlement in Australia'. This success, he believed, 'has blunted the edge of radical critiques, which have, in any case, not been very common or persuasive in recent years'. Comparing Australian settlement policies with those of other countries, he observed that they:

> compare most favourably with those of some other immigrant recipients, most notably Britain and the USA. They are comparable with many initiatives taken in Canada, although provincial variation and responsibility is more important there. The elaborate welfare states of Sweden and The Netherlands give more detailed attention to vulnerable groups such as refugees, using local government much more widely than would be feasible in Australia. Some Australian programmes have aroused interest and even admiration from elsewhere—most notably the Telephone Interpreter Service and some aspects of direct method teaching under the Adult Migrant English Programme [sic].

Robert L. Bach's chapter in the same work highlighted areas in which the settlement policies of the US government diverged markedly from those of Australia. Bach characterised US government settlement policies as 'programmatically decentralized but financially concentrated'. His observation that in the USA 'Settlement policies involve institutional responses to broad-based social movements organised by and on behalf of both newcomer and established resident groups' is of particular importance to those inclined to generalise from the USA to the Australian experience, where community pressure for such services to 1975 was negligible.[34]

In contrast to Jupp, *An Overview of Australian Government Settlement Policy 1945–1992* (1992), produced in-house by Bureau of Immigration Research manager Oleh Lukomskyj, drew from published official and academic sources to present a generalised and rather negative picture of settlement services to 1975. It quoted without comment (and therefore appeared to endorse) the criticisms of government 'carelessness and neglect' presented by such authors as Jean Martin, David Cox and Andrew Jakubowicz. It described a reactive—not a proactive—government settlement policy, ignored the advocacy role of the Department of Immigration, and attributed changes in policy during the 1960s to research by academics without mentioning the Department's own considerable research activities.[35]

The Bureau of Immigration and Population Research commissioned four academics to produce *Australian Immigration: A Survey of the Issues* (1994). This book included a section on the social aspects of immigration which, like Jupp's 1992 work, concluded that Australia's immigration intakes had not threatened Australia's social cohesion and that non-English speaking migrants had largely succeeded in 'overcoming economic and social obstacles to upward social mobility and improved welfare, especially over the longer term'. Its analysis focused on the government's responsibility for the provision of migrant settlement and its changing philosophies and objectives over time. While referring, not uncritically, to the principal academic studies which dealt in broad outline with migrant settlement since Jupp's 1966 work, it remarked that 'Much of this debate has been conducted through assertion of general propositions, rather than detailed empirical research', and stressed the need for detailed historical research into processes of policy formation based on archival material.[36]

Social Change and Cultural Transformation in Australia (1995), by Adam Jamrozik, Cathy Boland and Robert Urquhart, included an overview of the Australian immigration program since 1940 which focused on 'changes in policy and attitudes towards migrants' and 'the difficulties which monocultural Australia has experienced in accepting the cultural diversity brought in by immigrants from various non-English-speaking countries'. The principle guiding the policies of successive

Australian governments, the authors claimed, was the immediate needs of the labour market, 'and little thought [was] given to longer-term social and demographic implications and outcomes'. Whatever the successes of the immigration program may have been both for the immigrant and the host country, in their view 'the negative outcome for both has been a great waste of human resources created by early immigration and settlement policies'. Their black picture of 'irretrievable loss' was based on Egon Kunz' 1988 account of pre-1952 policies in relation to refugees, which they generalised to later non-refugee immigrants. The authors erroneously claimed that not only displaced persons but Italians, Greeks and Yugoslavs did not have their skills recognised, were classified according to gender either as labourers or as domestics, were placed on a two-year contract, and were provided with no English-language instruction. Drawing on another 1988 secondary source they confidently claimed that well into the 1970s the government had an 'unstated policy' of importing unskilled rather than skilled workers. Governments and public administrators, they asserted, 'have hindered rather than facilitated the process of utilising imported talents and skills ... After nearly half a century of conducting an immigration program, the progress the country has achieved in this area has been minimal'.[37]

Although archival sources to 1965 became freely available to researchers by 1995, little use has been made of them to study the development of settlement policy. The collection of historical documents published by John Lack and Jacqueline Templeton, *Bold Experiment: A Documentary History of Australian Immigration Since 1945* (1995), did not draw on archival sources. Templeton's historical introduction to the selection of documents illustrating aspects of migrant settlement reiterated a familiar account of deprivation and neglect. The Department of Immigration was mentioned only as a purveyor of unsubtle assimilationist propaganda, as an instrument of a government determinedly striving to separate migrants from their cultural baggage, which overcharged assisted migrants in its hostels. She made no attempt to distinguish between the responsibilities of State and Commonwealth governments, and her few references to the Department's settlement services were sketchy and inaccurate. While the lack of access by migrant workers to adequate English instruction was deplored, the Adult Migrant Education Scheme was mentioned only in the context of the 1978 Galbally Report, to which the creation of the Grant-in-Aid scheme (initiated by the Department of Immigration in 1968) was erroneously attributed. The Telephone Interpreter Service, conceived of and developed within the Department in the early 1970s, was credited entirely to the Labor government. Not surprisingly, Templeton baldly asserted 'Australia did not confront the migrant presence . . . Until the late 1960s and the 1970s when migrants and their children could begin to make their own criticism heard, all problems were stubbornly denied or blamed on the migrants'.[38]

In December 1995 a former officer of the Department of Immigration, George Kiddle, completed a manuscript entitled 'Post arrival services for migrants 1947–1981'. Although unpublished, it is available in the Department's library. As Assistant Secretary of the Settlement Services Branch of the Department from 1973 to 1980, Kiddle prepared background papers on migrant settlement for the 1981 review of post-arrival programs commissioned by the Galbally Report. The section of the manuscript covering this period drew on these papers. It dealt only with the welfare areas with which Kiddle had particular responsibility and did not, therefore, discuss language services. Its usefulness to researchers is limited by the failure of the author to identify his sources. He appears to have derived his information for the period before 1975 largely from the records of the Immigration Advisory Council rather than from Departmental files, although he may also have used later secondary sources.

Drawing principally on archival sources, this book analyses the considerable if inadequate efforts of one government department to respond to the settlement needs of migrants at a time when there were few other government or non-government agencies with which it could constructively collaborate. It is intended to provide a more complete and accurate picture of the role of the bureaucracy in the provision of settlement services to non-English speaking migrants in the period 1945–75 than has been previously attempted.

CHAPTER 2

The two faces of the Department of Immigration: social workers and selectors

THE Department of Immigration reflected the culture of the society from which its officers were drawn. The largely female staff of its Social Welfare Section reflected the compassionate face of Australia to needy and often traumatised aliens in Departmental accommodation and to the victims of the 1952 recession. They were, however, a small and relatively uninfluential minority within the Department. The power in the Department during the period 1945–75 lay largely with those who implemented government policy—the migration planners and selectors. They mirrored the values of mainstream Australians, who saw their national identity as inseparable from Anglo-Celtic ethnicity and culture. This was evident in the racist administrative practices adopted during this decade to restrict the intake of southern Europeans. The gender discrimination institutionalised in Australia's male-dominated society during this decade was evident in the selection and placement in employment of migrant women workers.

P.M. Rice, a professional social worker who began his career in the South Australian Department of Aboriginal Affairs, joined the Department in 1966 as a social worker in the Adelaide regional office, and from 1967 was an administrator in the Integration Section of Central Office in Canberra. He has identified separate cultures within the Department of Immigration—

the 'getters' and the 'keepers'. The former were concerned with assessing applicants, bringing people into Australia, and controlling their movement on arrival. They were unconcerned with issues of welfare and settlement, which they believed were not the Department's problem. They were most powerful within the Department's hierarchy and were responsible for the closure of most of the Department's post-arrival accommodation centres in the late 1950s and early 1960s. The 'keepers' were concerned to encourage the social absorption of migrants after their arrival—to provide and develop services for migrants. He felt that they were never quite accepted (although tolerated) by the hardline migration people who regarded them as 'do-gooders', on side with migrants. The 'keepers' kept a low profile and avoided publicity, thus their contribution was not widely understood or recognised by academics or others concerned with migrant settlement. They learnt to manage the 'getters' where necessary, and were generally allowed to get on with their work unhindered.[1]

The Formation and Role of the Social Welfare Section 1948–52

The Department of Immigration pioneered the employment of professional social workers by the Commonwealth in Australia. From 1949 social workers presented the human face of the government's assimilation policy to thousands of migrants around Australia. They helped them with their personal problems and provided them with information and advice so that they could access much-needed services. Initially intended to service the needs of aliens, from 1952 they were also required to provide social welfare services in Department of Labour and National Service hostels, which in the early 1950s accommodated mainly British migrants.

Social workers also provided their Department with what was probably its most reliable source of information on the difficulties migrants experienced in attempting to restructure their lives in Australia. Many of the problems with which they were presented were the result of systemic discrimination against aliens and an unpreparedness of Australian institutions to meet the needs of non-English speaking people from non-British cultures. They were, therefore, well placed to offer their Department practical policy advice based on first-hand observation. They made visible and comprehensible in Canberra the problems of marginalised groups of migrants, particularly those of women in its accommodation centres, mentally ill aliens, and migrant workers in rural areas of Australia. Through the detailed written reports submitted by its social workers, the Department first came to appreciate fully the obstacles to the assimilation of aliens into an Anglo-Celtic-dominated society.

The Department's Social Welfare Section was established in 1949 on the recommendation of Hazel Dobson, a qualified and experienced Departmental social worker. Her advice was included in a research report she had prepared on alien migrants in late 1948. She had investigated the living conditions of aliens already in the community and those of recently arrived IRO refugees in the Department's Reception and Holding Centres. Her report revealed a range of problems, but emphasised the need to find suitable employment for refugees with psychiatric problems resulting from their wartime experiences. It also pointed to the need for aftercare for difficult cases leaving the Centres and moving into the community.[2]

Dobson had made the suggestion somewhat tentatively, as she recognised that hers was a relatively new profession and thought that she would probably have some difficulty in demonstrating its usefulness. The report was, to her surprise, taken up with enthusiasm, as it had presented an unfamiliar and disturbing view of the migrant settlement experience to the senior officers of her Department. In forwarding her recommendations to the Assistant Secretary, Encouraged Migration Division, G.C. Watson commented that the development of the Displaced Persons' Scheme 'has brought in its train many problems that have previously not been encountered in this Department'. As Dobson later observed, 'The fact that this Department early recognised the need for trained people to deal with the problems of migrants, and was prepared to commence with a fair-sized establishment right from the outset, has frequently been commented upon by the Social Work profession'.[3]

Dobson was aware that the task ahead had no precedent, and that her solution was a totally new experiment. She recommended flexibility, and advised that the Department 'keep a close watch on developments, and be prepared to meet needs as they arise and as experience dictates. This is equally true of staff requirements, of organisation, and of social welfare policy as a whole'. Watson supported her proposal, and recommended the appointment of one social worker to each of the Department's Reception and Training Centres and in the proposed Holding

Centres for dependants, coordinated by a senior social worker in Central Office in Canberra. He also recommended the appointment of Commonwealth Migration Officers (CMOs) in each State 'to deal with aftercare problems of migrants who have passed out into the community'.⁴

Hazel Dobson had worked in Canberra with Arthur Calwell before the foundation of the Department of Immigration, and maintained close contact and had considerable influence with him when he became Minister for Immigration. Social workers in various States remembered her differently. To Pauline Griffin, a junior social worker in the Department's Sydney office between mid-1949 and the end of 1951, she was a distant figure, always immaculately dressed in a suit and gloves complemented by a feminine hat and blouse. Stephanie Charlesworth (née Armstrong), the first social worker appointed by the Department of Immigration to its Melbourne office in March 1949, described her as a tall, handsome woman with shortish iron-grey hair, decisive but gently spoken, approachable and not at all intimidating, who was supportive of her staff and gave them a great degree of autonomy. Sydney social worker Sylvia Lyons, however, remembered her as a slim, attractive woman who was overbearing, 'would not let you ask her things but just told you', and who 'got on everybody's nerves'. It is possible that her early links with Calwell did not endear her to her male colleagues in Canberra during the 1950s, many of whom regarded her as a nuisance. John Tarbath, a social worker recruited by Dobson in 1950, described her as a 'visionary with ideas which were long before her time and not acceptable to the public service'. There is oral evidence to suggest that the Secretary of the Department, Tasman Heyes, severely undermined her efforts and refused to let her into his office.⁵

In June 1949 a Social Welfare Section was created, and the Aliens Control Division was now renamed the Aliens Assimilation Division. This changed nomenclature reflected an important shift in conceptualising the relationship of the Department with aliens. The Section had an approved establishment of 39 social workers—considerably more than Dobson had originally proposed. She was appointed Officer in Charge in Canberra, and one senior social worker was appointed in each State except Tasmania. Between them they were allotted 26 Grade II and six Grade I positions. Under Public Service Board regulations all appointees were required to have a Diploma in Social Studies, for which two years' study at university in political science and economics was a prerequisite. Most had another degree before enrolling in social work. Grade II workers had to have a minimum of two years' experience after graduating and senior social workers a minimum of five. Only sixteen of the positions were allocated to city offices, nineteen positions required the officer to live full-time in the Centres, and fifteen positions were earmarked for remote country areas. It was intended that each Centre have its own full-time social worker.[6]

From the outset, Dobson recognised the inadequacy of the Department's services to meet the complex needs of migrants. She therefore recommended the formation of a voluntary community support network in the form of Australia-wide Good Neighbour Committees. She also advised the referral of cases to relevant voluntary and statutory bodies providing welfare services, as a means of bringing migrants 'into touch with the ordinary community facilities, and encouraging the community, in turn, to play its part in Australia's huge migration programme'. She was aware of the special needs of the alien migrant and of the necessity for administrative coordination. She wrote:[7]

> In his case, the problems of the ordinary citizen are multiplied many times . . . Most cases reveal, not one single problem, but a variety which are dealt with by different Departments and voluntary bodies. It is particularly necessary in the case of these newcomers that each individual should be treated as a whole person, and not as a series of isolated problems to be dealt with in unconnected fashion by a number of different organisations and Departments.

All Departmental social workers were women, except for four ex-servicemen who qualified at Adelaide University under the Commonwealth Reconstruction Training Scheme. One of these, John Tarbath, was inspired to study social work by the desperate suffering of the refugees he had witnessed while in the airforce in Europe. Most were Anglo-Celts and largely monolingual, although Nora Brack in Sydney, the daughter of a Swiss diplomat, was fluent in French and German. Others, such as Pauline Griffin in Sydney and Stephanie Charlesworth in Melbourne, taught themselves enough 'DP Deutsch' to communicate with those of their clients from camps in Europe, where German was the lingua franca. Many from the Baltic countries, Griffin recalled, spoke English.

Social workers did not, however, have to rely on their own linguistic skills. The Department provided its regional offices with two or three paid multilingual interpreters, and all social workers quickly built up a network of voluntary interpreters in the languages the paid interpreters could not speak. None of the early social workers interviewed found lack of interpreters a problem. As well as the two paid interpreters employed in the Sydney office, Pauline Griffin identified interpreters in other languages whom she regularly contacted, usually by telephone. Interpreters were also available to social workers residing in or visiting Department of Immigration Holding Centres and workers' camps. From 1949 social workers in the Department's Melbourne office had three full-time interpreters, each fluent in six languages, for their exclusive use. Stephanie Charlesworth could not recall any time when she was not able to get an interpreter. In the absence of appropriate English-language training courses, and because Australian universities did not recognise non-British educational qualifications, migrants at this time faced great difficulties in qualifying as social workers.[8]

The Social Welfare Section was both the Department's most important source of information on the difficulties experienced by migrants and its 'front line' in responding to them. Stephanie Charlesworth recalled that in the period to 1952, when she left the Department, Central Office in Canberra was responsive to her suggestions for change as well as to her requests for advice and assistance. Sylvia Lyons described the help she received from the Chief Migration Officer in Sydney to frame her submissions to Canberra in terms that would be persuasive to bureaucrats.[9]

Casework

The social workers' primary function was casework. Clients were referred to them from various sections of the Department of Immigration, the Commonwealth Employment Service, the Department of Social Services, by teachers of migrants employed by the Commonwealth Office of Education, and by managers of Migrant Workers' Hostels. They dealt with migrants with difficulties obtaining housing and employment; with mental illness, tuberculosis and other medical conditions; suffering bereavement, domestic violence and marital problems. They helped them to comply with laws relating to adoption, maintenance, child welfare, house and land purchasing, eviction and debt repayment, taxation, and to access such services as vocational guidance, tertiary education, baby health centres and English classes. They also dealt with migrants by correspondence, replying to letters from country areas asking how to bring relatives from Europe, to cope with banking, to apply for admission to courses or to claim social welfare benefits.

From December 1950 they were required to meet all ships arriving in Sydney and Melbourne carrying Commonwealth-nominated migrants and to escort them to Reception and Training Centres. Sydney social worker Sylvia Lyons recalled that about three ships arrived every week, each carrying about 13 000 people, and her colleague Pauline Griffin remembered clambering up the sides of ships in Sydney harbour from pilot boats. At Mascot airport Nora Brack met the pregnant women and the aged, who were sent to Australia by air, and accompanied them to the Holding Centres. In Melbourne, Department of Immigration social worker Stephanie Charlesworth accompanied migrants on the train to Bonegilla, offering advice and assistance en route. In South Australia social workers met the trains and, until March 1950, were responsible for tracing lost luggage. One of Brack's many tasks was to bring children who had been hospitalised after shipboard illnesses to rejoin their mothers in Holding Centres. She also ensured that minors who had arrived in Australia without any family were allocated suitable employment, and found families for them to live with in areas where they could pursue further education. They assisted migrants to cope with the legacies of past trauma, with the inflexibility of their new environment, and with community facilities ill-prepared to meet their needs. Although in retrospect this appears to have been an impossible task, it did not appear to them that way at the time. Most social workers were young and full of energy and enthusiasm. As Pauline Griffin commented, 'I don't think when you are in your twenties you ever think anything is impossible; just difficult'.[10]

Monitoring migrant accommodation

The shortage of suitable accommodation for alien families and the Department's policy of housing the wives and children of alien workers separately in Holding Centres was, observed senior social worker in Sydney Jean Scott in her first report for 1949–50, the source of most of the cases she had to deal with. Scott was a highly experienced, capable and assertive social worker who got on well with the Departmental hierarchy. She also had great compassion for her clients, as she herself had experienced hardship in Scotland during the Depression. In attempting to solve their problems she liaised with a wide range of State departments and welfare workers in most available social service organisations. Her section head, Hazel Dobson, endorsed her observation, stating that 'accommodation is without doubt the most widespread and serious problem of all those experienced by migrants'. As well as providing on-site personal advice in the Centres controlled by the Department, social workers visited and reported on conditions in migrant work camps, such as those maintained by the Railways and Water and Sewerage Boards. Pauline Griffin visited all the Department of Immigration Holding Centres in NSW as well as such work camps as those for the migrants building the Warragamba Dam. While the Holding Centres were run on hierarchical lines, generally by ex-servicemen employed by the Department, she observed more self-management among the migrants in the work camps.[11]

Liaison with other Commonwealth and State bodies

Departmental social workers drew attention to the inappropriateness of provisions in social welfare legislation discriminating on the grounds of nationality against aliens in the grant of certain social welfare benefits. The Sydney social worker Sylvia Lyons, who visited the Princess Juliana Sanatorium regularly from January 1950, for example, discovered that aliens could not claim the special tuberculosis allowance. Her submission to the Department of Social Services resulted in the granting of this allowance to aliens from July 1951, and in the retrospective payment of sickness benefits by the DSS to previously ineligible patients.[12]

They also drew the attention of other departments to the insensitivity of their staff in dealing with migrants. G.N. Hunter, a social worker in South Australia, reported in March 1950 to Hazel Dobson in Canberra that officers of the Commonwealth Employment Service (CES) stereotyped migrants as 'arrogant'. He complained that a uniformed policeman was placed on full-time duty at CES offices next to the room where migrants were interviewed and in full view of those waiting to be interviewed. He suggested that the Department of Immigration arrange meetings with the CES, employers of large numbers of migrants, and trade unions, to enable them to understand how their officers could be helped to adjust their behaviour and attitudes to migrants. This was not true, however, of all government agencies. Sylvia Lyons found that the General Post Office was excellent at placing unskilled migrants or those who had had problems in other places of employment.[13]

Departmental social workers were sometimes called in to mediate in industrial disputes. In September 1949 Jean Scott was required to liaise with the management of King George V Hospital in Sydney, where the Hospital Employees Association had complained about the employment of 45 refugee women. Although three were qualified doctors, three were dentists and one was a third-year medical student, they were employed as nursing aides and paid as domestics. The union objected to their not being paid award wages. The women, only eight of whom were single, endured poor conditions and heavy work. They felt alienated from the nursing staff and wanted someone to explain to their colleagues the wartime experiences from which they were still suffering and their hopes for the new country. None had been in an Australian home and none had homes of their own; they lived and worked in the hospital. Scott interviewed the union, and after her intervention with the sister in charge of nurses the women were given a recreation room in which to rest and meet their husbands when off duty.[14]

Liaison with non-government welfare agencies

It is likely that the degree of cooperation Departmental social workers obtained from non-government organisations varied from State to State. There were few ethnic organisations anywhere in Australia in these early years and few, apart from the well-developed Jewish bodies, were capable of providing welfare services for their compatriots. However, as Sydney social worker Pauline Griffin recalled, there were groups centred around individual migrants who could be called on to help clients of the same nationality.[15]

Griffin's colleague, Sylvia Lynch, saw linking migrants with the community as her most important function. However, the experiences of social workers in various States differed when they sought to refer their clients to mainstream welfare organisations. Adelaide social worker G.N. Hunter became acutely aware of the passive attitudes prevailing in mainstream organisations towards the assimilation of migrants. He believed that successful assimilation would result not so much from adjustment by migrants, but from the active re-education of such organisations. In November 1952 he reported on the 'still great reserve in regard to the acceptance of migrants as an integral part of our community' among the institutions or organisations from which he had sought cooperation. He had found that such institutions commonly expected migrants to fit into the 'ordinary pattern of life followed by Australians and that they as a particular organisation (profit making bodies excluded) do not have to worry about migrants'. It was commonly believed that migrants should show immediate and tangible evidence of their becoming assimilated: 'we've brought them here—they should now feel they are one of us, and do as we do' was the prevailing attitude he encountered. All but the aged were expected to assimilate as soon as possible. He suggested that a panel of competent and trained 'assimilation advisers', attached to the Assimilation Division of the Department of Immigration, be sent to liaise with employers, voluntary and statutory organisations, to enlarge community understanding of the effect of migration on the Australian community. Reform, he believed, could not be relegated to any one State, as it was a Commonwealth responsibility. He warned his Department that: 'The current public and official attitude(s) held in regard to the assimilation of migrants . . . hold potentially grave and alarming implications for the future effects of the migrant body of our population on the Australian nation'.[16]

This was not the experience of social workers in all States. Pauline Griffin remembers a considerable degree of sympathy towards migrants and willingness to help on the part of the mainstream organisations with which she dealt in Sydney, such as schools, churches, child welfare and family service agencies, and hospitals, where migrant nursing aides acted as interpreters for hospital social workers. She found their cooperation remarkable in a society that had no idea how it was going to be transformed by migrants who came from countries few Australians had heard of. Stephanie Charlesworth found mainstream agencies in Melbourne, and religious leaders, such as the Catholic migrant chaplain and the Polish and Dutch chaplains, very responsive to requests to help migrants in the period to 1952. The Dutch community was particularly well organised in responding to cases of need, while she found groups associated with the Good Neighbour Movement to be good at organising social events for the more outgoing and better adjusted alien migrants. By 1951 she observed that the problems of migrants in Holding Centres, particularly those of Yugoslav and Maltese couples, were changing from legal, psychological and medical to marital. Her work involved fewer responses to emergencies and became more focused on personal relationships.[17]

Coping with male prejudice

As women in a predominantly male world, Departmental social workers had to be prepared to deal with male prejudice. Pauline Griffin remembers that her colleagues got on well with male administrators. The latter were, however, preoccupied with the practical challenges involved in the movement of large numbers of migrants from the ships to their places of employment and accommodation, and were 'somewhat bemused' by the role played by social workers, who often advocated on behalf of their clients with their Department, drawing attention to the problems created in particular cases by Departmental restrictions. Nora Brack initially experienced considerable sexual harassment as the first social worker appointed to Bonegilla. The camp's administrators were unhelpful until the senior social worker was sent from Melbourne to insist that adequate working conditions be provided.[18]

When Jean Scott travelled from Sydney to Cooma in October 1952 to establish a branch of the New Settlers' League there, she found that the representative of the Canberra Good Neighbour Council had done nothing to prepare for her visit as arranged. The representative relieved himself of the opinion that the lack of assimilation in Australia could be attributed to the Department's decision to appoint 'highly trained social workers with the latest brand of psychology when what was needed was the interest of motherly women who had reared families', and left before the meeting finished. The CMO in Sydney reported dryly to Central Office that this remark 'was adequately dealt with'.[19]

Promoting departmental propaganda

Departmental social workers were also responsible for encouraging ordinary Australians to overcome their fears and prejudices and to welcome migrants into their communities. Wherever they went they lectured groups such as Parents and Citizens Associations, Apex, Legacy clubs and churches, showing the films 'Mike and Stefani' and 'No Strangers Here', and leading discussions on migration issues. They gathered information from local government authorities, teachers, ministers of religion, employers, police and any others in a position to advise on migrant welfare, as well as interviewing migrants themselves in their homes or workplaces. This function was largely taken over by the Department's Public Relations Section, created in Canberra in 1955. Before that date, journalists from the Australian News and Information Bureau had been seconded to the Department of Immigration. From 1954 the Department began to spread the message of assimilation by distributing monthly 42,000 copies of its magazine *The Good Neighbour*, and by recycling its articles to whatever magazines would publish them. It mounted an immigration display on the Jubilee Train which toured Victoria and South Australia, illustrating 'the types of migrants Australia is receiving and the contributions they are making to Australia', and distributed 15,000 copies of a leaflet entitled 'Why Migration is Vital to You'. They provided assimilation bodies with the film 'No Strangers Here', and sent information to children for school projects on immigration.[20]

Restructuring and rethinking 1952

By December 1951, the Department of Immigration recognised that its Social Welfare Section as currently structured would not be able to cope with the enormous demands created by the immigration program, which that year brought 185,000 migrants to Australia. It therefore asked the Commonwealth Immigration Advisory Council (IAC) to conduct an inquiry into 'the scope and nature of an adequate social welfare service to all immigration centres and workers' hostels', and to suggest an appropriate establishment within the Department to deal with social welfare matters.[21]

This inquiry was largely dominated by women. Chaired by Ada Norris, representative of the National Council of Women on the IAC, it included F.G. Krumm, president of the Young Women's Christian Association, representatives of the Australian Council of Social Workers, the Australian Council of Social Services and its Victorian and South Australian branches, the Department of Immigration's Social Welfare Section and Olga Leschen, supervisor of the Free Kindergarten Union of Victoria. Professor G.W. Paton, Vice-Chancellor of Melbourne University and President of the Victorian Council of Social Service, joined the Committee in April 1952.[22]

The review was conducted in the context of a recession which created unemployment for the first time since the Depression of the 1930s. The migrant intake, planned in August 1951 at 150 000, was curtailed by Cabinet in July 1952, and the intake from all sources for 1953 was limited to 80 000. Government expenditure on migration was reduced, and three migrant Reception Centres were closed. In January 1952 the management of migrant hostels was taken over by Commonwealth Hostels Ltd, a company responsible to the Department of Labour and National Service. This body accepted that the Department of Immigration was responsible for assimilation activities, and looked to it to provide social welfare services to migrants in its hostels. This division of responsibilities disappointed the Victorian Council of Social Services, which believed that social problems of migrants in hostels should be the responsibility of the relevant hostel administrators.[23]

One of the principal problems with the original allocation of social workers had resulted from the female domination of the profession. Many were married with families. Like all married women they were, until 1966, prevented from holding permanent positions in the Commonwealth Public Service. This made their employment conditions insecure. Nora Brack, one of the first social workers employed in 1949 by the Department of Immigration in Sydney, recalled that she was refused re-employment after her marriage because she might become pregnant. Family responsibilities prevented those like Sylvia Lyons, who already had children, from residing in the Reception and Training and Holding Centres. The single social workers appointed to those centres found that their working conditions varied considerably, and most lacked the privacy necessary to interview clients. While the commander of the Bathurst Centre provided the necessary room, interpreting staff and equipment, Nora Brack found nothing prepared for her arrival at Bonegilla. In a period when all forms of accommodation were at a premium, better conditions for social workers were not a priority with the Department. The Holding Centre at Greta was divided into two 'cities'—'silver city' (the corrugated iron huts) and the slightly more comfortable 'chocolate city' (the wooden huts). When the resident social worker there in early 1952 asked for partitions for privacy in her office and linoleum on the floor, her request was refused because of the recent funding cuts in expenditure on migration.

As members of a profession not long established in Australia, social workers were in demand by agencies offering city employment and better salaries and employment conditions than the Commonwealth. The Department of Immigration was, therefore, unable to fill all its 39 designated positions. By April 1952 it had employed a maximum of 30 social workers at any one time. By that year, 575 000 immigrants had been brought to Australia since January 1947.[24]

In January 1952 the Citizenship Convention had urged the government to appoint trained social workers to hostels and Holding Centres to undertake casework and to 'promote group work for adults and children' which would 'inculcate democratic principles and self-help'. The Social Welfare Section, however, recommended that the proposed inquiry into the Department's welfare services should also consider the needs of migrants in the general community. The Social Welfare Section's solution to the Department's inability to attract social workers to its Reception and Training and Holding Centres was to centralise its staff in the capital cities, and have them regularly visit Centres but not live in them. It hoped that the IAC inquiry would suggest that more social workers be employed, and it advised that they work with groups as well as individuals. It also suggested that professional social workers be supplemented by unqualified but trained 'mature women experienced in community welfare work'. There was, it believed, room for 'almost indefinite expansion' in the use of voluntary agencies to supplement the work of paid staff. An information service was needed to relieve social workers of general inquiries and to place migrants in touch with community facilities. The provision of social welfare to migrants should be the responsibility of the Department of Immigration, it stressed, as dual control with any other department would be undesirable.[25]

The lengthy report prepared by the Social Welfare Section for this inquiry not only outlined the extent of the social problems disclosed by its social workers—it warned that the economic costs to the Department of reorganisation and staffing would be insignificant compared with the political costs of not dealing adequately with integration difficulties of immigrants:[26]

> These problems not only present a serious threat to the successful assimilation of the individual or groups concerned, but they are also focal points for the spreading of dissatisfaction among the migrants, or amongst the general public where anti-social behaviour is involved or community resources over-burdened.

It also called attention to the needs of 'new alien groupings', a term it used to refer to the 'considerable degree of alien concentration around essential industries and special projects', which it regarded as 'inevitable for the present' despite 'the most earnest efforts to avoid it'. It argued for the provision of specialised services for alien migrants, arguing that 'their ignorance of the language and customs of the country and . . . total lack of knowledge of the many facilities available to meet various needs in the community' caused the problems of the ordinary citizen to be multiplied many times for the alien.[27]

The lobbying of the Social Welfare Section was partially successful. The inquiry recommended that Departmental social workers should extend their services to Department of Labour and National Service hostels, which at this time housed only British migrants. The following year the Public Service Board approved the placing of the majority of social workers in the capital cities and deploying them from there to serve in Centres and hostels; however, the number of positions was reduced from 39 to 28 (by 1958 only 23 positions remained). In Sydney, three social workers were appointed with primary responsibility for working with the staff and residents of Commonwealth Hostels Ltd, in particular to assist in the planning of social committees. They surveyed community resources near a number of these hostels, and sought to involve local voluntary organisations in providing social and recreational activities for residents. In Victoria and South Australia, Departmental social workers accepted cases from Commonwealth Hostels but staff shortages remained, and a regular visiting service could not be provided. Stephanie Charlesworth spoke of her reluctance to deal with British migrants. She found them full of complaints, much harder to relate to, and reluctant to seek help from the same people who were helping aliens.[28]

Responding to the effects of the 1952 recession on alien workers

The restructuring of the Social Welfare Section prepared it to cope better with the distress caused among alien migrants by the recession that began in 1952. Although the unemployment rate was only 2 per cent, it affected migrants unevenly. Unskilled migrants, women, and those with poor English suffered most. Sydney social workers reported that by mid-1952 hundreds of unemployed migrants were sleeping in the Domain because the Salvation Army Hostel and the City Mission had reached saturation point. The Department agreed to receive them back into migrant centres.[29]

Reports by the Department of Immigration's Welfare Section suggest that the recession affected some sections of the migrant workforce for a number of years. In 1956 they observed that the employment situation had deteriorated steadily in all States, particularly among recent migrants, who had language difficulties and were subject to the 'last to come, first to go' union rule, and general reductions in staff. Older men (over 40), women, and those with physical or mental disabilities were almost impossible to place in employment. In some States public works had come to a standstill and the railways, previously a large employer of migrant labour, were fully staffed. Apprenticeships for migrant youths with language difficulties and without the necessary educational qualifications or above the required age for apprentices were almost non-existent. The worst cases of distress were among unemployed independent immigrants, who were ineligible for income support because they had a guarantor. In 1956–57 approximately 40 per cent of the time of Departmental social workers in all States was taken up with problems that were either directly or indirectly related to unemployment.[30]

As the CES employed only one social worker in NSW and one in Victoria to deal specifically with the disabled, migrants turned to Department of Immigration social workers in growing numbers or were referred there by the CES. In the most populated States, NSW and Victoria, unemployment was placing a heavy strain on non-government organisations—churches, voluntary welfare agencies and national groups (migrant organisations)— with which Departmental social workers liaised.

The recession expanded the role of social workers employed by the Department. They collaborated with the CES in surveying unemployed migrants, assisted in arranging special language classes, trade tests, or even with housing when voluntary agencies were no longer able to provide emergency accommodation for the homeless. They followed up newspaper advertisements for migrants with language difficulties, gave them lists of firms they could contact, and used their personal contacts to get them jobs. They exploited every agency, both statutory and voluntary, in order to alleviate the distress of unemployed migrants. Hazel Dobson's report for 1956/57 concluded by reminding the Department that the numbers seeking her officers' assistance represented only a small proportion of unemployed migrants.[31]

Unemployed migrant women 1952

Alien women were in a particularly vulnerable position during the recession because of the Department of Immigration's housing and English-teaching arrangements, the government's social welfare policy, and prevailing cultural attitudes towards their employment, which limited them to unskilled domestic work in private homes and institutions or in factories. Many married women were housed in Holding Centres, which were converted former military establishments located far from centres of employment. Departmental social workers who regularly visited these Centres, as well as the hostels run by the Department of Labour and National Service in urban and rural areas, reported that women migrants had difficulty finding employment during this period.[32]

Both the selection criteria applied to women and the rights they had on arrival reflected the attitudes towards women prevailing in Australia's post-war culture. Quotas for women workers were much lower than for male workers, and selection criteria were applied to them which did not apply to men. The CMO in Cologne responsible for the selection of 100 German women brought out in 1952 with funding from the Provisional Intergovernmental Committee for the Movement of Migrants from Europe (PICMME), for example, was advised by the Secretary of the Department of Immigration that when selecting these women he should 'take into account their general presentability and appearance . . . as it is felt that the favourable impression we hope they create will help to "sell" the proposed German migration scheme to the Australian public'.[33]

The only occupational categories recommended for female assisted migrants in 1951 were factory work, employment in institutions, or as domestic servants. They were employed in hospitals and convalescent homes as wardsmaids, kitchenmaids or waitresses. Female domestics employed in private homes or institutions were not usually covered by industrial awards. Government policy was that they were to be paid according to Australian rates and to be housed in conditions acceptable to Australians, but it is doubtful whether this was effectively monitored. However, as Stephanie Charlesworth recalled, many women workers quickly became aware that if they were not treated well in their employment as domestics they could complain to the Department and they would be moved. They would often visit the Department's Melbourne headquarters which, she observed, they regarded as their embassy.[34]

In addition to the usual disadvantages of aliens, women migrants shared the legal disabilities common to all women in

Australia, particularly unequal rates of pay. For example, in 1952 the weekly rate of pay for women domestics in private homes was £3.10.0–£4 with keep and £6 in institutions, with £1.1.0 deducted for board and lodgings. The male basic wage at this time was £10.5.0–£10.16.0. All married women were ineligible for unemployment benefits.[35]

Reports by Department of Immigration social workers suggest that the situation did not improve after the 1952 recession. Of all the categories of migrants for whom they sought work in 1956–57, women were most difficult to place—particularly if they had language problems or were supporting mothers. The provision of language classes at night limited the opportunity of most women with families to learn English. Many migrant households, however, increasingly relied on the wages of their women members to keep above the poverty line.[36]

The range of employment open to alien women was limited by perceptions of them—occasionally echoed by Members of Parliament from both sides of the House—as being chiefly suited for domestic work. W.C. Coutts (ALP QLD) recommended the importation from Vienna of more German girls 'many of whom would take your breath away', to solve the marriage problem of German migrants. He also observed that 1200 'talented girls' from that city, 'many of whom speak four languages', had recently lost their jobs as typists and stenographers when the USA ended its occupation of Austria. He asked that they be brought to Australia for temporary employment in the Australian Public Service (aliens were barred from permanent employment in the Public Service). Holt, who confirmed that his government was 'making efforts to bring to Australia a larger number of female migrants from Germany as domestics', replied that the issue of employing skilled women 'is being carefully examined'. H.A. Bruce (ALP QLD) saw women migrants as a cure for homosexuality and a tendency to 'fly to the knife' in regions of high male concentration, such as that around Cloncurry (where migrants worked in the Rio Tinto uranium mine), the Mount Isa mines, and the surrounding cattle country.[37]

Discrimination against Southern Europeans by Departmental Selectors

The work of Department of Immigration social workers in presenting the friendly face of their department to alien migrants was undermined for many southern European migrants by the racial and ethnic discrimination they experienced from those of its officers responsible for migrant selection. These Departmental officials reflected the culture of the society of which they were part and, because of their responsibility for managing the political acceptability of the immigration program, had to take this into consideration when selecting migrants and planning the program's composition. Both the selection and integration of immigrants from southern Europe were affected by racist assumptions that northern Europeans were 'a better type of migrant', and that southern Europeans were perhaps not quite 'white'.

Australia's racially discriminatory migration policy initially applied to southern Europeans as well as Asians. In 1921, after the introduction of discriminatory immigration restrictions by the USA, the Australian government feared an influx of southern Europeans. Between 1923 and 1929, therefore, it progressively excluded Maltese, Italians, Greeks, Yugoslavs and Albanians. A policy that discriminated against all aliens was not introduced until 1930. After that date, while British migrants could come to Australia without restriction, all aliens had to be sponsored by immediate close relatives and needed to obtain a landing permit before departing for Australia. The conditions demanded by these permits, and the visas by which they were replaced, were varied from time to time as the government thought fit. Considerations of 'colour' were more important than nationality. Citizens of the republics of Eire and South Africa, for example, were regarded for immigration purposes as 'British', whereas Cypriots, who were British subjects, were processed as 'aliens'.[38]

The attitude that southern Europeans were not 'desirable types' persisted after the war, and influenced Australia's selection of workers. Selection officers in Mediterranean regions were given the task of picking the difference between 'colour' and suntan. One, selecting Greeks, used to refer doubtful cases to the medical officer, who had them strip to see if they were dark all over. This 'racial' consideration overrode political alignment during the war, as it applied as much to Greeks, who supported the allied forces, as to Italians, who fought against them.[39]

Greeks

During the period 1946 to 1954, only 8963 permanent settlers came from Greece. Greek ex-servicemen led the protest against what they perceived to be discrimination against Greek immigration in October 1948. At their request, the Greek Consul-General approached the Australian government through Allan Fraser MP. He argued unsuccessfully for the inclusion of Greece in the assisted passage agreements for ex-servicemen and their dependants, being negotiated by Australia with other allied nations. In February 1949 a group of Queensland Greeks who had served in the Australian forces during the war appealed, again through their Consul-General, for the right to nominate their relatives from Greece under the assisted passage scheme. They were told that the scheme was not for ex-members of the Australian forces.[40]

The announcement of the government's intention to conclude migration agreements with Italy and the Netherlands in 1951 aroused further resentment among the Greek community in Australia. The Greek Consul in Melbourne informed the Secretary of the Department of Immigration in January 1951 that 'there is a strong undercurrent of resentment among the Greek Community that 20000 Italians should be brought out here free of charge while no similar scheme operates in respect of Greeks'. At this time there was considerable agitation among Greek workers in Rome, where there was a 22–28 per cent unemployment rate, to migrate to Australia. Greek diplomatic representatives, Greek Orthodox clergy and the Greek branch of the RSSAILA continued to make representations to the Department on behalf of the Greek community. The *Hellenic Herald* in Sydney complained the Greeks were being treated less favourably than they deserved, given the assistance they had extended to Australians during the war.[41]

Objections to Greek immigration were, however, not solely based on racial prejudice. A 1952 Departmental assessment of Greece as a potential source of immigrants, which drew on Australian, American and International Labour Organisation (ILO) sources, advised that statistics of pre-war Greek emigration indicated a high rate of return. Emigration was seen by the ILO as a short-term solution to the current economic problems in Greece. Also integration problems were anticipated, resulting from the current 27 per cent illiteracy rate and the fact that 60 per cent of the workforce was employed in largely small-scale farming, which demanded very different agricultural practices from those required in Australia. Of the 12 000 Greeks in Australia at the 1947 Census 4500 were not naturalised, it observed. Bureaucratic inefficiency, corruption and lack of records on right-wing extremists were seen as obstacles to effective security screening. It concluded that Australia was unlikely to be able to recruit from Greece the 'quantities and types' of skilled workers demanded by the Australian economy.

The government decided to ignore these Departmental objections and, although no formal approach had been received from the Greek government concerning the negotiation of an immigration agreement, the Minister for Immigration decided in November 1951 to appoint migration officers in Athens. In January 1952 the Consul-General for Greece in Australia requested an interview with the Minister, Harold Holt, to discuss the negotiation of an assisted immigration treaty. These discussions were deferred until after the Minister had signed the agreement in August 1952 with the PICMME to accept 500 Greek migrants. An important reason for accepting this group of mostly single male rural workers from Greece was to deflect criticism that Australia was favouring ex-enemy nationals over former allies. While the target intake under this agreement in 1953–54 was for 2000 Greeks, they were greatly outnumbered by former enemy aliens (7000 West Germans, 3000 East Germans, and 750 Austrians).[42]

Single women were initially excluded from the PICMME agreement, as the Department anticipated 'considerable difficulty' in placing 'single Greek girls with a rural background into suitable rural employment'. By 1953, however, the Department of Labour and National Service was seeking Greek and Italian 'girls' because of the reluctance of women from northern Europe to accept positions in Australia as domestics. They were required to be childless, 'of good appearance and character', under 35, experienced as domestics, have some knowledge of English, and to agree to accept placement in country districts with Australian families. This was another example of the selection criteria for the only category of female worker acceptable to Australia being more rigorous than for male workers.[43]

Male workers were also difficult to place in rural Australia because of their lack of English and of the prevalence of discrimination against southern Europeans 'from the "colour" angle'. Employers did not accept Greeks readily, preferring Dutch and German rural workers. Greek men resisted separation from their families. Although the Director of Bonegilla Reception Centre was very positive in his report on the Greek migrants sent under the PICMME agreement, he believed that they had not been adequately informed on Australian accommodation arrangements before leaving Greece. 'They are very reluctant in all cases to move other than as a family unit', he observed. In a speech of welcome to newly arrived Greek migrants in Melbourne in April 1953 the Greek envoy, Dimitri N. Lambros, spoke of the 'lack of discipline and stamina' among young married Greeks who had arrived on an earlier ship and had deserted their work in Mildura to return to their wives in Bonegilla.[44]

In June 1953 the Secretary of the Department of Immigration sent Mr Lambros a draft migration agreement based largely on the migration agreements entered into with other countries. By this time Australia was looking to Greece to make up a substantial shortfall in Dutch migration and an anticipated shortfall from Germany and Austria. They wanted to attract Greek skilled as well as rural workers, although non-recognition of Greek trade qualifications by Australian employers and trade unions was anticipated. While under this treaty the Australian government did not accept any obligation to provide or obtain work for the migrants selected, it guaranteed that, if placed in positions, the immigrant would be entitled to 'the same wages, accommodation and general conditions of employment as apply to Australians engaged in the same type of employment'. Although regarded as temporary residents for two years, these migrants were subsequently entitled to apply for permanent residence and were encouraged, after five years' permanent residence, to apply for full citizenship status.[45]

Italians and the restriction of sponsorship rights

The Italian government, gravely concerned about its surplus population, had begun discussions with the Australian government on a migration agreement by August 1950. The Department of Immigration was enthusiastic about the type of worker this agreement would make available, although it had reservations:[46]

> Southern Italians, particularly Sicilians and Calabrians, are not the most desirable types from an Australian viewpoint, but there is no doubt that there are many thousands of both skilled and unskilled Italians in central and northern Italy who would be very suitable for settlement in Australia. In addition to rural workers, they include skilled men over a wide industrial field and would be particularly useful for employment in developmental and constructional work in Australia, such as the Snowy Mountains Hydro-Electric Scheme, where for example a vast amount of tunnelling, in which Italians are acknowledged experts, will have to be undertaken.

As with German migration, the Department had to proceed carefully in negotiating an agreement with Italy. Some powerful community leaders and advisers to the government on immigration planning were prejudiced against Italians. In August 1950 the Secretary of the Department of Immigration, Tasman Heyes, met with J.C. Neagle, General Secretary of the RSSAILA, a body represented on the Immigration Advisory Council, and Albert Monk, President of the Australian Council of Trade Unions and member of both the Immigration Planning Council and the Immigration Advisory Council, to discuss the migration of ex-enemy aliens. Heyes reported to Holt that 'Mr Neagle . . . personally dislikes Italians and I know is opposed to any large influx of them into this country. Albert Monk has similar views, particularly in relation to Southern Italians'. Heyes advised his Minister that:[47]

> The case for Italian immigration is on a par with the German one. We have signed a peace treaty with Italy, and in accordance with long established government policy, Italians are technically entitled to the same treatment as other European nationals if they wish to settle here under their own arrangements . . . It would be to our advantage to select the best offering and not just accept those who are fortunate enough to have relatives abroad who can nominate them. In our selection policy we would place main emphasis upon the recruitment of Northern Italians of suitable type.

In reviewing the migrant intake in March 1952, however, Heyes became alarmed by the possibility that Italian migration to Australia might come to dominate the immigration program. He advised his Minister that steps should be taken to curtail it, as had been done in the 1920s. Although Italians had comprised only 5.7 per cent of the intake from October 1945 to December 1950 (compared with over 48 per cent British and 36 per cent displaced persons), Heyes feared that, as the IRO scheme had closed and the flow of British migrants had slackened, the numbers of Italians might rise disproportionately to the rest of the intake. He believed this might 'cause public alarm, having a detrimental effect on our overall immigration programme'.[48]

The conclusion of the migration agreement with Italy in March 1951 had made 20 000 Italians eligible for assisted passage, and the numbers of applications from full-fee-paying migrants had escalated each year from 1762 in 1947 to 25 302 in the first ten months of 1951. Heyes feared the impact this might have on Australian national identity. He warned Holt that: 'Unless precautions are taken the flow of alien migrants could be overwhelmingly Italian and it could happen that they could outnumber British migrants. This could lead to the creation of a situation which would not be in the best interests of the Australian community'.[49]

The Department had taken some steps to limit the numbers of Italians sponsored by gaining ministerial approval for the imposition of a literacy test, 'because of the extent of illiteracy amongst Italians and other Mediterranean races'. At a recent meeting the Immigration Advisory Council had recommended that restrictions be placed on their nomination rights, particularly those of wage-earners without substantial assets. Although new tactics needed to be devised, Heyes hoped that:[50]

> These measures and the selective methods which will be taken by our immigration officers in Italy will, no doubt, effect a considerable reduction in the number of Italians admitted, will ensure that those admitted are of a better calibre and will no doubt also lead to a reduction in the number of nominations submitted, the rapid growth of which is becoming an embarrassment in some State offices.

Heyes sought a way of curtailing unassisted Italian migration which would not endanger the agreement with Italy by leaving Australia open to accusations of discrimination. At the same time, care had to be taken that any administrative arrangement limiting Italians should not adversely affect the immigration of unassisted central and northern Europeans. To distance his Department from the solution he had in mind, Heyes successfully recommended to Holt that a subcommittee of the Immigration Advisory Council be set up. Entitled 'Committee on the Control of Alien Immigration', it comprised Neagle, Monk, Ada Norris (representative of the National Council of Women) and Colonel R.S. Ryan, MP (Liberal VIC), a veteran of the 1914–18 war, former diplomat and grazier, as chairman.[51]

Heyes carefully prepared a paper for the information of the subcommittee which showed that the Italian component of the total alien intake had risen from 0.3 per cent in 1946 to 28 per cent in 1951. He stressed the danger to Australian culture and prevailing notions of national identity that might result if this escalation was not checked, and emphasised his Department's determination to preserve the British character of Australian society:[52]

if unrestrained, Italian immigration could not only constitute an overwhelming proportion of our alien migration but would outnumber British migrants. This, with their penchant for community settlement and their greater resistance to assimilation than the general run of foreigners, would ultimately lead to the creation of a situation which would be opposed to Australian interests . . . The Department's view is that . . . the over-riding principle of our immigration policy is that nothing shall be done to endanger the predominantly British constituent of our population, or which would tend to the creation of any considerable alien minority of a particular nationality.

He advised the subcommittee not to consider the imposition of quotas on Italians, as that 'could provide room for criticism by Asians on the ground of racial discrimination'. Placing an arbitrary limit on the number of Italians could also be perceived as discriminatory. His solution was to introduce regulations which would appear even-handed—as they would limit the sponsorship rights of all groups in Australia—but which could be administered by Departmental officers in a way that would discriminate against southern Europeans. He suggested that the sponsorship of friends should be forbidden irrespective of nationality, and that, while the sponsorship of close relatives (wives, children, parents and siblings) should continue unchanged, evidence of relationship should be required when other relatives were sponsored. These rules, he suggested, should 'be strictly applied where the admission of southern Europeans is concerned, but with wide discretion in the case of northern and central Europeans'.[53]

Heyes personally addressed the subcommittee when it met in Melbourne on 3 April 1952, on his 'serious concern' about the efficacy of current restrictions 'to stem the flow of the Mediterranean types'. The subcommittee not only endorsed Heyes' discriminatory recommendations—it made them more restrictive. It rejected Ada Norris's suggestion that southern Europeans should be restricted to sponsoring close relatives only, on the grounds that this would appear discriminatory. The subcommittee decided to recommend that all non-British migrants be prevented from sponsoring other than immediate family. It specified, however, that a 'wide discretion should be exercised in the case of Northern and Central Europeans'.

In forwarding these recommendations to Holt, Heyes stressed that the limitation of sponsorship to immediate family would, in practice, be restricted to 'the Mediterranean type of migrant and not extended to nationals such as Dutch, Scandinavian, German, etc.'. He indicated that, if approved, he would send confidential instructions to migration officers in all States. The Minister approved these recommendations on 14 May 1952 with the proviso that exemptions should be allowed for southern Europeans sponsoring relatives to work in rural areas or essential industries. His decision was endorsed by the IAC at its next meeting in June 1952 which, on the recommendation of the Department of Immigration, further restricted the definition of 'close dependent relatives' by removing siblings. Regional offices were informed of the changes in October 1953.[54]

It was not until May 1958 that the government admitted that the regulations restricted family reunion by southern Europeans to dependent relatives but were more generous for migrants from northern and eastern Europe. In answer to a question by Jim Cairns in May 1958, Minister for Immigration Alexander Downer claimed that these regulations had been adopted in May 1956, and that:[55]

> The dependency clause applies principally to those countries bordering the Mediterranean, from where there has always been a large number of applications for migration to Australia. It was necessary to introduce this requirement early in 1956 to ensure that, within the numbers of migrants we may receive each year, the immigration programme as a whole maintains the necessary degree of balance between types and occupations.

Through these revised sponsorship regulations Australia was able to control the numbers of full-fare-paying aliens, and to regulate the flow of Europeans from particular regions by selective application of these regulations. It also limited the numbers of assisted southern Europeans through the treaties negotiated with the Italian and Greek governments. Only 16.6 per cent of Italians and 33.4 per cent of Greeks and Cypriots who arrived in Australia between 1947 and 1973 were assisted. This meant that the great majority of southern Europeans did not receive the initial settlement assistance provided by the government to, for example, British migrants, 86.5 per cent of whom were assisted, or to Germans, 75.3 per cent of whom received aid.[56]

It was possible to regulate migration flows by the use of discriminatory provisions during a period when migration regulations were not codified and not publicly disclosed, when there were still strong push factors in Europe, and when it was not electorally damaging to make public statements such as that expressed by South African-born grazier C.G. Anderson (Country

Party NSW), who explained to the House in September 1958: 'In Europe there are three different types, the Nordics, the Mediterraneans and the Alpines. I think we should concentrate on the northern Europeans because I believe they can be assimilated more easily than southern Europeans'. His racist theories were echoed from the Opposition benches by Queensland farmer H.R. Bruce, who believed that 'Building a population is like breeding thoroughbred horses. We must have an infusion of new blood from time to time . . . We have had a very large infusion of Latin blood, and I think it is necessary to have Nordic blood'.[57]

These racist theories which disparaged southern Europeans were, however, challenged from both sides of the House by such Members of Parliament as W.C. Coutts (ALP QLD) and A.S. Hulme (Liberal QLD), who had substantial numbers of Italians in their electorates. Discrimination and secrecy were also being questioned. Lawyer and future Minister for Immigration B.M. Snedden (Liberal VIC) appealed in September 1958 for the codification of migration regulations:[58]

> we should include in our legislation the inviolable right of family re-union . . . such a code should clearly enunciate also the exclusions that will prevent a person wishing to nominate another from having a nomination considered . . . and, perhaps more important than anything, a definite statement in legislative form should be provided to the migrant showing that he is free from any discrimination and shall enjoy social equality.

Criticism of the Department's discriminatory family reunion policies was also expressed in 1966 by Melbourne academic James Jupp. In his book *Arrivals and Departures* he quoted a Melbourne Italian on the importance of his family's presence to his happiness in Australia. 'Perhaps this southern Italian former farm labourer understands more about assimilation than the Immigration officials who have been reluctant to encourage Southern European family migration by the means used to attract the British and Northern Europeans', he remarked acerbically.[59] This was, however, soon to change.

The diminution of racism within the mainstream community towards southern Europeans by the late 1960s, combined with the Department's perception that increased prosperity within the EC caused falling interest in migration to Australia from northern Europe, resulted in more equitable sponsorship regulations for southern Italians. The granting of equal assistance with passage costs and settlement benefits to southern

Europeans came only after years of determined negotiation by the Italian government, including a temporary suspension of its migration agreement with Australia. In July 1969 the wives and dependent children of any breadwinner who had come to Australia as an unassisted migrant became eligible for assisted passage. This increased the proportion of southern Europeans receiving assisted passage from 24.5 per cent between 1947 and 1969 to 53 per cent between 1970 and 1983. On its return to power in December 1973, the Labor government adopted a global non-discriminatory immigration policy and set about removing existing discriminatory laws and regulations. It did not, however, extend assisted passage to non-Europeans, and such assistance was abandoned in 1982 for all but humanitarian entrants.[60]

Conclusion

In the period before the development of ethnic community bodies with the organisational capacity to deliver welfare services, Departmental social workers provided a unique personal service to hundreds of thousands of distressed, needy, ill and confused migrants throughout Australia. Their achievements were all the more remarkable when one considers their handicaps. Social work was a new profession in the post-war period. It was dominated by women at a time when the professional expertise of women was undervalued in almost every area of Australian life. They were middle-class, largely monolingual Anglo-Celts attempting to understand and solve the problems of migrants from an enormous range of cultures whose various experiences of the cataclysm of World War II they could only imagine. As the Department of Immigration was the only Commonwealth agency to employ such large numbers of social workers, it was difficult for them to set up a support network for their clients in the wider community.

Most of the personal problems which Departmental social workers attempted to tackle were either caused or exacerbated by legislative and administrative discrimination against aliens rooted in Australia's British origins and its conception of itself as an ethnically British country. This conception of Australian national identity, for example, sanctioned the provision of inferior on-arrival accommodation to aliens and the systemic disruption of their families. It was sustained by a network of discriminatory legislation and administrative practices (such as those regulating the intake of Greeks and Italians), which deprived aliens of important social welfare benefits and prevented hospitals, psychiatric services and other necessary public facilities from being responsive to their needs.

The commitment of the Department of Immigration to assisting all migrants to become part of the host community was clearly evidenced by the work of its professional social workers. They helped migrant planners to identify major obstacles to the successful absorption of migrants, and suggested ways to remove these obstacles. The effectiveness of their advice was, however, limited by the cultures of those they were advising. Despite their responsibility for administering the government's policy of migrant assimilation, the image of Australian national identity which most influential bureaucrats shared with the rest of the community during the 1950s prevented them from appreciating the practical and psychological effects of discrimination on aliens in general and on specific ethnic groups.

CHAPTER 3

Non-compliant women in Holding Centres

NON-COMPLIANCE is often described as 'the weapon of the weak'. Rather than being the ineffective reaction of a victim, it can be a powerful spur to administrative reform and sometimes even cultural change. Laws and regulations that cannot be complied with, which are structured in ways which deter compliance or which are deliberately and publicly flouted, erode the authority of the state. One of the principal tasks of bureaucrats, therefore, of is to monitor compliance and remedy the causes of non-compliance, either voluntary or involuntary. Sometimes, in the process of dealing with a particular problem, more widespread and similarly neglected community needs are highlighted, and the solutions arrived at contain the seeds of profound cultural change. The Department of Immigration's response to non-compliance by alien supporting mothers in its Holding Centres illustrates this point.

One of the most intractable problems identified by Hazel Dobson in her 1948 survey of refugees was that created for the Department by refugee women who were pregnant or caring for preschool children. Supporting mothers were possibly the weakest and most vulnerable group among the refugees brought to Australia from 1947 to 1954 under the IRO agreement. Male and female refugees (unlike British migrants) were required to work wherever they were directed by the Department of Immigration for two years. Both married and single women in advanced pregnancy or caring for infants were unable to comply. In the process of searching for a solution to the problem they posed, administrators were required to examine some of their basic cultural assumptions about women, and to recognise the importance of providing adequate child-minding facilities if these women were to work. By involuntary non-compliance with their obligation to work, alien women highlighted systemic obstacles to the exercise of the rights and fulfilment of responsibilities of Australian citizens who were supporting mothers. Solutions to their problems, however, were much slower in coming.

Just as today, the majority of all post-war refugees were women. The gender composition of refugees in the western zone of Germany in 1946 was estimated to be 44 per cent male and 56 per cent female. By 1949, Britain had brought 5600 German women to the United Kingdom to work for two years as domestics, nurses, in institutions or in industry. Their medical examination included a test for pregnancy.[1]

Between 1947 and 1954 Australia's intake of 170 700 refugees included 70 678 women, either unattached or as dependants of men. Like all refugees these women were selected on humanitarian grounds, without reference to their work experience or skills. Whatever their qualifications their two-year contract required them to work as domestics in either private homes or institutions or in factories. Male workers were accommodated either in Department of Labour and National Service workers' hostels or in accommodation provided by their employers, both of which were regarded by the Department of Immigration as unsuitable for women and children. Alien women with children, either married or unsupported, were housed in Department of Immigration Holding Centres, which were former army and airforce bases, mostly located far from centres of employment. Wives found themselves sometimes hundreds of miles from their husbands, and not infrequently in another State.[2]

The problem of non-compliant refugee women was an interdepartmental one. As it was a question relating to employment, it involved the Department of Labour and National Service's Commonwealth Employment Service (CES). As it also concerned the assimilation of aliens, it was the responsibility of the Department of Immigration, whose regional director was required to approve all allocations of aliens to employment in his State. The many tasks of the newly appointed social workers in the Department included both 'cooperation with the Commonwealth

Employment Service in the placement in employment of special or difficult cases in reception and training centres', and 'dealing with the social problems of pregnant women and mothers of young children (both married and unmarried)'. These tasks were made almost impossible in the case of married mothers with young children by the accommodation arrangements, which caused most of the problems by disrupting their families.[3]

Married Women

In August 1948 the CES sought advice from the CMO in Sydney on women refugees who were unable to comply with the terms of their contract because they were pregnant or nursing infants. The problem was discussed at a conference of CMOs on 23–25 August 1948, which recommended that married women in this position be released from their employment obligation. This was approved by the Secretary on 27 October 1948. From then on, a married woman refugee who could not take up work or continue working because of pregnancy, and whose husband could find independent accommodation for her, was released from her contract. If her husband worked in an area where housing could not be found, he would be transferred to a region where it was available. If she was in an advanced state of pregnancy and her husband could not provide her with accommodation, she was sent at her husband's expense to a special maternity centre. If in an earlier stage, she was sent to a Holding Centre to await confinement in a community hospital.[4]

Administrative arrangements were initially harsh, even for British women. The Department of Labour and National Service (DLNS) in 1949 insisted that only single workers and married couples without children could be housed in hostels for British migrants. A married woman could remain until her confinement but not return after the birth of her child. In September that year the Secretary of that department, W. Funnell, asked the Department of Immigration to establish maternity hospitals for migrants, and approved visits to DLNS hostels by Department of Immigration social workers.[5]

Family reunion was not high on the agenda of immigration planners in the early 1950s. The leaders of industry, who manned one of the most influential bodies advising the Minister for Immigration, the Immigration Planning Council, expressed their belief in August 1951 that, unlike British migrants, alien dependants 'would accept separation from the breadwinners and could be housed in Holding Centres established in existing former service camps'. This assumption was made despite considerable evidence to the contrary. There had been incidents in several States since 1949 of wives defying administrative arrangements by leaving Departmental Holding Centres, often with their children, and 'squatting' in their husbands' work camps and DLNS workers' hostels. These non-compliant women were threatened with deportation, and in the ACT were intimidated by police presence. 'The continuance of camp life, the separation of families and the improbability of any real home life for many years is the biggest disappointment for migrants to this country', the Department of Immigration's senior social worker in Adelaide observed in her first report in July 1949.[6]

The situation was worse in South Australia, as at first there was no hostel for displaced persons, and the DLNS discouraged their integration into its two hostels because the British hostel occupants would resent their introduction. The need to provide for the families of alien workers allocated to South Australia was at last recognised in April 1950, when the DLNS's hostel at Gawler was allocated to alien women and children only. At first husbands were totally excluded, but the DLNS later relented and allowed husbands to visit their wives at a cost of 2/- per night. This prompted wives to leave Holding Centres in other States to join their husbands in South Australia. Although these women from interstate were excluded from Woodside and Gawler hostels, they refused to return. They somehow found accommodation nearby and put their children into foster homes.[7]

Reports from all States in 1950–51 revealed widespread concern among social workers with the frequent breakdown of migrants' marriages and the institutionalisation of children. Most found the prolonged separation of husbands and wives in hostels a precipitating factor, and recommended the establishment of hostels for alien families. Although lack of adequate support from mainstream organisations made dealing with these problems extremely difficult for Departmental social workers, this did not prevent one such organisation from criticising the Department. In early 1952 the Victorian Council for Social Services condemned the Department's policy of separating alien families, arguing that 'A pronouncement of policy is required as to whether the Government is prepared to mitigate a hard headed business deal by some element of sentimental alleviation in cases of hardship of this type'.[8]

Unmarried Mothers and Widows

While the problem of mothers with male financial support had been solved, the problem remained of non-compliance by single mothers (generally referred to as 'widows') with their contractual obligations. In July 1949 the Victorian Council for Social Welfare drew the attention of the Social Welfare Section to the numbers of supporting mothers in the Department of Immigration's Reception and Training Centre at Bonegilla seeking to place their children in Victorian institutions so that they would be free to work. The Secretary replied with unwarranted optimism that the number of widows was small and their separation from their children could be avoided through liaison between non-government organisations and Departmental social workers.[9]

Non-government agencies were not always cooperative. Jean Scott reported in December 1949 the reaction of Burnside Homes when an unemployed Latvian woman in the Cowra Holding Centre sought to place her three sons aged 6, 10 and 12 there. A qualified dentist, she 'could see no future for herself or her boys without employment'. She had found work as a domestic in the home of an Australian dentist, but to take the job she had to place her sons in care. The secretary of Burnside, who wanted only British migrants, complained about the Department's policy of bringing women with children to the country. He agreed to accept these boys but warned that he would not accept others so readily.[10]

Department of Immigration social workers in the various States took different approaches to the problem of getting supporting mothers to work. In South Australia they initially looked to orphanages run by charitable institutions. Children could not be admitted into State homes unless they were placed under the control of the Child Welfare Department by the court. In July 1950 the South Australian social worker reported that:[11]

> some of the unmarried mothers with children have proved unsatisfactory in employment and in two cases it has been necessary to place the children in voluntary organisation homes. Another case of alleged prostitution has been placed under supervision in a Roman Catholic Refuge and the child in an orphanage.

By April 1950 there were plans to extend the child-minding centre at the Woodside Holding Centre provided for the children of women who were ill or in hospital, to care for the children of widows employed as staff by the Centre. Apart from a woollen mill five miles from the Centre, and seasonal potato picking, there were few employment opportunities for women in that area of South Australia.[12]

The annual report of the Social Work Section in Perth noted that in the 1950/51 financial year it had placed 28 children of widows in institutions or homes either permanently or temporarily, thus freeing their mothers for work. This was not the preferred solution, as they reported that widows did not want to be separated from their children and the institutions were overcrowded. Child-minding centres were therefore established in Western Australian Holding Centres, for which widows paid £1 a week for each child. These centres were overcrowded and could not give the children the attention they needed, but there were no community agencies to help.[13]

In Victoria, widows with more than one dependent child were a major problem. Bonegilla's crêche was only for mothers in hospital, and at the Benalla Holding Centre, where work was readily available, those with children under three years could not take advantage of it as there was also no crêche for infants. In Victoria the Social Welfare Section had discussed with the State Department of Health the provision of baby health centres and crêches for working mothers from 1950 to 1951, without success. While the State was willing to provide these facilities it would not fund them. As a result, the Section had daily inquiries from migrant parents wishing to place their children in schools or institutions so they could work. This was thought to be unwise even in extreme cases. Unmarried mothers who decided to keep their children were encouraged to spend several months before and after their confinement in religious-run maternity homes, and then to place their children under the Child Welfare Department's Infant Life Protection Scheme, for which they paid 15/- per week. As a short-term measure, both responsible departments issued a public appeal by their Minister, Harold Holt, which resulted in the CES and the Department of Immigration finding employment for 800 supporting mothers by March 1951. Many were placed as staff in immigration centres, or continued to live there while working in adjacent towns. Of these, only twelve had more than one child.[14]

Almost 700 more remained in the centres unemployed, untrained and with a poor knowledge of English. They met their specially reduced weekly accommodation fees of 22/6 from child endowment of 5/- per child, unemployment benefits of 30/- or, in the case of women who had never worked, special benefits.

Aliens were ineligible for widows' pensions—a restriction on their social rights which, when it came to be reviewed by the Department of Immigration in 1963, was found by the Secretary to be unfair, counterproductive and irrational, as it dated from a period before large-scale alien immigration. Many supporting mothers fell into debt.[15]

Towards a Structural Solution

Research

In early 1951 Departmental social workers in a number of States were requested to conduct a survey of single parents in particular hostels and to suggest solutions to their problems. Trained to deal with problems on a case-by-case basis, Hazel Dobson initially tended to see both the causes and the solutions to this problem as lying with the individual women, not in the structural discrimination they all confronted. She recommended the provision of more social workers to research and analyse the problem. Until a permanent solution was arrived at, the assistance of voluntary organisations to teach hobbies, handicrafts, childcare and hygiene, she believed, would prevent time hanging so heavily on the women's hands. As marriage was the only really satisfactory solution, social and church workers and Good Neighbour Councils should be urged to create opportunities for widows to meet suitable men, she concluded.[16]

One of the few male social workers, attached to the isolated Cunderdin Holding Centre in Western Australia, regarded all but three of the 30 women he interviewed as unemployable because of their lack of English and their resistance to placing their children (a total of 56) in orphanages. As no employment offering accommodation was available, he recommended their employment on the staff of the Centre, or in day work in the town. He also believed that they should be encouraged to do dressmaking and knitting to produce handicrafts to be sold in the Centre. His preferred solution was to make the children wards of the State, as that would offer them permanency. This might, he observed, create resentment in the mothers. Allowing them to work in the city while living in the Centre where a crêche could be provided would, he anticipated, arouse criticism that migrant widows were treated better than Australians.

The social worker from Bonegilla, Victoria, the only Department of Immigration Centre in that State to which a social worker had been specifically attached, reported that there were 40 women with 66 dependent children there. She also observed that women with more than one child (half of the group) were almost impossible to place in employment. A number had found employment only by putting their children in orphanages at their own expense. Some kept the youngest child and institutionalised the older. Some siblings were placed in different institutions because of their ages. Women who had tuberculosis were especially difficult to place, as most openings for women found by the CES were as domestics and it was illegal to employ tuberculosis sufferers as domestics or in the preparation of food. Without child-care facilities these women could not work in factories. Few were willing even to consider having their children adopted, and most showed 'a great desire to work and support their families themselves', although most were by education and experience qualified to work only as domestics or in factories. The reports of social workers from other States were similarly dismal.[17]

The results of this inquiry were presented by Dobson to the Secretary on 9 October 1951. Her report suggests that she was beginning to look for systemic solutions to this problem. She indicated that if widows from elsewhere in Australia were transferred to Benalla, where there were already 90 widows and employment available at a newly established factory almost opposite the Centre, it might be possible to establish a crêche there. She did not, however, favour the concentration of widows in one camp, as it would impede their chances of meeting husbands. She recognised that formal two-hour English classes at night were unsuitable for women with dependent children who worked all day. At Benalla only 10 per cent of widows attended them. She recommended shorter and more entertaining classes run by voluntary groups.[18]

Another survey of all Departmental Holding Centres at the end of 1951 revealed that approximately 2500 of the 6000 mothers housed in them had little chance of leaving. This 'hard core of permanent residents' comprised women whose husbands were no longer under contract or widows who, even if they had employment, had little chance of being able to afford unsubsidised accommodation. The director of the Cunderin Holding Centre in Western Australia believed that the only solution lay in systemic reform. He advised the Secretary that 'the assimilation of widows and unmarried women with children depends upon a change of government policy and the expenditure of money upon a scheme to provide housing, schooling and care for children to enable these females to become absorbed into industry of some kind'.[19]

Also in late 1951 Olga Leschen, supervisor of the Free Kindergarten Union of Victoria, and G.E. Pendred, Federal officer of the Australian Association of Pre-School Child Development, prepared a report for the Department of Immigration on the provision of preschool facilities for migrant children in Holding Centres and workers' hostels. Their recommendations could not be implemented, however, until the Commonwealth decided what its responsibilities in this field might be.[20]

Recommendations by advisory bodies

The 1951 Citizenship Convention had drawn attention to the need for child-care centres for migrants. The Department of Immigration responded that it was the policy of the government to provide crêches, kindergarten and child-minding facilities in family hostels (run by the Department of Labour and National Service for British migrants), and that provision would be made in all new hostels for them. It showed less commitment to providing adequate child-care facilities for aliens. While it remarked that 'some progress' had been made in organising play centres in Department of Immigration Holding and Reception and Training Centres, it expressed the somewhat vague hope that there would 'ultimately' be such amenities in all migrant accommodation.[21]

In order to reach a decision on the provision of preschool care in its Holding Centres for aliens, in February 1952 the Department of Immigration referred Leschen and Pendred's report to the Immigration Advisory Council. As whatever preschool care provided for the 5000 children in these centres was run by untrained people, the Secretary, T.H.E. Heyes, now believed that his Department should fund trained staff to ensure preschool training to acceptable standards. He intended to appoint a senior preschool officer to manage the program. The Council recommended to the Minister for Immigration that the Commonwealth provide preschool facilities of a uniform standard at all Holding Centres and workers' hostels.[22]

Action by Commonwealth Hostels Ltd

The Department of Labour and National Service, with its responsibility for the assimilation of migrants into the workforce, had been more active in providing facilities for British working mothers than had the Department of Immigration for aliens. In 1950 it had sought from the Commonwealth Department of Education advice on the buildings, equipment and staffing necessary to establish child activity centres for preschool children in all migrant hostels. The Department of Education recommended that the Departments coordinate their inquiries on the preschool requirements of the migrant population. While it had passed on its estimates of the costs of providing such centres to both Departments and the Treasury, by mid-1950 it had received no response. Such centres had to be funded, staffed and supervised by the Commonwealth, it argued, for although State Education Departments contributed to organisations conducting such centres they did not control them. If States were to establish child-care centres at hostels for migrants, it was feared that they would be pressured to provide similar centres for women in the general community.[23]

The Commonwealth Hostels Ltd, the company that took over the running of Department of Labour and National Service hostels in January 1952, established a child-minding service for the British migrants in all its hostels. This decision was both economically rational and administratively convenient. The company argued that such a service was essential because it assisted the national economy by 'facilitating women going to work in a period of rising employment, and because of its effect upon the rate of movement of families from hostels'. The facilities provided, however, were far from perfect. The staff provided for these child-minding centres was inadequate and poorly trained and the centres were ill-equipped. They also did not cater for children under three years.[24]

Action by the Department of Immigration

The Department of Immigration aimed at a much higher standard of preschool accommodation than that provided in Commonwealth hostels, which was described as 'deplorable' by one unidentifiable senior officer of the Department of Immigration in 1952. This officer believed that child-minding centres should be set up in Department of Immigration Holding Centres only if they were suitably housed, equipped and staffed by qualified and supervised child-minders. They should be only for children over the age of two and a half, as 'children under three need close parental contact'.[25]

A meeting of Departmental social workers in Canberra in early 1953 recommended the establishment of fee-based baby-minding centres and free preschools in Department of Immigration hostels. The Department accepted the recommendation on preschools for children between three and five, and appointed Olga Leschen as officer-in-charge of its preschool services. It did not support the need for crêches for children under three. In November 1952 Leschen reported that 1420 children attended play centres in the Department's fourteen Holding Centres. They provided two sessions daily for classes of never more than 50 children, with a ratio of one adult to every fifteen children. Untrained staff were given practical experience by working in a free kindergarten for two weeks. While only seven of the centres had trained preschool teachers, the others were regularly visited by two divisional officers. They were equipped from an amenities fund; some effort was made to brighten the buildings in which they were housed and to provide them with toilets and washing facilities. The children received medical inspections each week and a thorough medical examination by the Department of Health every three months. Unfortunately for working mothers these centres were closed during school vacation periods in 1952 as a cost-cutting measure, and the children were expected to stay at home with older brothers and sisters. The focus was on the welfare of the child, not on their working mothers. As Leschen explained:[26]

> ... my experience in Immigration work has convinced me that the migrant child in Holding Centres, with his lack of normal home life, his background of insecurity through changing environment and parental anxieties, has an even greater need of our consideration than has the average Australian child.
>
> Pre-school training is essential to the migrant child to ensure that he enters school life with confidence. Confidence that will be gained by a familiarity with the Australian way of life and language and a feeling that he is on a fairly equal footing with the Australian child, a footing which may well colour his whole future life.
>
> We cannot afford to neglect these children during the formative pre-school years.

Crêches were not considered necessary, even in the Benalla Holding Centre which in 1953 housed the majority of Victoria's supporting mothers. There unsupervised and unregistered private child-minders cared for the babies of those women who went to work in order to pay their accommodation fees and to save enough to provide for their children's future. Linda Dickson, social worker at Greta, argued passionately for their provision. There the numbers of single mothers had grown from 25 in 1952 to 80 in 1953. She complained to Central Office of exploitation of single mothers by child-minders and argued that, while children under three were generally better off with their parents, supporting mothers were in a different position. Unemployed mothers' financial strain and fears about their future often detrimentally affected their children. 'I have found at Greta that the best kind of women in this group have always tried hard to secure employment, even before their child was 12 months old', she observed.[27]

While migrant supporting mothers were in assisted accommodation, clogging up the system by remaining indefinitely in what was intended to be temporary accommodation, they were the concern of administrators who had the responsibility for facilitating their integration into the workforce and into Australian society. In attacking systemic obstacles to their integration, these administrators for the first time came to realise the immensity of the task of administrative reform and innovation which lay ahead of them before they could achieve the government's policy goal of absorbing all alien immigrants into Australian society and encouraging them to take out Australian citizenship.

Once alien supporting mothers became sufficiently independent to move out of hostels into the mainstream community they were confronted with the economic difficulties faced by Australian citizens who were supporting mothers, for whom no administrator was responsible. The plight of alien women for the first time drew the attention of administrators to the unresponsiveness of Australian culture and administrative structures to the needs of working women in general, and in particular of women in the community attempting to provide for children without male support. By 1969, when child-minding facilities were only beginning to become available to working women in the wider community, they had already been provided for migrant women for sixteen years. By the end of 1975 there were child-minding facilities and after-school care in all hostels for working women. The demands placed on the bureaucracy by migrant women contributed significantly to the cultural change that was taking place in Australian attitudes towards the participation of women in the workforce.[28]

Conclusion

During the late 1940s and early 1950s British workers were housed by their sponsors—largely State governments. When the Commonwealth was able to build hostels specifically designed for migrants, British migrants were given priority. Most of the existing accommodation available to the Commonwealth to house alien migrants was in the form of large army camps, far from centres of employment and therefore unsuitable for migrant workers. While some of these camps, such as Bonegilla in Victoria, provided temporary accommodation for alien families immediately on arrival, once a man was allocated work his family was sent to Holding Centres in other army camps, as the Department of Immigration considered the accommodation provided for male workers too primitive for women and children.

Alien mothers who had no male breadwinner were also sent to Holding Centres, where they were unable to comply with their obligation to work because of their need to care for their children, and because the former army camps had been located in areas where work, especially for women, was generally unavailable. Their non-compliance with their obligation to work was clearly involuntary. The solution to their problem—locating them in areas where employment was available and providing them with adequate child-care so that they were free to work—was arrived at with difficulty because of prevailing cultural assumptions about aliens, and about women in general. These assumptions initially inspired impractical or unacceptable suggestions, such as encouraging mothers to give their children up for adoption or to find husbands to support them.

The solution to the problem presented to Department of Immigration administrators by migrant supporting mothers was relatively quickly arrived at. The provision by the early 1950s of child-minding facilities to enable such women to work was a radical departure from prevailing cultural norms, and clearly demonstrated the effectiveness of involuntary non-compliance as a means of forcing administrative change.

CHAPTER 4

Marginalised migrants: the mentally ill and aliens in rural areas

As the post-war migration scheme was intended primarily to provide labour for industrial expansion, the focus of the Department of Immigration was principally on the social absorption of migrants into urban communities. Its social workers were, therefore, located either in capital cities or in migrant hostels and Holding Centres, making it difficult for the Department to monitor the welfare of those geographically isolated by their employment in rural areas.

Because many were single men without family support, mentally ill aliens in urban areas were more obvious in public places than mentally ill Australian citizens. Thus, despite their smaller numbers, Departmental social workers were required to respond to the problems they presented, both for humanitarian reasons and to protect the political acceptability of the migration program. Australian cultural attitudes towards the mentally ill, the unresponsiveness of psychiatric services to the needs of migrants, the shortage of multilingual psychiatrists (due largely to the political power of the British Medical Association) and lack of support from migrant organisations made their task extraordinarily difficult. During the 1950s, many of those unable to cope with the combined stress of migration and the psychological legacy of wartime horrors walked the streets of Australian cities by day, and at night sought shelter in refuges for the homeless.

MENTALLY ILL ALIENS 1950–72

The mentally ill had no place in the imagined community of Australian citizens. They were largely invisible, their needs were marginalised and their rights as citizens largely ignored. Mentally ill migrants, however, were one of the principal categories of clients of concern to social workers employed by the Department of Immigration—the only Commonwealth department to accept responsibility for their welfare. The needs of mentally ill migrants highlighted and exacerbated the inadequacies of the state mental health system. These were described in the detailed reports received by the Department from its Social Welfare Section in all States. In her report on psychiatric cases seen in the metropolitan area of New South Wales during 1950–51, Departmental social worker Madeline Keary commented:[1]

> The whole question must be seen against the Australian situation regarding psychiatrics, i.e. the inadequacy of Mental Hospitals to meet the increasing numbers of mentally ill people, the lack of resources in the community for helping them adequately to rehabilitation, the social stigma attached to people who have been in Mental Hospitals and the prejudice and even superstition existing in the minds of the general public regarding them. That situation has an exaggerated significance where migrants are concerned.

As a consequence of the Depression and budgetary restrictions necessitated by World War II, mental hospitals in all States (except those catering specifically for ex-servicemen) were grossly overcrowded by 1950. The standard of basic patient care had deteriorated to such a point that royal commissions or major inquiries into mental hospitals were set up in most States. In 1955 the Federal government commissioned a survey of mental health facilities in Australia. Its report revealed appalling standards and a paucity of early treatment units and outpatients departments. As a consequence, the Commonwealth became directly involved in the field of mental health care. The *States Grants (Mental Institutions) Act 1955* provided assistance in capital works for mental health facilities, which enabled a major building and renovation program to be undertaken. There remained, however, many problems, as the royal commission into Callan Park Mental Hospital revealed in 1961. Because of these funding arrangements the Commonwealth refused hospital benefits to those in institutions for the mentally ill. Such patients were, therefore, ineligible for either State or Commonwealth social benefits. Minister for Health A.J. Forbes explained in 1970 that, while in certain circumstances they were paid pensions, 'traditionally the government has regarded the care of the mentally ill as primarily a State matter'. As migrant care was seen as the sole responsibility of the Commonwealth, however, mental illness among the migrant population became a source of criticism of the Federal government. During the 1950s some Opposition members of Parliament attacked the administration of the migration program by drawing attention to the numbers of migrants who sought psychiatric help, or who were committed to mental hospitals. The government responded by attempting to minimise the problem. There were far fewer mentally ill in the migrant population than in the population as a whole, it argued, as it staunchly defended prevailing selection procedures.[2]

In 1950–51, 91 migrants were certified for admission to NSW mental hospitals, only seven of whom were British. Given the obstacles placed by the medical profession in the way of migrant doctors seeking registration, it was extremely difficult for non-English speaking migrants to get the psychiatric assistance they needed, because patients requiring certification needed to be assessed by two independent doctors who did not work in a mental hospital. Monolingual doctors, who could not understand what their patients were saying, were understandably reluctant to accept responsibility for their committal. Of those who were able to gain admission, most were sent to Gladesville Hospital, which had no doctors who spoke foreign languages. Those sent to Callan Park in 1950 were more fortunate. That hospital had two migrant doctors who between them spoke thirteen languages and who supervised the learning of English by their migrant patients. Parramatta Hospital also had a multilingual doctor. Four-fifths of Madeline Keary's 51 mentally ill clients were unmarried and without relatives or friends, and all but seven of them were men. Lack of family support made their discharge difficult. A small non-government body, the After Care Association, provided accommodation for homeless cases recommended by hospital superintendents. Their funds were limited and they had a long waiting list. Migrant organisations, Keary reported, shared the general prejudices against the mentally ill and were reluctant to assist their institutionalised compatriots.[3]

Less seriously ill migrants voluntarily admitted themselves to the Broughton Hall Psychiatric Clinic which had, Keary reported, recently lost its only multilingual specialist. Like those committed to institutions, those who volunteered for psychiatric help also lost their social welfare benefits. Mentally ill migrants who did not seek help often fell foul of the Department of Immigration or the police, through their failure to comply with laws and regulations. If they rejected a job they lost their unemployment benefits. About one-third of the cases seen by this social worker came from country areas of the State: 'Those who can get to Sydney are probably in a more fortunate position than those who are admitted to country Mental Hospitals'.[4]

In reporting on the situation Australia-wide between 1949 and 1951, the head of the Department's Social Welfare Section, Hazel Dobson, remarked that 'In many instances the language difficulty is so great that in some States the visit of the Social Worker, accompanied by a skilful interpreter, constitutes one of the few opportunities which the psychiatrist has of assessing the degree of insanity and recovery'.[5]

Aware of the need for specialist assistance to help them deal with their mentally ill clients, social workers in Sydney successfully appealed to Canberra for the appointment of a consulting psychiatrist who spoke languages other than English. He would examine their mentally ill clients and sign a schedule which enabled them to be examined for admission to a mental hospital. Departmental social workers were often the first point of reference for mentally ill migrants. They arranged for interpreters and sometimes escorted the patient to hospital.

John Tarbath, the only Departmental social worker in Tasmania from 1950 to 1963, brought men from isolated work camps suffering from mental illness or alcoholic psychosis to the local mental hospital. He became a consultant at the hospital and was given the right to admit voluntary patients. He avoided having migrants certified as he had identified a number of non-English speaking patients who, because they had no friends or relatives, had been forgotten by the system and were avoided by their fellow countrymen because of the stigma attached to mental illness. In the 1950s he discovered a Danish seaman who had been institutionalised since 1919, and in the early 1960s a Chinese former prisoner of war of the Japanese who had been certified in 1945. Both were found to be sane. Tarbath advocated on behalf of such patients with mental health authorities, the Department of Social Security, ethnic communities and, if appropriate, with their diplomatic representatives in Canberra, requesting that they be repatriated. When he moved to Brisbane in 1964 Tarbath worked with the Public Trustee, arranging for the repatriation of patients who had been involuntarily committed to mental institutions but who were assessed suitable and wanted to return home. Social workers also maintained contact with the patient's family and friends (if any) and attempted to gain support for him or her from migrant and other organisations. They contacted the Commonwealth Employment Service on the patient's behalf, tried to ensure that their living and working conditions on discharge would not be too stressful, and made follow-up visits. Sometimes they arranged temporary financial help and suitable accommodation. During 1951 a total of 279 such cases were assisted by Departmental social workers.[6]

Despite its assurances in Parliament about the soundness of its screening processes, the government's lack of confidence in them was indicated by its engagement in late 1956 of Sir Harry Wunderly, an Australian expert on tuberculosis. He was sent overseas to survey medical screening procedures used to detect tuberculosis and mental disabilities in both British and European migrants. The Department of Immigration initiated closer cooperation with the Commonwealth Department of Health to obtain a more reliable basis for recording the incidence of mental illness in the migrant population.[7]

Although the *Migration Act* provided for the deportation of a person who had become an inmate of a mental hospital or charitable institution within five years of immigration, this was not obligatory and the provision was rarely used. In 1958 the government agreed with a recommendation of the Immigration Advisory Council, and formally adopted as policy its general practice of deporting the mentally ill only in cases where the illness existed before the entry of the migrant to Australia and had been 'knowingly and deceitfully' concealed by them. This proviso, Minister for Immigration Alexander Downer admitted, would be difficult to prove. The Department of Immigration would approve such a deportation only if it was in the interests of the migrant to do so—for example if they had no family in Australia but had relatives in their own country willing to care for them. In the three years to 1958, approximately 30 persons were deported on the grounds of mental health, and between 1950 and 1962 the government deported a total of 297 mentally or physically ill persons.[8]

By 1960 Labor immigration spokesmen were more inclined

to attribute mental illness among migrants to their on-arrival difficulties than to failures in the selection process. Assimilation, observed Leslie Haylen, 'can be Gethsemane for the migrants', and was a two-way bargain to which the government was not contributing its share. It had, he claimed, a selfish approach to immigration:[9]

> we have the numbers, they will help us to fight our wars, to reap our crops and to develop our country, but we will not get much out of them unless we give them the same standards as we enjoy ourselves. Poor housing, horribly insanitary conditions and exploitation by landlords and sometimes by employers are not the ways to encourage assimilation. These are not the ways to encourage migrants to become part of the nation, to cast away for ever their European background and become Australians in the strongest sense of the word.

In 1961 the Immigration Advisory Council published its 'Report on the incidence of mental illness among migrants', the first of a number of reports on this topic throughout that decade. Although the immigration of displaced persons ceased in 1953, its legacy of mental illness persisted. The level of schizophrenia among Eastern Europeans, particularly among Poles, Hungarians and Yugoslavs, was considered by the Department in the late 1960s to be 'alarming'. In 1962 a study found that, while the incidence of this disease among Australian-born men was 21.2 per 100 000 and 28.6 among women, the figures for men and women born in Eastern Europe were 121.9 and 159.9 respectively.[10]

A 1966 Department survey of psychiatric patients in Australian institutions found that in metropolitan Sydney 887 (16 per cent) of a total population of 5500 patients were migrants. This, it somewhat defensively argued, was not an unfavourable percentage when compared with the percentage of overseas-born in the State's population (17.3 per cent). Such a survey was, of course, unable to estimate how many migrants in the community needing such care were not receiving it. Mentally ill migrants were clearly still regarded in Central Office as potential political problems to be countered. P.M. Rice recalls that during the course of this survey he found a German in an Adelaide psychiatric hospital who had objected violently to being interned at the outbreak of World War II. Unable to speak English, he had been institutionalised and forgotten for almost 30 years.[11]

The tendency of parliamentarians, bureaucrats and the community in general to conceptualise aliens as an amorphous group of 'migrants', or to lump them into broad categories such as 'Eastern Europeans', was abandoned as the cultural, ethnic and historical complexity of the migrant community was better appreciated. This was greatly assisted by the increased use of computer processing by the Department of Immigration in the second half of the 1960s, and by the establishment in 1967 of a special Integration and Education Section to analyse the information provided by Departmental social workers.[12]

A Departmental study of psychiatric admission rates to New South Wales hospitals in 1967 showed a significant over-representation of Poles, both men and women. While the admission rate of the Australian-born of both sexes was 0.3 per cent of the population, it was 0.9 per cent of the population of Polish men and 0.8 per cent of Polish women. While the number of Polish-speaking psychiatrists had significantly improved, in hindsight P.M. Rice admitted that 'more could have been achieved at the preventative level by more careful planning of the resettlement of all refugees coming to Australia'.[13]

By 1970 the numbers of mentally ill immigrants had increased, and Rice expressed his concern at the standard of migrant selection overseas. He complained that:[14]

> There are some selection officers who tend to put their migrant interviewees on a desert island, and perhaps inadvertently look on them as unrelated to the human species. These officers appear to be assessing applicants to a set of criteria aside from the practical realities of life . . . Instances where migrants move directly from the ports of arrival to mental hospitals are not now uncommon.

John Tarbath, a Departmental social worker who was involved in analysing migrant mental health statistics during the 1960s, has warned that State statistics of migrant admissions should be regarded with caution. They were probably inflated by the policy of some States of recording a separate admission every time the same person was readmitted during the course of one year, and by classifying as migrants overseas-born people suffering senile dementia who may have spent most of their lives in Australia.[15]

In 1972 the Integration Branch conducted a survey of medical or mental breakdown of migrants prior to their arrival in Australia. The medical screening procedures in place by 1972 were described in Parliament. British and alien applicants were required to sign different declarations concerning their own and their family's medical history. Their mental soundness was assessed at the interview and at the general medical examination.

If applicants did not reveal a past history of mental illness there was little that could be done. The government considered that detailed psychiatric assessment was not cost-effective.[16]

Aliens in Rural Areas 1947–56

Because migrants were largely selected for work in secondary industry, most settled in urban areas. As the Secretary of the Department of Labour and National Service, H.A. Bland, explained to the Secretary of the Department of Immigration, T.H.E. Heyes, in May 1952, 'the policy of this Department in regard to the allocation of directable migrants has been aimed at helping to overcome bottlenecks in the manufacture of important basic materials'. The Department of Immigration always had considerable difficulty, not only in providing settlement services to migrants who settled in rural areas but even in understanding what their settlement problems were. Between 1950 and 1956 the Department's Social Welfare Section made heroic efforts to survey their needs, but it was left to local voluntary organisations (usually those affiliated with the Good Neighbour Movement) to meet them.[17]

Between 1947 and 1955, immigration introduced 435 000 workers into Australia. By the end of 1953 one in ten workers in Australia was a post-war migrant. Of these only 78 000 were farm workers. Many more immigrants, often with their families, were directed to rural areas to work for public facilities such as Commonwealth and State railways, or in the mining or timber industries. By 1952, for example, 20 per cent of all the wages staff of the South Australian railways were migrants.[18]

An analysis of a sample of 12 000 non-refugee immigrants who arrived in 1952 from the United Kingdom, Holland, and Italy revealed that 16 per cent were employed in rural production, 2 per cent in timber and forestry and 2 per cent in mining. Almost 50 000 immigrants who came to Australia between January 1949 and June 1953 indicated that they intended to take up rural employment; this represented over 14 per cent of the worker component of the intake. Migrants selected under bilateral agreements included a proportion of rural workers. The Department of Immigration's 'shopping list' of German workers for 1953–54 included 700 rural workers out of an intake of 2125. During the first three months of 1954, 25.4 per cent of all male workers under assisted passage schemes had rural occupations.

At this time only 17.9 per cent of male Australians were rural workers.[19]

Between 1947 and 1951, 41.4 per cent of all immigrants were British, and they could not be compelled to work in country areas. Of the 163 443 assisted British immigrants who came to Australia during this period, only 3341 went into rural occupations. They were, however, the group preferred above all by rural employers. When the Queensland branch of the RSSAILA at the League's 36th Annual Congress in 1951 urged the government to try to attract experienced British rural workers and help them develop farming properties, the Department of Immigration replied that, while the Commonwealth Nomination Scheme provided for the selection of experienced rural workers, the response had not been particularly heartening. Advice from the Department's London office had indicated that because conditions in the United Kingdom for rural workers were quite good, and rural work was regarded as of extreme national importance, British rural workers were reluctant to emigrate.[20]

Obstacles to retaining migrants in rural areas

Perceptions of rural employers
Despite the recession, which began in 1952 and caused considerable unemployment and hardship for most of the decade, particularly among unskilled migrants in secondary industry, the chambers of both Houses of Parliament in the 1950s echoed with frequent complaints from Members representing rural constituencies that the government was not sending enough migrants to rural areas, and that those that came soon deserted the country for the bright lights of the city. The latter complaint was most eloquently expressed by Labor Senator A.M. Benn from the sugar-growing area of Queensland in the form of a parable on cane toads:[21]

> I remember that some years ago when beetles were very bad in the cane crops in Queensland, the government found it necessary to import a kind of cane toad from the Argentine for the purpose of keeping down the beetle pest. The toads did very good work for a while after liberation, but then found that by going into the townships where there were electric lights, they could get their meals without going out and catching beetles in cane crops. They thereupon congregated under the lights in the streets. When moths, mosquitoes and other insects became affected by the heat of the electric lights and fell to the ground, the toads had their supper. It was not long before

all the toads went into the townships. I suggest that we are now having a similar experience with immigrants. They are coming to Australia and it appears that most of them are settling in the cities and entering secondary industries. Very few are going on to the land.

Many of the obstacles to the social engagement of migrant workers in rural areas resulted from the cultural attitudes of rural communities towards migrants in general, and to aliens in particular. Some rural employers were reluctant to pay award wages and supply accommodation, and there was a general lack of settlement services for non-English speakers in rural areas. This was recognised by Minister for Immigration Harold Holt, who, in his address to the 1952 Citizenship Convention, suggested four strategies to improve the supply and retention of migrant rural labour: careful selection and placement of migrants; the provision of suitable living accommodation, 'a willingness on the part of farmers to accept European migrants'; and the adoption by State governments (and acceptance by farmers) of a policy of land settlement for migrants. There were, he added, 'understandable reasons why few farmers are inclined to admit European migrants as permanent residents in their homes' but, he warned, significant numbers of British rural workers could not be expected to emigrate. The Department passed on the relevant sections of the Convention's four resolutions on the subject of encouraging migrant workers in rural areas to the National Farmers' Union of Australia, to the Graziers' Federal Council of Australia and to the Department of Agriculture for comment, but little practical action resulted.[22]

Rural employers continued to communicate their dissatisfaction to government through the 1954 Citizenship Convention, which resolved:[23]

> That this Convention, concerned at the tendency of people, Australians and New Australians, to move to the cities with the resulting deprivations of national life and character, urges that more be done to bring to Australia a target number of migrants who are willing to live and work on the land, and that conditions be liberalised to make it possible and more attractive for additional people so to live and work.

A small but very practical recommendation of this Convention—that bilingual agricultural officers be appointed to visit migrants in rural areas—was not supported by the Department of Immigration. It argued that there were not sufficient concentrations of migrants of the one nationality in rural areas to warrant the expense, and that rural migrants could learn English by following correspondence lessons. In 1952, however, it assisted the NSW government in fostering the assimilation of Italian migrants in the Murrumbidgee Irrigation Area by funding an Italian-speaking liaison officer to its Extension Service. In 1972 a former Italian-speaking officer of the NSW Department of Agriculture's Murrumbidgee Irrigation Area Agriculture Extension Service, A.J. Grassby, became Minister for Immigration.[24]

Most migrants who were directed into or who chose rural employment were aliens who had to attempt to 'assimilate' into monolingual, conservative, Anglo-Celtic communities which had little understanding of, and less sympathy with, their needs, expectations and cultural backgrounds.

Pay and conditions
In April 1948 the Queensland Dairymen's Organisation approached the Department of Immigration with the suggestion that immigrants not be paid award wages for a period after commencing employment, because 'in most cases they will not be competent to do the work efficiently' without 'a period of tuition'. Their suggestion of a training wage was flatly rejected by the Department, which pointed out that the basic adult wage took no account of previous knowledge or experience, and applied as much 'to inexperienced Australians as it does to inexperienced migrants'. It condemned the suggestion on the grounds that it would not only defeat the national object of 'absorbing desirable new settlers into our communities, but would also tend to undermine the standards of living of which we Australians may be so justly proud'.[25]

Although the succeeding Liberal government adhered to the principle of equal rates and conditions for migrant workers in rural industries, it was more willing to consider suggestions for variations. The Minister for Immigration told the House in May 1952 that some consideration had been given to the provision of 'a special wage rate' owing to 'the immigrants' lack of experience of Australian conditions'. He suggested, however, that employers in rural industries apply to the appropriate tribunals for an award to govern such cases.[26]

In 1952 both Labor and Liberal politicians accused farmers of not wanting migrant labour. Senator Buttfield pointed out that, although Italians had proved to be satisfactory workers in the sugar industry, Queenslanders complained that too many Italians were being brought to their State. Sugar farmers must provide accommodation and offer off-season work if they wanted to attract migrant labour, she pointed out. Little seems to have changed by 1953, however, as the NSW New Settlers' League reported that it was difficult to find accommodation on farms for migrant families, and that farmers and graziers were generally unwilling to pay recognised rates to migrants without a period of probation to learn Australian methods.[27]

Commonwealth government initiatives to promote migrant settlement in rural areas

While the Department of Immigration recognised that the removal of legislation preventing the acquisition of land by aliens was a matter for State governments, and that they alone could decide the basis of eligibility under land settlement schemes, it took some initiatives to encourage the settlement of migrants in rural areas. During his visit to Europe in 1952 the Minister for Immigration discussed with the Intergovernmental Committee for European Migration (ICEM) the possibility of that body's funding a pilot scheme in Australia under which a limited number of families from a number of European countries would be placed on farms. If successful, the scheme would be extended. The proposal was placed on the agenda of the ICEM's fourth session in Geneva in October 1952, which viewed it favourably and asked its member governments to produce definite proposals for pilot land settlement schemes for its next meeting in March 1953. The Department was helped to formulate its policies on migrant participation in primary industries by the Immigration Planning Committee on Rural Production, established in 1951 under the chairmanship of Professor S.M. Wadham.[28]

In March 1952 the Department of Labour and National Service began a drive to promote the employment of migrant labour by farmers. It circulated 40 000 leaflets to them and contacted 7000 personally. During the first eight months of this drive approximately 4500 vacancies were located of which 3000 were filled by migrants, in addition to the normal vacancy rate of about 100 a week. Two years after it began, this initiative had identified 11 000 rural vacancies and had filled 7500 with specially selected migrants. The remainder were filled by Australians or by migrants who had been in other employment.[29]

Aliens in rural areas as seen by Departmental social workers 1950–56

Although in February 1953 Holt had painted a rosy picture of the efficacy of the Good Neighbour Movement, through which 'every immigrant can readily find a friend and a helping hand in any part of this country to which he or she may go', the reality as seen by officers of his Department was far less than the 'wholehearted cooperation in the carrying out of a great national policy' of which he spoke.[30]

By that year, the New Settlers' League had established 27 branches in the country in New South Wales; however, the Commonwealth Migration Officer in Sydney had considerable reservations about its ability to bring migrants in contact with people in their rural communities. This view of the Movement was reinforced by a number of Departmental social workers who travelled widely within other States between 1950–56. Their reports afforded their Department a rare insight into the practical impediments to the integration of migrants in rural areas, and clearly explained why many displaced persons did not stay in rural areas once their contract had expired. Their supervisor, Hazel Dobson, was far from being Canberra-bound and was aware from experience of the 'difficulties of distance and isolation . . . which must be overcome in the work with migrants'. Soon after her appointment she visited remote areas in Queensland and South Australia, and in 1953 she accompanied the Western Australian social worker on his tour of the southwestern regions of that State.[31]

Social workers visited towns and camps where immigrants were employed and gave what assistance they could to cases of need. They found much alienation and little encouragement to assimilate. Most found little overt hostility to migrants but a great deal of indifference to their needs.

South Australia

The Department's social worker, G.T. Cuddihy, travelled extensively throughout rural areas in South Australia from 1950 to 1952 by public transport. His supervisor's repeated requests that he be given funds to hire a taxi or car were consistently ignored by Canberra. He began in 1950 and 1951 visiting the Mount Gambier district. There were approximately 1200 aliens in this area, and during his first visit he concentrated on interviewing employers rather than the aliens themselves. He noted the resentment directed at them when they spoke in their own languages and the absence of any local sources of advice or assistance. If their district employment officer could not help them, they had to travel to Adelaide and stay overnight to obtain the information or help that they needed. 'The average Australian tolerates the New Australian but will not go out of his way to make them feel at home', he observed. He attributed the departure of most workers from the area on the expiry of their contract to their general isolation. Camps were located far from large towns and 'even those living near towns find a large degree of rejection by the local townspeople', he observed. Marital problems were growing and affected wives and children received little support from the local community. He alerted the Department to misinformation on hospital services provided in Departmental pamphlets, which told immigrants that such services were free in Australia. This was true only of capital cities, not country areas.[32]

The following year Cuddihy returned to this area, interviewing 122 individual aliens as well as groups in each employment centre. He noted their general lack of interest in naturalisation: 'Country people complain that New Australians return to the city, however few private firms make any attempt to house families'. In March and April 1952 he visited the Port Lincoln district and interviewed 180 aliens in various camps and hostels, commenting on their living and working conditions and their relations with the local community. He observed that since his last visit a year earlier there had been a marked decline in the numbers of aliens employed in the area. Almost half had moved to the city once their contract had expired, and replacements were not readily available. Not even the churches assisted migrants to assimilate, although previously some voluntary organisations had made an effort when the migrants first moved to the district. They 'now take no interest . . . no doubt due to the lack of response by the newcomer in the early stages', he reported. English classes were not functioning due to the failure of migrants (mostly shift workers) to attend.

The local police were 'inclined to be hard on migrants' and, as they seldom wore uniforms, migrants had difficulty identifying them. This led to fights. Two aliens had lost legs in accidents and received no support from the community. 'Local people and organisations in country areas still have not realised that many of these people are completely on their own in Australia and as a consequence are at a loss to know what to do with them more often than not', he complained, adding that Port Lincoln was no worse than other places. Regretfully, he reported that staff shortages had prevented him from visiting rural areas between July 1952 and June 1953. One-quarter of the alien population of South Australia lived outside the metropolitan area and 'to assume that these people have made a more satisfactory adjustment or settlement than those living in the metropolitan area is wishful thinking,' he warned.

Western Australia

In 1953 Ray Vincent, the senior social worker in Western Australia, travelled the length of the Trans-Australian Railway on the 'Tea and Sugar Train', which carried supplies to the migrant workers and their families living in the isolated camps in the harsh climate of South and Western Australia through which the railway ran. They were largely German 'special project workers' under contract to the Commonwealth Railways, although there were some displaced persons, Italians and British migrants. Most were single men, but there were at least 50 families with 100 children on the Western Australian side. Their main problems arose from their lack of settlement services. They could learn English only by correspondence, and many in areas where secondary education was unavailable found supervising their children's correspondence lessons difficult. They had problems filling in Departmental forms, particularly those requiring the signature of a justice of the peace, who was often two days' travel away.

While locals were not antagonistic to migrants, local organisations such as the Country Women's Association just ignored them. Vincent observed in 1954 that in rural areas where Good Neighbour Councils had been established to help local community organisations understand and respond to the needs of migrants, they were not working as intended. Although local organisations sent representatives to Council meetings, they felt no obligation to promote integration, which they saw as the task of the Council in Perth. During his visit to the Kalgoorlie region in 1956, Vincent found the activities of the Council largely ineffective. Their main project was collecting English-language magazines and other literature for distribution to the migrants on the Trans-Australian Railway line. They had no way of knowing whether the magazines were of any use—even if they were collected by their intended recipients. He thought the practice should, however, be continued 'as an expression of goodwill'. Only a few Kalgoorlie residents met migrants who visited the town for shopping or to receive medical attention. One woman, herself a migrant, acted as an interpreter. On the whole, he observed, most organisations such as Parents and Citizens felt that the migrant should make the first approach to joining them, and he was aware of no occasion where any organisation had attempted to contact isolated groups of single migrants in camps where the need for contact was great. 'Some of these migrants are very young and have no opportunity of entering any house or having contact with any family group', he reported. Migrants mixed with Australians only at work and were socially segregated otherwise.

Vincent also found union officials distinctly suspicious of aliens. When interviewed in 1954, the secretary of the Collie Miners' Industrial Union of Workers said that:

> the position was watched carefully to make sure that they (migrants) did not threaten the position of the Australian worker, and if it is felt that too many migrants are being admitted to the Union an attempt will be made to close the books in order to preserve a safe position for the Australian worker.

The secretary's fellow workers were upset by migrants talking in their own language in the presence of Australians—particularly underground, where failure to speak English was seen to endanger workers. It was also felt that aliens tended to become 'bosses' men' and were too anxious to work overtime.

Vincent's reports revealed the failure of the government's assimilation strategies in Western Australia. He suggested ways of improving the provision of information and accommodation to rural migrants. In his 1953–54 report, he drew attention to the need for 'some kind of Advisory Service' to answer the questions of migrants on naturalisation, the health scheme, and obligations connected with building, as they were anxious 'to plan for more adequate accommodation but did not know what to do'. In preparation for such a service he began to develop an 'information index' on the contacts he had made and the organisations he had visited throughout the State. Lack of accommodation for migrants, he observed, was a disincentive to their employment by local farmers, who would rather manage alone than house a stranger and his family on their farms. Vincent advised that if migrants could be accommodated in country regions and some organisational support was provided, they would form a pool of employment on which local farmers could draw. In the absence of such planning, farmers limited their work and 'did not seem inclined to make any great effort to obtain employees unless they were on the spot'. Although he had found no real antagonism towards migrants, most 'had failed to obtain any real source of inspiration and advice in their district' and were rarely invited into Australian homes. He characterised local attitudes towards migrants as a lack of enthusiasm and indifference 'coloured by a tolerance of them because of their usefulness'. Migrants tended to find their own recreation in their own national groups.

In 1956 Vincent and an officer of the Migrant Education Department travelled 1500 miles by car in the Kalgoorlie area. While Vincent attempted to check compliance with the *Aliens Act 1947* his colleague established English classes. From 1 January 1948 this Act obliged all aliens 16 years and over to register on arrival in the country and notify the Department of Immigration of any change in their address or occupation. It also forbade them to change their surname without the written consent of the Minister for Immigration. Separate lists of aliens were kept for the Commonwealth by the Department, and by each State. State indexes were kept alphabetically and by nationality, occupation and locality (which coincided with Federal electorates). The government hoped that these indexes would provide readily accessible information which would enable it to monitor 'the flow of aliens to any area and to watch how they are being absorbed'. Vincent's report indicated that the Act was almost impossible to administer. Compliance relied largely on the voluntary cooperation of the alien, was not effectively monitored, the lists were difficult to use and almost impossible to keep up to date. A register of aliens' changes of address or occupation could not be obtained through their place of employment because of the frequency with which they changed jobs and because much of the hiring and firing, especially on the railways, was decentralised. It was, he advised Canberra, undesirable to request employers to note the status of aliens, as it involved considerable clerical work for them and could thus encourage discrimination and prejudice their opportunity for employment. Unless brought to notice by a welfare organisation or some authority it was difficult to identify aliens, and they could not be easily distinguished from naturalised migrants, some of whom had been in the Kalgoorlie region up to 20 years, he remarked.[33]

Tasmania

John Tarbath, who had studied social work at the University of South Australia with Cuddihy and Vincent, was appointed to Tasmania in January 1950 and remained there until 1963. When he arrived he was the only Departmental social worker for 330 aliens who had migrated before the war, for 1000 Polish ex-servicemen who had been brought to Tasmania after the war by the hydroelectric scheme, and for growing numbers of displaced persons for whom a camp had been established. He had an office in Hobart, but spent one week in every three visiting migrants working in the hydroelectric camps or mines. He found that the hydroelectric scheme had made little provision for their migrant workers. There was little for them to do outside working hours apart from the films screened for them by the Young Men's Christian Association, and there were no libraries or public transport. Because the canteens served alcohol, drunkenness was a problem, and Hazel Dobson had advised Tarbath before he left for Tasmania that she was concerned about the numbers of suicides there. Migrant workers were treated with considerable antipathy by the local community. 'We had to show that somebody cared for them and was interested in their future', Tarbath commented.

Tarbath undertook an advocacy role on behalf of migrants. He attended the weekly meetings of the Good Neighbour Council, which he found was prepared to talk but not to do much work. It referred any problems encountered to him. He suggested that the Council enlist ethnic groups to provide interpreters to visit the migrants in camps, but it showed little understanding of the need for interpreters. Tarbath identified a number of people within the migrant communities who would act as unpaid interpreters, particularly in the courts. As there were no consuls in Tasmania (apart from the Greek Consul), Tarbath was responsible for informing all migrants who came before the courts of their legal rights and for finding them legal representation where necessary. Later, funds were provided for a professional interpreter, a Pole who spoke several languages. English language teaching for migrants was impeded by lack of accommodation for classes, as many headmasters were reluctant to make school premises accessible after hours. Very successful English classes funded by the Department of Immigration were, therefore, begun in the hydroelectricity camps by professional workers, mainly engineers. Tarbarth found that the staff of the CES were largely those who had run the manpower program during the war, and their attitudes towards the early migrants who came under a two-year contract were excessively harsh. Tarbath intervened in cases where old or malnourished men had been allocated heavy work, obtaining a medical certificate from a private doctor, and advocating on their behalf with the CES which was initially strict in enforcing the rule that migrants should work where directed. Tarbath recalled the case of an engineer with pre-war experience in a canning factory. Allocated by the CES to work with the local council he took holiday work at a local canning factory, where he was found to be the only worker who could keep their somewhat antiquated machinery going. Despite the wishes of both the worker and his new employer, the CES insisted that he return to his original job and applied for a deportation order when he refused. When the order arrived from Canberra Tarbath did not serve it.

As well as his advocacy role, Tarbath undertook casework, dealing with unemployed, homeless, mentally ill migrants and those with marital problems, particularly deserted wives who were ineligible for social security benefits until they had been deserted for six months. As he lived in an almost exclusively migrant area of Hobart he developed valuable contacts within non-English speaking communities, which enabled him to strengthen their efforts to assist one another. Transferred to Brisbane in 1963, Tarbath largely worked with mentally ill migrants. There he found the Good Neighbour Council much better organised than it had been in Tasmania.[34]

German Special Project Workers

The first group of Germans to arrive in Australia were special project workers, who although under contract to work for two years met their own passage costs themselves. Immigration selection officers, who were hard at work in Germany by March 1951, were favourably impressed with these workers, finding them superior in every way to the displaced persons they had processed. Approximately 5000 Germans had arrived under this scheme by September 1952. These workers, who arrived without their families, were sponsored by sixteen private firms and public instrumentalities such as the Department of Railways in Victoria and South Australia, the Commonwealth Railways, and the Snowy Mountains Authority. They became indebted for the cost of their passage to their sponsoring employers, who deducted repayments fortnightly from their wages. Most of these workers settled permanently in Australia and became further indebted to their employers to bring out their families and to house them. They were possibly the most disadvantaged immigrants in Australia.[35]

The Department of Immigration gained a valuable insight into their problems from G.T. Cuddihy, who visited groups of special project workers employed in South Australia by the State and Commonwealth Railways in January 1952. They had a number of complaints, all of which this officer believed to be totally justified. Although each had initially agreed to repay a passage fee of £150 and they had been detailed for duties on board the ship coming to Australia, they were told on arrival that, as the vessel had been changed, they had to repay transport costs of £197. They had also been promised fully furnished rooms with a bed, wardrobe, chair, and some sort of floor covering. Most were housed in dormitory accommodation, supplied with inadequate toilet facilities, and given poor food. Those in the hostel at Port Augusta were required to share rooms which were furnished only with beds. Although the South Australian Railways had brought only single men, the Commonwealth Railways had attracted married men with a verbal promise that they would help them bring out their families. This was not incorporated into their contract. No time limit had been set, but many gained the impression that this assistance would be provided soon after their arrival. In some cases a period of six months was mentioned. By the time they were interviewed by Cuddihy, many had come to believe that the Commonwealth Railways would not honour these statements made in Berlin, so they had made up their mind to break their contract and seek employment elsewhere. To add to their woes they were denied the taxation concessions allowed at that time to married men, although most were supporting families in Germany. They were not taxed as married men until they had been joined in Australia by their families, but they were unable to fulfil the Department of Immigration's requirements for nominators. Although most were 'good types and would settle down satisfactorily if given the chance', many wanted to return to Germany and few were interested in applying for Australian citizenship, Cuddihy reported.[36]

Following the signing of an assisted migration agreement with Germany in August 1952, dependants of special project workers who had not already been sponsored (approximately 236) became eligible to have their passage to Australia paid. This was of little use to those workers who had already become indebted to bring out their 536 dependants, or to those who had already arranged the passages of 269 relatives. Despite the advocacy of the Lutheran World Federation, which had advanced £30 000 for travel loans, the Commonwealth Railways, which had lent £25 000 to 88 of its workers, and the Australian Workers' Union, their appeal for assisted passages for those relatives already en route was rejected. The German Ambassador did not support them, and he assured the Department that it could rely on his support to explain the position to his nationals. While legally correct, the Department's decision created perceptions of procedural unfairness and increased the likelihood of non-payment of these debts. Departmental administrators had achieved a small financial saving by prolonging the financial difficulties and alienating a useful group of potential settlers. On arrival, their families were housed in Departmental Holding Centres, for which they were also charged. This further handicapped their debt repayments.[37]

The Departmental social worker who visited special project workers in their isolated camps along the Trans-Australian Railway in October 1953 reported that this decision had resulted in poor morale among the group. Some were indebted for about £500 and were very depressed when they worked out how long it would take them to pay their commitments. 'They are tending to become timeservers and are looking forward to the time they will be able to leave the railways', he reported. They had no complaints about their working conditions but felt deeply about their financial burdens. They had no money to socialise with Australians and became withdrawn and neurotic.[38]

Conclusion

The integration of migrants into rural communities was hindered by entrenched cultural attitudes and the inability of the responsible government department to monitor and respond to their settlement needs. The 1966 Census revealed that only a small proportion of each State's migrant population lived in non-metropolitan areas. The successful social engagement of those who settled outside Australia's cities owed more to changes in their bargaining position resulting from their becoming landowners, employers, and Australian citizens with voting rights than to active intervention by the Department of Immigration.

Their political representatives were then required to articulate their views and advance their interests, along with those of their other constituents.[39]

The reports by Departmental social and welfare workers on the mentally ill and migrants in rural Australia illustrate their value to the Department. Despite the overwhelming dimension of the task they tackled and their own linguistic and cultural limitations, they were a unique source of information on the practical difficulties faced by migrants and provided sound practical advice. They made visible previously marginalised groups within the migrant community.

CHAPTER 5

Communicating with migrants: teaching English to adults and children

THE Commonwealth government saw the provision of English language training to adult migrants as the key to their successful social and economic integration. While it generously funded an imaginative range of English-language services from 1948, the culture of the service-providers initially presented considerable obstacles to the Commonwealth's efforts to establish effective communications between migrants and the host community. Administrators and most politicians initially assumed that a minimal command of English could be acquired fairly easily, and would be sufficient to allow migrants to participate fully in everyday life. They were largely unaware of the difficulties confronting migrants attempting to learn English at evening classes or by correspondence after a long day's work. They could not see that teachers untrained in teaching English as a second language might have had difficulties making their classes interesting and relevant. Radio, and later television language teaching, while innovative, was programmed at times that precluded many migrants from taking advantage of it.

As funding increased, participation levels declined. Part of the reason for this lay in the reliance of government on mainstream community organisations to publicise these classes among non-English speaking migrants. Until the late 1960s, administrators neglected to monitor class retention rates and to consult consumer representatives to discover the causes of declining participation. They relied too much for advice on policy and planning on elite and monolingual members of the Australian establishment, whose background and experience prevented them from perceiving the practical problems confronting migrants. The philosophy of the party in power for most of this period led it to rely too much on the voluntary efforts of mainstream community organisations to encourage migrants to learn English, and to expect too little of major employers of migrants (both government and private). Those who benefited most from migrant labour were never required to allow Adult Migrant Education Scheme (AMES) classes to be conducted in the workplace during working hours, although a number of employers did so voluntarily. Significant sections of the migrant community did not utilise the language services provided, and many who did did not persist to a level at which their understanding of English was adequate to allow them to gain access to the community services to which they were entitled, although instruction was free and available for as long as participants felt they needed it. These groups were at risk of being socially marginalised and economically disadvantaged. Their inability to participate fully in Australian society was reflected in the reports of major government inquiries in the early 1970s, in the statistics of eligible migrants who did not apply to become citizens or who applied but were rejected on language grounds, and of those who left Australia permanently.

THE CULTURAL CONTEXT

European immigrants to post-war Australia entered a monolingual society. The principal foreign language taught in Australian secondary schools was French, the relevance of which to Australians was unquestioned. Few Australians needed to use French, and most rapidly forgot it on leaving school. As William Lawrence, Liberal Member for Wimmera in Victoria, lamented to the House of Representatives in September 1953, 'Those of us who gained a smattering of languages such as French and German in the course of our studies at school, have forgotten nearly all that we learned because we have not had an opportunity to converse with Frenchmen and Germans in their own language'. The few Australians who travelled overseas almost invariably made the long and expensive journey 'home' to

England. Australians at every level of society, therefore, had no understanding of what it was like to live in a country whose language was foreign and whose laws, regulations and institutions were unknown and therefore inaccessible. The combination of goodwill and lack of understanding that was to confuse the large numbers of non-English speaking migrants soon to enter Australia was articulated in Parliament in 1945 by Leslie Haylen (ALP NSW), an ex-serviceman and prominent promoter of migration. While he urged the provision of basic English classes on migrant ships because lack of English would lead to isolation and segregation on the migrants' arrival, he opined that all commands and instructions on board should be in English.[1]

Australian monolingualism had been reinforced by censorship regulations during both world wars, which produced fear and suspicion of those using foreign languages in Australia. In 1945 newspapers could not be printed in Australia in a foreign language except by permission of the government on the recommendation of the security service. An Italian newspaper published in Sydney, *Il Risveglio*, which had received such permission, was criticised in Parliament by Dame Annabelle Rankin (Liberal QLD) for its stated intention of helping Italian workers defend their rights to equal pay and treatment with Australian workers, particularly those employed in the Civil Constructional Corps. Dame Annabelle complained that two-thirds of the paper was printed in Italian and asked Dr Evatt, the responsible Minister, to 'consider the danger to national security of newspapers in certain foreign languages circulating in Australia, and prohibit their publication unless printed wholly in English'. This attitude persisted long after wartime regulations had ended. It was clearly articulated in 1958, for example, by former postmaster Dominic Costa (ALP NSW), who told the House that his party believed that 'there could be a danger in having newspapers published in Australia in foreign languages', and suggested that 'if a newspaper must be published in a foreign language, each foreign language component should be accompanied by an English translation'.[2]

The need for migrants rapidly to master English to assimilate into the host society and its workforce was well appreciated, and from 1948 considerable effort at Federal and State levels was put into providing them with a basic knowledge of spoken English. The inadequacy of basic English to migrants in their daily interaction with this society was not, however, sufficiently appreciated. Neither the mainstream community nor the administrators responsible for their welfare understood the difficulties they faced when they attempted to exercise the rights and gain access to the services to which they were entitled, or to understand and comply with the many laws and regulations to which they were subject as residents or citizens. It was not until the late 1960s that the department responsible for the absorption of migrants into Australian society began to appreciate the extent of the need for more varied and professionally staffed language teaching, and for translating and interpreting services throughout Australia, and to take a positive role in the provision of services to meet this need.

The Adult Migrant Education Scheme

Aim and administration

A proposal to initiate English language training for the influx of refugees expected after the July 1947 agreement between the Australian government and the International Refugee Organisation (IRO) was approved by the Minister for Immigration Arthur Calwell, put to the information department on 21 November 1947, and publicly announced on 3 March 1948. At this time only 8230 non-British migrants had arrived in Australia. A sum of £10 000 was earmarked in the 1948/49 Budget for the 'education of displaced persons from Europe after discharge from reception centres', but only a little over half of this was actually spent. Initially intended only for refugees, the scheme was extended to all aliens by Cabinet on 6 December 1948 after a recommendation by the Immigration Advisory Council (IAC), which described it in April 1948 as 'an experiment the like of which, so far as is known, has not been attempted previously anywhere else in the world'. The scheme offered free English instruction in four different forms—class instruction, correspondence courses, radio programs, and shipboard education.[3]

The aim of this range of AMES courses was to give migrants 'an elementary knowledge of the English tongue and to meet their practical everyday wants, and in addition some knowledge of Australian civics'. Its operation involved both interdepartmental and Commonwealth–State cooperation. Responsibility for policy development, management and funding lay with the Department of Immigration (despite an attempt in March 1949 by the Department of Education to take control of the scheme). The Commonwealth Department of Education accepted responsibility for assisting the Department of Immigration by providing professional and technical advice, developing special teaching methods, designing and producing special teaching and learning materials, and for teacher training. After an agreement between the Commonwealth and State Education Departments at the end of 1951, the administration of the scheme became the responsibility of the State Education Departments. They enrolled students, appointed teachers, provided classrooms, corrected correspondence lessons, and supervised the day-to-day operation of the various courses.[4]

Classroom education

All adult migrants were eligible to attend four hours of class instruction weekly without cost, for as long as they needed. Classes were established in metropolitan areas, where twelve migrants were enrolled, and in country areas, where a class of six could be formed. The State Education Department closed classes when enrolments fell below nine in metropolitan areas and four in country areas. Instruction was given by school teachers who were paid extra for working after hours according to prevailing rates (which were the same for male and female teachers except in NSW and Victoria, where women teachers were paid less than men).[5]

These classes were held at night, which precluded the attendance of shift workers and most married women. Although early enrolments were disappointing, Harold Holt as Minister for Immigration resisted suggestions that English classes be made compulsory. A suggestion made by the IAC in March 1951 that an incentive be provided in the form of a remittance of part of the refugees' two-year employment contract was rejected by the Citizenship Convention. In an attempt to improve accessibility, daytime classes for women were held in some preschool and baby health centres by 1954 (such classes were not permitted in NSW baby health centres). It was not, however, until 1972 that language classes specifically tailored to special groups such as women and adolescents were introduced. The Department was unsuccessful in its attempts to persuade employers to allow classes on their premises during working hours.[6]

The teaching method employed quickly developed into what soon became known as 'the Australian situational method'. In order to enable migrants to speak English and to understand it in the shortest possible time, and because many migrants, particularly from southern Europe, were illiterate in their own language, there was no systematic teaching of grammar, and reading and writing in English were not stressed. Everyday situations were employed to develop the use of sentence patterns, in preference to translation of single words and phrases. Teachers followed a two-part textbook entitled *English for Newcomers to Australia*, which initially had 140 units (the number of units was reduced to 114 when it was found that few students remained in classes beyond that level). Although the teachers were not specially trained to teach migrants English, some attempt was made to assist them by supplying them with a special version of the textbook, holding demonstrations of the method during vacation periods, and sending advisory teachers to visit their classes two or three times a year. The Commonwealth Office of Education offered them suggestions in the form of two circulars, 'English—by way of introduction' and 'English—a new language'.[7]

Correspondence lessons

Free correspondence lessons for migrants who could not attend classes began in May 1949. They followed 34 separate lesson booklets entitled 'Correspondence course for New Australians', and the only prerequisite was a knowledge of the English alphabet and script. For those who were illiterate in or who had a limited knowledge of their own language, four special introductory lessons were offered.[8]

Radio broadcasts

The use of radio for the teaching of English was suggested by the Director of the Office of Education to the Secretary of the Department of Immigration in May 1948. Classes began in April 1949, with the Australian Broadcasting Commission (ABC) broadcasting two language lessons weekly, without charge to the Commonwealth. A booklet produced by the Education Department containing the script of forthcoming broadcasts, 'For New Australians', was posted monthly to enrolled migrants. The ABC broadcast its 15-minute migrant education programs very early in the morning. In 1952 it refused a Department of Immigration offer to fund more frequent programs at times more convenient for migrants, on the grounds that such changes would interfere with the entertainment of its mainstream listeners. Until November 1954 the Commonwealth Office of Education designed and controlled the programs. After that date it continued to supply the script, but the ABC took over production. An ABC survey of clients in 1959 found that the classes attracted fewer than 1 per cent of listeners in capital cities throughout Australia.

Later other media were employed. In 1966 the government issued records based on the radio/correspondence course, and for five years from 1967 the ABC screened a British Broadcasting Commission Television English language series entitled *Walter and Connie*, sponsored by the Department of Immigration. In September 1971 the government began to enlist regional commercial television channels in the dissemination of locally produced language programs. WIN Channel 4, in the industrial city of Wollongong, NSW, began to broadcast the first in a series of 40 one-hour television programs, which taught English language according to the situational method and elements of Australian citizenship. They were directed specifically at migrant women, although it was hoped that they would also give mainstream viewers an appreciation of the traditions, values and problems of migrants. By 1974 they were being also shown in the Newcastle and Ballarat regions, and were scheduled for broadcast in the capital cities. Production had commenced on a further 78 half-hour programs. As migrant women had a higher participation rate in the workforce than non-migrant women in the 1970s, the efficacy of such daytime television programs in reaching its target audience was limited.[9]

Pre-embarkation and shipboard education

A shipboard education scheme was conducted for refugees brought to Australia under the IRO, from the middle of 1948 to the end of 1951. Education officers not only taught English—they also did a good deal of welfare and liaison work. Their numbers were never sufficient, and of the 99 ships that sailed for Australia, only 53 had education officers on board. As Pauline Griffin, a Department of Immigration social worker in Sydney during this period, recalled, migrants who attended these classes learnt very little English from them. This particular shipboard education scheme lapsed with the demise of the IRO.[10]

Shipboard education was revived in 1954, when the Australian government negotiated an agreement with the International Committee for European Migration (ICEM) whereby Australian government-funded language teachers travelled on migrant ships as ICEM staff. The first six Australian teachers sailed to Europe in March 1955. One (sometimes two) usually bilingual language teacher(s) travelled on each ship, assisted by volunteers from among the English-speaking passengers. A publication, *English on the Way*, containing 36 units for use in the shipboard classes, was introduced in March 1955. It was not until 1970 that the first in-service training course was held for shipboard education officers, at the Canberra College of Advanced Education. By 1973 there were 21 shipboard education officers, who conducted classes for both assisted and unassisted migrants and lectured and showed films on various aspects of life in Australia.[11]

Except for a brief period between mid-1949 and February 1951, initial hopes of establishing pre-embarkation language classes in refugee camps in Europe were not realised. Pre-embarkation language instruction was, however, again introduced in 1969, and by 1972 extended to France, Scandinavia, Yugoslavia and Turkey. An additional $150 000 was contributed to ICEM in 1972 for language teaching in Greece, Italy and Germany and to a lesser extent in Malta, Belgium and the Netherlands. The Spanish Institute of Emigration introduced language classes for intending migrants, the major costs of which were met by the Australian Department of Immigration. Only about half the amount budgeted between 1970 and 1973 for pre-embarkation and shipboard language teaching was actually spent.[12]

The home tutor scheme

As a result of a series of reports to government by the Migrant Education Committee of the IAC in October 1972, October 1973 and June 1974, the Department of Labour and Immigration produced a series of 'home tutorial' kits for use by voluntary organisations such as the YWCA, the CWA and the Good Neighbour Councils. The scheme was modelled on that initiated by the Wandsworth Council for Community Relations in the UK. It was launched early in 1974, and at the end of 1974–75 some 1334 unpaid tutors (largely of Anglo-Celtic origins) were involved in teaching English to migrant families, particularly women. Tutors were given brief training, and the two-hourly tutorials were conducted in either the tutor's or the student's home. Administrative arrangements varied. In New South Wales and Victoria the Commonwealth funded full-time coordinators, but in the ACT and Tasmania the scheme was coordinated solely by the Good Neighbour Councils. By 1975–76 the scheme had a total of 3947 students, 1733 tutors, and the average cost of each student to the Commonwealth was $10.[13]

The Debate about Advanced English: Needs vs Costs

In advisory bodies

From late 1952, concern was expressed by a number of bodies at the adequacy of the level of English-language training being offered to migrants. In August 1952 the issue was raised by the State Education Authorities at a meeting of the government departments involved in administering the scheme. The meeting agreed that the existing course provided a reasonable but not adequate standard of English, and that it was desirable that twelve advanced course lessons be prepared to be offered only to genuinely isolated students. In January 1953, delegates to the Citizenship Convention also discussed the adequacy of the level of instruction offered by the scheme. They recommended that a more advanced course be offered to enable migrants to gain access to education designed for native-born adult Australians. In response, the IAC in April 1953 appointed a subcommittee to investigate the standard that should be offered to migrants. Its members were English-born and Oxford-educated J.R. Darling, headmaster of the exclusive Geelong Church of England Grammar School since 1930 and vice-president of the Royal Empire Society of Victoria, J.G. Norris MA, president of the National Council of Women, and C.J. Austin.[14]

The report of this committee acknowledged the limited goal of the Commonwealth government in establishing the AMES, and that it had made 'a substantial financial commitment' to enable migrants to overcome the 'initial language barrier as a first step towards their integration into an English-speaking community'. At that time only 27 000 of the approximately 390 000 non-English speaking migrants in Australia were enrolled in either evening classes or correspondence courses, and £280 507 was spent on language teaching in the 1952/53 Budget. Nevertheless, the committee expressed its belief that the requirements of the majority of migrants who needed English 'to meet their everyday needs' were being met. It felt, however, that those of a minority of young migrants in the 16–21 age group who wanted to pursue further vocational education were not being met. It also pointed to the absence of bridging courses for native-born Australians who had been unable to proceed to higher education at the normal age. On the initiative of Mr Darling the committee added a third group—those who wanted to 'be introduced to the wider aspects of the English language and its literature so that they may share fully in the cultural life of the society in which they now live'. The committee felt that vocational training institutions and existing adult education services should provide such bridging courses, but until they did it recommended that the needs of migrants be met by providing advanced classes for selected students within the framework of the AMES and by placing more emphasis on the acquisition of reading skills. It anticipated that demand for advanced classes would not be great, and could be met by providing two or three such classes in the larger centres. Students should be required to contribute to the cost.[15]

By 1956 the number of non-British migrants in Australia increased to over 576 000. Class attendance grew from almost 11 000 in 1951 to nearly 16 500 in 1956, and enrolments in correspondence courses grew from over 6000 to 12 641. The cost per head of correspondence lessons escalated from £9.6.0 in 1951/52 to £13.5.0 in 1956/57, and by 1956/57 the budget for the whole AMES had risen to £434 000. Although the Minister for Immigration rejected suggestions that knowledge of English should be made a precondition of entry to Australia, authorities looked at ways of reducing the cost of the scheme, despite warnings in Parliament that failure by migrants to learn English would disadvantage the national economy and exacerbate the 'subconscious hostility which large numbers of Australians have towards foreign-speaking people'.[16]

The question of the effectiveness and expense of the AMES was raised in the October 1956 meeting of the Commonwealth IAC. The Secretary of the Department of Immigration, T.H.E. Heyes, insisted that its educational goal and level of expenditure was a matter for the Commonwealth, not the States. Darling suggested that migrants should be asked to contribute to the cost of the scheme, and reiterated his view that it should be used to promote the study of English literature. This latter suggestion did not receive the support of Darling's colleagues, who affirmed that the standard should be limited to that 'sufficient to meet daily requirements' (without discussing what these might be), and stressed that 'no preferential treatment should be afforded to migrants'. The IAC appointed a committee to review the costs, benefits, and scope of the scheme. Other advocates of the 'user pays' principle were vocal in this committee. Air Marshall Sir Richard Williams expressed his opinion that migrants should have to assume some portion of the costs personally, as 'some of the best types were not coming forward to these classes because of the present policy of providing free services and tuition'. Charging even a nominal sum would 'help to attract the better element amongst the migrants'. Senator Dame Nancy Buttfield (Liberal SA) also supported a fee. The committee recommended the establishment of a small interdepartmental committee of three experts from the Commonwealth, NSW and Victorian Departments of Education to advise it.[17]

While the experts focused almost entirely on the possible effects of proposed cost-cutting measures, they also looked for the first time at some AMES clients. While it was impossible to assess client satisfaction with the quality of the language instruction offered, as statistics were not kept by AMES on retention rates, NSW Department of Education officer A.H. Pelham analysed the progress of 340 students in correspondence courses who enrolled in March 1955. He found that they remained on course for approximately 13 months, but that only 60 (18 per cent) of the group completed all 34 lessons. Most (40 per cent) completed the first twenty lessons only. The committee of experts did not favour the introduction of a fee on the grounds that it would discourage the involvement of the less well educated migrants, who needed English-language training most, and poured cold water on most of the other cost-cutting alternatives. The IAC committee appointed to examine the AMES accepted the experts' recommendations, subsequently concluding that no major savings could be made without reducing the value of the scheme, although the Minister, Athol Townley, remained concerned at its cost.[18]

At no time in these discussions was the number of migrants enrolled in AMES courses related to the numbers of non-English speaking migrants in Australia. A preoccupation with cost-saving strategies prevented sufficient attention being given to the adequacy of the scheme to meet the basic settlement needs of such migrants, and the question of the level necessary to meet the 'basic everyday needs' of migrants was never examined. Discussion within the IAC tended to reflect the cultural values of mainstream community leaders on the committee rather than the objective needs of the client community. The opinion of education administrators, who at least made some attempt to assess migrant responses, however, prevailed with decision-makers. The failure of government to provide more than a minimum level of English was dramatically highlighted in

November 1962 by a Belgian woman in the Department of Immigration's Holding Centre at Bonegilla, who went on a hunger strike over the inability of her husband to pursue his teaching career. As Senator Henty pointed out, the level of English offered at the hostel was inadequate to equip him for his profession.[19]

In Parliament

At the heart of the debate on the costs of teaching migrants English lay pro-British and assimilationist cultural values. Such a perspective led to a passive attitude among some politicians towards the provision of settlement services. Australia should have as many migrants as it had 'capacity to absorb', declared NSW ALP parliamentarian Dominic Costa in 1958, adding:[20]

> We believe that British immigrants should constitute 60 per cent of the total. We do not adopt this view because of any prejudice, but because we think it is wise to preserve the British outlook and the British stock of this country. Another advantage is that British immigrants are easier to assimilate than non-British immigrants, because they understand our language and our laws. They are like us in every way.

Another of his right-wing Catholic colleagues, Francis Stewart, wanted to submit migrants to a mandatory English test after two years' residence in Australia, but these attitudes towards migrant languages were not representative of the attitudes of the ALP as a whole. The Victorian ALP in 1960 conducted segments of the radio program 'Victoria's Labour Hour' in migrant languages, but abandoned this after representations to the Minister for Immigration from grazier and ex-serviceman Winston Turnbull (CP VIC), who opposed foreign language broadcasts on the grounds that 'we want migrants in this country to speak the English language'.[21]

These views were shared by some government members but not all. Hubert Opperman, grandson of a German migrant, who was to become Minister for Immigration from 1963 to 1966, had an entirely different perspective. He estimated in 1959 that he had approximately 10 000 migrants from a number of language groups in his electorate, and warned his parliamentary colleagues that 'we who have lived here all our lives should not expect the newcomer to put on the cloak of citizenship and fit into our way of life without some difficulty'. He criticised the insensitive and parochial manner in which migrants were often discussed in the press and in Parliament 'as though they were a new breed of cattle, oblivious to human feelings', and argued that they should not be required to be able to speak English before being granted citizenship. '[I]f migrants desire to become Australians it does not matter very much whether they pronounce their words correctly or put them into the correct sequence. Let them become Australians and belong to Australia', he urged.[22]

Politicians became increasingly concerned at the failure of migrants to become Australian citizens. In 1960, Edward Gough Whitlam (ALP NSW) asked the Minister for Immigration how many eligible aliens had not applied for citizenship and how many applications for citizenship had been refused. The reply revealed that 215 622 eligible aliens had not sought citizenship and 8286 had been refused, 3947 because of their inadequate knowledge of English and the 'responsibilities and privileges of citizenship'. The Labor Party at this time was, however, more concerned about the 194 migrants who had been rejected on security grounds than with pursuing the reasons for the failure of large numbers of migrants to master sufficient English despite their desire to become Australian citizens. Only later did the ALP shift its focus to language-related obstacles to citizenship. Complaining about a proposed cut of over £78 000 in expenditure on migrant English in the 1962/63 Budget, Senator James McClelland (ALP NSW) pointed to the disparity between migrant intake and the numbers taking up citizenship, claiming that only one-third of eligible migrants had become Australian citizens. Lack of 'an adequate knowledge of English', or of 'the responsibilities and privileges of citizenship', was responsible for the rejection of 9102 applications for citizenship between 1961 and 1970.[23]

The Diversification of the Adult Migrant Education Scheme 1960–75

Part-time continuation classes

As the table on p.116 indicates, the number of students participating in part-time English classes or correspondence courses declined from the early 1960s. This information became more publicly available from 1966, when the Department of Immigration began publishing annual statistics of migrants attending language courses in its *Quarterly Statistical Summary*. In 1968–69 the Department reviewed the AMES and found that by 1969 there were only approximately 22 000 students in classes, correspondence and radio courses. This, however, prompted it to introduce in 1969 a range of innovative solutions which brought a greater flexibility into the scheme, thus allowing migrants a wider choice of classes. Continuation classes were subsequently diversified to include day classes for women equipped with child-minding facilities, family classes at community centres, tuition for members of various ethnic organisations, English classes for the parents of children attending classes in their first language in ethnic schools, courses for long-term patients in hospital, and classes that emphasised literacy. While many migrants initially enrolled (total enrolments in continuation classes rose from approximately 34 000 in 1973 to almost 46 000 in 1975–76), there was a high dropout rate, and many classes were closed (approximately half of enrolled students discontinued their studies in 1975–76, and 477 classes were closed). These classes were free for the migrant, and relatively cheap for the government to provide—the average cost per student during the early 1970s was $133. These multilevel part-time continuation classes had been the only form of face-to-face teaching provided until 1969 when other, more costly, professionally oriented courses were introduced to cater for the different vocational needs of migrants.[24]

Full-time intensive classes

Full-time intensive English courses for professionally trained and other educationally advanced migrants were introduced at the University of New South Wales for the first time in 1969, largely as a result of the influx of skilled migrants from Czechoslovakia. Migrants were paid a living allowance to enable them to maintain themselves and their families while studying eight hours a day, five days a week, for eight weeks (approximately 320 hours). By April 1970, there were 280 students in two courses, and by July the following year nine courses were operating in Melbourne, Sydney, Canberra, Perth, Adelaide and Hobart, catering for 1640 students annually. The funding more than doubled, from over $218 000 in 1969/70 to over $448 000 the following financial year. Demand was great; there was a waiting list in 1970 of 5000, and it was planned to extend the courses to the industrial centres of Newcastle and Whyalla. Annual vacation courses were also held at Monash University and the University of Queensland. By 1972–73 intensive English courses were available in all States at fourteen different centres, and catered for 1764 students annually. By 1975–76 the number of students and centres had declined slightly, to 1520 students in nine centres around Australia. They were receiving 5.2 per cent of the AMES budget at an average cost of $321 per student.[25]

Part-time accelerated English classes in Migrant Education Centres and hostels

Part-time accelerated courses were introduced in October 1969. These accelerated classes covered in three to four months the curriculum followed over eighteen months in the normal continuation classes. Flexible teaching hours enabled adults to attend classes at various times of the day and evening to suit their working schedule, and special daytime classes were provided for women. Classes of between eight and twenty hours weekly were held over sixteen to twenty weeks, and they catered for about 4000 students annually. As they were working, students did not receive an allowance to attend the classes. By March 1971 Migrant Education Centres providing accelerated English courses had been established in Westbridge, Cabramatta and East Hills hostels. Such courses were also provided at State Migrant Education Centres in Melbourne, Sydney, Wollongong, Darwin and Geelong, and were planned for Brisbane, Mount Isa, Newcastle, Adelaide and Perth. The curriculum taught in hostels followed on from the pre-embarkation and shipboard classes, and children were given from four to six weeks' language training before they entered mainstream schools. By 1975 they occupied 12.6 per cent of the AMES budget.[26]

Full-time accelerated courses

In January 1973, full-time ten-week courses, based on the normal continuation curriculum, were introduced for migrants who required English quickly for employment. Like the professionally qualified students attending intensive courses, they received a living allowance. By June that year these courses catered for 940 students in Sydney, Melbourne and Perth, and were planned to increase as Migrant Education Centres opened in other State capitals. By 1975, 10.2 per cent of the AMES budget was devoted to such courses.[27]

Advanced English

From the 1969/70 financial year, migrants already proficient in English could attend advanced language courses over a period of three terms. The courses, conducted by both State Adult Migrant Education Services and by some other (mainly tertiary) institutions, were mainly part-time, and lasted from ten to twenty weeks. Although the students paid fees, the cost of the course was subsidised by the AMES. By 1971, 200 places were provided annually at the University of Sydney, the Council of Adult Education in Melbourne and the Australian National University Centre for Continuing Education in Canberra, and 410 were provided by AMES. By 1975/76 the number of places had grown to 2520 AMES enrolments and 590 in other institutions. The average cost per student was $65.57.[28]

English in the workplace

The Liberal government, in power from 1950 to 1972, made no attempt to require the major firms that benefited most from migrant manpower to encourage their employees to learn English by allowing AMES classes to be conducted at the workplace during working hours. This had been recommended by the 1954 Citizenship Convention but rejected by the Department of Immigration, which believed that 'employers are understandably reluctant to allow classes during working hours and migrants are reluctant to attend classes during their lunch hour'. AMES teachers were supplied to any private firms or government agencies which, like Myers department store in Melbourne or the NSW and South Australian Railways, chose to allow them to teach in the workplace. Some 50 courses, held in the employee's time, were then running in factories in New South Wales, Victoria and South Australia. Pauline Griffin, who moved from the Social Welfare Section to become personnel officer and manager in various branches of Bradmill Industries in NSW and Victoria from 1953 to 1973, recalled that language classes were held in most Bradmill workplaces in the 1950s. They were conducted by teachers provided by the AMES and held in the employees' time (during a one-hour period before or after shifts). While their degree of success and patronage varied from mill to mill, classes were generally small because relatively few employees attended, mostly women. This service was regarded as worthwhile by the management, which made facilities available for classes but did not rely on its employees' knowledge of English, particularly to convey information on safety regulations. Highly experienced and competent bilingual migrants were employed as instructors, one for each language group. Lack of English, therefore, did not place the Bradmill worker at a disadvantage in the workplace, although it was a considerable handicap outside work.

Arthur Marshman, of the Queensland State Migrant Office, recalled a number of unsuccessful efforts by his government to encourage employers to hold English classes in the workplace, particularly in General Motors car factories in the 1960s. He attributed its failure not to opposition from the unions, but to resistance from English-speaking employees to giving migrants time off for this purpose. By 1968, an English course designed for use in places of employment was being used in 26 firms in NSW, and by 1971 the AMES was developing textbooks specially adapted for language classes in factories and other places of employment.[29]

This was too little, too late. Consequently, there was a great and unmet need for interpreters in places of employment, and for the provision of information in translation for workers. The Coalition government did nothing to require firms to provide interpreters and translators, largely because it began to appreciate this need only in the early 1970s, shortly before losing office. The succeeding Labor government was more proactive but also stopped short of compulsion, because Australia had entered a period of growing unemployment and the government now feared that, if required to hold language classes in working time, employers would be disinclined to engage migrants. In March 1973 a new six-week course was developed, adapted to the specific needs of individual factories in consultation with their management. For six hours each week the language classes included information on factory rules, safety factors, and the specialised vocabulary needed for that particular industry. Conducted by teachers provided by State Education Departments, it was operating in 25 factories in Victoria, and plans were being made to extend it to other States. The government expected, but did not require, that these courses would be held during working hours, and no financial incentives were provided for employers. In 1974 the Department of Labor and Immigration published 50 000 copies of a leaflet 'English in industry', to encourage their employers to conduct English classes for employees and to encourage migrant workers to join these classes. The leaflets were translated into Arabic, Turkish, Greek, Italian, Serbo-Croat and Spanish.[30]

The IAC, in a series of reports on migrant education during 1972–74, urged the government to set the example to private industry by arranging courses in its own factories and institutions, which employed significant numbers of non-English speaking migrants. The Department of Labor and Immigration approached the relevant departments and authorities, and by October 1975 had succeeded in having such courses established by several departments. The introduction of workplace English classes in non-government industries, however, was slow. Between 1972 and July 1974, 192 courses had been conducted, largely in employers' time, for 2500 workers, mostly in Victoria. By 1975 just under 1 per cent of the AMES budget was devoted to courses in industry, 59 organisations participated in the scheme (43 private, 2 statutory and 14 government), and 2293 students attended (about one-quarter of whom were women), at an average cost per student of $30.42.[31]

Cultural Change and Political Embarrassment

The significant cultural shift that had taken place in thinking about migrant language requirements by the end of the 1960s was reflected in the terminology used both within the Department of Immigration and in Parliament. No longer was the issue of language teaching discussed in relation to 'assimilation', but as a strategy to promote 'integration'—a process that was seen as involving various government instrumentalities and as a matter of ethnic and cultural as well as linguistic differences. In his Department of Immigration budget statement for 1971/72, the Auditor General for the first time referred to funding for the education of 'language handicapped adults and children in Australia'.[32]

The first in a series of reports on migrant poverty, published by Professor Ronald Henderson in 1970, provoked a defensive reaction within the Department of Immigration. 'The basic fallacy involved in extrapolating from the survey is that while it gives a fair picture of those poor who are migrants, it ignores those migrants who are not poor', the Programme Development Subsection commented. However, the appointment by Prime Minister William McMahon of Professor Henderson to a non-parliamentary commission of inquiry into poverty in Australia on 29 August 1972 meant that the focus on the causes of poverty, including migrant poverty, would only intensify in the coming years.[33]

Parliamentary pressure to account for the increasing numbers of migrants departing permanently from Australia resulted in reports on this topic by the IAC's committee on Social Patterns in 1967 and 1973. A Department of Immigration survey of migrant employment problems completed in November 1971 for the second inquiry on the causes of migrant departures revealed that the most important single employment problem among the migrants surveyed was language and communication. Only a small percentage of migrants studied, however, were attending English classes. It also found that Commonwealth Employment Offices had inadequate numbers of appropriately qualified multilingual staff, and that referral and counselling services for migrants were inadequate. In 1973 a survey of 7700 families in five capital cities whose heads had arrived in Australia since 1963 was conducted by the Australian Bureau of Statistics on behalf of the Department of Immigration. It was analysed by the Australian Population and Immigration Council, which found that there had been some improvement in migrants' fluency in English during the ten years since arrival. Of those who claimed on arrival to speak fair to poor English, 36 per cent were assessed as fluent to good at interview, as were 12 per cent of those who had spoken no English on arrival. However, there was still a large group that had made little progress in learning English. Of these, more than half had been either unable or unwilling to attend any form of English classes. Non-English speakers were found to be migrants who had had a low level of formal education in their country of origin, were not well qualified, enjoyed lower wage levels than other migrants, and were less committed to staying in Australia. They were disproportionately from Mediterranean countries, and many had emigrated from rural areas with little or no industrial experience.[34]

By 1972–73, when approximately 11 per cent of the Australian population was born in non-English speaking countries, the budget for part-time adult English classes was almost $2 million, over $1 million was spent on full-time intensive English classes, and over $5 million on child migrant education. The proportion of the budget spent on part-time courses as opposed to full-time courses by 1975 reflected the government's growing desire to utilise the talents and experience of skilled migrants. Of the 36.8 per cent of the budget spent on part-time courses, only 21.2 per cent was devoted to the old continuation classes—the rest was divided between part-time accelerated, advanced, and industrial classes. Services for migrants who could not attend classes—television, radio correspondence courses and the home tutor scheme—occupied 13 per cent of the budget. Full-time courses—intensive, accelerated and bridging courses for ethnic teachers—occupied 35.9 per cent (20 per cent of which was taken up in providing living allowances for the students). Despite this growth in expenditure, the numbers of migrants attending continuation classes progressively declined throughout the early 1970s. While classes had attracted 15 581 migrants in 1970, this declined to 10 751 in 1973 and to 8601 in 1975. The numbers enrolled in correspondence courses remained fairly constant, at between 7000 and 8000, over this period. On 14 June 1974 responsibility for migrant education was removed from the portfolio of the Department of Immigration.[35]

By 1975 AMES was an innovative, flexible, and fairly well-funded program, but it had not been accessed by all migrants who needed it. In 1978 the Galbally Report estimated that approximately 400 000 of the 1.5 million migrants in Australia from non-English speaking countries had a low level of fluency in English. Probably the most important reason for the scheme's inability to attract the migrants who needed it lay in the failure of successive governments to market this service adequately among migrants. Liberal philosophy, as Senator Greenwood explained in 1969, looked to community bodies to supply and support migrant settlement services. Although the Department of Immigration attempted to publicise its language classes in the form of posters and pamphlets, it largely looked to the predominantly Anglo-Celtic Good Neighbour Movement to encourage migrants to attend them.[36]

For a growing number of migrants from an increasingly diverse range of language groups who were unable or unwilling to attend AMES classes, access to the range of community services to which they were entitled and compliance with the myriad laws and regulations to which they were subject as citizens or permanent residents was extremely difficult. Although the post-war expansion of industry had depended substantially on migrant labour, by 1975 the government had missed its opportunity to require employers in times of full employment to provide English classes. As the Commission of Inquiry into Poverty remarked in 1975:[37]

> Little time or effort has been spent by industry on induction procedures, training information or safety instruction designed specifically for migrants. In practice safety information or instruction is usually presented only in English and often the employer does little to encourage the employees' proficiency in that language. Frequently industry copes with the language barrier simply by putting members of the one ethnic group together in the same section of the industry, with a bilingual overseer for that group. This solution, however satisfactory for the employer, does little to help the migrant. On the contrary, segregation of migrants effectively removes them from contact with Australians and makes it even more difficult for them to learn English and to understand more of the society in which they live.

ENGLISH-LANGUAGE TRAINING FOR MIGRANT CHILDREN

As, under the Australian Constitution, responsibility for the education of children lies with the States, the Department of Immigration did not initially become involved in the education of migrant children. State governments, however, saw the task of facilitating alien settlement as a Commonwealth responsibility, and failed to perceive the problems migrant children and their non-English speaking parents were having in gaining access to educational services. It was not until the 1960s and early 1970s, when political embarrassment was caused by Labor Party spokesmen and mainstream community bodies concerned that the cycle of poverty and social disadvantage was repeating itself in the second generation of migrants, that solutions were sought. These solutions required Commonwealth–State cooperation, a process that was fraught with difficulties.

Pressure for Commonwealth intervention during the 1950s

Mainstream culture hindered the adaptation of migrant children to the host community. The widely held assumption that language learning was easy for children was articulated by Minister for Immigration Harold Holt in 1956. He told Parliament:[38]

> The children present the least of our problems . . . because we have found that they are readily adaptable to the Australian

Table 5.1 Adult Migrant Education Scheme: participants and costs 1951–75

Date	Classes	Correspondence courses	Immigration Department budget	Total alien settler arrivals since 1945
1951	11 000	6000	£163 925	190 842
1952	18 238	9336	£280 507	390 000
1953	15 212	12 395	£303 513	430 053
1956	16 500	12 641	£415 000	576 000
1961	20 228	11 015	£503 596	887 553
1962	17 169	9074	£443 097	943 802
1963	16 500	8700	£447 845	994 104
1967	13 003	6223	$968 381	1.2 m
1970	15 481	7608	$1.4 m	1.3 m
1972	11 874	8134	$2.1 m	1.4 m
1973	10 751	7481	$2 m	1.5 m
1975	8601	7871	N/A	1.7 m

Sources: Commonwealth of Australia *Budget Paper*, Government Printer, Canberra, 1951–75; Department of Immigration *Statistical Bulletin*, no. 1 January 1952–no. 39, July 1961; Department of Immigration *Australian Immigration Quarterly Statistical Bulletin*, vol. 2, no. 1, November 1961–no. 20, 1966; Department of Immigration *Australian Immigration Quarterly Statistical Summary*, vol. 3, no. 1, September 1966–vol. 3, no. 35, December 1976, AGPS, Canberra.

way of life, and quickly acquire a knowledge of the language. Certainly they do so once they begin their schooling, and, indeed, the facility with which the children pick up the language often enables them to assist the parents to acquire a working knowledge of English.

Although James Cairns (ALP VIC) raised the question of the teaching of English to children in school hours in 1963, it was not until 1966 that the issue was more actively pursued in Parliament by the Opposition. William O'Connor (ALP NSW), whose electorate of Dalley included three major migrant hostels with more than 2000 migrants, argued for more Commonwealth funding to meet the demands created locally by large-scale migration. The impact of immigration on two high schools in his electorate had produced a situation which was 'becoming nothing short of a national scandal', he claimed. About 40 per cent of students at the Port Kembla High School had migrant parents, and 32 classes had to be conducted in eighteen classrooms. Berkley High School, designed to accommodate 800 students, had an enrolment of 1020 and fourteen classes with no permanent rooms.[39]

In 1967, Gordon Scholes (ALP VIC) drew the attention of Prime Minister Harold Holt to the educational handicaps experienced by migrant children because of their lack of English, and asked the Commonwealth to make grants to the States to allow special schools to be set up for the teaching of English. Holt expressed his satisfaction with the success with which Australia had absorbed more than 2 million migrants, and claimed that no complaints about problems encountered by migrant children had come to his notice. However, less than two months later, Holt revised this somewhat cavalier answer, informing the House that 'this is a matter with which both the Department of Immigration and the Department of Education and Science are concerned, and about which discussions have been had with State Education authorities', adding:[40]

> There is no doubt that a child who comes to Australia from a country where English is not spoken does meet with difficulties, particularly where his parents do not speak English. However, I am informed that all States have introduced some special provisions to cope with the language problems of migrant children and the relevant Commonwealth Departments will, of course, continue to maintain their interest in the question.

The Opposition pursued the matter of Commonwealth funding for special language teaching for migrant children in 1968. It was informed that nothing would be done until the results of a year-long experiment by the NSW Department of Education, on the best method of teaching English to school children, were available and had been circulated to all the States for their comment. The government obviously did not think the problem was an urgent one.[41]

The following year Gordon Bryant (ALP VIC) painted a graphic picture of the plight of migrant children in inner Melbourne schools. In one Malvern school there were sixteen language groups ranging from half a dozen Turkish-speaking children, none of whose parents spoke English, to 500 newly arrived Italian children. 'It is a problem that the education system in Victoria is not equipped to tackle. The Commonwealth is the only authority which can do something about it', he argued, as it was a problem the Commonwealth had created. He pointed out that in 1968, 35–40 000 migrants between 5 and 19 years of age had arrived in Australia. As the average school in metropolitan areas accommodated about 800 children, he argued, there should be between 45 and 50 new schools constructed to cater for this influx, and some 2000 additional teachers employed. Most pressure was on the older schools in inner-city industrial areas. 'It is a Commonwealth responsibility. We cannot shirk it. We cannot duck behind the smokescreen of State rights', he concluded. By 1969 a group of inner-city residents had formed the Carlton Association to push for better schooling in that inner-city suburb, particularly for migrant children. Their concerns were brought before the Senate by a government member, Senator Ivor Greenwood (Liberal VIC), who also suggested Commonwealth funding to remedy the problem.[42]

The Immigration (Education) Act 1971

As classroom accommodation in areas with high migrant populations was an obvious problem and probably the easiest to tackle, in March 1970 the Department of Immigration proposed to Cabinet that Commonwealth funds be provided to supply classrooms in these areas, or to allow new sites to be acquired for schools unable to expand beyond existing boundaries. Victoria had been the only State to have pressed the Commonwealth to provide school accommodation, as most of the 63 schools within a three-square-mile area of inner Melbourne had high migrant populations and were badly in need of repair and modernisation. Probably because of the lack of interest from other States, Cabinet rejected this proposal.[43]

On 12 March 1971 the Commonwealth government finally intervened in the education of migrant children by passing the *Immigration (Education) Act*. This attacked the problem on a number of fronts, although it did not provide for improved accommodation. On 23 April the Commonwealth announced that it would fund the salaries of teachers in special language classes for migrant children in State and independent schools, that it would fund training for these teachers in English as a second language and provide language laboratories and educational materials. Over $1.7 million was to be spent on child migrant education in 1970/71 out of a total budget allocation of $16 million for migrant education over four years.[44]

The results of past neglect were, however, not quickly remedied, and now tended to attract criticism to the Commonwealth government. Although the first report on migrant poverty published by Professor Ronald Henderson in 1970 had included only a brief comment on the inadequacy of schools to meet the needs of migrant children, a study by M. De Lemos, on behalf of the

Australian Council for Educational Research and submitted to the Department of Immigration in August 1971, found that English-speaking children in 262 schools achieved better than children of non-English speaking backgrounds. The Department's Program Development Subsection suggested defensively that 'migrant problem schools' were not typical of the migrant scene, but existed in areas in which migrants had formed enclaves, and that the problems of migrant children were largely the result of children still working out their initial adjustment to Australia.[45]

The Secretary, R.E. Armstrong, however, was concerned by the degree of criticism his Department and Minister A.J. Forbes were receiving as the result of problems confined to relatively small areas of Sydney and Melbourne. He suggested that if the Department could make a concerted effort to solve the problems in these two areas it would have solved a high percentage of its integration problem cases. He ordered the preparation of a paper on the specific problems in the teaching of English in inner-suburban schools, indicating any other factors that might lead to their being described as 'problem schools', and suggested that 'some thought' be given to developing a concentrated program for inner-suburban areas in Sydney and Melbourne to overcome existing integration difficulties. He also suggested that the proposed study might reveal inadequate accommodation as the chief cause of migrant children's disadvantage.[46]

An embarrassing survey 1972

The Department became alarmed in February 1972, when the Department of Education and Science (DES) decided to survey schools in the inner-metropolitan areas of Melbourne to evaluate the effectiveness of Commonwealth-funded initiatives, without consulting the Minister for Immigration. The Department believed that it was 'clearly wrong' for the DES to be taking the initiative in an area which was the Department of Immigration's financial responsibility, and believed that the situation was the result of the divided control over migrant education and pressure on the DES by their Minister, Malcolm Fraser. This interdepartmental conflict was resolved by April 1972, when Fraser wrote to Forbes proposing a joint study on child migrant education in inner-Melbourne schools. The DES proposal focused firmly on the operation and adequacy of special English classes for migrant children. In his reply, Forbes stressed that the joint study should be taken without commitment. The study was made in October and November 1972 by representatives of the Departments of Immigration, Education and Science, the Education Department of Victoria and the Melbourne Catholic Education Office, in 63 schools in the Melbourne inner-metropolitan area. The results were dismal. Although in August 1972 the Minister for Immigration had assured the House that '[t]he rate at which we have been able to develop this program has . . . considerably exceeded our original expectations', the survey found that after 31 months of Commonwealth funding only one-third of children with learning difficulties attributable to inadequate English were attending special classes, and of those who attended 40 per cent were not getting sufficient instruction.[47]

The main problem, as the Department of Immigration had anticipated, was accommodation. Two-thirds of the schools surveyed were very poorly placed, only 29 per cent of rooms used for English language classes for migrant children were proper classrooms, the rest being held in converted corridors, store rooms, staff rooms, cloakrooms, under stairs, and even in a converted shower block. The number of teachers was also inadequate, with 500 teachers provided for 16 000 migrant pupils in Victoria. The survey estimated that the 63 schools surveyed needed 400 additional teachers. Although a four-week training course in teaching English as a second language (ESL) was provided for teachers, it was not a prerequisite for employment as an ESL teacher. Only 65 teachers in the 63 schools surveyed had done the course, and all thought it had not been long enough. The teaching materials supplied were inadequate and were often inappropriate for children, and the language laboratories provided by the Commonwealth were condemned as a largely useless gimmick. The provision to migrant parents of translated information, and of adult interpreters, was found to be inadequate, and consequently attendance by migrants at parents' meetings was poor.

The report was particularly sensitive for the Victorian government. Its several drafts reveal a number of strongly worded criticisms were watered down, and the representative of the Victorian Education Department contested the report's findings. He argued that these findings were the result of the 'natural propensity' of teachers and principals 'to inflate the dimensions of the problem', and unsuccessfully attempted to prevent its tabling before the State elections in May 1973. In his statement to Parliament on the report on 5 April 1973, Kim Beazley acknowledged the need to reverse the 1970 decision of Cabinet not to grant Commonwealth assistance for accommodation in State schools. The budget allocation in 1973/74 for this program was increased by 100 per cent. By June 1973 there were approximately 43 000 children receiving instruction in special classes.[48]

After the recommendations of a series of reports by the IAC, the Commonwealth organised a seminar on the need to include instruction on special needs of non-English speaking children in all teacher-training courses in 1974. It also funded studies of the educational experience of such children and of ways of assessing their progress in English learning. The urgency of their language needs caused the teaching of citizenship to migrant children—in State and independent schools, also provided for in the Act—to be completely ignored.[49]

Conclusion

The government's determination to address the language problems of migrants from 1948 was not primarily inspired by economic considerations. Most of the major employers of migrant labour appear not to have valued an English-speaking and literate workforce, otherwise they would more actively have encouraged government-sponsored English-language classes in the workplace. Language-related settlement services were not provided in response to demands from the migrant communities themselves. In the period under consideration most migrant organisations were still social clubs, and few had made the transition either to service-providers for their communities or to political lobby groups.

The determination to remove the linguistic obstacles to the integration of aliens into Australian society was largely cultural. It can be related both to the way Australians perceived the role of the state and to their understanding of Australian national identity. The formation of the Australian state was influenced both by utilitarian philosophy and by a later form of social liberalism than the earlier rights-based contractarian liberalism so influential in American political history. Australians invested the state with an ethical role as the vehicle of social justice. They were also political pragmatists. Their expectation that the government should respond to legitimate demands led to a tradition of bureaucratic creativity which was manifested in the solutions provided by the Department of Immigration from 1948 to the communication needs of non-English speaking migrants.[50]

While Australia's success in absorbing migrants lay in its political institutions and its culture, so also did the obstacles it had to overcome. As aliens could not hold permanent positions in the Public Service, the Anglo-Celtic majority dominated the administration of services to migrants within the bureaucracy at Commonwealth, State and local government level. They also dominated the mainstream organisations to which the bureaucracy delegated much of its settlement tasks. Their lack of understanding of minority cultures and their monolingualism left a legacy of disadvantage. This became most evident in the early 1990s, when many migrants with a poor command of English were retrenched as a result of the radical restructuring of those industries they were brought to Australia to develop.[51]

CHAPTER 6

Towards access and equity: interpreting and translating services

THE level of migrant English instruction considered adequate by the government during the 1950s, and the small proportion of the migrant population willing or able to take advantage of the Adult Migrant Education Scheme (AMES), made it inevitable that translating and interpreting facilities would be needed. Cultural assumptions, however, prevented decision-makers from perceiving the social disadvantage and exclusion experienced by large numbers of migrants. The failure of both government and non-government bodies to provide information in languages comprehensible to non-English speaking migrants provided a major obstacle to their exercising their rights and accessing the services to which they were entitled as permanent residents. The Department of Immigration rejected totally a resolution by the 1952 Citizenship Convention that mainstream media be used to communicate with migrants in languages other than English, arguing that: 'particularly in view of the large numbers of languages which would be involved, quite apart from other difficulties, it is impracticable that the medium of expression designed for general use and appeal should present press columns and radio sessions in languages other than English'.[1]

The need for adequate interpreting and translating services was not understood until their absence had created situations that brought great personal tragedy to some migrants and considerable political embarrassment to the government. Administrators failed to appreciate the compliance costs to departments and instrumentalities at all levels of government of large numbers of migrants who were either unaware of laws and regulations or had no idea how to comply with them. Monolingual bureaucrats not only failed to see the need to provide migrants with interpreters and translators for a long time—they also did not appreciate the skills involved. This was reflected in a resistance to paying allowances to migrants employed in other work but used as interpreters and in the low wages and unrealistic expectations of those employed primarily in this capacity.

By the late 1960s, a number of important service-providing agencies were becoming aware of their own urgent need for interpreters and translators, and looked to the Department of Immigration to provide them. A small group of bureaucrats within its Integration Section, drawing on the experiences of departmental social workers, conceived of and developed an imaginative and innovative telephone interpreter service. The task then confronting the Department, and one with which it made little headway before 1975, was to persuade other government and non-government bodies to provide their migrant clients with in-house interpreters and information about their services in translation.

THE DEPARTMENT OF IMMIGRATION'S INTERPRETING SERVICES

Although the Department was slow to perceive the need of migrants for interpreters, it was quick to perceive its own need for them in order to communicate with and monitor the activities of migrants. From 1950, migrant interpreters were employed in the Department of Immigration. They were also increasingly called on by other Federal and State bodies to help them relate to the migrant community. The Department was, therefore, forced to formulate policy to regulate their availability and payment.

In May 1950 the Chief Commissioner for Police in Victoria asked Minister for Immigration Harold Holt to allow a Czechoslovakian clerk employed at the Williamstown Hostel to interpret for police when interviewing migrants in hostels. He asked if similar arrangements could be made in other parts of the State. Holt agreed, but pointed out that the proposed rate of 10/6 an hour was considerably less than the clerk's current remuneration. The Secretary of the Department of Immigration, however, informed the Chief Secretary of Victoria that the terms of employment with the Commonwealth Public Service Board prevented the particular migrant nominated by the Chief Commissioner from being employed as an interpreter. Instead, the Department arranged for the employment of a full-time interpreter on the staff of the Commonwealth Migration Officer (CMO) in Melbourne, who would be paid at a rate appropriate to Commonwealth interpreters.[2]

Not only were there insufficient interpreters available, but the standard of interpreting was often inadequate. Untrained migrants were often called on to interpret in highly specialised fields where accuracy was essential. The Victorian Attorney General complained to the Minister in June 1951 that the judges of the Supreme Court of Victoria were dissatisfied with the lack of proficiency of interpreters used in the court, and asked for a list of reliable interpreters. Heyes informed the Department of Labour and National Service that there was only one official interpreter in the Department's Melbourne office, and that he had always been made available for Supreme Court work. Heyes indicated, however, that he might be able to supply other interpreters from among the Department's 'temporary New Australian staff' (only British subjects and Australian citizens could be permanent employees of the Public Service).[3]

By October 1951 there were four migrants employed in the Melbourne office, who between them 'covered the majority of European languages'. This, in the opinion of the CMO, would meet most of the requirements of Crown authorities in Victoria. The CMO had considered supplying to State authorities a typist with linguistic qualifications, but decided against it on the grounds that 'it would do little to satisfy their overall requirements as it is most difficult to obtain a girl with other than three or four major languages and, in addition, it is undesirable to use female interpreters in many Court actions'. It was not until July 1951 that the Department formulated a policy on the use of Departmental interpreters by outside bodies. The Department would refuse requests to supply interpreters to courts (except where the Crown was involved) and other public bodies, such as municipal councils, throughout Australia. Senior officers in the Central Office in Canberra, however, were authorised to make exceptions in the case of requests by local bodies in the region, such as courts in the ACT and Queanbeyan, the

Commonwealth Police, and Kenmore Psychiatric Hospital at Goulburn. The Department argued that the supply of interpreters to other bodies was outside the responsibility of a Commonwealth department, and organisations requiring interpreters should engage them through the Commonwealth Employment Service.[4]

Interpreting and the Provision of Information in Translation by Other Agencies

Other Commonwealth and State departments were relatively slow in recognising the importance of providing the interpreters and information in translation needed to facilitate migrant compliance with Australian laws and regulations. In 1963 the Minister for Customs and Excise informed the Senate that, while his department employed its own multilingual staff as interpreters and engaged outside interpreters when necessary, it had only recently begun to consider having a number of its publications and forms translated into various languages.[5]

One of the most urgent areas of need for information in translation and interpreters was that relating to compliance with traffic regulations. By 1951 the Road Safety Council was considering publishing a booklet in several languages incorporating important aspects of the *Traffic Act* to issue to applicants for drivers' licences. The Department of Immigration also included information on traffic laws in its 1951 English-language booklet 'Australia says welcome'. Although most States by 1973 allowed migrants to explain the road rules in their own language by means of an interpreter when being tested for a drivers' licence, Victoria, Western Australia and the Northern Territory did not. A Melbourne study conducted that year found that six out of every ten migrants who sat the test failed. Many, therefore, drove unlicensed, and there was a flourishing trade in forged licences for which extortionate sums were charged. This situation also encouraged police corruption.[6]

Pressure for Interpreting Services for Migrants

Although the Department of Immigration was responsible for coordinating English language teaching throughout Australia, it did not seek a similarly proactive role in the provision of interpreting and translating services. The ethnic press, however, was not silent on the need for adequate interpreters in the Australian community. In September 1953 the journal *Magyar Ujsag* published an article by a former leading Hungarian jurist, S. Edvi-Illes LLD. While he praised the impartiality of the Australian judiciary, Edvi-Illes argued that the inadequacies of official interpreters supplied by the Department of Immigration impeded the just application of the law in cases involving migrants, because they were often unfamiliar with legal terminology and with the subtleties of the English language. He suggested that the Crown Law Department conduct examinations for interpreters, or that migrants should be allowed to bring their own interpreters into court. While the Department had no scale of fees for interpreters, by the end of 1953 it had become normal practice to pay them at rates applied by the Supreme Court in each State.[7]

Pressure to establish an interpreting service for the community funded by the Department of Immigration also came from within its own Social Welfare Section. In April 1963 the senior social worker in the ACT, Stephanie Lindsay Thompson, cleverly turned one of the Department's own publications against it. A booklet entitled 'Organisation and functions of the Department of Immigration', published in February that year, rather rashly claimed that:

> Translations are undertaken by the Department in all cases where a direct migrant benefit exists—in all matters affecting immigration or integration . . . The centralised service adopted to arrange translations enables each State branch office to provide translations free of charge to migrants, government departments and such organisations as the Good Neighbour Movement and the Australian Red Cross Society.

Lindsay Thompson expressed her surprise that, given the above statement, the Department did not make any provision for an interpreter service. She noted that the highly valued interpreting services provided by Departmental officers in the ACT had recently been curtailed and social welfare services had subsequently suffered. 'Interpreters are indispensible to a migrant welfare service', she asserted. In the ACT, she pointed out, the Department of the Interior had no interpreters and relied on those of the Department of Immigration. Volunteers from the Good Neighbour Council could meet the needs of only 25 of the 40 nationalities in the region, very few were well qualified, they were mostly unavailable during working hours, and were often either unable or unwilling to interpret correctly. She argued for the establishment of both an interpreting and a translating service to assist her Section in the assimilation of aliens into the local community. This lively communication was taken seriously in Central Office, and other Sections were consulted. The officer who did most of the interpreting for the ACT region was asked to detail recent requests for his services. The senior social worker in the Sydney office, when questioned, informed Central Office that during her visits to Wollongong she used Commonwealth Bank interpreters and conducted interviews in their offices. Outside interviews were carried out using friends or family as interpreters.[8]

Although there was no interpreting service in Central Office, by 1964 the Australian community increasingly looked to the Department of Immigration in Canberra to meet its interpreting needs. In February that year, for example, the Australian Corriedale Association asked the Department for assistance in finding simultaneous English/Spanish interpreters with knowledge of sheep terminology for its forthcoming world conference. This matter involved various officers of the Department until June that year.[9]

THE DEPARTMENT OF IMMIGRATION'S TRANSLATION FUNCTIONS

From 1953 to 1957 the Department of Immigration farmed out its domestic foreign-language correspondence to its migrant accommodation centres, where translators were usually available. This led to long delays and complaints about the quality of translations. Central Office took over this translating function in June 1957, and by December 1958 it had assumed the translating functions which had been performed for Commonwealth government departments and the Red Cross by the Commonwealth Investigation Service since 1947. Although policy defining the Department's translating role was adopted in November 1959, responsibility for its foreign-language translating functions was transferred to the Citizenship Branch only in 1963. In 1964 the Department approached the Public Service Board for assistance in establishing a Departmental translating and interpreting service. It sought the establishment of full-time interpreting and translating positions to do the work previously done by Departmental officers as 'extra duty'.

Regional perceptions of need

In 1968, through the Integration and Education Section, the Department instructed the State Directors of Migration to review interpreting and translating services in their regions. NSW reported that there was no official establishment of interpreters in the Department of Labour and National Service's hostels, but as most staff were Europeans they were usually called on to fulfil that function. In the absence of an appropriate interpreter the hostels relied on the Commonwealth Bank which, by 1968, provided migrant information and interpreting services in the cities of Sydney, Wollongong, Newcastle and Fairfield, had bilingual staff in areas of high migrant concentration, and offered a free translating service at any of its branches in NSW. The ANZ Bank in Sydney also had a small migrant service, and provided interpreting and translating in most major European languages and Arabic. The Sydney CMO informed the Department in May 1968 that he proposed to seek approval from the Public Service Inspector to establish an interpreting and translating service in his office, as he opposed the use of his staff for this purpose and reliance on the banks or other outsiders to perform 'our duties'.[10]

The Department's attention was drawn to the problem of the lack of interpreting and translating for small language groups by the Finnish Ambassador in 1969, in the context of a proposed migration agreement between Australia and Finland. The Ambassador's concerns prompted the Department to ask all State and Territory branches what they believed their interpreting needs to be. Although the Secretary himself believed that the Department should have in each of its offices in the State capitals at least one person capable of translating the language of each of the countries from which migrants came in any substantial numbers, the replies to the Australia-wide inquiry revealed that in most regions (except in NSW and the Northern Territory) there was little appreciation of migrants' needs for interpreting and translating services. Tasmania, Western Australia and South Australia did not believe they needed a full-time interpreter, and Queensland supported its argument that it did not need a translator by statistics showing the small numbers of translations it had been asked to provide. It admitted, however, that most migrants were aware that the office did not provide translations, and used the migrant advisory services of the banks. The Commonwealth Director of Migration in

Brisbane saw only periodic need for an interpreter when large numbers of migrants arrived, and believed that this need 'could be best covered by approval to employ an interpreter for a limited period to assist in the initial settlement of the group and in associated problems which may arise'.

George Pridannikoff, an Australian-born Russian-speaker who joined the Brisbane office of the Department of Immigration in 1965, confirmed that at this time his office believed that interpreting was not a skilled profession and that anyone could do it, in four or five languages if necessary. It was not perceived as a Departmental priority; it was widely believed that it could be adequately performed for migrants by their relatives or friends and that the free migrant services sections of the Commonwealth and ANZ banks, with which the Department worked closely, was adequate. Interpreting in the 1960s he observed was conducted on an ad hoc basis: the police, for example, generally sought an interpreter in the local pub. Other agencies relied on informal networks they had created. Victoria focused entirely on the question of remuneration for its staff engaged in extra interpreting and translating duties. No State saw a need for interpreters fluent in Finnish.[11]

Community pressure for interpreters

This general complacency evident within most State branches of the Department of Immigration, about the adequacy of existing interpreting and translating services to meet the needs of the migrant community, was soon eroded by community groups concerned about the failure of government departments to deliver their services to migrants, particularly in the areas of health and education. This push initially came not from ethnic but from mainstream community organisations, and mostly from the southern States of Australia.

The senior social worker in Sydney warned the Department in May 1968 of concerns about inadequate interpreting and translating facilities expressed by several committees of which she was a member. These were the Good Neighbour Council, the Welfare Planning Committee, the Mental Health of Migrants Committee (a standing committee of the Association for Mental Health) and the Migrant Care Committee, chaired by Dr Yeomans of the NSW Health Department. Questionnaires sent out to doctors in hospitals and private practices by the Good Neighbour Council, and a survey of interpreting needs in 28 public hospitals in Sydney conducted by the Mental Health of Migrants Committee, revealed that complacency was widespread. The NSW Department of Health replied that, while it recognised the difficulties, it considered neither the appointment of interpreters nor the training of staff to be justified. Although that Department was preparing a list of NSW psychiatrists with one or more foreign languages, zoning arrangements prevented them from being consulted by patients outside their catchment area.[12]

Powerful health administrators had begun mobilising their forces. In December 1967 Mr Justice Rae Else-Mitchell, president of the Association for Mental Health, had written to the NSW Minister for Health F.H. Jago conveying that organisation's resolution on the need for the appointment of professional interpreters in public hospitals. The Minister informed him that most used their own bilingual administrative or domestic staff as interpreters, or engaged voluntary or commercial interpreters. Since 1958, public hospitals had relied on a booklet, 'Foreign Language Phrases', produced by the Victorian Red Cross. 'Whilst I agree that there may be some difficulties between migrants and the staff of hospitals', the Minister conceded, 'I do not consider that the appointment of professional interpreters is justified at this stage'. He included an undated list of languages spoken by the 'medical staff' in NSW mental hospitals (which did not indicate in what capacity the staff was employed).[13]

Professor of Obstetrics and Gynaecology at Monash University Dr Carl Wood joined the fray in February 1968 with a letter to the Minister for Immigration, B.M. Snedden. The Queen Victoria Memorial Hospital in Melbourne delivered several thousand Greek and Italian patients of babies each year and, he pointed out, the majority of mothers could not speak English. The hospital needed interpreters so that these patients could be adequately cared for during labour. 'Many of these patients are extremely frightened or frankly terrified during childbirth and the small hospital resources for providing paid interpreters is always over-strained', he argued. He suggested that the government give recognition and financial support to migrant groups so that they could assist in solving that problem. The Italian Assistance Committee already provided some interpreters to hospitals, but its service was limited by lack of support.[14]

In March 1969 Senator J.A. Mulvihill (ALP NSW) drew the attention of Parliament to the need for interpreters in baby health centres near migrant hostels to enable migrant mothers to care properly for the health of their children. He tabled a letter from the NSW Minister for Health F.H. Jago (which he later described as 'evasive') that listed hostels in his State with baby health centres and described the various limited arrangements made to provide interpreting for migrant mothers. Mulvihill, who had visited two of the hostels, urged the appointment of qualified interpreters. He also highlighted the lack of value placed on the skills of interpreters in the bureaucracy, quoting a recent advertisement for an interpreter at Sydney Airport which offered $56 a week for an interpreter to work on call with customs, health and immigration officers. The applicant was required to be fluent in Italian, Spanish, French, German and Dutch and have a knowledge of Russian, Polish, Yugoslav and Asian languages. 'A person would have to be a pretty hot shot to be reasonably conversant with all the languages mentioned', the Senator remarked laconically. 'There is a lack of communication and not enough interpreters', he stated, expressing his mystification at the continued priority placed on the teaching of French when there were so few French migrants in Australia. He urged the employment of more multilingual post-war migrants as interpreters instead of resorting to ad hoc use of untrained migrants working in other capacities.[15]

The concern of the peak welfare body, the Australian Council of Social Services (ACOSS), about migrant welfare was made manifest by its formation of a Joint Committee on Migrant Welfare in conjunction with the Australian Council for Overseas Aid (ACFOA) on 7 May 1968. This Committee comprised representatives of fifteen mainstream welfare organisations (most of which were also affiliated with the Good Neighbour Movement) but no ethnic groups. Its submission on interpreting needs for the Department of Immigration's survey recommended the establishment of a national school for interpreters offering a two- to three-year course for professionals, a one-year course in Colleges of Advanced Education to solve the more immediate and pressing needs, and the initiation of a comprehensive program of community education to emphasise the need for skilled interpreters.[16]

In May 1970 ACOSS sponsored a conference on psychiatric illness in migrants attended by psychiatrists, physicians and social workers representing a wide range of government, university and voluntary agencies. Its findings also indicated an acute lack of suitably skilled interpreters in mental hospitals. It declared the use of hospital attendants and cleaners by psychiatrists when interviewing and treating migrants 'quite unsuitable', and not infrequently the cause of wrong diagnoses. Chairman of the ACOSS/ACFOA Joint Committee on the Welfare of Migrants Walter Lippmann commented at its 34th council meeting in August 1970 that government departments had 'only recently become more aware of' the specific interpreting problems of migrants in relation to health, preschool and school education. The committee expressed its concern at the lack of interpreting services, and the Department of Immigration accepted its invitation to send a representative to committee meetings as an observer.[17]

The issue of adequate interpreting was also discussed at the 1970 Citizenship Convention, where H. Souter of the Immigration Planning Council suggested that a register of people with linguistic skills be made available to hospitals, doctors and lawyers and at police stations, in the same way as lists of justices of the peace were available. Walter Lippmann, also a member of this Council, stressed the need for skilled interpreters to assist migrants in medical and social counselling, and particularly at police stations and in lower courts.[18]

Department of Immigration responses to community pressure

This pressure began to have results. The issue of interpreters in hospitals was raised at the conference of Commonwealth and State Ministers for Immigration on 12 February 1969. In 1970 the Department of Immigration conducted its own survey of migrant patients in government psychiatric centres in Sydney, and found that inability to communicate was a major factor leading to psychiatric breakdown and impeding subsequent recovery. One-third of all non-British patients spoke little or no English and only half of the Greek, Italian and Yugoslav patients spoke English. The report's recommendation that a survey be undertaken of interpreting needs not only in psychiatric hospitals but in the community generally was communicated by the Department to the meeting of the Commonwealth/State Immigration Ministers in October 1970.[19]

On 25 February and 30 October 1970 the Department of Immigration put proposals before the Public Service Board for the creation of three positions in both its Sydney and Melbourne offices for interpreters. They would form the nucleus of an interpreter service for both routine Departmental matters and for emergencies, such as in hospitals, psychiatric centres and police courts. It also requested allowances for its staff employed as casual interpreters. It was considering extending this service to other States 'where the need is seen to exist'. On 23 November 1970 two Clerk Class 1 positions were approved for interpreters in Melbourne, but the question of allowances for existing staff engaged in interpreting was still unresolved. The Public Service Board did not think such payments appropriate. Although the Queen Victoria Hospital in Melbourne now employed interpreters, there were still no Commonwealth or State policies on the provision of free interpreting services for migrants needing to gain access to medical or legal facilities. Nor did employers of large numbers of migrants see the need to provide interpreters for their staff. There was an obvious need to delineate State–Commonwealth responsibilities to fund adequate interpreting facilities.[20]

In March 1971 the Secretary raised with the Minister the need for a system in Australia whereby professional interpreters could gain accreditation. He urged the Commonwealth to take the lead by creating the classification of interpreter within the Commonwealth Public Service. That month the Minister was able to report to Parliament that his Department had an establishment of ten translators in Central Office (as well as other clerks with linguistic skills who could be used when needed) to meet its own demands, and those of other Commonwealth departments and of certain community agencies such as the Red Cross. There was also one interpreter in Canberra to meet the requirements of the ACT. State offices had 106 clerks with linguistic skills who could be called on when required as translators and interpreters. He referred to the current applications before the Public Service Board to create positions for interpreters in NSW and Victoria, and announced his intention to provide an interpreter unit to meet Departmental needs and emergency situations arising in the community. He added that he expected the community to develop its own interpreter services and that the proposed Departmental survey was expected to assist in identifying areas of greatest need.[21]

Although the need for adequate and skilled interpreting services was firmly on the agenda by 1971, the government had introduced no practical initiative to demonstrate that it was doing anything constructive. Despite this, it continued to present the situation in a favourable light. When asked by Senator Willesee (ALP WA) in October 1972 whether the Minister for Immigration would give urgent consideration to providing interpreters in major public hospitals, Senator Greenwood, representing the Minister for Immigration, continued to stress that it was not solely a Commonwealth responsibility, commenting that 'it is significant to note the extent to which commerce and industry is already active in this regard'. He also revealed that the Department was currently considering the findings of its own Australia-wide survey of interpreting and translating needs in the community, and was seeking means to remedy the situation.[22]

Department of Immigration survey of interpreting and translating needs 1971–72

While the research conducted by non-government bodies in 1970 had revealed the desperate need for adequate interpreting services in certain areas, there was no information on the situation Australia-wide. From 1971 to 1972, therefore, the Department of Immigration's Survey Section sent 2515 questionnaires to 34 different types of organisations in all States in areas with a high migrant population. The insight its 'Report on the survey of interpreting and translating needs in the community' provided into the inadequacy of current services for migrants was so potentially embarrassing to the government that in 1972 its distribution was restricted to academics with a special interest in the field, and to State governments and Commonwealth departments providing personal services to the community. It showed that, due to inadequate language services, many migrants had been unable to access many essential services to which they were entitled, or to comply with laws and regulations to which they were subject in everyday life. Significant numbers of organisations working in the areas of employment, accommodation, welfare, health education, law, finance and insurance, local government and transport reported occasions on which non-English speakers could not be assisted because no interpreter was available. Despite the focus of many of the recent complaints on migrants' lack of access to medical services, the greatest problems were found to lie in access to educational guidance services. The second most difficult area to access was that providing welfare services. While most organisations had problems arranging for interpreters, those providing employment and accommodation services were handicapped most severely. Each major group surveyed believed that accuracy and precision of interpreting was vital, but this was seen to be most important in the legal and law enforcement areas.

If the survey highlighted the inadequacy of the Department's regional directors' appreciation of the need for interpreters in their States, it disclosed an even greater lack of awareness of interpreting needs in the general community. Not one of the organisations contacted had either full-time interpreters or staff that could be drawn on as interpreters. All relied on migrants to supply their own interpreters, who were sometimes children, usually untrained, and often inadequate. Reliance on such interpreters was often embarrassing to clients and sometimes compromised confidentiality. Migrants had to have their documents translated through banks, consulates or other sources.[23]

The death of a baby and the birth of an emergency telephone service

In 1972, in response to a request from Ted Charles for ideas for a Cabinet submission, Director of the Integration and Education Section P.M. Rice put forward a suggestion that had originally been made by Brisbane social worker Nancy Anderson in a paper she presented to a meeting of departmental social workers in 1967, and which Rice had long thought about. He proposed that the Department establish a telephone interpreter service for migrants on the lines of the existing Lifeline telephone counselling service for people in crisis. He envisaged that, unlike Lifeline, it should be available for a wide range of interpreting needs, not just life-threatening personal emergencies, and it should not have to rely on a large body of trained people. It would be staffed by a small number of people who could recognise the caller's language and transfer him or her to an appropriate interpreter. He suggested that the service be piloted in Sydney and Melbourne, and worked out the number of new staff and the budget that would be needed to support such a service. The Department, initially lukewarm, considered his estimates too high and reduced them.

Rice's argument for such a service was tragically reinforced by an incident in Melbourne. A Turkish migrant who could not speak English and whose wife was in labour hailed a taxi, and eventually managed to communicate to the taxi driver their need to find a hospital. After being turned away from several hospitals that did not comprehend their plight, the woman gave birth to the child in the taxi and it died. This was reported in several

Melbourne newspapers. Rice used this incident to argue at a meeting of divisional heads that in the absence of a telephone interpreting service such incidents were bound to occur in the future, and would inevitably attract criticism of the Minister. He realised that if he had argued 'we need to look after these people, they need our help', he would get no support. The need to protect the Minister from 'getting egg on his face' would be totally convincing. His meeting lasted three minutes; he had won the support of the 'big brass' for his proposal.[24]

In late April 1973 the case came before the Coroner's Court in Melbourne, it was widely reported in the press, and Alan Matherson of the Ecumenical Migration Centre used it to argue that 'the supply and availability of competent interpreters is not geared to the ethnic groups with the greatest needs'. When the inevitable question was asked in Parliament by Senator Mulvihill on 27 April, Senator Greenwood, representing the Minister for Immigration, referred to, without specifically identifying, 'a tragic incident' which 'had occurred in Melbourne'. He argued that in addition to the interpreters provided by State governments, some 400 qualified interpreters were provided by the Commonwealth—through the State branches of the Department of Immigration, the Department of Labour and National Service's employment officers in areas of high migrant density, and through Commonwealth hostels. He was also able to refer to the Department of Immigration's plans 'to introduce an on-call telephone interpreter service to provide, in the languages causing the greatest problems, a 24-hour service for urgent community needs'. Its establishment was now guaranteed by ministerial support. The proposal was put to Cabinet, which approved the funding, and the Public Service Board then approved the new positions. It was mentioned in the immigration budget speech that year.[25]

For reasons of departmental politics Rice insisted that the new service should be named the 'Emergency Telephone Interpreter Service', although he had intended from the outset that the service be available for more general inquiries. Once the service had demonstrated its value the adjective 'emergency' was dropped. This was an important illustration of the 'keepers' in the Department using the growing community pressure for improved settlement services to reinforce their arguments with the more powerful 'getters'.[26]

Interpreting and Translating under Labor 1973–75

The Emergency Telephone Interpreter Service begins

Although the Department of Immigration's senior policy-makers remained largely the same under the Labor administration, they became more proactive in the area of migrant welfare, as the political ideology was more favourable to the 'keepers'. Whereas the conservative Liberal–Country Party coalition that had governed the country for the previous 22 years had defended the perceived 'social homogeneity' of Australian society, Labor stressed the need to help migrants to join 'the family of the nation' by integrating Departmental settlement activities with those of the community.

The change of government freed up the Department of Immigration and facilitated reform. It was no longer obliged to defend the previous government's increasingly dismal performance in the provision of language services, and could focus on providing solutions. The new Minister for Immigration was A.J. Grassby. Although of predominantly Anglo-Celtic origins he spoke Italian, and had strong links with the Italian community in his rural electorate of Riverina, where he had earlier worked with non-English speaking farmers as an agricultural extension officer. He was, therefore, sensitive to the need for interpreters. On 19 February 1973 he announced the introduction in Sydney and Melbourne of the Emergency Telephone Interpreter Service (ETIS). As has been described above, this service had been planned under the previous administration. It was first mentioned in Departmental files in February 1972, and its introduction was foreshadowed in the Senate in April, August and October 1972, but it was never commenced, due to administrative delays in gaining approval for staff and funding. The Labor government, therefore, gained the credit for its introduction. A technical problem also delayed its introduction—it was illegal to divert calls from one telephone handset by putting it together with another (this had been done by Departmental social workers and others for many years when using the telephone to link migrants with interpreters). A box-like device (known as a one-to-one divertical) had, however, recently been invented which would transfer a caller from the first number dialled to another, for the cost of one call. The Post-Master General's department was keen to try it, but needed a good argument to have the legislation changed. It was fortunate that the interests of two Commonwealth departments coincided on this matter.[27]

The ETIS was an entirely Australian innovation. Rice could find nothing like it anywhere else in the world. It provided a widely advertised interpreter service, initially in sixteen languages 24 hours a day, seven days a week. Offices in capital cities were at first staffed by four interpreters, who could call on the services of private interpreters in the suburbs when required. These contract workers (of whom there were 120 by 1976), answered most inquiries by telephone but, when required, travelled to wherever a migrant was in difficulty. They were given one week's training in Canberra, two weeks' local training in their State office, and two hours a week in-service training for three months. Cases requiring the advice of social workers were handled by Departmental social workers and welfare officers. This required the appointment of additional staff. The service was extended to Perth in March 1974, to Brisbane in November 1975, and to Adelaide in December 1975, by which time it had become the responsibility of the Department of Social Security.[28]

This service revealed the enormous community need for interpreters. By 31 July 1973 between them, the three services had received 130 000 calls. By September 1975 its function had been expanded to include an information referral service in some 50 languages or dialects. This drew on data collected by ETIS and migrant welfare workers to provide newly arrived migrants and refugees with information on local services. It did not attempt to meet all the interpreting needs of the community; for example, it did not deal with routine hospital admissions. It did, however, provide contract interpreters for migrants needing to communicate with a hospital or a doctor.

Professional status for interpreters and translators

The Department of Immigration's survey of interpreting and translating needs had been so thorough, and its findings so appalling, that in October 1972 the Immigration Advisory Council (IAC) appointed a subcommittee to study it, to consider matters arising from it and to make recommendations to the Council on these. The subcommittee, which first met on 26 January 1973, agreed that the Department should not be responsible for meeting all migrant communication needs, and that the onus for providing language services lay with the community at large, including State and local governments and statutory authorities, as well as commerce and industry generally. It emphasised that interpreter services should be seen as part of normal community services, with the cost being borne by the user except in cases of hardship.

At its second meeting on 19 March 1973, the IAC discussed various option papers. It agreed that government and non-government agencies and major employers should be encouraged to establish skilled interpreter services appropriate to their needs and financed from their own resources. It also advised that educationalists be consulted to develop a two-tiered training structure—short courses for generalist interpreters and twelve-month courses for persons already competent in languages. It recommended the establishment of a national committee or board to set standards, approve qualifications, to act as a registration authority and to recommend salary levels appropriate to the status accorded to graduates. The Department of Immigration was given the task of investigating details of interpreting courses overseas, and the IAC reviewed classifications of interpreters employed in the Commonwealth Public Service. Their rates of pay were to set the standard for other employers of interpreters. The IAC aimed at initiating a comprehensive program to educate the community to recognise situations in which interpreters should be used, to provide interpreter services, and to appreciate the need for interpreters to be professionally qualified. Although it agreed with the Department that responsibility for providing adequate interpreting facilities lay with the community, it observed at its third meeting in July 1973 that the government was in the best position to provide a lead, and urged the Department to coordinate action to provide interpreters throughout the community.[29]

On the recommendation of the IAC, the Minister for Immigration in May 1973 discussed with State Ministers for Immigration the provision of interpreters in State government administration, health and legal institutions. The Commonwealth argued that the provision of adequate interpreting should be seen as a normal part of communicating with the community, and that State and local governments must each play their parts. It also sought to stimulate community interest in the importance of interpreters.[30]

In August 1973 ACOSS chaired a meeting in Canberra of representatives of various government bodies and educational institutions on the need for a national interpreters' school. It argued that the findings of its own 1968–70 inquiry into interpreter needs and those of the Department of Immigration demonstrated the grave shortage of skilled interpreters, not only in welfare agencies but in a wide range of essential services. This meeting established a working party to make a detailed examination of the need for a national school for interpreters. ACOSS was seen as the most appropriate body to lead such an inquiry, because of its wide community base and because it was seen by the government departments involved as being 'more neutral'. ACOSS released its own 'Report on interpreter facilities' in September 1973. In its annual report for 1972–73 it stressed the 'severe shortage of interpreters', and recommended the establishment of interpreter schools at State and national level. As the over 120 bilingual officers employed in the Central and State offices of the Department of Immigration were still heavily involved in translating material for a wide range of Commonwealth departments and approved outside agencies, the Department welcomed this report as a community response to a pressing migrant need for professionally trained interpreters, rather than as one that looked to the Department to solve the problem.[31]

On 30 October 1973, on the recommendation of the IAC, the government publicly released the Department of Immigration's report on interpreting and translating needs, which had been so potentially damaging to its predecessor that it had been suppressed. The Council advised that the report should be more widely available to community organisations and other agencies involved in interpreting activities. In releasing the report, Grassby described the lack of interpreting in Australia as a 'national disgrace' and 'among the worst in the world'. He told Parliament in September 1973 that 'the position in regard to interpreter services generally in Australia is deplorable'. Migrants had not been able to receive treatment in hospitals, and one man had gone to gaol because there were no interpreters. Interpreters had been 'dragged in off the street to give assistance in the courts on most complex matters', a situation that was prejudicing the administration of justice. The Commonwealth and the States must cooperate, particularly in the fields of health and justice. 'I am not satisfied at all that justice is being done at the present time or that it has been done in the past', he concluded.[32]

On the recommendation of the November 1973 Commonwealth–State conference of Ministers for Immigration, Grassby approached Dr D.M. Myers, Chairman of the Committee on Overseas Professional Qualifications (COPQ). He suggested that, although it was not within COPQ's terms of reference, that body was admirably suited to establish professional standards for interpreters and translators and to help them obtain recognition as a professional group. Grassby indicated that efforts by ACOSS and some universities and colleges to solve the interpreting problem had been 'uncoordinated'. He outlined his department's aims of establishing carefully defined standards for interpreters, a regulatory body to maintain a professional level of services, an association of professional interpreters, and sufficiently attractive terms and conditions of employment for interpreters. COPQ agreed to become involved in a working party with other interested groups to establish an accreditation structure for interpreters. In November 1973 Grassby announced in Parliament that discussions were taking place to establish proper professional standards for interpreters and translators, and to set up a body that would police those standards and determine appropriate levels of pay and conditions for them. He hoped that a national school for interpreters would be established in Canberra.[33]

While Grassby's national school never eventuated, in 1975 three tertiary institutions, the Royal Melbourne Institute of Technology, the Canberra College of Advanced Education and the University of New South Wales, introduced courses for interpreters, financed initially by the Department of Labor and Immigration. The Department asked the State Ministers for Immigration and the Australian Minister for Health to encourage suitable personnel to apply for admission to these courses. A national Accreditation Authority for Translators and Interpreters was eventually established by the Coalition government in 1976-77.[34]

Devolution of responsibility from the Department of Immigration 1973-75

In August 1973 the Department of Immigration saw indications of the success of its efforts to get other Commonwealth bodies to accept responsibility for language services. The Department of Social Services decided to develop its own interpreter service in Sydney and Melbourne, with help from the ETIS in those States. In October 1973 Grassby was even more heartened by the insistence by Mr Justice Moore, President of the Australian Conciliation and Arbitration Commission, to make his decision in a recent compensation case available in the languages of the migrant workers involved in the dispute. He described this decision as the 'greatest breakthrough' in the quest to have migrants informed of their rights and privileges as Australian workers. A recent study had, he added, revealed that industrial accidents were highest among recently arrived migrants, and that safety advice was not displayed in factories in languages comprehensible to the migrants employed there. Once injured, migrants were unaware of their compensation rights, because this information was also unavailable in translation. The Minister undertook to ensure that the example set by Mr Justice Moore was followed in all State and Commonwealth arbitration tribunals, and that non-English speaking migrants were made aware of their rights and responsibilities under industrial awards.[35]

Extension of responsibility for the provision of language services to other agencies was, however, a slow and uneven process, and the position in 1974 was still unsatisfactory. The Telephone Interpreter Service was not established in Adelaide until December 1975 and in its absence, as the Administrator of the Royal Adelaide Hospital informed the South Australian regional director of the Department of Labor and Immigration in August 1974, the interpreting needs of many of the hospital's patients were unmet; nurses, domestics and orderlies were being used as interpreters, and there was a lack of appreciation among all staff of the need for interpreters. He perceived that Aborigines as well as migrants shared this need. There was no translating service within the hospital and no funds to pay for outside assistance. Crown Street Women's Hospital in Sydney had unsuccessfully requested that State authorities provide trained interpreters and by November 1974 was still using untrained cleaners, nurses and clerical staff to interpret for its migrant patients. Few ethnic organisations could meet the interpreting and translating needs of their own communities, and they looked to the State to provide such services. TIS was often overloaded as, despite Department of Immigration advocacy for a higher classification for interpreters and translators, inadequate remuneration made it difficult to get experienced staff for such positions.[36]

The danger to public health created by failure to provide information in translation to migrants on health regulations was clearly perceived by at least one Melbourne doctor. A general practitioner in the inner-Melbourne suburb of Coburg, Dr

Grimblat, reported that none of the newly arrived Turkish parents in his area had complied with the requirement that they have their children immunised against polio, diphtheria or whooping cough. He wrote to *The Medical Journal of Australia* expressing his fears that such non-compliance might lead to an epidemic of these diseases. The Victorian Minister for Health denied that there was a problem, arguing that 87 per cent of children in migrant hostels had been immunised and that leaflets in ten languages, including Turkish, were being distributed at infant welfare centres. Dr Grimblat pointed out that Turks neither lived in hostels nor took their children to health centres. The Department of Immigration reacted by translating its pamphlet 'We're safe, we've been immunised' into Greek, Serbo-Croat, Italian, German, Arabic and Turkish, but the problem of distribution to its target readership remained.[37]

A number of major inquiries increased the pressure to devolve responsibility for interpreting and translating from the Department of Immigration. The IAC's Community Relations Committee's inquiry into discrimination against migrants resulted in the provision of funds to establish full-time courses for interpreters and translators at the Royal Melbourne Institute of Technology and the Canberra College of Advanced Education and part-time courses at the University of New South Wales throughout 1975, pending the creation of permanent courses.[38]

The first main report of the Australian government Commission of Inquiry into Poverty, released in April 1975, linked the economic disadvantage of migrants to poor English. It criticised the provision of language classes, pointing out that only 40 per cent of non-English speaking family heads attended post-arrival English classes, and urged the provision of interpreters and information in translation. Although the Department of Social Security (DSS) by now produced some of its basic information in fifteen languages, it pointed out, no State health or welfare department provided information in translation. While acknowledging that the responsibility for providing information in translation lay with all government departments, it criticised the Department of Labor and Immigration for not taking more initiative to encourage this. Another 1975 report by the Commission, entitled 'Migrants and the legal system', attributed much of the disillusionment by migrants with life in Australia to the community's failure to recognise and respond to their language needs. The 1971 Census had revealed that a large proportion of the migrant population was barely literate. It severely criticised the inadequacy of community interpreting after a quarter-century of immigration.[39]

The focus of criticism on this issue was removed from the Department of Immigration to the DSS, to which the settlement functions of the former department were transferred from 12 June 1974. This sudden devolution prompted protests from some ethnic organisations, and not without cause. The transfer of the Migrant Services Section to the DSS in February 1975 found it ill-prepared for such responsibility. The Section suffered from lack of clerical and administrative support and had no permanent full-time interpreting and translating staff. The Telephone Interpreter Service, which had drawn heavily on the linguistic skills of the Department of Immigration's Translating Unit (which remained with the Department of Labor and Immigration), was transferred to the DSS. The DSS immediately surveyed its staff in regional and district offices, as well as State headquarters, to discover what linguistic skills it could draw on. Some State directors insisted that Departmental staff used as interpreters should be adequately trained and remunerated.[40]

George Pridannikoff, a Department of Immigration officer in Brisbane who transferred to the DSS in order to supervise the establishment of TIS in that State, welcomed the change. He found certain advantages in being a new appendage to a large and better resourced department which knew nothing about the service, and which gave its newly acquired staff a liberty they might not have had in their old department. He observed that TIS flourished in his State under these new administrative arrangements. He believed that there was no particular community pressure in Queensland for the service, but that it was introduced into that State as a consequence of the success of its trial introduction in Melbourne and Sydney.[41]

By 1975 other government and non-government bodies were increasingly acknowledging the need to inform migrants of their social rights and to provide this information in translation. By 1975, the NSW Department of Education provided interpreters for migrants enrolling their children, and the NSW Police had its own interpreters supported by the NSW Court Interpreting Service. The Australian Government Information Service produced 'Newcomer and the law' in eight major migrant languages and distributed it widely through the DSS, the Department of Labour and Industry, Good Neighbour Councils, migrant hostels, ethnic clubs, bank migrant information services, legal aid offices, State branches of the Federal Attorney General's department and

State police headquarters. The Victorian Council for Civil Liberties also produced a pamphlet entitled 'Your rights', which was translated into six major migrant languages.[42]

Conclusion

The reconceptualisation of the relationship between the State and its clients, formulated in 1985 as Access and Equity Policy, clearly had its roots in the struggles of the Department of Immigration from the 1960s to comprehend and respond to the obstacles confronted by non-English speaking migrants seeking to access services to which they were entitled. This understanding was slowly communicated to other agencies by a department that had recognised that migrants' need for information about all their rights and responsibilities as members of the Australian community was far beyond its capacity to meet. Eventually, a policy was developed based on the premise that government agencies were responsible for making their services accessible to all in an equitable manner, benefiting all Australians.

Arthur Calwell, the chief architect of the post-war migration program and the first Minister for Immigration (July 1945–December 1949), at the first citizenship ceremony in the Great Hall, Melbourne University, 1949. Calwell saw the alien migrant not as a mere guest worker but as a potential citizen, who would share all 'the privileges and benefits which derive from Australian citizenship . . . a partner in our great Commonwealth'. He established two important bridges to Australian society for alien migrants—the Adult Migrant Education Scheme, and an Australia-wide network of professional social workers. (DIMA 49/12A/2)

Hazel Dobson, professional social worker and head of the Social Welfare Section from 1948 until the late 1950s, with Arthur Calwell at a reception marking the arrival of the 250 000th ICEM migrant in 1954. She recommended that the Department of Immigration establish a regional network of professional social workers to help aliens with settlement problems. (DIMA 54/4/11)

Tasman Heyes, the first Permanent Head of the Department of Immigration (May 1946–November 1961), was an experienced and astute bureaucrat. While he supervised the assimilationist period of his Department, he also successfully recommended the 'modification by degrees' of the 'white Australia policy', gaining Cabinet approval for the admission of highly qualified non-Europeans in 1956. (DIMA 58/28/1)

Harold Holt, on retirement as Minister for Immigration in 1956, being farewelled by Tasman Heyes and his successor, Athol Townley. Holt reported that during his period as Minister, the migration program achieved most of the demographic and economic goals set by the Labor government in 1945. (DIMA 56/25/4)

The Department of Immigration accommodation centre for assisted alien migrants at Bathurst in 1951 was one of the best-run and most pleasantly situated. The Department provided English-language classes, interpreting and translating facilities, settlement information, and social workers at its centres. (DIMA 51/22/31)

Department of Immigration social worker, M. ('Bunty') King, interviewing an Italian client, Ricardo Treven, at Bonegilla Reception and Training Centre in 1956. Social workers presented the welcoming face of their Department to alien migrants, sensitised other agencies to their needs, and were an invaluable source of policy advice. (DIMA 56/22/7)

As the accommodation provided for Commonwealth-assisted male workers was considered unsuitable for families, alien women and children were housed separately in former army camps. These women at Bathurst in 1951 have tried to make their quarters as homely as possible. (DIMA 51/22/28)

Alien supporting mothers in Holding Centres could neither fulfil their obligation to work for two years, nor move out of what was intended to be temporary accommodation. On the recommendation of Department social workers, pre-schools were established in migrant accommodation centres, allowing mothers to work. Playtime in one such centre in 1958. (DIMA 58/22/27)

A child minding centre in a Nissen hut at the Scheyville Holding Centre, NSW, in the 1950s. (Australian Archives 1969/441)

Minister for Immigration Alexander Downer (March 1958–December 1963) with his family at his mansion Arbury Park, South Australia, in 1960. Although two-thirds of the migrant intake by 1959 was non-British, that year Downer reduced his Department's establishment of social workers to fifteen Australia-wide. As the displaced persons program had ended, he argued, 'the principal object for which these social workers were originally appointed has evaporated'. (DIMA c60/25A/2)

Mentally ill migrants, many traumatised by years of suffering in concentration and refugee camps, were referred by Department of Immigration social workers to hospitals like this at Rydalmere, NSW. They exacerbated the existing inadequacies of such hospitals, which were found by a Federal Government survey in 1955 to have appalling standards. (National Library of Australia 20620)

Migrants were selected mainly to work in secondary industry. Aliens seeking work in rural areas, such as these Italian cane cutters working in Queensland in 1956, found largely seasonal employment and inadequate accommodation. The Department of Immigration could offer them little assistance. (DIMA 56/4/47)

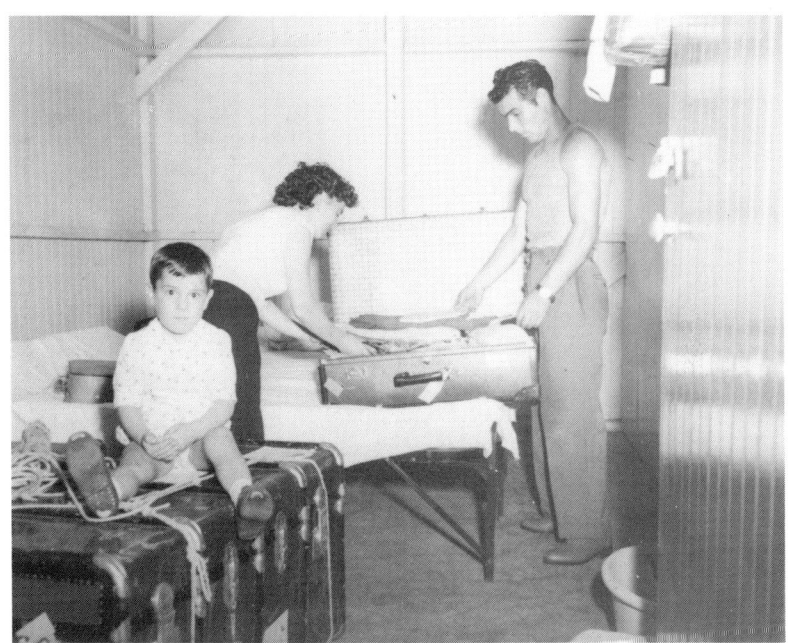

Top: An Italian cane cutter and his family unpack in their cramped quarters on a Queensland farm in 1956. (DIMA 56/4/46) *Above:* The Department of Immigration funded Adult Migrant Education Scheme, designed to give non-British migrants 'an elementary knowledge of the English tongue . . . and some knowledge of Australian civics', commenced in 1948. It offered classes, correspondence courses, radio programs and shipboard education. Migrants near Sydney learn English by gramophone in 1949. (DIMA 49/24/3)

German Special Project Workers labouring on the Transcontinental Railway and housed in isolated camps in the desert between South and Western Australia, were visited in 1953 and 1954 by a Department of Immigration social worker who travelled on the 'tea and sugar train'. This train was still bringing supplies and welfare to migrant workers in 1968, when these photos were taken. (DIMA 69/19/19 & 22)

Top: An English class at the Bathurst Reception Centre in 1951. (DIMA 51/22/34)   *Above:* Mothers at Woodside Hostel in South Australia learn English in 1952. (DIMA 52/24/1)

Top: Dr Eva Haarmann from Vienna teaches English to an Austrian class en route to Australia aboard the *Fairsea* in 1955. (DIMA 55/32/21)
Above: Although no government during the period 1945–75 required employers to provide English language instruction to their workers, some major employers of alien labour allowed Department of Immigration-funded classes in workers' time. Displaced persons employed by South Australian Railways learn English in 1951. (DIMA 51/24/1)

Top: Full-time intensive English classes for professionally trained migrants commenced in 1969. Migrants were paid a living allowance while attending the eight-week course. Migrants in Hobart at an intensive English course in 1971. (DIMA c71/24A/6) *Above:* From the late 1940s, translating and interpreting services were available to assisted migrants in Department of Immigration accommodation centres. In 1973, the Department of Immigration established an innovative 24-hour interpreting and translating service. (DIMA 74/50A/3)

By 1966, 38 000 non-Europeans and persons of mixed descent were living in Australia and 17 550 were citizens. The introduction in 1964 of special criteria for the assessment of mixed race applicants was a major milestone in the erosion of the 'white Australia policy'. Faye Joy Morris from Jamaica became a citizen in 1967. (Australian Archives A1200/19 L64547).

Hubert Opperman, Minister for Immigration (1963–1966), was the grandson of a German immigrant and a champion cyclist. He collaborated closely with Heydon in undermining the 'white Australia policy'. He is shown here in 1963 with his son Ian and his son's friend Jan Jansen, a Dutch migrant. (DIMA c 63/25A/4)

Above: Peter Heydon, Permanent Head of the Department of Immigration (1961–1971), regarded Australia's racially discriminatory migration policy as an embarrassment. An adroit and practical-minded bureaucrat, his ability 'to test the water and then to proceed as far as the Minister's toe was able to stand the heat', was demonstrated by his success in undermining the 'white Australia policy' in 1966. (DIMA 68/28A/1)

Left: Jewish welfare worker Frederick Frank with his family in Perth 1964. Jewish organisations sponsored over 11 000 post-war Jewish refugees and provided them with the support they needed to settle in Australia. (DIMA 64/13/1)

Above: By the late 1960s, increased prosperity in Europe made migration to Australia less attractive, and numbers of former migrants returned home. The government sought migrants in other regions, who introduced greater cultural diversity to Australia. A migration agreement with Turkey in 1967 brought significant numbers of Moslems to Australia for the first time. Turkish migrants at prayer in Broadmeadows hostel in 1969. (DIMA 69/22/82) *Left:* Throughout most of the thirty years from 1949, migrants granted citizenship were given a naturalisation certificate bearing an image of the Queen, which described them as both Australian citizens and British subjects. This is a naturalisation certificate as issued in 1961. (DIMA 61/12/25)

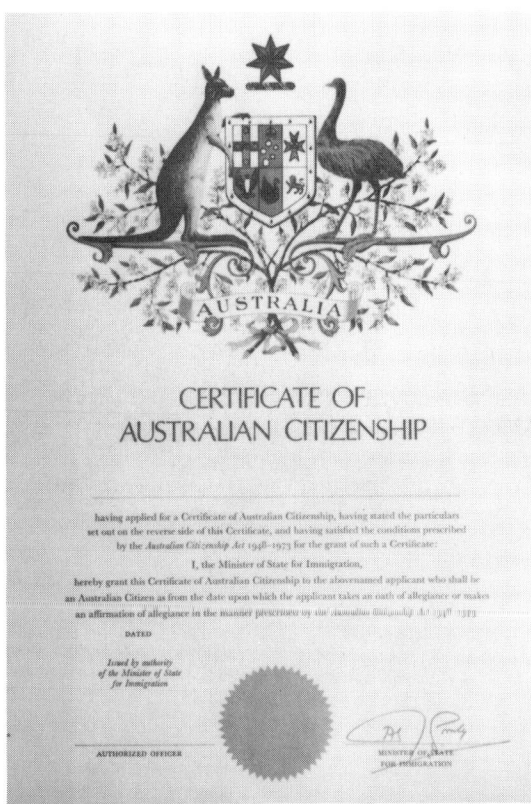

Left: The Labor Government, elected in 1972, presented the Australian public with a new image of their national identity. It defined Australia as a multicultural society and issued a certificate of Australian citizenship which replaced the image of the Queen with the Australian Coat of Arms and omitted all references to British subject status. A citizenship certificate as issued in 1973. (DIMA 73/12/12) *Below:* These Queensland migrants who became citizens in 1953 could have had no doubt that they were entering a society which saw itself as ethnically and culturally British. (DIMA 53/12/5)

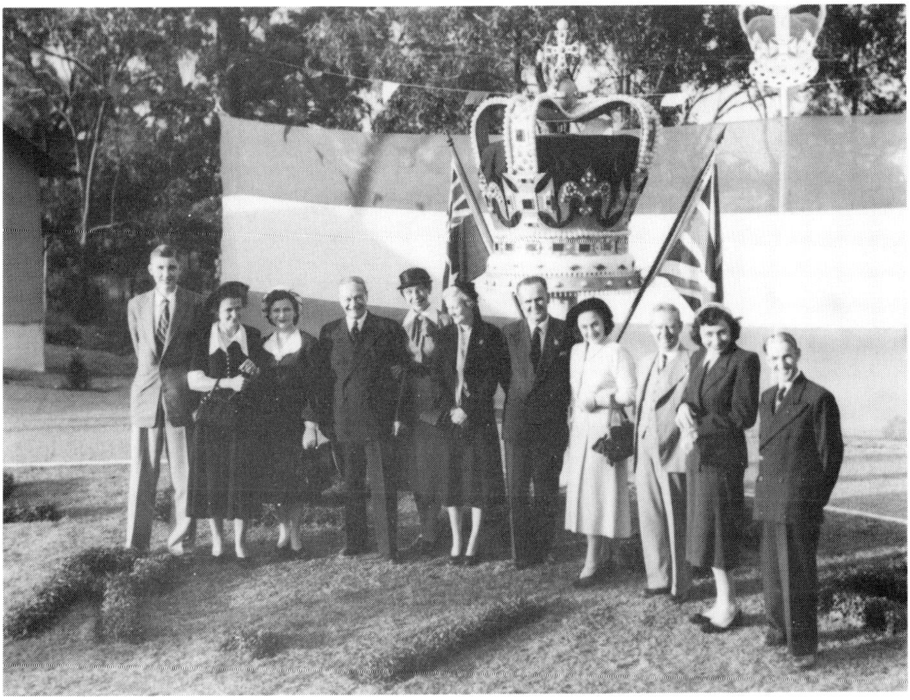

Top: Al Grassby, Minister for Immigration (1973–1974) was the first to redefine Australia as a multicultural society, and strove enthusiastically to disseminate this vision during his brief time in office. In March 1974 he became honorary member of the Italian Club of Western Australia. (DIMA 74/18/2) *Above:* E.G. Whitlam at a ball held by the Harmonie German Club in late 1972, shortly before he became Prime Minister. He disliked the Department of Immigration, which he saw as too closely identified with the previous administration, and dismantled it in June 1974. (DIMA 72/18/36)

7

From assimilation to integration

THE ultimate success of Australia's program of mass migration depended on the commitment of the Australian government to the social absorption of migrants. While the contribution of organised and informal groups of migrants and non-migrants in helping individual migrants settle into their communities was important, the wider context in which they operated was determined by the effectiveness (or ineffectiveness) of the Department of Immigration in devising solutions to the systemic problems faced by migrants. This varied over time, as both the way in which the ethnicity of the mainstream community was conceived and the manner in which migrants were expected to relate to it changed radically in the years between 1947 and 1975. While most Departmental officers reflected the mainstream attitudes of their political masters and worked within the parameters they set, others, particularly the minority working in the less powerful settlement-related areas, became agents of change. The Department's first attempt in 1952 to predict the future ethnic composition of the Australian population revealed clearly its assumptions that Australians were British in ethnicity, that 50 per cent of the migrant intake would come from Britain, and that the children of alien migrants born in Australia could be described statistically as British.[1]

The expected intake of British migrants did not eventuate

in the 1950s. The understanding of Department of Immigration officers in settlement-related areas of the nature of ethnic minorities and of the migration experience expanded during the 1960s. By 1964 the Department as a whole had developed a less fearful attitude towards the existence of ethnic minorities and their organisations. This cultural change was reflected in the terminology it adopted. In 1964 it officially abandoned the term 'assimilation' and substituted 'integration'. Later it adopted the terms 'ethnic organisations' and 'ethnic communities' to replace the rather negatively conceived 'national groups'.

THE DEPARTMENT OF IMMIGRATION'S ROLE IN ASSIMILATION

Discouraging 'national groups'

Initially the Department discouraged the formation of 'national groups', particularly within its Holding Centres and in workers' hostels. The term 'national group', used throughout the 1950s to refer to both ethnic communities and their clubs and societies, reflected mainstream fears that migrants would remain isolated from Australian society in ethnic enclaves, and that their organisations would perpetuate the political and social problems of their homeland in Australia. As the Department explained in response to a resolution of the 1951 Citizenship Convention on the topic of 'national groups', it discouraged the establishment of political or nationalistic organisations if they appeared to have the objective of separating their members from the Australian community. Although it had no objection to social or cultural clubs, it preferred that 'New Australians' (a term coined by Calwell as a more welcoming substitute for the popular 'reffo' or 'Balt') joined existing Australian organisations with similar aims and ideals.[2]

In 1952 the Secretary of the Department wrote to a number of sporting organisations, indicating that every effort should be made to include migrants in Australian sporting activities. By December 1954 the Department was preparing a pamphlet on sporting facilities in Australia, which it translated into German, Dutch and Italian, for distribution to migrants on embarkation for Australia. It listed the sports played in Australia and the address in each State for the various sporting bodies. This principle of organisational inclusion extended even to Boy Scout groups in Holding Centres. Although their parents exhibited 'a national consciousness and are endeavouring to form their own little national cliques in the various Centres', the controller of Migrant Accommodation Centres reported in 1952, 'every endeavour is made at all times to stamp this practice out'. Every Boy Scout group had to be open to all nationalities in the Centres, and their directors ensured that management committees included adults of all nationalities. 'It is very definite that children under the age of 16 at present in Australia will have only one nationality within the next few years, namely Australian', he concluded. The director of Scheyville Holding Centre also reported in 1954 that he had disbanded a Boy Scout group that had begun in his centre three years earlier because it had developed into a national group. The Department was consistent in its opposition to any form of social exclusion. On discovering that one Centre had organised a recreation club that restricted membership to Australians and other British persons, it issued an instruction in August 1951 to all migrant centres banning its employees from organising groups which excluded 'New Australians' as 'contrary to the spirit of the Department's assimilation activities'.[3]

The Department was reluctant to be too explicit with migrants about assimilation. A recommendation of the 1953 Citizenship Convention, 'That publicity be directed towards explaining to migrants what is meant by assimilation', was rejected on the grounds that:[4]

> ... the deed may be more important than the word, which, if over-emphasised, could come to be resented or ignored by migrants. The view has been expressed that a migrant who is assimilated without knowing it, is a good migrant, whereas one who is continually being told that he is being assimilated may develop a defensive attitude against his well-meaning assimilator. An indirect approach, e.g., through publicising stories of successful social and economic adjustment, might carry more weight.

This caution was understandable given the Department's far less well publicised assimilation strategy of discriminating against those they assumed would be less easily absorbed. In his address to the 1952 Citizenship Convention, Holt referred to the 'important element of restriction' in Australia's immigration policy: '[I]t is not a policy based on any notion of racial superiority but on a frank and realistic recognition that there are important differences of, for example, race, culture and economic standard which make successful assimilation unlikely'. Although he was referring specifically to Asian migration, as has been outlined in chapter 2, this discrimination was directed also at southern European migrants. The desired British component was outnumbered by European refugees up to 1953, and by German, Italian and Dutch migrants entering independently and under negotiated agreements until 1958. It gradually became dominant in the 1960s, increasing from 37.9 per cent of the intake in 1958–63 to 51.0 per cent in 1963–67.[5]

By the end of the 1950s the cultural assumptions underlying assimilation were being questioned. In October 1959, Opposition spokesman on immigration Leslie Haylen criticised the use of the word 'assimilation'. He felt it drew attention to differences between the migrant and the host community instead of 'creating a bridge over which we both can walk and assimilate each other and get to know each other. "Assimilation" is an ugly word. We want the migrants to become Australians in the broadest possible sense with an understanding of our different backgrounds'.[6]

Identifying migrant organisations 1951

Departmental social workers quickly recognised that migrant community organisations could be of great assistance in helping their members settle in the community. There was, however, no information available on them or on their activities in the early 1950s. The Directory of Social Agencies, compiled by the Australian Council of Social Services (ACOSS), was out of date by 1951 and made no reference to services available to migrants. In 1951, with the assistance of ACOSS and the Sydney Board of Social Studies, Margaret Ramsay, the social worker at Bathurst Reception Centre, compiled what was possibly the first directory of ethnic organisations in New South Wales. She intended it to form the basis of an information service for migrants wanting to learn about community facilities in the districts in which they would live and work. Hazel Dobson hoped that the Bathurst Information Service would become the forerunner of other information services prepared in collaboration with ACOSS or similar organisations in other States. If compiled in the form of a card index, not a published volume, it could easily be updated and would provide an invaluable source, not only to service-providers in Australia but to Department of Immigration officers when counselling applicants for migration overseas, she pointed out.[7]

Ramsay collected information on 30 clubs representing ten

different nationalities, and personally contacted fifteen of them. She also discussed national clubs with 29 representatives of ten other ethnic groups. It was important, she observed, to understand the nature of these organisations before referring a client to them:

> Some are welfare groups while others have a wider programme embracing the promoting of cultural activity and social intercourse, while others represent a difference in political thinking or social status. If these clubs are to be used constructively to help New Australians their policies must be thoroughly known, for in referring a client to a group opposed to his ideals and way of life more harm can be done than good.[8]

Of the seventeen Polish groups she identified, the Polish Welfare Society was the most receptive to the referral of problem cases. If they could not help a client they agreed to refer him or her to the appropriate Polish organisation. The Ukrainian Association was the most cooperative of the three Ukrainian bodies contacted. The Yugoslavs, Hungarians and Czechoslovakians, she found, were too divided along political, ethnic or class lines to collaborate. Lithuanians, Latvians and Estonians did not seem to find as much difficulty in assimilating as some of the other groups, and although the Greek Orthodox Church provided general advice on language and employment problems through its Community Central Office, Greeks were mostly helped financially through their families.

THE DECLINING ROLE OF DEPARTMENTAL SOCIAL WORKERS 1959–67

Like that of the Cheshire Cat, the friendly face of the Department of Immigration faded and became largely invisible to migrants after a reduction in the Department's establishment of social workers in 1959. There appears to have been no officer or section in the Department with enough influence or interest to argue against the Minister, Alexander Downer, who informed Parliament in 1959 that as the result of a Public Service Board review Departmental social workers would be reduced from 23 to 15, on the somewhat specious grounds that they had been appointed to deal with the specific problem of displaced persons and, as that category had now virtually disappeared, 'the principal object for which these social workers were originally appointed has evaporated'. Although Hazel Dobson did not leave the Department until 1961 she had, according to John Tarbath, become a spent force. Her insistent advocacy now fell on deaf ears at a time when the government was on an economy drive. 'When Hazel left, we people in the States were left entirely to our own resources', he commented.[9]

As Department of Immigration-funded accommodation diminished throughout the 1960s, social workers spent most of their time in offices in urban regional centres and their peripatetic ventures into country areas ceased. Their reduced numbers made them less able either to help migrants or to advise Canberra on settlement problems and strategies than their predecessors had been. This period in the history of Departmental settlement services shaped the perceptions of academic writers like James Jupp and his successors. As George Kiddle commented:[10]

> The government no longer had the resources to provide other than a nominal welfare service nor had one been developed to any significant extent by the voluntary sector. Migrants largely had to fend for themselves, which, to their credit, most did very well. It was probably this period, rather than any other, which gave rise to later criticism that little, if anything [was done] for migrants until the early 1970s, criticism which is largely unjustified if the whole picture is looked at over the post war years.

INTEGRATING NATIONAL GROUPS 1964–72

In 1964 the Department of Immigration replaced 'assimilation' in its official documents by 'integration'. P.M. Rice, at that time working with the South Australian Department of Aboriginal Welfare, was conscious of the change in terminology in this area also. He defined Aboriginal integration as meaning 'Aborigines in their own right were to be accepted as integral parts of the community'. The word was never adequately defined within the Department of Immigration, and Rice observed that the terminological change took a long time to be accepted by some people in the Department. Departmental officers seem to have taken little interest in the international and academic debate about the term 'assimilation' at this time. Rice was not aware of the 1959 UNESCO conference in Havana which recommended the substitution of the word 'integration' for 'assimilation', although he had read the paper T. and G.J. Van Keulens had presented to the 1959 Citizenship Convention on the topic. Like his colleagues, who were involved daily in developing practical strategies to assist migrants settle in Australia, he was little interested in theory or terminology. He was merely aware that the assimilationist expectation that migrants become like Anglo-Celtic Australians did not work. A Departmental paper entitled 'Citizenship and settlement' in 1973 interpreted integration as meaning:

> that migrants should be accepted into the community without prejudice and they should retain their cultural identity if they wish. The policy of the Department is to encourage migrants to seek maximum freedom of expression in their social, religious and political aspirations, subject only to normal legal and other restraints common within the Australian society. It endeavours to remove any impediment which places the newcomer at a disadvantage to the established citizen and which might restrict him in making his full contribution to the well-being of the community.

By 1973 the Department clearly had made considerable progress towards recognising cultural pluralism, and had adopted a less defensive attitude towards the traditional construction of national identity. However, as W.G. Kiddle, another officer who worked in the settlement area of the Department from the early 1970s, explained in 1981, the term 'integration' 'lacked (and still lacks) any degree of precision being synonymous in the view of many people with assimilation yet being equated by others with concepts as far advanced as multi-culturalism'.[11]

Whatever the meaning of 'integration', the officers in Rice's Integration and Education Section during the 1960s and early 1970s, with considerable support and encouragement from their senior officers, made a number of practical contributions to facilitating migrant integration, which they saw as both necessary and achievable. They were responsible for originating the Grant-in-Aid scheme, the Telephone Interpreter Service, the data collection system, translating and interpreting, the repatriation of migrants with serious settlement problems, upgrading settlement staff and recruiting ethnic welfare officers. They developed administrative structures which enabled their Department to monitor migrant groups directly, thus making it less dependent on information supplied through Citizenship Conventions and the Good Neighbour Movement. Their systematic research into the nature and extent of migrant organisations enabled the Department to provide ethnic communities with the funds and organisational structures they needed to improve their provision of settlement services to the members of their communities. As a new relationship between migrant organisations and the bureaucracy developed, the integration activities of mainstream organisations were increasingly viewed as irrelevant. Politicians of both major political parties at this time supported the provision of settlement services to their constituents.

Improved information collection

The Survey Section

Until the early 1960s, the only body dealing with migrants which kept adequate statistics on its services was the migrant information service of the Commonwealth Bank. By 1968 the Bank of New South Wales migrant advisory service was interviewing approximately 1600 migrants a month, providing its clients with information on migration and citizenship, helping them to obtain temporary accommodation and advice on housing purchase, translating documents required by employers, and helping them with 'domestic problems'. Until that year, when the Taxation Department asked it not to, it had helped migrants comply with their taxation obligations. In 1967 the Australian and New Zealand Bank set up a similar advisory centre for migrants but had not begun to keep comprehensive records, and the majority of its clients were British.[12]

In 1962 the Department of Immigration set up a Survey Section within the Citizenship Branch of its Entry and Citizenship Division, to enable the Department to collect and analyse its own information on the settlement experiences of migrants. Its nine staff prepared recommendations and reports on 'the habits and behaviour of migrants within the community, the practical difficulties they experienced during the process of integration, the attitudes of the native-born to the migrant, and research into motivation and personality factors'. Their work helped the Department to formulate policy to assist integration, particularly by improving the delivery of welfare to migrants and their selection by its officers overseas. Much of the information used by this Section was extracted from reports and statistics supplied by the remaining Departmental social workers in the various States. When it began to analyse this material, however, it found that poor definition of terms and the absence of a standard form of case-reporting were obstacles, particularly to longitudinal research. While early attempts to get regional staff to comply with standardised recording procedures had failed, in May 1967 the Survey Section eventually succeeded in convincing the Department's senior social workers to adopt a standardised format for their reports. This was based on a system developed in Adelaide by Departmental social worker P.M. Rice.[13]

Computerised data-processing by the Integration and Education section

In late 1967, P.M. Rice was transferred to Canberra to join the newly created Integration and Education Section. The role of the Section was 'to focus attention predominantly on settlement problems of migrants and the steps necessary to resolve these through counselling and an optimum use of Australian community resources'. It was able to give considerable attention to cases where settlement had seriously broken down. In September that year the director of the branch, S.J. Rooth, who was investigating the number of repatriation cases, suggested the introduction of a basic index card, coded for electronic data-processing. After discussions at the conference of Commonwealth Directors of Migration in 1968, the Integration and Education Section developed a case record envelope. This facilitated the collection and computerised processing of information on clients collected in the regional offices, such as length of residence, nationality, nature of problem, gender and occupation. A pilot project was set up in the Adelaide office on 16 April 1968 and the procedure was introduced nationwide (except for Darwin and Townsville) on 1 May 1970. The information collected was initially processed for the Department by the Commonwealth Bureau of Census and Statistics. It was expected that this system would assist in the assessment and treatment of cases, as well as facilitating future planning.[14]

The usefulness of statistics compiled from cases presenting to social workers as a means of understanding the wider migrant experience was debated within the Department. One senior officer warned his colleagues not to expect too much in conducting research, or to draw too many conclusions from these statistics 'about why settlers depart, or why they form ghettos, or why they don't become naturalised—simply because case records relate to only a very small proportion of migrants'. Another officer defended the system, arguing that it was not meant to be a theoretically perfect survey machine but a system for gathering pragmatically based information on the types of problems presented to Integration Sections in each State, and that it had already proved itself invaluable. Information on migrant settlement problems was also collected from Departmental employment and accommodation officers, and from the staff of Department of Labour and National Service hostels. While Rice read all the academic criticisms he could find, including James Jupp's 1966 work on migrant settlement *Arrivals and Departures*, he found academic analyses of migrant settlement problems generally out of touch with current issues, based on outdated information, and of little use as they were 'quite negative in their criticisms, while we were flat out trying to get things going so they would get better'.[15]

The first report using the new data-processing technique was on the integration difficulties of French migrants. It was intended to inform the overseas post of the problems encountered resulting from their selection methods. The second report was on the problems of aged migrants, and the third in 1970-71 compared problems across all States. From its inception in 1962 until December 1972 the Survey Section produced 41 research reports on various aspects of the migrant experience. None of these were released or published under the Liberal administration.[16]

P.M. Rice regarded computerised data collection and analysis as an enormous asset to both the Department and its Minister. It was abandoned under the Labor administration which, he believed, felt it could develop its policies without the assistance of such social research. It was one achievement of the Integration and Education Section which was never restored by the Liberal government after the November 1975 election. Perhaps the data it had collected on migrant settlement problems was too revealing for comfort.[17]

Grants-in-Aid

At the same time as the collection of data from Departmental social workers was being improved, the Department introduced a new and much more finely targeted system of involving community agencies in migrant welfare than was possible through the Good Neighbour Movement. It also, for the first time, provided a structure by means of which ethnic organisations could be recognised and included, and which required professional rather than untrained voluntary assistance from community organisations. According to Nancy Anderson, a newly appointed social worker in the Brisbane office in 1966, the ideas that gave rise to the Grant-in-Aid scheme were generated at a conference of Departmental social workers from all States held in Canberra in 1967, which attempted to identify the reasons migrants returned to their countries of origin. Participants discussed in particular the problems they experienced in referring their clients to welfare-providers outside the Department. In a paper she delivered at the conference, Anderson pointed out that many migrants in Brisbane were referred to the telephone crisis service Lifeline, and argued that the Department should fund ethnic organisations, which had the required linguistic and cultural skills, to enable them to employ professional social workers. She gave a copy of her paper to her assistant secretary, John Dempsey.[18]

The ground rules for the grants were developed that year by P.M. Rice, and the scheme was successfully implemented by John Dempsey. This achievements of this Section were remarkable, given the need to develop new settlement policies in a context of growing pressure on the Section from both government and Opposition parliamentarians, who were beginning to appreciate the electoral advantages to be gained by intervening in cases on behalf of their migrant constituents. As there was no separate policy development section, Rice found himself working 16-hour days and developing policy proposals on weekends for five or six years. He felt it was the one chance he would get to develop these highly significant innovations.[19]

In 1967 the Survey Section conducted a survey in all States of the scope, size and function of community-based agencies and of the Department's own State offices. It assessed the suitability of various agencies for inclusion in a greatly expanded scheme to assist migrants with their settlement problems. From this survey came the realisation that voluntary ethnic and other 'suitable' organisations in the community could be encouraged to develop their own services with Commonwealth financial assistance. As Rice later explained, the development of the Grant-in-Aid scheme was a belated acknowledgement by the Department of the value of the services being provided by both organised and informal ethnic groups to the members of their communities by the late 1960s. Another important development from this survey was the upgrading of settlement staff (especially social workers and welfare officers) in all States. This was done in collaboration with the Public Service Board and expanded the Department's migrant settlement facilities, which had become seriously depleted since 1959.[20]

In its 1967/68 budget the Department put aside a small sum to set up grants to community agencies so that they could employ qualified social workers to give skilled assistance to migrants with social problems. Although this vote grew every year, it was always considerably less than the funding provided to Good Neighbour Councils. (In 1972/73 the budget for Grants-in-Aid was $234 600, compared with up to $620 000 for the Good Neighbour Movement.) The first two grants were made by the Minister on the recommendation of the Department of Immigration on 1 July 1968 to the Family Welfare Bureau in Sydney and the Italian Assistance Association in Carlton, Melbourne (Co.As.It.). By July 1969, 27 agencies were approved to receive Grants-in-Aid (eight in NSW, six in Victoria and in South Australia, four in Queensland, and three in Western Australia). Although they were funded to pay a social worker and to meet associated costs, including secretarial assistance, only fourteen of these agencies had been able to recruit a social worker by July 1969. By late 1970, Good Neighbour Councils in Sydney, Adelaide and Perth were receiving additional funding under this scheme.[21]

The case-recording system, which combined the reports of Grant-in-Aid social workers with those of its own social workers, permitted the Department to get a better understanding of the main settlement difficulties of migrants. Employment was the main problem encountered by both sources. The analysis of Melbourne case records for the year 1968–69 included those of Co.As.It., from which most Italians sought help. It was found that 60 per cent of the migrants consulting Departmental social workers had lived in Australia for less than two years. The Italian welfare service dealt with more established migrants. By September 1971 the number of grants had been increased to 38, and 28 social workers were employed by funded agencies. By then, four other ethnic organisations had been approved for funding—the Australian–Jewish Welfare and Relief Society, South Yarra; the Australian–German Welfare Society in Melbourne and Sydney; and the Italian Committee of Assistance, Sydney. In 1972–73 the 49 agencies funded by Grants-in-Aid saw 20 000 migrant clients. All funded bodies were situated in urban areas.[22]

In 1973 the Department argued for the continued funding of mainstream organisations, pointing out that newly arrived groups from new source countries, particularly refugees, were most in need of assistance but had least opportunity to establish viable organisations capable of delivering welfare services. It was also, it added, difficult to fund all sections of some more established communities, which were fragmented along linguistic, political or religious lines. By 1974 the number of grants had risen to 60, but a ceiling of 49 was set which was not changed until the implementation of the recommendations of the 1978 Galbally Report on migrant services and programs. From 1975, however, a lively debate developed on the need to fund ethno-specific organisations as opposed to mainstream bodies, and on the provision of community-based social workers as opposed to those attached to the Department of Immigration. Although the progressive increase in the number of grants gave some scope to the funding of new ethnically based agencies, the limited number of professionally qualified bilingual social workers available restricted the effectiveness of the scheme. By July 1981 the equivalent of 111 grants had been allocated under the Grant-in-Aid scheme, 49 to ethnically based organisations and 43 to traditional non-ethnic voluntary agencies.[23]

Compliance monitoring, although not perfect, was much more rigorous for agencies in receipt of Grants-in-Aid than for agencies registered with the Good Neighbour Movement. Like Departmental caseworkers, funded agencies were required to submit daily activity sheets with monthly abstracts and comments for checking by the Department's senior social workers in State offices. These reports were then sent to Central Office in Canberra and the payment of grants was dependent on their receipt. The failure of the Department to provide enough staff to analyse this information, and therefore to provide feedback to reporting agencies, proved to be a disincentive to their compliance with these time-consuming requirements. P.M. Rice observed that initially the Department was very even-handed with ethnic groups, and this made it difficult to target those which were particularly needy. By 1976, he believed, politics was intruding on the grants program, and on occasions the Prime Minister overrode Departmental advice in relation to particular grants. This tended to politicise the public service. Until 1978 grants were allocated for one year but were renewable subject to satisfactory performance. This proved to be inflexible, as it was politically difficult for the Minister to reallocate grants from relatively well-performing groups, where the need had lessened, to new areas of need. The Galbally Report recommended that an increased number of three-year terminating grants be provided for which agencies should be required to compete. The adoption of this recommendation helped to remedy this problem.[24]

Grants-in-Aid to ethnic organisations provided them with important signals from government that it recognised their value as agents of integration. Government recognition gave the sort of status and prestige to the members of their voluntary committees previously only awarded to the leaders of mainstream community organisations associated with the Good Neighbour Movement. This strengthened the likelihood of compliance by ethnic community leaders with the government's policy of social inclusion, and assisted the development of formally structured and politically skilled ethnic organisations in the 1970s. It was, however, potentially divisive, as it pitted organisations against each other in the search for government funds, and some were more astute in applying for grants than others. George Pridannikoff, who was Ethnic Affairs Officer in the Brisbane office of the Department from the late 1970s, observed that the Vietnamese community in that State quickly became skilful political lobbyists and took advantage of government funding arrangements, whereas the Muslim community was much slower in seeking assistance from the bureaucracy. Considerable skill was required of Departmental managers of Grants-in-Aid, he observed, to prevent funding from dividing communities.[25]

THE REVIVAL OF DEPARTMENTAL SOCIAL AND WELFARE WORKERS 1968

From 1968 the Department rectified the mistake that had been made in 1959 and increased the numbers of its social workers and welfare officers. Unlike in 1959, the Department had P.M. Rice to argue the case for more settlement services, and to point out that that a caseload of more than 40 was unrealistic. State directors were also more subject to pressure from migrants for better welfare service than they had been ten years earlier. Much of this pressure came from British migrants, who could vote and were therefore of interest to politicians. However, the Department made another mistake when it began to computerise the information obtained from its social workers, by subordinating their advising role to the requirements of the Survey Section in Central Office, which was staffed by psychologists who knew nothing of social work.[26]

While earlier reports tended to group aliens as 'migrants', the new processing techniques enabled the Department to distinguish between the various ethnic groups. The information processed by its computers told the Department nothing about migrants in rural areas, and policy-makers received none of the first-hand policy advice from officers intimately involved with clients such as social workers had provided in the previous decade. Non-government organisations could not be looked to to fill this information gap. 'Welfare service organisations active in outlying areas don't seem to keep records of social problems, and I fear do not even appear to be able to identify them', Rice complained in 1970.[27]

The number of professional social workers employed by the Department in its regional offices had risen slightly to eighteen by October 1970 (six in Sydney, five in Melbourne, two in Brisbane, Adelaide and Perth and one in Canberra); however, 25 others were employed by agencies funded by the Commonwealth. The caseload of all social workers funded to work with migrants steadily rose, from 8556 cases Australia-wide in 1970–71 to 10042 the following year. The numbers of welfare officers also rose.[28]

Although Department of Immigration-funded social workers were available to migrants no matter how long they had been in Australia, by 1971 the Department was encouraging them to use normal welfare services once they became settled into the community. This happened only slowly for, as a survey of the sources of referrals undertaken by its social workers in 1971–72 revealed, newly arrived migrants still tended to look first to the Department for help, and mainstream welfare organisations and more established migrants continued to refer migrants seeking their help to Departmental social workers. Most of the 7602 migrants who sought the Department's welfare services within the first two years of their arrival did so of their own accord. Those seeking help who had been in Australia longer were generally referred by professional services, relatives, friends or voluntary agencies. Few learned about the service from the media or the Department's literature, and hardly any were referred by employment agencies or by their employers.[29]

Devolution of the provision of personal advice to migrants from the Department of Immigration to other agencies was only gradually achieved through Grant-in-Aid funding. By July 1973, the Department was funding 49 agencies to employ social workers. These professionals were, however, reluctant to accept that lesser-qualified welfare workers could be entrusted to carry out welfare and counselling work without close professional supervision. It was not until 1976, therefore, that the Grant-in-Aid scheme funded agencies to employ subprofessional welfare workers. In 1973 the Department's own welfare staff included about

65 per cent overseas-born or Australian-born officers of ethnic background fluent in community languages. It also planned to supplement its own 21 university-trained social workers and 18 welfare workers by appointing 48 multilingual welfare officers. After completing a twelve-month course at the Prahran College of Advanced Education, which included practical work experience under the supervision of Departmental social workers, these new officers would provide welfare and interpreting services to migrants at home, in schools and in the workplace.[30]

In 1981 W.G. Kiddle observed that there had been no significant drop in the demand by migrants for Departmental social workers. The following year, in reviewing the effects of changes introduced on the recommendation of the Galbally Report, the Australian Institute of Multicultural Affairs noted that, rather than declining as expected, the number of welfare staff employed by the Department of Immigration in 1981 was actually higher than in 1977. The recommended transfer of casework to non-government welfare bodies had not occurred, as the Department did not believe that they were ready to meet the demand.[31]

THE NATIONAL GROUPS LIAISON UNIT

In 1968 the Department of Immigration established an administrative structure, the National Groups Liaison Unit, headed by James H. Houston, to enable it to deal directly with migrant organisations. In 1967, in preparation for the formation of this unit, an index of ethnic associations throughout Australia was compiled. Concurrent with the formation of the unit, a subcommittee of the Immigration Advisory Council, which included Houston, was established in August 1969 to study the part ethnic groups could play in future in the settlement process and to identify what kinds of help they needed to carry out these functions. This subcommittee recommended an important change in Departmental terminology—that the term 'ethnic groups' be substituted for 'national groups'. This had originally been suggested by Professor Sol Encel, Professor of Sociology at the University of New South Wales, who had carried out his own studies of such groups.[32]

The National Groups Unit contacted ethnic organisations Australia-wide, initially by mail, to discover the types of activities and services they provided for their members and to obtain a better understanding of the problems they experienced in assisting migrants. It also attempted to assess their willingness to collaborate more closely with the Department. Migrant spokesmen, usually the president or secretary of their organisations, were presented with a detailed questionnaire intended to clarify that organisation's role. They were asked about its membership, aims and objects, and the facilities and amenities it provided (such as social welfare counselling, information on employment and housing, English language classes and interpreting or translating services). They were also asked whether they wanted their organisation to be included in a published directory of ethnic organisations. Their responses were analysed statistically. Officials of the 905 bodies found to be relevant were interviewed by Departmental officers. A further 1050 organisations were identified but not interviewed. Some were found to be cultural clubs, others were defunct, some did not regard themselves as a 'national group'. The confidence of these organisations, many of whom were initially apprehensive about working with a government department, was gained by the Integration Section's promise to preserve the confidentiality of this information. It vigorously resisted a suggestion by a senior officer that the information obtained be referred to the Australian Secret Intelligence Organisation, and subsequently kept the files it generated locked in a safe, restricting access to them to approved officers only.[33]

In March 1970 Houston asked all representatives of national group organisations what they perceived the most important needs of their members to be, and how they thought the Department might be able to help. This encouraged the establishment of a dialogue between the Department and such bodies. It helped ethnic community leaders to focus on the settlement needs of their communities, improved the Department's understanding of migrants' perceptions of their settlement needs, and encouraged ethnic organisations to look to the government for solutions. Most importantly, it was the first formal signal to ethnic communities that government saw them as having a major role to play in fostering the integration of their members into Australian society.[34]

The letter that accompanied the survey communicated the Department's 'desire to develop a closer partnership with the many national group organisations in Australia'. It affirmed that the Department recognised the contribution they were making to the successful resettlement of migrants as well as to preserving cultural and social traditions, 'which can be a bridge rather than a barrier between the former homeland and the adopted land'. When analysed, the survey revealed that most existing migrant organisations were far from being effective service-deliverers. Only a few communities were receiving adequate settlement assistance from them, apart from the large and well-established Italian, Jewish and German bodies which were receiving Grant-in-Aid funding.[35]

In addition to the research conducted by the Department, the Immigration Planning Council set up a Migrant Studies Committee. It included the eminent demographer, Professor W.D. Borrie of the Australian National University, and sociologist Professor Jean Martin, as well as officers of the Department of Immigration. At its first meeting on 1 March 1971, the Committee began planning a survey over time of the changing attitudes of 10 000 migrants on such issues as health, welfare, income, employment and their past history.[36]

Towards a directory of national groups

The usefulness of Department of Immigration research to service-providing bodies became evident to the Department even before it was completed. In November 1971 the Migrant Welfare Committee of the non-government Australian Council of Social Services (ACOSS) requested a list of all migrant organisations throughout Australia with staff dealing with migrant welfare problems. ACOSS was supplied with data collected on those of the 516 service-providing migrant organisations which had been identified by the National Groups Survey by that time, and which had agreed to publication, to enable it to expand its existing State directories of social services. Although the survey of national groups was completed by June 1972 the Department's directory was not published that year, as its scope had been widened from purely welfare-oriented bodies to all types of migrant organisations—social, cultural and religious—so that migrants seeking any form of assistance could be referred to an appropriate organisation.[37]

Unfortunately, by the end of 1973 the grand vision of developing a computerised directory—for use by State and regional offices, by the Telephone Interpreter Service to locate interpreters, by ACOSS to supplement its State directories, by the Department to compile and maintain an index of ethnic organisations classified under various headings—had not been realised. Progress on all projects had been poor, the final survey report had not been completed, and the only concrete product was an

ACOSS directory in South Australia. As P.M. Rice remarked gloomily, 'the service to our migrants through ethnic organisations and our relationship with the organisations themselves remain much the same as they did prior to August 1969'. Computerisation of the information was, however, underway by June 1975, and the first directory of ethnic organisations was published that year by the Department of Social Security (which had by then become responsible for settlement matters). It appeared in the form of a bound book entitled *National Groups in Australia*, not as the easily updated loose-leaf computer printout Rice had suggested in 1973.[38]

The cultural change that had occurred within the Department of Immigration by the end of the 1960s towards 'national groups' and previously mistrusted 'ethnic enclaves' was reflected in the speech to Parliament in September 1970 by Minister for Immigration Phillip Lynch. He employed the term 'ethnic concentrations', which he described as normal, benign, and temporary:[39]

> Concentrations of persons of the same nationality initially offer to the migrant and his family an opportunity to be with compatriots. They also offer a migrant a sense of fellowship with members of his own nationality. This serves to provide a cushion or barrier to the normal cultural shock which the difficult transition of migration and resettlement from one country to another involves. In this sense ethnic concentrations can be seen as advantageous to migrants in the short term, before they move into outlying suburban areas.

THE DECLINE OF THE GOOD NEIGHBOUR MOVEMENT

As the Department of Immigration developed its own sources of information on the settlement needs of migrants and its own ways of communicating with ethnic organisations, it became less dependent on, and more critical of, the Good Neighbour Movement which it had established in 1950 and continued to fund. The Movement did change with the times, and attempted to enlist ethnic communities. By 1970 its Councils had begun to encourage migrant organisations to apply for affiliation, and a number of the Council's contact workers in the community and in hostels spoke relevant community languages.[40]

The cultural change in thinking about migrants that was transforming Councils by 1974 was reflected in the distaste with which the NSW Good Neighbour Council regarded a proposal from the commercial sector to foster multiculturalism. It lobbied vigorously against a proposal by the management of Lend Lease shopping centres, which operated eight large complexes in New South Wales in which one-tenth of the total retail sales in the State were transacted. Lend Lease offered the use of its premises for ethnic groups to organise national gatherings, such as folk dancing and outdoor concerts. Referring to the proposed entertainment as 'side-shows' the Council remarked that 'such shows tend to confirm the widely held Australian suspicion that migrants are "a race apart". They could also be demeaning to migrants who generally do not cavort in this way in their own countries'.[41]

By 1973 the Movement had become more decentralised. It had over 600 branches and representatives in regional centres, as well as organised teams of voluntary workers in the metropolitan zones of the larger Australian cities. Decentralisation had resulted in an increase of staff and consequent rises in cost to the Department of Immigration. Its eight State Councils now employed 74 full-time staff, including 18 welfare officers, and four Councils employed full-time social workers. In April 1973 the Councils reformulated the role of the Movement as welcoming new arrivals and assisting them settle and learn English, advising the government on migrant integration, and encouraging community services and organisations to meet the needs of migrants. They also included the more political objective of encouraging public acceptance of the importance of immigration to national development and of the notion of a 'family of the nation'.[42]

All its attempts to encourage migrant participation, to decentralise and to reformulate its aims, however, were not enough to save it in this new climate of multiculturalism and devolution, and with a funding body that now saw it as a relic of the assimilationist era. In his evidence to the Immigration Advisory Council's Committee on Community Relations in 1975, one of its former coordinators commented that, although it had successfully cultivated community acceptance of migrants and educated newcomers in the Australian way of life in the past, 'Over recent years, the momentum of this campaign has slackened and its effectiveness has diminished. The Good Neighbour Council generally can no longer claim to be significant community educators paving the way for multi-cultural social development'. The Committee's report to the Department of Immigration observed that there was 'a consensus that the Good Neighbour Councils as presently organised are not equipped to be structurally involved in the development of a community relations program on the lines envisaged by the Committee'. It did, however, see it having a 'grass-roots' role to play in subordination to the Community Relations Council and its committees. A conference of senior assistant directors of the Department of Social Security, which by now had responsibility for migrant settlement services, officers in charge of Migrant Service Sections and senior social workers from all States was held in May 1975. It decided to undertake a comprehensive reappraisal of the Good Neighbour Movement, but also noted that, while considerable emphasis was placed on the role ethnic organisations could play in introducing recently arrived migrants into the community, many were not geared to this purpose.[43]

In 1975, when the staff of the Movement had reached 78 and its funding was costing the government $1 million, a comprehensive reappraisal of the organisation was made and a new statement of its functions formulated which attempted to push it into more practical activities. The Bailly Report in 1976 reflected the new thinking, which looked to ethnic organisations to replace the settlement role of the Good Neighbour Movement. Foreshadowing the demise of the Movement, it commented:[44]

> There is no way in which government departments could have provided the range and sensitivity of service which the Councils offer. However . . . [they] have not always managed to cope as effectively with non-British migrants, and it seems that the implications for their functions of the development of distinct ethnic groups within the community need to be thought through.

Galbally's review of post-arrival programs and services in 1978 delivered the final death blow on behalf of a Department which found it no longer useful. Although it listed ten areas in which the Councils were by 1975 offering important services to migrants, it observed that the notion of the organisation providing a bridge between the host community and migrants may have been appropriate in the past, when there were no other non-governmental or major ethnic organisations active in migrant settlement. It was, however, inconsistent with the multicultural nature of Australian society in 1975. The Galbally Report concluded:[45]

> It is not possible to envisage a suitable role which would neither duplicate our other proposals nor inhibit the role which we believe the ethnic communities must have. We could therefore find no reason to justify continued funding of Good Neighbour Councils by the Commonwealth government.

In May 1978 the Council was notified that the Commonwealth government had accepted this advice. The mainstream community structure which the Department of Immigration had created in 1950 but did not control was seen as superfluous. It intended that the Council's role in fostering the social absorption and acceptance of migrants should be taken over by ethnic organisations which the Department was now attempting to foster, sustain and monitor. The organisation was not extinguished totally in all States. In 1979–80 the Queensland government funded the Good Neighbour Council of Queensland as an interim language service unit. It was replaced in 1982 by the Division of Migrant Services Translating and Interpreting Unit. The organisation itself was revitalised and restructured, with State government funding, as the Queensland Migrant Settlement Association.[46]

Had the structure provided by the Movement been retained and an attempt made to integrate ethnic organisations within it, the government might have had an Australia-wide organisation of citizens in place to disseminate at local level its new vision of Australia as an equal and multicultural society. After the dismantling of the Good Neighbour Movement, the task of promoting the political acceptability of immigration and multiculturalism was left to bureaucrats and ethnic communities, and the opportunity for promoting its new vision of Australian national identity to Anglo-Celtic Australians through this network was lost.

Conclusion

Within two decades the Department of Immigration's interaction with non-British migrants had caused its institutional culture to change profoundly. It no longer saw its settlement role as that of encouraging aliens to become an indistinguishable part of an essentially British community. By the early 1970s, through its improved understanding of migrant groups, it had lost its initial suspicion of them and begun to enlist them as agents in the social integration of their communities. The benign neglect with which the 'keepers' had long been regarded within the Department worked in their favour. Ignored, they were allowed to get on with their job and to develop arguments for settlement services which the more powerful 'getters' were unable to counter, and which politicians from both parties found persuasive. By the late 1960s they found they were getting support from the powerful people in the Department. Also, younger people were recruited who reflected changing attitudes towards Australian society.

The Department gradually became aware that the task of absorbing migrants into the community lay beyond one government department and the good will of untrained volunteers. The obstacles to migrants' accessing mainstream community facilities had to be removed by getting all relevant bodies to provide information about their services in translation, to provide interpreters, and to train their staff to be sensitive to the needs of migrants. Its more complex understanding of the migration experience and of minority cultures led it to believe that migrant organisations were best equipped linguistically and culturally to deliver social welfare services to their members. The activities of the Anglo-Celtic-dominated Good Neighbour Councils were thus seen by the Department as increasingly ineffective. As the arrangements through which they were permanently funded had not required them to report, the Department had no control over the way its money was spent and found monitoring the effectiveness of the Movement extremely difficult.

The short-term funding arrangements, through which it enlisted mainstream and ethnic organisations to supplement the efforts of its own social workers, incorporated exacting reporting requirements which enabled the Department to evaluate their cost-effectiveness. The development during the 1970s of ethnic organisations from social clubs to welfare-providers and political lobbyists on behalf of their communities was, in part, attributable to the provision by the Department of Immigration of seed-funding for welfare services. Through conforming to the guidelines set down for organisations applying for Grants-in-Aid, they not only became more structured than they had been in the 1950s and 1960s, they became more attuned to the Department's policy goals and more compliant with its instructions, because of their need to compete with each other for limited funding. By 1974, however, few were equipped to meet the needs of their communities and would not be for many years.

The task of managing the political acceptability of the

migrant presence and of creating bridges between migrants and the mainstream community, which had for so long been left largely to the Good Neighbour Councils, was increasingly delegated to ethnic organisations and the bureaucracy. They now became the only avenues for disseminating the government's new vision of Australia as a multicultural society, in which the previously favoured Anglo-Celts were to be treated equally with other ethnic groups.

CHAPTER 8

Promoting Australian citizenship

ALTHOUGH by the mid-20th century most Australians would have regarded and referred to themselves as 'Australians', their nationality was solely that of British subject until 25 January 1949. The *Nationality and Citizenship Act 1948* created a new status of Australian citizenship, in addition to that of British subject. This change had not been brought about by any particular nationalistic pressure to create a new and different national status. It was imposed on an almost entirely indifferent Australian population from above, as a consequence of Canada's moves to create a separate Canadian citizenship. In late 1945 the Australian government accepted a submission put to Cabinet recommending that, at the proposed conference of experts on nationality to be held in London in February 1947, Australia support the principles embodied in the Canadian Citizenship Bill.[1]

No Australians—including the officers of the Department of Immigration, which was given portfolio responsibility for administering the Act—had any conception of what being an Australian citizen as distinct from a British subject actually meant. This was because citizenship was conceptualised in relation to British culture and ethnicity, not in terms of the rights and responsibilities of the citizens of an autonomous state. This culturally normative conception of citizenship was clearly reflected in the definition of 'alien' embodied in the Act. A nation's understanding of itself is revealed by the categories of people it regards as foreign, alien, and 'other'. From 1948 to 1987 Australia's citizenship legislation defined an alien as 'a person who does not have the status of British subject and is not an Irish citizen or a protected person'. The image of Australians enshrined in the Act, therefore, was that of an Anglo-Celtic people.[2]

Two years before Australian citizenship was created, the first Minister for Immigration, Arthur Calwell, was enthusiastically planning to promote it. In November 1946 he outlined to Parliament his vision of more elaborate and dignified citizenship ceremonies and his fledgling Department's efforts to help the Immigration Advisory Council (IAC) to prepare a booklet which would:[3]

> give the alien an outline of our historical and cultural background, our social structure and mode of government, an appreciation of our way of life, and what Australia stands for as a nation. It will bring home to him the privileges and benefits which derive from Australian citizenship, and will better fit him to take his place as a partner in our great Commonwealth.

America, to which Calwell's Irish great-grandfather emigrated in 1775, provided him with models for both the ceremonies and the booklet. His understanding of citizenship, however, owed far more to his grandfather's immigration to Australia in 1853 and his subsequent naturalisation as a British subject in 1876 than to the American rights-based conception. The understanding of citizenship which Calwell and the ex-servicemen who comprised the staff of his Department brought to the management of the *Nationality and Citizenship Act 1948* was clearly based on the norm of British culture and ethnicity and on notions of 'privileges and benefits', not on equality of rights.[4]

Apart from an unsuccessful attempt in 1953–56 by its Secretary, Tasman Heyes, to give content to the term 'Australian citizen' by promoting discussion of a charter of Australian citizenship, the Department of Immigration focused entirely on decision-making in relation to migrants' access to or loss of Australian citizenship. Neither the 1955 Citizenship Convention to which the question was referred nor the IAC had anything useful to contribute, and the charter idea was dropped into the 'too-hard basket' by Minister Harold Holt in 1955.[5]

In 1958 a similar concept was suggested in Parliament by

Liberal member Billie Mackie Snedden, a former migrant processing officer in London who became Minister for Immigration in 1967. He outlined a more rights-based than ethnically defined notion of citizenship and called for a comprehensible 'code' that would clarify for the migrant what 'he may do' on being admitted as a resident of Australia. It should also, he urged, state very clearly 'what will be their political rights in Australia . . . what their social benefits will be . . . And, perhaps more important than anything, a definite statement in legislative form should be provided to the migrant showing that he is free from any discrimination and shall enjoy social equality'. Such a code, he believed, would attract migrants because they would know 'precisely what their powers and limitations would be'. Probably because of his fellow parliamentarians' and his Department's inability to come to grips with such a rights-based notion of citizenship, this idea also came to nothing.[6]

This lack of understanding of what it meant to be an Australian citizen as distinct from a British subject made the Department's task of promoting it to aliens extraordinarily difficult. Australians only slowly developed an understanding of citizenship based on equality of rights rather than on British culture and ethnicity. This meant that those who conceived Australian national identity as being inseparable from their British origins were also reluctant to accept the legitimacy of cultural diversity. One of the most important (although unintended) spurs to the development of a rights-based notion of citizenship in Australia was the Department of Immigration's responsibility for facilitating the social and economic absorption of alien migrants into Australian society. In the process, it learnt to understand and work with ethnic minorities from a wide range of cultures.

Throughout the post-war period, Australian politicians and bureaucrats anxiously monitored the numbers of aliens who became Australian citizens and attempted to understand why many chose to retain their former nationalities. Considerable manpower and funds were directed into surveys, citizenship campaigns, and into devising strategies to promote Australian citizenship. The driving force behind this activity was not economic. Except for a few highly skilled workers who were debarred on the grounds of nationality from practising their professions, the productivity of post-war migrant workers was unrelated to their citizenship status. Neither was it political. Despite the arguments of some Labor politicians convinced that government was refusing citizenship to migrants it knew would never vote for it, the numbers of left-wing migrants excluded on 'security' grounds were so small as to be politically insignificant in elections. The motivation was primarily cultural. Acceptance of Australian citizenship by aliens was seen as an indicator of successful assimilation—of their social, political and cultural absorption into the mainstream community. In order to encourage this process the government gradually eased the requirements demanded of aliens seeking citizenship. In 1954 and 1962 it removed most of the obstacles caused by the complexities and insensitivities of the application procedures. In 1966 Liberal politician Sir Keith Wilson argued for further simplifications—the reduction of the residential qualifying period for citizenship from five years to one or two, and the abandonment of the English language requirement on the grounds that 'we want to build an integrated Australian nation in which all people, or substantially all, are Australian citizens. We should not, therefore, have any unnecessary barriers on the obtainment of Australian citizenship'.[7]

As the Department of Immigration believed that the reluctance of aliens to abandon their original citizenship status was caused by their ignorance of the benefits of Australian citizenship, it channelled much of its efforts into strategies designed to disseminate information on citizenship. For each migrant, however, the decision to relinquish his or her former nationality involved a calculation of costs and benefits which was only slowly understood by Australian bureaucrats and politicians. Many who came to Australia as refugees long cherished the dream of returning when things improved in their homeland. Others had contributed to pensions which they would lose on becoming Australian citizens, or wished to retain the option of retiring to a country whose language, institutions and customs were familiar. For many, the costs of relinquishing their former citizenship were obvious, and the benefits of attaining Australian citizenship remained obscure. They did not understand the political system in which they found themselves, and could not comprehend why they were required to take an oath of allegiance to the British monarch before they could become Australian citizens. For many migrants, the requirement that they renounce their former allegiance was either a psychological disincentive to acquiring Australian citizenship or completely meaningless, as the laws of many countries did not allow them to relinquish their citizenship. As their needs were often ignored by local and

State governments, and only a few Federal politicians actively intervened on behalf of aliens who could not vote for them, many had no practical understanding of Australian political processes.

Those whose command of English was a barrier to accessing educational, health welfare or legal services to which they were entitled, or who had been barred from practising trades or professions for which they were qualified, tended to believe that nothing much would change even if they did become Australian citizens. The introduction of conscription for aliens in 1967 during the Vietnam War conferred on them what was generally perceived to be one of the major responsibilities of citizenship, whether or not they wanted to become naturalised. It was only after mainstream culture and institutions had undergone considerable readjustment that many migrants felt able to make the psychological commitment involved in accepting Australian citizenship.

ADMINISTRATIVE RESPONSES TO ALIEN NON-COMPLIANCE 1952–73

Research

Believing that 'a high rate of naturalisation would be evidence of the success of our immigration policies', in November 1952 Secretary of the Department of Immigration T.H.E. Heyes launched his Department on its long and somewhat fruitless process of monitoring compliance with the citizenship 'bargain'. In effect, this was an attempt to quantify the success of the government's policy of assimilation. His officers were set the task of devising methods for calculating the numbers of aliens who did not become Australian citizens, of assessing their reasons for non-compliance, and of devising strategies to promote citizenship. The failure of large numbers of aliens to manifest their contentment with Australian society by applying for citizenship had already inspired considerable concern in Parliament and some hostility in the popular press and in the Returned Soldiers', Sailors' and Airmen's Imperial League of Australia (RSSAILA).[8]

The Department estimated that by 1952, although approximately 180 000 adult migrants had been in Australia long enough to make a declaration of intention to become citizens, only 29 000 had done so. Although reminded by the Department,

75 per cent of the 29 000 who had signalled their interest in becoming citizens by lodging such a declaration had not applied for naturalisation when they became eligible. Of the declarations lodged in the first quarter of 1953, 70 per cent were by displaced persons, over half of whom had delayed their application until they had been in Australia over three years. In May 1953 Commonwealth Migration Officers (CMOs) in all States were asked to conduct a random survey of recently eligible migrants to discover what was deterring them from applying for citizenship.[9]

Although based on only a few interviews, the replies suggested some important reasons. The CMO in South Australia, who had addressed a number of 'national groups' on the advantages of naturalisation, believed that many refugees cherished the hope of returning to their homelands when the political order of Europe changed. He also pointed to perceptions among migrants of unfairness and discrimination in the allotment of housing and employment, and their belief that this would not be changed by naturalisation. Like his colleagues in Central Office he believed that migrants' lack of knowledge and 'lethargy' were important factors. The Melbourne office pointed to difficulties migrants found in filling in the documentation required, and Brisbane reported that a Czechoslovak was deterred by the requirement that the names of applicants for citizenship be publicly advertised, fearing reprisals against his family in Czechoslovakia. The director of the Holding Centre in Cowra, New South Wales, told the Department in 1954 that most of the camp residents who had been in Australia over three years had not applied for naturalisation. Displaced persons feared conscription for military service and that the government would not allow their Australian-born children, who were British subjects, to leave the country if they decided to return to Europe. Although Heyes recognised that the language requirement was an obstacle to the naturalisation of aged migrants, particularly women, he was reluctant to recommend that this requirement be waived. English was important to assimilation, he argued, and older aliens should be deterred from coming to Australia just to receive the age pension.[10]

In 1954 the Department of Immigration surveyed all its migrant accommodation centres in order to discover why they did not apply for citizenship. Out of more than 2000 aliens who had been in the Department's nine centres for over two years, only 128 gave reasons for not applying for citizenship. Most (70) said they intended to apply, 44 gave no reason, six said they lacked incentive and five intended to leave Australia.[11]

Reform of administrative procedures 1955–62

Simplification of application procedures
Migrants' compliance with the government's expectation that they become Australian citizens was probably deterred by the initial complexity of procedural requirements. Citizenship could be applied for only after five years' residence in Australia and two years after making a 'Declaration of Intention to Apply for Naturalisation'. In October 1953, Assistant Secretary H. McGinness questioned the need for the latter requirement, and both the Citizenship Convention and the Opposition in 1954 recommended its deletion. It was abolished in May 1955, although its abolition did not produce any noticeable increase in applications.[12]

Migrants were required to advertise their intention to become citizens in two newspapers in the district in which they lived, so that objections could be lodged by people who knew them. In 1954 the Opposition argued that the cost of this (approximately £10), on top of the £5 naturalisation fee, discouraged some applicants. In the past 36 years fewer than six protests had been made against applicants for British subject status in Australia (before 1949) or for Australian citizenship (after January 1949). It described the requirement as 'vexatious and futile' and 'an unnecessary singling out in the community, as an alien, of a person who is on the threshold of becoming a citizen'. It also recommended the abolition of the fee for citizenship. The 1954 Citizenship Convention recommended that these advertisements be abandoned. The government accepted these arguments and in 1955 abolished the requirement for advertisements and reduced the fee for the certificates of naturalisation from £5 to £1. 'Citizenship is something that should be earned and not bought', the Minister explained. Although it retained the requirement for applicants for citizenship to produce character references, it extended the categories of persons eligible to supply them to executive officers in Good Neighbour Councils and New Settlers' Leagues. In 1959 the fee for naturalisation was abolished.[13]

In 1962, 244 972 aliens were eligible to apply for citizenship, and their failure to do so was raised in both Houses of Parliament. Migrants were again surveyed to discover their reasons for not applying. It was concluded that the two main reasons were the result of administrative requirements—the forms were too difficult for non-English speakers to complete, and many migrants could not obtain the required certificates of character from Australian citizens who had known them at least a year. Senator J.F. Fitzgerald (ALP NSW) cited recent correspondence in newspapers and articles, which described the approaches to migrants from the Department of Immigration as 'cold', and referred to the fear experienced by many migrants on receiving official letters. The forms were simplified, and new procedures introduced which not only made the process easier for the applicant but reduced the cost to the Department of monitoring applicants. Much correspondence and the need for second interviews were eliminated. These reforms did result in increased applications.[14]

In 1966 Labor politician and founder of the Australian–Italian Association of Western Australia, Richard Cleaver, proudly compared the simplicity of Australian administrative requirements with the complexity of those in the USA and Canada. However, Minister for Immigration Hubert Opperman warned against making the process too easy. If the language requirements were eliminated or the residence requirement shortened, he feared the grant of citizenship to migrants might be perceived by the general public as lax and their acceptance of the immigration program endangered.[15]

Renunciation of former allegiance

In 1917 the Australian government had enacted legislation that required that aliens renounce all former allegiances before being granted British subject status in Australia. This wartime precaution was dropped from legislation in 1921, but subsequently retained as an administrative requirement. The effect of this requirement appears to have been largely misunderstood, for example by the Leader of the Senate, Senator Keane, who in 1945 mistakenly informed his parliamentary colleagues that 'the laws of most countries provide that a citizen who takes the oath of allegiance to a foreign power loses his rights of citizenship of his country'. In fact, the legal effect of this requirement on the original citizenship of aliens becoming Australian citizens varied widely. For some it meant automatic loss of their former citizenship, for others it had no effect at all, as the citizenship laws of their country of origin either required further steps before citizenship could be relinquished or did not allow their citizens to divest themselves of their citizenship. Its necessity was questioned only in the 1960s as the result of a better appreciation among some parliamentarians of ethnic minorities and of the migration experience.[16]

Migrants accepting Australian citizenship were expected to be loyal to Australia. Initially, to many Australians this was synonymous with loyalty to Britain. Complaining in 1950 that Union Jacks were not supplied at naturalisation ceremonies, Liberal parliamentarian W.R. Lawrence urged that at these ceremonies 'the love and attachment that we have for the mother country should be stressed emphatically . . . migrants should be encouraged to forget their national prejudices and contentions'.[17]

By the early 1960s, parliamentarians from both major political parties were beginning to appreciate the difficulties renunciation of former allegiance posed for many migrants. The arguments employed between 1961 and 1966 by Senator Buttfield (Liberal SA), Senator G.S. Davidson (Liberal SA), Senator N.H. Henty (Leader of the government in the Senate), Tasmanian Labor Senator J.H. O'Byrne, Senator J.F. Fitzgerald (Labor NSW), and in the House of Representatives Labor member Keith Jones and F.M. Daly, Chairman of the Opposition Committee on Immigration, displayed considerable understanding of the legal and emotional complexities involved in the requirement. There was also pressure from outside Parliament. In 1963 and 1965 the IAC recommended the deletion of the renunciation requirement, and a number of prominent religious and other mainstream community leaders spoke against it at the 1965 Citizenship Convention.[18]

Despite these pressures, in 1966 the government actually strengthened the requirement by incorporating the renunciation into the oath of allegiance to the Queen. Opperman explained that this shortened form would 'eliminate the emotional disturbance felt by candidates due to their natural and rightful love of their homelands'. Labor vainly opposed the amendment, arguing that the legislation did not require renunciation of former allegiance and that the oath was a far more onerous form of renunciation than was the previous statement. A Department of Immigration survey conducted in 1971 found that this requirement was a deterrent to citizenship applications. Even after coming to power in late 1972, the Labor government was unsuccessful in its attempt to abolish the requirement. Despite the unanimous support of the IAC's Committee on Citizenship, the government's Bill to remove it was twice rejected in the Senate in 1973, and it was not excised from the oath of allegiance until 20 August 1986.[19]

Disseminating Information and Promoting Citizenship

Within the senior ranks of the Department of Immigration it was initially assumed that the failure of migrants to apply for citizenship was the result of their ignorance and apathy. It was, therefore, a problem to be solved by the provision and dissemination of information, and through friendly discussions between migrants, its officers, and members of the Good Neighbour Movement. More active efforts were opposed by some senior officers, who feared that the Department would appear to be 'selling' citizenship. By July 1953, the Department had extended its publicity efforts on citizenship to ethnic and provincial newspapers, as well as to 'national groups'. Most foreign-language newspapers cooperated. Their attitudes varied from tacit approval, indicated by fairly neutral accounts of naturalisation ceremonies without comment, to more obvious approval and direct advice to migrants to seek naturalisation. Changes in the *Nationality and Citizenship Act* were often reported by migrant newspapers.[20]

The Department's failure to understand the impact of discriminatory legislation on the practical lives of non-British migrants was revealed by its pamphlet 'This is how you can help someone to become an Australian citizen', 50 000 copies of which had been circulated by March 1953. It listed one of the benefits of citizenship as: 'You are eligible for ALL social service benefits'. When the Good Neighbour Council of Melbourne complained that this was misleading as, apart from the citizenship requirement there were lengthy residency requirements, its complaint was dismissed as unimportant.[21]

In 1956 the Department calculated that only 77 670 (35.2 per cent) of the 220 380 aliens who were registered in June 1951 had applied to become citizens. Although uncertain how other countries compiled their statistics, it compared this with application rates for citizenship in the United Kingdom (6.5 per cent), New Zealand (20.1 per cent), Canada (45 per cent), and the United States (31.1 per cent). It argued that Australia was 'well ahead of the UK and New Zealand and practically on par with Canada'.

It incorporated this somewhat questionable conclusion into the Minister's speech to the 1957 Citizenship Convention.[22]

Public criticism of naturalisation rates in the 1950s

Although the annual naturalisation rate had increased dramatically from under 2000 in 1950–53 to over 20 000 in 1955 and more than 41 000 in 1957, complaints by the Opposition, the media and vocal mainstream organisations constantly spurred the Department of Immigration to further efforts. When articles appeared in the Sydney press in November 1955 alleging that many migrants refused to become Australians, would not 'have any truck with the Australian way of life', and 'did their utmost to bind their children with old national ties', the Department suggested to its Minister, Harold Holt, that he respond publicly, as it regarded such statements as anti-migrant propaganda. Holt refused.[23]

In 1958 the government's failure to encourage more aliens to become citizens drew criticism from important mainstream organisations. The RSSAILA demanded an inquiry into the failure of aliens to apply for citizenship, alleging that many of them sent money home in preparation for leaving Australia. At its annual conference that year, a resolution was moved by the New South Wales representatives urging the government to ask eligible migrants to state their reasons for not applying for naturalisation. The Associated Chamber of Manufactures of Australia also intervened, claiming that two-thirds of eligible migrants were not naturalised and that they enjoyed the privileges but shirked the responsibilities of citizenship, especially the defence of Australia in times of national emergency. It urged employers to encourage them to become Australians as soon as possible. In September that year Minister for Immigration Alexander Downer firmly rejected a suggestion by Country Party member Winston Turnbull that migrants should be required to apply for citizenship by a specified period as a condition of entry to Australia. In Parliament, Western Australian Senators Agnes Robertson (Country Party) and G.H. Branson (Liberal) warned of the dangers to Australia of having large numbers of aliens of questionable loyalty.[24]

While largely drowned out by more powerful voices, at least one migrant contributed another perspective to the debate. In 1959, a Greek-language newspaper *The Torch* reported a speech by F.F. Wheener, public relations officer of the All Nations Club,

Sydney. Wheener, a naturalised Australian from Czechoslovakia, pointed to the failure of government and private enterprise to employ migrants in administrative positions. Trade unions had refused them membership, they were never found in the senior ranks of the Public Service or in managerial positions in insurance companies, banks or heavy industry, and they were to be found on none of the industrial boards, he complained. One-tenth of the Australian population was treated as 'second-class citizens', he concluded.[25]

Letters of invitation to aliens 1956–65

In 1956, after some internal debate, the Department accepted a recommendation of the 1954 Citizenship Convention that all aliens should be advised by letter when they were eligible to apply for citizenship. Some officers still feared the Department would appear to be 'hawking' citizenship, and that the effort involved in contacting approximately 376 000 registered aliens would not be cost-effective. Its main strategy by 1956 had been to distribute reply-paid cards in five main migrant languages inviting expressions of interest and its pamphlet directed at Australians in contact with migrants—'How to help someone become an Australian'. In 1957, the letter of invitation was distributed to both male and female aliens in all States who had been in Australia four and a half years. It was not sent to non-Europeans, or to those who had convictions for offences punishable by sentences of six or more months. It pointed out that they were eligible for naturalisation, told them how to apply, and explained that they might lose their original nationality but would become Australian citizens and British nationals. The results were disappointing: only one-quarter of those contacted requested forms.[26]

Subsequently, letters were sent only as aliens became eligible for naturalisation. By February 1958, 48 549 letters had been distributed and an estimated 100 000 aliens remained to be contacted. Despite these efforts, the number of citizenship applications lodged in 1957 fell by 8 per cent. Heyes saw the problem as one caused by lack of information and poor communication, not as a response to discrimination. 'It is not considered that the recent allegations by certain groups of discrimination against naturalised Australians had any marked effect, if any effect at all, on the position', he wrote.[27]

In 1959 the annual naturalisation rate had grown from 4781

in 1953 to 52 000. The Department believed that by June 1959 approximately 206 000 alien migrants had been naturalised, and about the same number were eligible but had not applied. Alexander Downer launched another citizenship drive with the statement that 'Acceptance of citizenship is the aim of our migration program and of all our very considerable efforts to aid the assimilation of migrants'.[28]

By 1959 it was clear that many European refugees had abandoned their earlier hopes of returning home. The groups with the highest percentage of citizenship applications came from communist countries, with Hungarians leading at 62 per cent, and applications from Czechoslovaks, Romanians, Russians, Ukrainians, Latvians and Estonians all exceeding 60 per cent. Apart from Britain, the largest numbers of migrants came from Holland, Italy and Germany. Of the numbers eligible from these countries, 47.2 per cent, 42.4 per cent and 36 per cent respectively became Australian citizens. By 1960 the Department had arrived at a fairly accurate formula for assessing the numbers of eligible migrants who failed to apply for citizenship. By June 1960 it estimated that 52.22 per cent of eligible aliens had applied for citizenship, leaving 215 622 who had not. Statistics of applications by gender were not provided until January 1963.[29]

In 1962 the government began yet another campaign to promote citizenship. It distributed to eligible migrants application forms with a reply-paid envelope accompanied by a personal letter from the Minister for Immigration. It also enclosed a pamphlet and poster directed both at migrants and at Australians in a position to explain to migrants the benefits of citizenship. It initiated a survey which it was hoped would provide information on the reasons eligible migrants did not apply for citizenship. Its results were not made public. In 1965 letters were sent to aliens who had been in Australia seven years without applying for citizenship, in addition to the usual letters to those who had been in Australia four and a half years.[30]

Involving community leaders—ethnic and mainstream

In 1962 the government created the Immigration Publicity Council, a body which it hoped would improve its ability to communicate with aliens. Chaired by J.R. Darling, former headmaster of Geelong Grammar School and now chairman of the Australian

Broadcasting Commission, its function was to advise the Minister on all public relations aspects of the immigration program, and to assist with the integration of migrants into the Australian community. It was also to inform the Australian public on immigration policy, programs and procedures. The committee included A. Schuurman of the *Dutch–Australian Weekly*, Dr Costanzo of the Italian newspaper *La Fiamona*, J. Dunin-Karwicki of the *Polish News* and A. Sourdin of the French *Le Courier*. In 1965 the Council suggested that the Department of Immigration replace its letters inviting aliens to become citizens by advertisements in foreign-language newspapers. The Department decided instead to supplement its letter with such advertisements.[31]

During the 1950s the Department had enlisted the cooperation of all Rotary Clubs in Australia and of the Good Neighbour Council of Victoria in distributing its promotional material. General Motors Holden allowed an officer of the Department to address its employees during their lunch hour; other firms employing large numbers of migrants were not so cooperative. The Department employed a wide range of strategies to encourage aliens to take up Australian citizenship—country tours by naturalisation officers, posters, window displays, pamphlets, migrant English classes, advertising in picture theatres and newspapers, and radio broadcasts. The Secretary looked to his senior officers in the States to provide further suggestions. Most felt by 1957 that they had exhausted all avenues. The Department was still puzzled by what it believed to be lagging citizenship applications.[32]

Non-Compliance with the *Aliens Act* in 1965

The various letter-writing campaigns conducted by the Department of Immigration disclosed widespread non-compliance with the *Aliens Act 1947*. This legislation limited the civil rights of aliens by requiring them to notify the Department of changes to their address, occupation and marital status. In Melbourne, the Aliens Index was overhauled when it was discovered that 52.7 per cent of the 2000 circulars in a 1957 pilot survey had been sent to inaccurate addresses. In New South Wales, 20 per cent of aliens sent letters had not notified the Department of changes to their address as required. In 1963 the Department breached the privacy requirements of the *Aliens Act* in its anxiety to enlist the services of NSW Apex Clubs in its citizenship campaign. Apex abandoned the campaign by July 1965, as many of the names and addresses it had been given from the Aliens Index were inaccurate, causing a considerable waste of its time. George Pridannikoff, an officer who worked in the Aliens Registration Section of the Brisbane office of the Department of Immigration in the 1960s, expressed his view that the registration of aliens was 'an absolute waste of time and resources'.[33]

This widespread non-compliance was acknowledged by the government in 1965 when it amended the Act to require aliens to notify it annually of changes in their address, marital status and occupation, instead of within a fixed period after these changes had occurred. The Opposition doubted that this procedural change would improve compliance, particularly as the government did not intend to notify aliens of their obligation in languages other than English. The Minister for Immigration, Hubert Opperman, rather optimistically hoped that with the aid of English-speaking friends 'the message will get about'. However the change did improve compliance. By April 1966, the Opposition spokesman Mr Daly admitted that as a result of this change between 85 and 90 per cent of all aliens required to register had done so.[34]

Reduced Incentives to Take Up Citizenship from 1965

On 11 November 1964 the government introduced a scheme that required all 20-year-old Australian citizens and British subjects to register for conscription. If balloted in they had to serve two years in the army, and from 1965 they were liable to be sent into combat in Vietnam. As aliens were initially excluded from this scheme, increased popular pressure was placed on the government to encourage non-British migrants to take up citizenship. The 1965 Citizenship Convention recommended that all migrants who had been in Australia over ten years should be automatically recognised as Australian citizens. This was supported by J.F. Fitzgerald (ALP NSW), who pointed to the current exemption of aliens from conscription, adding: 'They enjoy such benefits as social services and industrial award conditions, but we believe that they should accept the responsibilities of citizenship as well'. The government, however, rejected automatic citizenship on the grounds that it was a privilege and an honour which should be sought. Eligibility for conscription was hardly an incentive to take up citizenship and probably served as a deterrent, particularly in the context of an increasingly prosperous Europe. A survey of 135 aliens and 137 naturalised migrants who had been in Australia at least six years, conducted by the Department of Immigration in 1965, revealed that about one-third were still undecided about staying in Australia, particularly the Germans, Austrians and Dutch. Most surveyed cared little about Australian citizenship and saw no real advantage in it. As Senator K.M. Anderson explained, 'A number of migrants indicated that their parents and speech brand them indelibly as migrants and that, irrespective of whether they became naturalised, they would still continue to be regarded as migrants'. The government responded to this general lack of interest in 1965 by appointing Naturalisation Promotion Officers in New South Wales and Victoria to liaise with migrant groups, Good Neighbour Councils, employer, employee and other organisations concerned with migrants. The government hoped that these officers would be able to persuade employers to allow naturalisation interviews in the workplace.[35]

In 1966 one of the major incentives to become a citizen disappeared when a permanent resident in Australia no longer needed to be an Australian citizen to be eligible for age, invalid or widows' pension. The Department of Immigration then began employing citizenship caravans, which travelled around regional areas and shopping centres. Late-night citizenship interviews were held in most capital cities. Despite accompanying newspaper and radio publicity, the results were universally disappointing. By 1970, the Department estimated that there were 208 230 aliens over the age of sixteen in Australia who had not applied for citizenship although residentially qualified. Annual naturalisation figures in South Australia had steadily fallen from a peak of 59 000 in 1956 to 1900 in 1971. Naturalisations Australia-wide for the second half of 1971 had dropped from about 35 000 a year in the 1960s to 12 579, and it was calculated that post-war migrants waited an average of 9.1 years before applying. Greeks, Italians and Yugoslavs were the largest groups granted citizenship, with Germans, Dutch and Poles well behind. Only a small proportion of eligible British migrants in Australia applied for citizenship.[36]

The Survey Section of the Department of Immigration continued to monitor migrant opinion in the hope of discovering reasons for the lack of interest in taking up Australian citizenship. A 1971 survey disclosed that some aliens were not aware that the nationality requirement had been removed for pensions, and still regarded social security benefits as the main advantage to becoming citizens. Few valued the right to vote. Most surveyed saw few disadvantages to being naturalised, but the objection most commonly referred to was the loss of their own nationality and of pension rights in their own country. Of those who commented adversely on the rights and obligations of citizenship, most said that the 'rights' accruing to naturalisation were of little practical value, that it was difficult to accept the need to swear allegiance to a non-resident English monarch, or that they found it difficult explicitly to renounce their country of birth.[37]

THE IMMIGRATION (EDUCATION) ACT 1971

This Act was intended to provide Commonwealth funding for the development of English language courses for adult and child migrants both before and after their entry to Australia, and for the Australian-born children of migrants. It also provided funding for citizenship courses, which would give adults and children 'an understanding of the rights and duties of an Australian citizen and the way of living of the Australian people'. This intervention by the Commonwealth in the education of migrant children, normally a State responsibility, was inspired by political pressures created by perceptions that the State governments were neglecting the educational needs of children from non-English speaking families. The language needs of migrant children therefore dominated the agenda, and citizenship education was not mentioned in the second-reading speech when the Bill was presented to Parliament. It was only rarely referred to during the lengthy debate that followed, and then only with considerable suspicion. At the height of opposition to the government's military involvement in Vietnam and conscription, Dr R.E. Klugman (ALP NSW), foundation member of the NSW Council for Civil Liberties, expressed his hope that citizenship education would not become military indoctrination. In fact, the funding provided by the Act was used solely for language teaching, and the idea of citizenship education for migrants and their children was never pursued.[38]

The implementation of the Act by the Department of Immigration clearly demonstrated its priorities. No thought was given to communicating the meaning of Australian citizenship to native-born Australians. The practical needs created by the migration program were uppermost, and ultimately the neglected language needs of migrant children completely supplanted any perceived need to explain to them or their parents the nature of the society to which they belonged.

Conclusion

Because responsibility for administering Australia's citizenship legislation was given to a relatively small department, whose other main responsibility was managing the enormously varied demands of a program of mass migration, Australian citizenship was thought about solely in relation to migrants. The assumption, shared by both the general community and the government, that the attainment of Australian citizenship was the final step in the process of assimilation and that citizenship statistics were therefore measurable indicators of the ultimate success of the immigration program, inspired the Department's constant search for effective ways to promote Australian citizenship to aliens.

While the Department managed its citizenship caseload, processing applications for Australian citizenship and determining who had forfeited it, it gave no thought to what citizenship might mean for those Australians, including Aboriginal Australians, who had attained their citizenship by being born in the country. The notion of Australian national identity as being culturally and ethnically British also meant that the Department neglected to target British migrants in its various citizenship campaigns. Most British subjects who came to Australia after 26 January 1944 did not automatically become Australian citizens, but because they had most of the rights and responsibilities of Australian citizenship, including the right to vote and the obligation to be conscripted, large numbers of British subjects in Australia erroneously believed they were Australian citizens.

Because they were unable to conceive of Australian citizenship as being anything other than full participation in an essentially British society, the officers of the Department who planned and participated in its citizenship campaigns were unable either to present the advantages of Australian citizenship in a way that would be attractive to an increasingly diverse ethnic community, or to understand the ethnic community's lack of interest in attaining citizenship. For this reason, the attempts of the Department of Immigration to promote Australian citizenship among non-British migrants by the early 1970s were largely ineffective.

CHAPTER 9

Towards a more equal citizenship 'bargain'

OVER 30 years, the presence of large numbers of non-British migrants in Australia slowly eroded the conception of Australian citizenship from a status based on British ethnicity and culture to one based on equality of rights and responsibilities. Although the Australian government was never interested in attracting 'guest workers', and expected both those it assisted to come to Australia and those who paid their own passage to remain permanently and to assimilate into Australian culture and society, until 1973 alien and British migrants were offered very different citizenship 'bargains'.

British migrants could exercise all the civil, social and political rights and the responsibilities normally associated with citizenship. Aliens were offered only a partial 'package' of these rights, with the promise of full rights once they renounced their former allegiance and became Australian citizens. Until then, their ability to participate in Australian public life was limited by a range of discriminatory Commonwealth and State legislation. Those wanting to migrate who were deemed unable to assimilate into a white, Anglo-Celtic Australia were excluded by racially discriminatory selection procedures. Those who passed the initial screening process but were subsequently found to be unassimilable were deported or repatriated.

Politicians, bureaucrats, and some mainstream spokesmen

during the 1950s assumed that aliens had entered into a form of unwritten citizenship 'bargain'. Regarded as potential citizens, they were granted partial access to the benefits available to Australian citizens, and in return they were expected to learn English and apply for the full 'responsibilities and privileges' of citizenship after they had been in Australia five years. By this time, it was assumed, aliens would have absorbed the prevailing culture. This notion, held by Australians of all political persuasions, was stated particularly clearly by Labor Senator Patrick Kennelly. Disturbed by the small numbers of migrants applying for citizenship in 1956, he remarked:[1]

> If a person from another country takes Australia as his country of adoption he has a responsibility to us, as we have to him. Our responsibility is to help the immigrant as much as we can by working with the Good Neighbour Councils to break down any class or race prejudices that we may have. We say to the immigrant, 'Conditions here are good. These conditions were not lightly won. We expect you to do the right thing. If you do, you will be one of us'. We expect him to show that he wants to become one of us by acknowledging Australia as his country.

The persistence of the conception of Australia as culturally and ethnically British was reflected in the government's lack of interest in getting British migrants, who also did not have Australian citizenship, to apply for it. Citizenship was made particularly easy to obtain for British migrants: they were permitted to apply for citizenship after only one year in Australia and not required to attend citizenship ceremonies. Although the government progressively made the application processes simple for aliens and had had considerable success in absorbing migrants into the economy, it was puzzled by the failure of large numbers of aliens to signal their satisfaction with the 'bargain' offered them by accepting Australian citizenship. Lacking an understanding of minority cultures and of the experience of migration, most Australians regarded assimilation as a relatively straightforward process. The legislative and systemic discrimination that sustained Australians' notions of national identity was largely invisible to them.[2]

By the late 1960s, however, authorities perceived that the bargaining position of aliens had improved. The economic prosperity created by the European Economic Community (EEC) had made temporary intra-European migration economically more attractive than permanent dislocation to faraway Australia. Even more alarmingly, statistics of those leaving Australia permanently suggested that Europe was attracting back the migrant workers on which Australia had built its industrial growth and economic prosperity. The rights and conditions offered by the EEC to its guest workers raised the expectations of those who did decide to emigrate to Australia, and forced guarantees of equality and a broader 'package' of citizenship rights to be spelt out in migration agreements. The Australia–Yugoslav Migration Agreement of 1970, for example, stated that 'The Yugoslav authorities and the Australian authorities shall co-operate in the activities which may facilitate the adjustment of Yugoslav workers and their families to their new environment in Australia'.[3]

Clauses like this in other international agreements strengthened the hand of the Department of Immigration in its efforts from the 1970s to persuade government departments to make their services accessible to migrants, particularly through the provision of interpreters and information in translation. The perception that aliens were in a stronger bargaining position served to shift the government's focus from the 'benefits and privileges' of British subject status to the 'rights and responsibilities' conferred by citizenship on all Australians without distinction by 1973. Only then did discrimination become clearly visible.

British Migrants and Australian Citizenship 1949–73

Initially, Australia was seen by almost all Australians as a British country, and some conservative politicians opposed the introduction of a separate Australian citizenship because they saw it as a threat to the British character of Australian society. Sir Eric Harrison, a Liberal politician who became Australian High Commissioner in London from 1956 to 1964, described the Act in November 1948 as part of 'a sinister plan—to liquidate the British Empire'. To Sir Josiah Francis it was 'pulling down the Union Jack'. Country Party politician Sir John McEwan believed that 'when the British people took steps to separate into different nationalities, it was a black day in their history'.[4]

Both major political parties recognised that there were few advantages to British migrants to taking up Australian citizenship, and because of their shared conception of Australian national identity neither party expected them to apply. In launching his citizenship campaign in 1959, Minister for Immigration Alexander Downer described citizenship for aliens as 'a prize which they must earn, and which they should try to achieve as a coveted honour'. However, his Department had no interest in getting British migrants to become Australian citizens. When asked the previous year what advantages there were for British migrants in becoming Australian citizens, Downer had admitted that there were none. British migrants were not expected to participate in any citizenship 'bargain'—their compliance was assumed. Labor spokesmen at this time reserved their criticism for the government's failure to persuade more aliens to take up citizenship. They did not contest its cultural values. As former journalist and Labor spokesman Leslie Haylen told the House in 1956:[5]

> I know it is the aim of the Australian people generally to preserve their national character . . . There are no great problems here for British immigrants . . . For them assimilation into the Australian way of life is like walking from one room to another. They give us no enduring problems in settling into this country, because they are some of us and because they are the most desirable immigrants of all . . . The Australian, following a century and a half of consolidation, is in general a good type. He stems from English, Scots, and Irish stock and the almost imperceptible change that will be wrought by this influx of immigrants . . . is something that we must consider on racial and ethnic grounds . . . Screening . . . is an important matter.

Although by 1964 there were an estimated 470000 British migrants in Australia who had not applied for citizenship, and only 3000–4000 annually had applied between 1962 and 1965, this was not a cause for concern to government. Labor Senator L.K. Murphy was the first to take up this issue. He warned the government that British migrants assumed that as they had the right to vote they were Australian citizens, and urged the Department of Immigration to make more active efforts to disabuse them of this view. As Senator K.M. Anderson pointed out in both 1964 and 1965, British migrants had all the rights and privileges of Australians and had no real incentive to seek Australian citizenship except access to an Australian passport.[6]

In 1966 Minister for Immigration Hubert Opperman made an important distinction. He drew attention to the difference between the aspect of citizenship that preoccupied his Department and citizenship as a reflection of national identity, an aspect with which it did not concern itself. The *Nationality and*

Citizenship Act, he told Parliament, was 'fundamental to our national status and from it stem the concept of Australian citizenship as well as the rules under which our citizenship may be acquired'. This perception did nothing to redirect his Department's attention from its practical task of processing casework to the more esoteric question of national identity.[7]

Labor's changed vision 1973

By 1973 the imagined community of Australians underpinning Labor's citizenship policies had become totally different from that of its Liberal predecessors. Labor abandoned the conception of Australia as a country of predominantly British ethnicity and culture, and promoted the conception of Australia as a 'multicultural' society. It clearly identified systemic discrimination as the principal cause of the failure of migrants to become Australian citizens. In 1973 the new Labor Minister for Immigration, A.J. Grassby, claimed that approximately 1 million migrants had not taken out Australian citizenship because they 'felt discriminated against by the previous government'. He created a new division within his Department in July 1973 which combined citizenship with settlement. This signalled a new recognition of the interrelationship between the post-arrival experiences of migrants and their desire to participate fully in Australian society, and drew an important distinction between the formal status of citizenship and the practical social and political participation normally associated with citizenship.[8]

Grassby succeeded where an earlier Minister, B.M. Snedden, had failed, in having the term 'naturalisation' removed from the terminology of his Department and replaced by 'citizenship'. This removed the distinction between British and other Commonwealth migrants, who were required merely to register as Australian citizens, and aliens, who were 'naturalised'. In 1973, for the first time, British migrants were made the primary target of a Department of Immigration citizenship campaign. The following year they were required for the first time to attend citizenship ceremonies. On the instruction of Prime Minister E.G. Whitlam, the Chief Electoral Officer began drafting a submission to Cabinet recommending the removal of the right to vote from British non-citizens. It was not, however, until 25 January 1984 that British and Irish non-citizens became ineligible to vote in Australian elections; those on the electoral role by that date retained this right. By 1975, over 822 000 of the post-war alien intake of approximately 1.7 million had become Australian citizens.[9]

Through these changes the Commonwealth government signalled the beginning of a reconceptualisation of Australian national identity as being other than British. It was an imagined community which now included non-British migrants, Asians and Aborigines. The term 'British subject status' was finally removed from the *Australian Citizenship Act* in 1984.

Removing the Unassimilable 1950–69

In attempting to identify and remove those who could not or would not comply with expectations that they would assimilate, the Department's attention was inevitably drawn to deficiencies both in its own selection procedures and in the management of social problems in the community in general. One of the first problems disclosed resulted from the assumption that the compliance of British migrants with Australian requirements could be assumed, and did not have to be monitored as carefully as that of aliens.

Inadequate British character and health checking 1950–56

The Australian government had initiated immigration from Britain without establishing any mechanism for character checking. British applicants for assisted passages were required merely to provide two character references, which initially were not checked. In May 1950 the CMO in Hobart drew the Secretary's attention to the numbers of British migrants with criminal records who were arriving in his State. Heyes immediately instructed the London office to check references of applicants for assisted passages. He considered it impractical to refer all applicants to Scotland Yard. As British migrants did not need visas there was no way of checking the character of those who arrived unassisted.[10]

The following year the Queensland Premier expressed to the Prime Minister his 'strong doubts' about the efficacy of both the character and medical checking of British migrants. He supplied a list of British migrants in his State who had been convicted of criminal offences, or who had been found to be medically unsound soon after arrival. One woman had died of tuberculosis on the voyage to Australia, and two other migrants were hospitalised with the same disease immediately on arrival. Heyes admitted that, because of the lack of facilities, applicants had only recently begun to be x-rayed. Criminal records in Britain, he maintained, could not be checked. The Premier subsequently requested the right to demand the repatriation of migrants without further investigation. Heyes insisted that the responsibility for deporting or repatriating migrants lay with the Commonwealth, but added that the States could recommend deportation. The dictation test could be used on those who would not return voluntarily, he informed the Premier. In 1953 Attorney General Senator J.A. Spicer assured several senators who queried the adequacy of health screening procedures that x-ray examinations were conducted at both ends of the voyage. The government's decision to dispatch Sir Harry Wunderly, an Australian expert on tuberculosis, to inspect screening procedures in Britain and Europe in 1956 indicated its continued concern about the efficacy of medical checking.[11]

Deportation

As Minister for Immigration Harold Holt explained in December 1953, before being granted citizenship an applicant should have 'proved his worthiness to be accepted as a member of the community'. The standards against which migrants were assessed were, however, not clearly defined. They were strongly suspected by the Opposition to be influenced by prevailing government notions of political acceptability, and were not applied equally to all migrants.[12]

The government attempted to reduce the numbers of migrants who could not become Australian citizens by removing those it regarded as unassimilable. The legislation through which this was accomplished applied more stringent conditions to aliens than to British subjects. The deportation provisions of the *Migration Act 1958* discriminated between British and alien immigrants by providing the former with greater protection against deportation. Whereas British subjects could be deported for offences carrying certain penalties committed within five years of entry, aliens could be deported for almost any reason after any period in Australia, even after becoming citizens. As B.M. Snedden pointed out in 1958, a great percentage of immigrants from certain European countries would fall within the provisions of the *Crimes Act*, which allowed for deportation on the grounds that:[13]

> He is a person who advocated the overthrow by force or violence of the established government of the Commonwealth or of a State of any other civilised country or of all forms of law, or advocates the abolition of organised government or the assassination of public officials, or advocates or teaches the unlawful destruction of property or is a member of an organisation which entertains and teaches any of the doctrines and practices specified in this paragraph.

Although, under section 13 of the *Migration Act*, migrants who became inmates of a mental hospital or a charitable institution within five years of entry to Australia could be deported, in practice the process was humane. The mentally and physically ill were deported only in the rather unlikely event that it could be proved that they had 'knowingly and deceitfully' concealed their condition before emigration. More usually, they were deported only if it was considered to be in their best interests, and where there was family or an overseas agency prepared to receive them. If necessary an escort was provided, generally a nurse or doctor going to Europe for further study who had their passage paid by the Department of Immigration.[14]

It was not until 1958 that the government put in place procedures for deportation, notified the migrant of the grounds on which he or she was to be deported, and instituted an appeals mechanism. Between 1950 and June 1962, 2951 persons were deported. By far the largest number (1436) were deserting seamen; 914 were deported for criminal activities, 297 on the grounds of mental and physical illness, and 303 on 'other' grounds. Initially, no record was kept of the countries to which they had been returned; however, by 1971 the government was able to give a breakdown of deportees by nationality as well as reason for deportation.[15]

Repatriation

Repatriation had been carried out since the inception of post-war migration. The process was formalised by incorporation into the majority of bilateral agreements that had been negotiated from the early 1950s. It was mainly used in cases where assisted migrants were unable to settle for medical, socioeconomic or humanitarian reasons. Only rarely were unassisted migrants repatriated by the Australian government; they were more often assisted by their own diplomatic representatives in Australia. If repatriation occurred within two years of arrival, the requirement that assisted migrants who returned within this period repay their passage costs was waived. From 1960 to February 1972, 3609 persons were repatriated at a cost of approximately $1.4 million. Of these, 75 per cent were repatriated for medical reasons, 17 per cent for humanitarian reasons, and 8 per cent for socioeconomic reasons. Of the medical cases, 67 per cent comprised migrants with mental and personality disorders. The creation of the Integration Section in 1967 had led to a sharp increase in the number of migrants repatriated and consequently in expenditure on the service. Computer analysis of repatriation records in 1972 revealed that most repatriation applications had been made because of problems that originated after the migrant had arrived in Australia—largely relating to employment, medical conditions, disorientation, or their domestic or marital situations. The largest number of applications came from migrants from the United Kingdom and Yugoslavia, and most were single or married without children, and between the ages of 20 and 30.[16]

The attention given to migrant problems made possible by the creation of the Integration Branch within the Department of Immigration was intensified in 1968 by the completion of the report of the Immigration Advisory Council's Committee on Social Patterns on the departure of settlers from Australia. This study, commenced in May 1966, concluded that migrants' problems rarely derived from a single, identifiable cause, and that economic and employment difficulties were of less importance than personal and psychological ones. This focus on the migrant, and not on the systemic difficulties he or she faced, was reflected in a report produced by the Integration Branch in December 1968. Based on an analysis of 225 letters and repatriation requests handled by the Integration Section over four months in 1968, it blamed the 'personal and psychological inadequacies' of migrants for their employment difficulties, and their mental and psychological problems on their 'low intelligence'. The examples it gave from the over 63 per cent of applications for repatriation from British migrants suggested that they were attempting to exploit the system to get free trips home. British social security and health provisions, and employment conditions for manual labourers, were better in Britain, it pointed out.[17]

A 1969 analysis of Sicilian and Italian repatriations revealed that the Italian government had repatriated 476 of their nationals between 1967 and 1969, most of whom had been assisted migrants. The Department of Immigration had repatriated only 91. The Department subsequently studied 43 cases it had repatriated from an intake of Sicilian earthquake victims. This analysis, based on data supplied by a small committee convened by its Sydney office, which included a representative of the Good Neighbour Council and an Italian priest, pointed to systemic causes for their problems. Most applicants were unskilled or semiskilled workers with only one breadwinner. Of these, 30 per cent had difficulty supporting their families on the incomes available to them in Australia, 23 per cent were severely handicapped by medical costs, and 14 per cent had experienced lack of interest and help from officials in coping with problems arising from differences between Sicily and Australia in employment accreditation. Within the Department this report was regarded as an indication that the Section was improving in its ability to analyse data. It concluded that because of the concern of Italian authorities 'about the social breakdown of their people soon after arrival in Australia . . . we should consider a variation in our selection procedures to screen out migrant families with a low economic survival potential'.[18]

As a result of the increased numbers of those repatriated on medical grounds, the Departments of Immigration and Health in 1969 set up a more efficient system for monitoring medical checking procedures before departure. Australian medical officers overseas were subsequently informed of medical repatriations, especially where previous conditions were disclosed. A detailed analysis of 68 cases repatriated in the first half of 1970 indicated that, although one case with intellectual and four with physical disabilities had been approved for migration after having been identified during the medical examination:[19]

> Nervous disorders form the bulk of the reasons for repatriation on medical ground. Such cases are difficult to eliminate by routine examination. It is doubtful whether the institution of more sophisticated screening methods for physical disorders would be worth the cost, time and administrative machinery involved.

Refusal of citizenship

Allegedly on political grounds
The requirement that the primary loyalty of those granted Australian citizenship should be to Australia lay at the heart of a bitter and unresolved dispute between the government and the Opposition which was begun by Jim Cairns in 1957 and continued through the 1960s and into the 1970s by Labor parliamentarians such as Senators Cavenagh, McClelland, and J.F.

Fitzgerald, and by Gordon Bryant in the House of Representatives, over the alleged denial of citizenship to communists. Although the government never admitted that it refused citizenship on the grounds of political affiliation, there were many within its ranks, such as Senator Buttfield, who were absolutely convinced that communists owed loyalty to another country and should therefore be denied citizenship. While carefully distancing themselves from communism, a number of Labor politicians persistently raised cases in Parliament which, they alleged, demonstrated that the government refused Australian citizenship to communists and even to those they suspected of being undesirably left-wing. They argued that as the Communist Party was not illegal in Australia, to deny otherwise qualified migrants the benefits of Australian citizenship because they belonged to it was discrimination against such migrants on political grounds. They also advocated the establishment of appeal procedures.[20]

From 1945 to March 1962 the Department of Immigration rejected applications for citizenship from 11 500 aliens. However, the numbers of rejections or deferrals of citizenship were increasing. In 1962 alone, 2364 applications were refused or deferred, and 2066 received the same treatment the following year. Most applicants were rejected because they had inadequate English or could not demonstrate an understanding of the 'responsibilities and privileges' of citizenship. A handful were rejected because they had not satisfied the residency requirements. The government would not, however, disclose the grounds on which it refused citizenship to migrants on whom it received adverse security reports, and they had no right of appeal. Although between 1949 and June 1958 only 136 persons were refused naturalisation on security grounds, the incidence of such rejections had grown rapidly throughout the 1950s, from four in 1953 to 33 in 1956 and 40 in 1957.[21]

Although the government denied that any applications were rejected on political grounds, Minister for Immigration Alexander Downer admitted in 1959 and 1962 that a person who was an 'active Communist', or was suspected of being a member of the Communist Party or of having communist sympathies, could be rejected on security grounds. In November 1962 he asserted 'unequivocally' that no migrant had been refused citizenship on political grounds, but added that 'If the evidence shows that an applicant for naturalization is most definitely a member of the Communist Party, this government will have none of him and will not clothe him with full-fledged Australian citizenship'.[22]

On 27 November 1962 representatives of various ethnic groups met at the Trades Hall in Melbourne. About 200 people of different nationalities who had been refused citizenship claimed that they had been:[23]

> victimised for their political, trade union and other democratic activities—legal under the Constitution—by the discriminatory use of the Immigration Act by the Federal government . . . This constituted a great danger for the harmonious democratic development and integration of migrants into the Australian community and the many spheres of social, cultural and political activities.

The meeting called upon the government to 'adhere to democratic principles guaranteed in the constitution and adapted by the United Nations Charter of Human Rights'. G.M. Bryant (ALP VIC), who represented an electorate with a large Italian population, argued that the denial of citizenship to these people was an offence against the 'democratic spirit of the Australian community'. He urged the government to inform applicants of the grounds on which their applications had been refused, and to institute a system of appeals. It 'ought to face up to the public criticism that would flow from such a policy' he argued, tabling the resolutions passed at the meeting.[24]

By early 1963, 213 applications for citizenship lodged since 1950 had been rejected on security grounds. The groups with the largest numbers of rejected applicants were Greeks, Italians, Russians, Yugoslavs, Czechoslovaks and Poles. During 1962-63, however, 36 migrants had their naturalisation applications either deferred or rejected on security grounds.[25]

While the government refused to disclose to applicants the reasons for their rejection on security grounds, it remained vulnerable to Opposition allegations that it refused Australian citizenship to applicants from the extreme left of the political spectrum but not from those of the extreme right. Senator Cavanagh continued in 1967 to bring to the attention of Parliament cases of migrants who had been refused naturalisation on grounds which the Minister for Immigration refused to divulge. Although in May 1968 the government released details of the numbers and nationalities of the 266 who had had their applications deferred or rejected since 1961 because of unfavourable security reports, it continued to insist that: 'In no case has naturalisation been withheld because of political views not involving security considerations'. The largest numbers of rejections on security grounds during that period were of Greeks, followed by Italians and Yugoslavs.[26]

The numbers rejected on security grounds were small. Between 1950 and 1969, of the 582 059 migrants naturalised only 529 had had their applications deferred or rejected on security grounds (124 of whom were later approved), and 20 022 were rejected on grounds other than security. Despite these small numbers, Labor parliamentarians, including Senators Georges and Cavanagh, continued to press the government on particular cases to clarify whether their rejection had been because of their political views. The debate got nowhere, as Senator Buttfield continued to insist that members of the Communist Party could not be loyal to Australia and should therefore be refused citizenship, and Labor spokesmen reiterated that, as a proposal to outlaw the Communist Party had been rejected at a referendum, to deny its members citizenship was discrimination on political grounds. When Labor came to power it reviewed the cases of over 200 applicants whom it believed had been refused citizenship for political reasons.[27]

On character grounds
Applicants for citizenship were also rejected on the grounds that they were not of 'good character'. Between 1961 and 1968, 1557 applicants were rejected for this reason. Italians comprised the largest group, followed by Yugoslavs and Germans. This was also an area susceptible to muddying by prevailing value judgements of moral worthiness, and which led to complaints against decisions in individual cases. In 1965 Senator F.P. McManus (Democratic Labor Party VIC) drew attention to the case of a migrant who had been in Australia fifteen years but had been rejected for citizenship on the grounds that he had been arrested occasionally for drunkenness: 'By withholding naturalisation from him, the Department is depriving him of certain rights that would come to him if he were naturalised'. This, McManus argued, was unjust. He had been punished twice for what was 'more a disease than it was a social evil'.[28]

Deprivation of citizenship

Until 1954 Australian passports issued to those who had been granted Australian citizenship were stamped 'naturalised Australian'. This was removed, as some migrants complained that it created the impression that this form of citizenship was a 'second-class' form of citizenship. The allegation was not, however, without some justification. Two Acts limited citizenship by grant, making it a less secure form of citizenship than citizenship by birth. The deportation provisions introduced into the *Crimes Act* by the Bruce–Page government in 1926 empowered the Attorney General to deport naturalised Australian citizens who advocated or incited the overthrow of governments, who participated in or encouraged others to take part in industrial disturbances, lockouts or strikes, or who joined an organisation declared by the high court or the supreme court of a State to be an 'unlawful association'. Sections 20 to 22 of the *Nationality and Citizenship Act 1948* provided that naturalised Australians who had lived outside Australia for seven years, and did not notify an Australian consulate annually of his or her desire to retain their Australian citizenship, would lose it. They also granted the Minister for Immigration power to strip naturalised Australians of their citizenship on the grounds of disloyalty towards the Sovereign; of unlawfully trading or communicating with the enemy in any war in which Australia was currently or had been engaged in the past; of not being of good character when naturalised; of being sentenced in any country within five years of naturalisation to imprisonment for twelve months or more; and of gaining citizenship through fraud.[29]

Although only seven out of the 150 000 post-war migrants who had been granted citizenship by 1958 had had their citizenship removed under these provisions, the Act was amended that year in order, as Minister for Immigration Alexander Downer explained, 'to erase from the Nationality and Citizenship Act every discrimination, except one, between naturalised Australians and people born in Australia'. The exception was in cases where citizenship had been acquired by fraud. Downer now proudly described Australian citizenship as 'a one-class train, without any suggestion of first or second class according to origin'. Spelling out the link between the grant of citizenship and the government's assimilationist expectations, he added:[30]

> Here, then, is another example of the government's determination to absorb, not by compulsion, but by opportunity, our new settlers into Australian customs, traditions, privileges and rights. Immigration in Australia will have a long history—this must be so, if we are to develop and survive. But we shall only succeed in this great movement of peoples from the old world to our own continent if we acclimatize them, and their children, sympathetically and speedily to our ways of living, and induce them to regard Australia as their home.

It was not, however, until the deportation provisions of the *Crimes Act* were removed in 1973, on the initiative of Labor Senator Lionel Murphy, that citizenship became in fact a completely 'one-class train'. Although it was doubtful whether any citizen had been deported under these provisions, it created the impression that citizenship by grant was inferior to that of birth. As the Acting Attorney General K. Enderby explained, 'The Bill gives effect to the policy of the Australian Labor Party that naturalised Australians are to be treated for all purposes as Australians and are not to be liable to deportation or cancellation of citizenship except for substantial fraud in applications for citizenship'.[31]

Although the amendments took place during a period of considerable public concern about alleged acts of political violence by the Yugoslav community in Australia, it had the wholehearted support of the Opposition. Opposition spokesman N.H. Bowen described the provision allowing for the deportation of naturalised Australians as 'inconsistent with the view we have of Australian citizenship today . . . Whether they are natural born or naturalised they ought not to be deported for any crimes against Australian law. They should be dealt with in Australia and according to our law'. The Austrian-born foundation member of the Council for Civil Liberties, R.E. Klugman, went even further and obtained an assurance from Minister for Immigration A.J. Grassby that even non-citizens convicted of some crime would not be deported 'to any totalitarian country if they had some political reasons to fear return to that country'.[32]

Awareness of, and Responses to, the Improved Bargaining Position of Aliens from 1965

From 1962 politicians and bureaucrats were becoming aware that conditions in a number of European countries that had been major sources of migrants in the past, particularly their social service benefits, were superior to those in Australia. This, it was believed, not only deterred immigration but was a major cause of migrants returning to Europe.[33]

By 1965 it was clearly recognised that Australia was not, in the words of Minister for Immigration Hubert Opperman 'a land of milk and honey' in comparison with Europe as revitalised under the economic restructuring of the ECU. This awareness shifted the focus within the Department of Immigration from removing potential non-compliers by repatriation, deportation and improving selection procedures, to removing systemic obstacles to the social absorption of aliens. It also resulted in clearer statements of migrants' social rights in migration agreements negotiated by Australia with migrant source countries. This formal statement of the citizenship 'bargain' strengthened the bargaining position of migrants, as it not only made them more aware of their rights but stimulated their diplomatic representatives to act as advocates for those of their nationals in Australia who believed that their rights had been infringed.

In October 1965, Opperman spoke in the House of Representatives of treaties recently negotiated with Malta, the Netherlands and West Germany, and of one currently being negotiated with Italy. He described the 'economic buoyancy' of northern Europe which had led it to import 'guest workers' from Italy, Greece and other countries of southern Europe. 'We must face the fact that these countries have opportunities and attractions balancing the opportunities available in this country which is 12 000 miles away', he warned. Despite an assisted passage scheme to which the government contributed £71 for every adult's £10, Opperman recognised that the new economic situation would force Australia to offer a more attractive bargain. 'We may have to make this assistance more generous as time goes on and may have to invest more heavily to face world wide competition if we are to secure the number and type of settlers which Australia needs', he advised. He recognised that the concessions demanded would be not 'just a matter of hard cash' and jobs. To attract migrants Australia had to explain the social rights and benefits it would offer to prospective migrants—to 'go into great detail about wages, overtime, working conditions, housing, social services, prices, transport and amenities in the areas in which the migrant will be living'. He admitted that this new bargaining position had already forced one important policy change in relation to southern Europeans. The former discrimination, which prevented them from sponsoring all but immediate family, had been relaxed and Greeks, Italians and other migrants in Australia from Mediterranean countries could now sponsor cousins and friends—a provision which had previously been restricted to northern Europeans.[34]

This new attitude towards migrants' rights was clearly evident in the migration agreement negotiated with Malta in June 1970. The approximately 54 000 Maltese migrants in Australia by that date had been subject to an onerous citizenship 'bargain'.

As British subjects they were liable to military conscription, but the treaty arrangements under which they were admitted to Australia subjected them to the same waiting periods as aliens when applying for pensions. In response to declining immigration from Malta the government renegotiated the treaty in 1970, providing much more favourable conditions and guaranteeing social and legal rights.[35]

Departures

Until 1959 it was impossible for the Department of Immigration to get an accurate picture of the numbers of migrants who had returned home. Until then, the departure statistics provided by the Commonwealth Statistician had included Australian residents leaving Australia for twelve months or longer, departing visitors who had been in Australia over a year, as well as former residents who had decided to leave permanently. On the basis of this information the Department estimated the departure rate for British migrants at 6 per cent and 3 per cent for aliens. The three categories were subsequently separated, and departure statistics became more accurate from 1959.[36]

At first, government members of Parliament tended to discuss statistics of migrant departures defensively, as these were often used by the Opposition to criticise the government's assimilation efforts—particularly its ability to retain British migrants. The government's position was weakened by the Commonwealth Statistician's method of compiling departure statistics before 1959. In August 1955 the Minister for Immigration Harold Holt argued that only 25 per cent of the 31 622 persons who left Australia over the 1954/55 financial year were returning immigrants, or others who intended to leave permanently. He also claimed that only 3.5 per cent of the total post-war intake had left Australia permanently. This was, he argued, 'not a very large figure and is certainly one that compared more than favourably with the experiences of other immigrant-receiving countries'.[37]

Opposition spokesmen contested these statistics, and regarded the arguments on which they were based as fallacious. In 1956, E.G. Whitlam tabled the arrival and departure statistics from 1946–55, and argued that:[38]

> Honourable members will see from these figures that, whereas the proportion of immigrants to Australia from the British Isles has declined to approximately one in four, the proportion of

departures from Australia to the British isles is two in five. The proper solution, I suggest, is to encourage British immigrants and skilled immigrants, first, by giving them the modern health and social services which they enjoyed in the countries from which they came, and, secondly, by making it possible for them to enjoy the housing conditions which they were able to obtain in the countries from which they came.

In 1965, E.N. Drury (Liberal QLD) drew the attention of the House to statistics which indicated that departures from Australia had been increasing at a rate almost equal to the increase in total arrivals. The main loss was a result of the permanent or long-term departure of Australian residents, but it was unclear whether this was only a temporary trend. In 1967 D.W. Duthie (Labor QLD) referred to 'reverse' migration, and quoted Immigration Advisory Council statistics showing that 78 419 migrants (8.9 per cent of all settlers) had left Australia permanently, and that the 'major culprits' (13.6 per cent) were British. In 1971 F.M. Daly described returning British migrants as having been on a 'working holiday' at the expense of the Australian government. One in four English migrants who had arrived in the previous year had returned, he pointed out, suggesting that the government review its selection methods.[39]

By the end of the 1960s the abandonment of the notion of assimilation, and the greater understanding of the migration experience, caused departure statistics to cease to be perceived as migrants' failure to comply with their responsibilities under a citizenship 'bargain'. The introduction of portable pensions and the consideration of reciprocal social security agreements in 1970 signalled that the government had abandoned its expectation that all migrants would make a lifetime commitment to Australia. By 1979 departure statistics were regarded more pragmatically, as indicators of Australia's ability to attract and retain desirable skilled workers in the increasingly competitive market created by a prosperous Europe. The focus shifted from migrants' failure to comply with the government's expectations to the government's ability to meet migrants' expectations by removing systemic discrimination and providing adequate settlement services. The Immigration Advisory Council followed its 1966 inquiry on settler departures with a much more comprehensive investigation of the topic from 1971 to 1973. Under the chairmanship of Polish-born academic Dr Jerzy Zubrzycki its task was to consider the rates and patterns of departure, its significance to the migration program, its reasons, and to recommend remedial action to reduce it. This study was based on Departmental arrival and departure statistics, data from the 1971 Census, and a much larger sample of passenger cards completed by both assisted and unassisted migrants leaving Australia than had been selected by the earlier inquiry. It also obtained submissions on the causes of migrant departure from both ethnic and mainstream organisations. It established that settler loss between 1966 and 1971 was between 22 and 24 per cent. It was estimated in 1977 that about one-fifth of migrants who had arrived since 1945 had subsequently departed, indicating that they were leaving permanently.[40]

Conclusion

By 1973, a new conception of the 'bargain' between migrants and their receiving community had developed within the Australian bureaucracy. The focus had shifted from the unwillingness or inability of migrants to conform to expectations that they would demonstrate their assimilation, particularly by taking out Australian citizenship, to the ability of the government to facilitate their social absorption by removing discriminatory legislative and administrative barriers and by providing settlement services.

The bargaining position of migrants had been considerably improved by a general awareness by the late 1960s that Australia's attractiveness had dimmed in comparison with the economic and social changes that had occurred in many traditional European source countries. These changes had resulted from the establishment of the EEC in 1957. Migrants had also been empowered by the spelling out in the texts of bilateral migration agreements, such as those negotiated in 1970 with Yugoslavia and Malta, of Australia's responsibilities to provide services and to guarantee the rights of migrants. The Australian government was most responsive to intervention by diplomatic representatives on behalf of their emigrant citizens in Australia, migrants became more aware of their rights and bureaucrats more conscious of their responsibilities to provide migrants with equitable access to services. By 1973 migrants could no longer be deported if after becoming citizens they committed crimes or engaged in other activities formerly considered to be in breach of the citizenship 'bargain'. An important factor in the development of a fairer citizenship bargain for migrants was, however, the growth within the bureaucracy of a more realistic understanding of the migrant experience, and an appreciation of the complex cultural impact of the demographic changes which they had supervised.

CHAPTER 10

The role of the Department of Immigration in eroding the 'white Australia policy'

THE Australian government persistently denied that it had a 'white Australia policy'. It achieved a racially restrictive immigration intake by administrative means. Until 1958 the government excluded those it regarded as undesirable (most commonly on racial grounds) by requiring them to pass a dictation test in a European language chosen to ensure that the applicant would fail. After 1958 the task of excluding non-Europeans fell to officers of the Department of Immigration responsible for selecting migrants overseas. If an applicant appeared to be less than 75 per cent European in appearance, he or she was rejected. All through the post-war years, non-Europeans—usually well-qualified Asians—were admitted to Australia at the discretion of the Minister for Immigration. By the 1960s, however, the 'white Australia policy' had become a source of embarrassment for many within government and in the general community, particularly those concerned with the way Australians were viewed in Asia.

Tasman Heyes and Peter Heydon, Secretaries who successively dominated Department of Immigration thinking from May 1946 to May 1971, shared this embarrassment. Cautiously and with as little publicity as possible, they put forward submissions for changes which, when accepted by Cabinet, gradually eroded the policy throughout the post-war years. Bureaucratic embarrassment was reflected in the dropping of the term 'white Australia' from official usage by the Department soon after the 1939–45 war. The term persisted unofficially, however, and was used by both opponents and supporters of the policy. In 1956 the Liberal Party considered a resolution by one of its branches that the term 'white Australia' be replaced in its policy statement by the officially accepted euphemism, 'the established immigration policy'.[1]

The first step in the long process of erosion was taken in 1947, when Minister for Immigration Arthur Calwell permitted non-Europeans who had been admitted for business reasons, and who had resided in Australia for fifteen years to remain without applying for periodic extensions of their permits. After World War II, Japanese were subject to greater entry restrictions than were other non-Europeans, but in 1952 Minister Harold Holt decided that Japanese wives of Australian servicemen should be admitted under permits valid initially for five years. In 1956 this additional discrimination against Japanese in particular ended, and they were treated the same as other non-Europeans.[2]

INTERNAL AND EXTERNAL PRESSURE FOR REFORM

In 1956 the Department of External Affairs urged the Department of Immigration to seek authority to allow a few distinguished Asians to immigrate without restrictions. At first the Department of Immigration was reluctant, believing that such a step was premature and might arouse racist controversy, which would further damage Australia's image in Asia. Late that year, however, the Department successfully recommended to Cabinet that certain categories of distinguished and highly qualified non-Europeans be admitted for 'extended stay' under a 'certificate of exemption' (from the dictation test). As Heyes later explained to his Minister in 1959:[3]

> These quoted words very thinly veiled the government's desire to be able to allow Asians to settle here permanently whose standing was such that rejection of their entry could cause outbursts of criticism, difficult to answer. In line with the general trend of 'modification by degrees', this particular point of the 1956 Cabinet review of our rules for the entry of Asians was not given any publicity initially.

The change was not, in fact, mentioned in public until July 1958, when Minister Alexander Downer referred to it in a speech to the Millions Club. Its announcement then aroused no controversy. By November 1959 no overseas post had referred to Canberra any cases of 'distinguished and highly qualified' Asians wishing to settle in Australia, although a few Asian doctors temporarily in Australia had been allowed to stay permanently as persons 'fitted to fill professional or high-grade technical positions for which qualified local residents are not available'.[4]

Critics of the policy grew in numbers and became more influential and vocal throughout the 1950s. The Department received letters and resolutions from community groups protesting against the racially based immigration policy, particularly from church and student groups in close contact with the growing numbers of Asian students studying in Australian universities either privately or with government sponsorship. At the 47th annual congress of the RSSAILA in Hobart in 1957, its South Australian branch recommended that, in response to pressure from certain groups, a 'token quota' of non Europeans be admitted to Australia; the number should be kept as low as possible, and preference should be given to soldiers who had fought with the British Raj. In December 1959 the national conference of the World Council of Churches in Melbourne unanimously endorsed a resolution that the government negotiate bilateral migration agreements with Asian countries. The Anglican synod of Sydney sent a cable to the Prime Minister in October 1960 urging the appointment of a citizens' committee to examine Australia's immigration policy, which it opposed as being based on racial prejudice. The Department of Immigration's files of correspondence and press clippings on the subject multiplied.[5]

In 1959 Cabinet decided to admit as permanent residents the non-European spouse and unmarried minor children of Australian citizens normally domiciled in Australia. In July that year the Department, in a paper entitled 'Entry of Asians for permanent residence in Australia' that it had prepared for distribution at the Commonwealth parliamentary conference, proposed the admission of some Asians as migrants—'even if only by way of token quotas'. In a memorandum to the Minister based on this paper, Heyes expressed his belief that 'the time could not be more propitious' for change, and argued that:[6]

> If we are to achieve any real 'break-through' against Asian misconception and resentment, I think it vitally important to be able to say to our critics that highly qualified Asians may be admitted as migrants without any immigration restrictions

and with the opportunity of becoming naturalised after five years, in the same way as Europeans.

Heyes used this paper to influence highly placed community thinkers. In November 1959 he gave a copy to an officer of the Department of Labour and National Service in Melbourne, who was preparing to give an 'in camera' talk to the influential Australian Institute of International Affairs on Australia's exclusionist immigration policy, and requested information on the outcome of the discussion.[7]

By the early 1960s Victoria—and Melbourne University in particular—had become a hotbed of agitation against the 'white Australia policy'. In March 1960 the secretary of Melbourne University's Student Representative Council forwarded a resolution to the Department. 'We acknowledge the desirability of maintaining social and ethnic continuity, and do not argue for any breaking up of the Australian way of life', it stated, at the same time as urging the liberalisation of the existing policy. On the advice of the Minister, the Department agreed not to reply to this letter. Later that year the Victorian State Conference of the RSSAILA refused to consider a motion put forward by the Melbourne University sub-branch delegate, Newman Rosenthal, that a quota of Asian migrants be allowed into Australia. A booklet, 'Immigration—control or colour bar?', was published in 1962 by 36 staff members and postgraduate students of Melbourne University calling themselves the 'immigration reform group'. Promoted as the first shot in the war against the 'white Australia policy', it argued from opinion polls that the percentage of the Australian population that supported the policy had declined from 60 per cent to 34 per cent in 1959. Like the World Council of Churches, it supported immigration from Asia by means of intergovernmental agreements. Like its hidden allies within the Departments of External Affairs and Immigration, it argued that the most important reason for change was the effect the policy was having on Australia's relations with Asia.[8]

In November 1961 Tasman Heyes was replaced as Secretary of the Department of Immigration by Peter Heydon, a career diplomat whose last posting had been as Australian High Commissioner to India from April 1955 to March 1959. Heydon regarded himself as a 'progressive conservative' in politics, and was seen by his senior officers as a strong tactician in policy matters—adroit and practical-minded—rather than a profound long-term strategist. According to academic, journalist, and later also Australian High Commissioner to India Bruce Grant, he was a pragmatist with no time for ideology. He admired scholarship, was excited by writing, and shared his predecessor's views on the need to reform Australia's racially restrictive immigration policy and his caution. He believed that Australia's sense of racial superiority damaged Australia's interests overseas. As one of his colleagues observed, 'his concern for Australia's image overseas led him at the beginning of the 'sixties to the fields of aboriginal discrimination where he helped to interest Ministers in cleaning up the Statute Books—and also in modification of the racial superiority formulation of Australia's immigration policy'.[9]

In July 1963 Heydon asked his Department to provide him with information on what countries had restricted immigration, how many Asians were admitted to Australia each year and on what terms and conditions. He asked if there were any specific arguments that could be put forward against allowing small quotas of Asian immigrants into Australia. According to journalist Maximillian Walsh, who interviewed Heydon shortly before his death in May 1971, Heydon's experience in External Affairs had led him to the opinion that Australia had more to gain internationally than it lost domestically by breaking down the traditional 'white Australia policy' and admitting well-qualified non-Europeans. In 1963, the Department of Immigration produced a paper entitled 'Brief notes on Australia's established immigration policy'. Not for general public consumption, it was designed to provide talking points for officers of the Department of External Affairs, particularly those attached to missions in Asia, for overseas officers of the Department of Immigration, and for those in State branches. It was, however, given to correspondents who specifically requested information on non-European migration.[10]

An early version of this paper, developed initially in March 1963 for the information of Chinese and other non-Europeans in Victoria, constructed an image of a unified nation as the authority for the policy. It referred to 'the national desire to develop within this country a homogeneous population in order that we may plan the full and proper development of our resources, and in doing so, avert the social difficulties which have become a feature of the growth of a number of countries'. Subsequent versions of this paper, which was regularly updated, argued that people coming to Australia should be capable of readily integrating both socially and economically, and therefore preference was given to people of European origin. It pointed out that Australia was not alone in seeking such homogeneity, and that each country had a right and duty to determine its own demographic composition. On the question of the admission of non-Europeans, it explained that they were not totally excluded, and that the immigration laws permitted the Minister to exercise discretion based on an individual's qualifications, the merits of each case, humanitarian considerations, and broad national interest. The paper proceeded to outline six ways in which non-Europeans were currently admitted for permanent entry, and estimated that in addition to Australia's indigenous population there were more than 30 000 people of non-European origin in Australia as students (12 000), temporary residents (8000), and 10 000 non-Europeans who were Australian citizens by birth, registration or naturalisation. The initial purpose of the paper was not fulfilled. In March 1963 the Department refused a request by T.H. Chou, Consul for China (Taiwan), that an officer of the Department address the Chinese community in Victoria on immigration. The Secretary also refused to have 'Brief notes' translated into Chinese, as he believed that the Consul's invitation was part of a renewed attack by the Taiwanese on Australia's immigration policy. The Assistant Secretary commented that he had no desire to encourage an interest in the current immigration policy among the Chinese, particularly as he expected it to be amended.[11]

Heydon gained unexpected support for his views on Australia's racially discriminatory entry policy after the appointment on 18 December 1963 of Hubert Ferdinand Opperman as Minister for Immigration. Opperman adopted a 'hands-on' approach to his portfolio, and brought insights to policy which were not always those of his government. Opperman and Heydon collaborated closely in preparing a submission to Cabinet which recommended that Asians living as temporary residents in Australia be allowed after five years to apply for permanent residence and to sponsor their immediate families, and that qualified non-Europeans overseas should be allowed to immigrate. On 4 May 1964 Opperman approached the Prime Minister, R.G. Menzies, with the proposal, which had been prepared in the Department of Immigration largely by Harold McGinness and Ted Charles. Menzies regarded it with disfavour, and Opperman had a battle getting his submission considered by Cabinet (Ministers for Immigration during Heydon's time as Secretary were not part of Cabinet, and attended Cabinet meetings only from time to time, when invited). The proposal was finally submitted in September 1964 and was, not surprisingly, rejected largely due to opposition from Menzies, Harold Holt and John McEwen. Opperman bided his time and Heydon continued informally to prepare some opinion and group leaders for the possibility of change.[12]

'MIXED-RACE' MIGRATION 1964

The next major milestone in the erosion of the 'white Australia policy' came in 1964, when special criteria were introduced for migrants of 'mixed race'. Previously, applicants had been judged on their appearance according to a subjective and ultimately embarrassing '75 per cent' rule, which required applicants to be European in appearance, '75 per cent or more European descent, fully European in upbringing, outlook, mode of dress and way of living', and capable of ready integration into the Australian community. The rule had been introduced in the 1950s to provide a margin of error for the interviewing officer in deciding whether an applicant for migration was more European than otherwise. Documentary evidence had been found to be so misleading as to be unacceptable. From 1964, special requirements concerning assessment of the skills of mixed-race applicants, their relationship with people already in Australia and their circumstances were introduced. These requirements were more liberal than those applying to 'non-Europeans', but more restrictive than those applying to Europeans. As Heydon commented to the Governor-General, Lord Casey, in 1966:[13]

> The immigration of mixed race people has been a significant factor in our non-European policy in the post war years, to an extent that may not generally be realised. We have admitted in excess of 15,000 people mainly from the mixed-race (Burgher) community in Ceylon, from India, and Pakistan, formerly from Indonesia and in more recent years from the Netherlands and Burma.

By 1970 approximately 30 000 mixed-race immigrants had been admitted to Australia since the war, largely from former British dependencies. To correspondents who complained of their presence in Australia, the Department routinely replied that:[14]

> Most are essentially British in education, traditions and customs. They appear to have found the transition to day-to-day life in Australia relatively simple and the demands they make upon officially provided integration and welfare

services are minimal. This reflects the careful application of responsible policies.

There was considerable divergence within the Commonwealth Public Service on the identification of race. This led to discrepancies between the statistics of non-Europeans in Australia provided by the Department of Immigration and those of the Commonwealth Statistician. While the Statistician used 'race' to refer to ethnic origin, irrespective of birthplace or nationality, the Department classified Syrians, Lebanese and Egyptians as southern Europeans rather than non-Europeans, and excluded Aborigines, Maoris and Torres Strait Islanders from its calculations. The Department estimated that between 1954 and 1961 the percentage of Australian-born 'full bloods' had remained unchanged (0.09 per cent of the total population), while overseas-born 'full bloods' had increased by 88 per cent (from 0.14 per cent to 0.23 per cent of the total population, or 33 097 persons) and 'half castes' by 39 per cent (7930 persons). The Census was a better indicator of the numbers of non-Europeans in Australia than the Department's statistics of admissions of non-Europeans for permanent residence. The Department's statistics could not identify the non-European spouses, dependent children or aged parents either of Australian citizens or of British subjects migrating to or permanently resident in Australia, and did not include those non-Europeans who had initially been admitted as temporary residents and who had subsequently qualified for permanent residence, or who had been granted citizenship.[15]

By 1965 there were 37 300 non-Europeans in Australia, including 10 300 Australian citizens by birth and 5000 by naturalisation or registration. While this information was distributed to Departmental officers overseas and interstate, and to the Department of External Affairs, it was not intended for general distribution to the public. This, in the opinion of journalist Maximillian Walsh and Kenneth Rivett, Chairman of the New South Wales Association for Immigration Reform, was the deliberate policy of Heydon, who did not wish to alarm potential opponents of his gradual program of reform.[16]

THE ADMISSION OF SKILLED NON-EUROPEANS 1966

The most important changes to the racial component of the image of 'Australian citizen' occurred after Menzies' retirement on 26 January 1966. He chose as his successor the former Minister for Immigration, Harold Holt. On 2 March Cabinet made two major decisions. The first was to reduce to five years the qualifying period for non-Europeans wishing to apply for resident status. (Previously non-Europeans had been admitted for long periods on temporary permits, and had been allowed to be joined by their families only after fifteen years in Australia.) The second reform permitted the entry for settlement of non-Europeans with qualifications in demand in Australia, who were likely to integrate readily into the community. They were allowed to bring their immediate families with them. This was an extension of the 1956 provision allowing for the admission of 'distinguished and highly qualified' Asians. Non-European wives and dependants of alien European residents also became eligible for admission to Australia. Having the Prime Minister's support rather than his opposition, as in 1964, made all the difference. The changes probably did not go as far as Heydon would have liked, but as one of his officers observed 'His biggest contribution (to policy development) was his ability to test the water and then proceed as far as the Minister's toe could stand the heat'. Menzies made his disapproval of these reforms explicit to Heydon. 'Clearly as a Conservative, he is finding this change hard to take, especially as he realises it is symbolic of great changes (to come) everywhere', Heydon observed prophetically.[17]

According to Maximillian Walsh, these radical changes were the result of 'a cynical lucky dip into Departmental ideas by Harold Holt'. Walsh's view, probably based on his interview with Heydon, was that, on inheriting the Prime Ministership on the retirement of Sir Robert Menzies, Holt wanted to develop policies that would distinguish him from his predecessor, so he called for ideas for change from his Ministers. Heydon and Opperman re-presented their previously rejected submission on skilled non-European migration; lacking any better suggestions, Holt now took it up with enthusiasm. Cabinet passed it, according to Walsh, as a piece of window dressing which changed nothing, and even critics of the 'white Australia policy' saw it that way until the early 1970s. Heydon encouraged this view.[18]

In his statement of 8 March 1966 on the revised policy, Holt stated that the changes had been prompted by Australia's increasing trade, aid, military, diplomatic and tourist involvement in Asia, and presence in Australia of over 12 000 Asian students. He stressed, however, that Australian standards, national characteristics and essential unity would be preserved, and that the basic policy that had been firmly established since Federation would be maintained, although modified, liberalised and more flexibly administered.[19]

In explaining this new phase in the policy to the Governor-General, Heydon emphasised that:[20]

> Throughout all the policy and administrative changes, the basic purpose of the policy remains unchanged. There is no wish to create in Australia the problems of a multi-racial or plural society, which are a feature of some other countries. The objective is to maintain broadly the present homogeneity of the Australian population.

The Department was besieged with protest letters. Correspondents disturbed by the decision were assured that there would be no departure from the fundamental principles of the current immigration policy, whose primary aim was an integrated and homogeneous population as opposed to a multi-racial Australian nation. It was, however, now believed that small numbers of Asians could integrate into Australian society without any great damage to society.[21]

This change in policy did not produce large increases in numbers of non-European immigrants, and State branches reported little immediate interest from non-Europeans in applying for permanent residence. At the end of 1966 there were 38 000 non-Europeans and persons of mixed descent residing in Australia, of whom 17 550 were citizens (11 150 by birth and 6400 by nationalisation or registration). There was no annual quota for Asian immigrants, and from March 1966 to March 1970 approximately 4800 well-qualified Asians and their dependants were admitted to Australia, largely from India, Hong Kong, Malaysia, Burma, Singapore, Indonesia, Ceylon and the Philippines. Of this group, 13 per cent were engineers, 10 per cent were teachers, 5 per cent university lecturers, 2 per cent medical practitioners, and among the 62 other occupations represented were 70 businessmen who engaged in substantial overseas trading.[22]

Whether non-Europeans temporarily resident in Australia were allowed to stay permanently, however, depended on how well they integrated. In fact, this decision had the effect of transferring the problem of refusing residence status to Asians within five years to the Citizenship branch of the Department. As one officer complained:[12]

> ... there is no logical reason why citizenship should be used

to control migration. Once we admit a man to Australia we should be prepared to grant him citizenship if and when he meets legal and policy requirements for the grant of citizenship . . . Citizenship is supposed to be the culmination of all integration activities—not an entry control measure.

The new policy was seen to increase the risk of non-compliance, by Asian temporary entrants who could not qualify for permanent residence, with the conditions on which they were granted entry. These conditions were the same for Europeans and non-Europeans, although deserters from ships were treated differently according to race. While European deserters were granted resident status if they remained in Australia for two years (sometimes less), non-European deserters were deported regardless of their period of stay.[24]

The Department was conscious that the racial discrimination still underpinning its selection criteria was a potential minefield in its relations with countries such as the USA, where racial discrimination had taken a dominant position on the political agenda throughout the 1960s. It also carefully monitored Australian press opinion and analysed the correspondence it received reacting to its policy changes.[25]

Departmental responses to correspondence

While carefully monitoring its correspondence on the topic, the Department did not take very seriously letters objecting to its new reforms. In forwarding at the Minister's request the 45 letters reacting to the modification of racially discriminatory entry provision received in the first nine months of 1970, Heydon observed that many of the 38 letters opposing non-European immigration appeared to be based on a common text, and most correspondents wrote only once. He interpreted their failure to pursue their complaints after being supplied with information on non-European entry provisions as indicating that these correspondents either were less disturbed by the policy, or that they had 'satisfied a primary urge to protest'. On forwarding to the Minister details of the 86 letters the Department had received on non-European migration for the whole of 1970 (73 of which had opposed reform), Heydon remarked that many had been instigated by anti-immigration organisations or were inspired by newspaper reports of specific incidents involving non-Europeans, and 'did not provide a sound basis for an analysis of general public opinion relating to our policies'.[26]

In dealing with groups that opposed racially discriminatory entry policies in the late 1960s, such as the Australian Council of Social Services and the Young Liberal Committee, the Department stressed that the policy and its associated rules and procedures would not remain rigidly fixed. 'On the contrary', the Minister informed the Liberal Party in 1968, 'as our population increases and our relations with Asian countries develop, one would expect continuing gradual development in entry conditions and in the categories of people who will be admissible'. This message was repeated to the Conference of State Ministers for Immigration in August 1968.[27]

Constructing a Departmental history of non-European migration 1971

Heydon carefully vetted the text of a speech prepared by the Department for the Minister on the history of Australia's non-European immigration policy, and had it published in March 1971 as a booklet for distribution to people writing to the Department on the issue. While the booklet claimed that US President John Kennedy's statement that his country was 'a nation of immigrants' applied equally to Australia, Heydon did not explore the challenge this notion posed for the image projected in the booklet of Australia as 'a socially homogeneous and cohesive population'. First Assistant Secretary H. McGinness recommended the removal from the draft speech of the phrase 'proud of cultural and social pluralism' and substitution of the more innocuous 'enrichment through migration', because of the overtones of 'pluralism'.[28]

Entitled 'The evolution of a policy', this booklet summarised the substantial but cautious erosion of the racially discriminatory entry policies which had taken place under the Liberal administration. The antithesis of the imagined 'cohesive' Australia put forward in this booklet was 'self-perpetuating enclaves and undigested minorities'. The latter were defined as:

> substantial groups of ethnic origin very different from the host community; proud of that difference and determined to perpetuate it; seeking to discourage intermarriage; desiring to have separate political representation; and ready to dispute the efforts of the national government to encourage integration.

The booklet concluded with a veiled suggestion that non-European immigration was inevitable:[29]

> After a century of British migration we undertook a large-scale

experiment in massive European Migration. While it is proceeding commendably, there is no compelling reason to add unnecessary problems to it without forethought or planning. But its success and resilience will continue to bear other elements flowing into it, gradually and cohesively as we meet real needs and absorb change in an intelligent evolutionary pattern.

Heydon died suddenly in May 1971. There was no further erosion of racially discriminatory entry policies under the Prime Ministerships of Holt's successors, John Gorton and William McMahon.

'WHITE AUSTRALIA' AND THE LABOR PARTY 1971–75

In the context of a coming Federal election, the Department of Immigration supplied its Minister, Dr A.J. Forbes, with summaries of Labor Party opinion on immigration. While immigration was not a topic for debate within Liberal Party ranks, where there was no pressure either for or against reform, it was an extraordinarily divisive issue within the Opposition. In early 1971 the Labor Party included spokesmen for a racially discriminatory immigration policy, such as Arthur Calwell and Fred Daly (shadow immigration minister), and those who opposed it, such as Don Dunstan (Labor Premier of South Australia), Keppel Enderby (ALP ACT) and A.J. Grassby (ALP NSW). The ALP platform at this time made no reference to race, and its immigration policy was largely indistinguishable from that of the government. Its Federal platform in 1971 favoured a policy that would avoid 'the difficult social and economic problems which may follow from an influx of peoples having different standards of living, traditions and cultures'.[30]

At the April 1971 Federal Labor Youth Conference, however, Gough Whitlam as Leader of the Opposition brought his party's divisions into the public arena by proclaiming his belief that it was impossible for a socialist party to distinguish between people on the basis of race or religion, and that Australia could not survive if it continued to discriminate on the grounds of colour. At the ALP Federal Conference in June, Whitlam achieved a change in his party's platform on migration, condemning discrimination and thus allowing him to mount a vigorous attack in the crucial pre-election months on the government's 'policy of fear'.[31]

The Department's advice to Minister Dr A.J. Forbes on this

shift in policy reflected uncertainty, and concern for the maintenance of bipartisan support of the program. As the ALP had not indicated the numbers of non-European migrants it might admit, the Department advised that it was possible that its policy would differ little from the government's, which it saw as having abandoned racial discrimination in 1966. If, however, the changed ALP policy implied that Labor intended to introduce large-scale non-European migration, the Department felt that it would probably be rejected by the public. It feared that debate on immigration along party lines would give rise to 'emotional and specious argument and distortion leading to grave misunderstanding not only within Australia but internationally'. In a press statement issued on 21 June 1971 based on this advice, Forbes drew attention to the ALP platform's vagueness about the numbers of non-Europeans it would admit, and concluded with the observation that ALP policy might not be very different from the government's, and if that was so the government welcomed this 'bi-partisan understanding'.[32]

The new Secretary of the Department of Immigration, R.E. Armstrong, a long-serving officer who was appointed on 25 May 1971, observed to the Minister that if Australia adopted a points system the numbers of Asians applying for immigration to Australia would be higher than to Canada, because of Australia's greater role in Asia and the Pacific, and for geographical and climatic reasons. Two months later the Department still had difficulty offering advice to the Minister on ALP policy because it felt 'their aims have not been precisely stated'.[33]

On Monday 12 October 1971 Whitlam almost precipitated a leadership challenge during a press conference in which he annoyed both the left and right wings of his party. The Right was offended by his announcement of the demotion of Fred Daly from the position of shadow immigration minister. The following Wednesday, Whitlam averted this crisis in a *This Day Tonight* television interview, during which he indicated that he would introduce a points system similar to Canada's, reduce the level of migration, and admit fewer non-European migrants than were currently being admitted. In a Departmental paper produced in October 1971 summarising recent ALP statements, W.G. Kiddle noted the discrepancy between Dunstan's estimates of a non-European intake under Labor of 27 000, and Whitlam's estimates of fewer non-European immigrants under Labor than under the Liberal administration. Kiddle believed that Whitlam's estimates were based on erroneous assumptions, particularly that 'Indians were not an emigrant people'.³⁴

In a speech to the Press Club on 24 October 1971, Whitlam attacked the government and indirectly the Department. If the government had valued a bipartisan approach to immigration it should have had a bipartisan migration committee, he asserted. It had staged no full-scale debate on immigration in Parliament for over five years, it had done little research on the economic and social effects of migration, and whatever information it had collected it had suppressed. He again expressed his belief that under a Labor government the numbers of non-Europeans would decline, but reiterated that a non-discriminatory policy was critical to Australia's reputation in our region.³⁵

The Labor government came to power in December 1972. Its immigration policy, tabled in Parliament by Labor's new Minister for Immigration A.J Grassby in December 1973, emphatically announced the end of discrimination on the grounds of race, colour or nationality in the selection of migrants, and the introduction of multiculturalism, a Canadian term which reflected a radically different way of imagining Australian society and a more complex view of Australian citizenship.³⁶

That month, the Department of Immigration for the first time stated clearly that the existing policy was in fact discriminatory, for while it did not exclude non-Europeans it demanded of them more rigorous conditions of entry, and except for a few exceptional cases withheld from them assisted passage. Discrimination in the granting of assisted passage under the Commonwealth Nomination Scheme remained throughout 1973. Also, procedures for deciding on applications from non-Europeans differed according to the race of the applicant. While overseas posts decided on unsponsored applications from Europeans, similar applications from non-Europeans were referred to Canberra for decision. In May 1973 the Secretary of the Department of Immigration advised all overseas posts of the revised rules of entry, and drew attention to these remaining discriminatory provisions. The Minister, he explained, was uncertain how much support there was among employers, trades unions and the community in general for the principle of non-discrimination, particularly in an increasingly tight labour market. The referral of non-European applications to Canberra for decision was, therefore, to continue. Nevertheless, in June 1973 Grassby embarked on a tour of Asia to publicise the death of the 'white Australia policy'.[37]

Sir Keith Waller, Secretary of the Department of Foreign Affairs, had transmitted Armstrong's May memorandum to all Heads of Mission of his Department overseas. However, in July he warned the Department of Immigration that their Minister risked loss of credibility, and that Australia's standing overseas would be damaged, if the discrimination in the processing of non-European applications and the granting of assisted passages was discovered. The Department of Immigration responded that these remaining discriminatory provisions were 'vestigial' and 'more apparent than real', and advised its Minister that both actions were designed to ensure that non-Europeans approved for entry would not encounter difficulties in employment on arrival. It was thought that the cost of the migrant's contribution to assisted passage, raised in June 1973 for the first time since 1947 from $25 to $75 for individuals and families, would discourage applications for assisted passage from poor non-Europeans. The problem of racially restricted assisted passage was overcome in October 1974 when it was restricted to sponsored spouses and dependent children of Australian permanent residents, refugees, workers with skills in demand in Australia and their dependants, and compassionate cases. Assisted passage was abandoned altogether for categories other than refugees in 1982. In February 1975 Grassby's replacement as Minister for Immigration, Clyde Cameron, announced that overseas posts would approve the entry of both non-Europeans and European applicants.[38]

The abolition of the 'white Australia policy' did not significantly alter the racial and ethnic composition of the intake under Labor. On coming to power in 1972, Labor had also announced the end of Australia's commitment of troops to Vietnam and the abolition of military conscription, which had supplied almost 20 000 of the Australian soldiers sent there. Whitlam reportedly referred to refugees from that country as 'Vietnamese Balts', a phrase which reflected his fears that, like many of the post-war European refugees from Communist countries, they would be unlikely to vote for a Labor government. Australia was, therefore, initially slow to respond to the refugee crisis created by the fall of the American-backed government in Saigon on 30 April 1975. Only 600 Vietnamese refugees had been admitted by 31 July 1975.[39]

Conclusion

The gradual introduction of highly educated and often very British non-European migrants from other Commonwealth countries from 1956 meant that the first Asians most Anglo-Celtic Australians met were either tertiary students or professionals, fluent in English, who made prevailing racist stereotypes appear absurd. While immigration from Asia had reached 5.2 per cent of the intake in the period 1961–66, it grew to 11.2 per cent in 1966–71 and to 21.2 per cent between 1971 and 1973. It was not, however, until the end of the Vietnam War in 1975 that substantial numbers of non-English speaking and less-educated non-European migrants came to Australia. The disasters anticipated by past opponents of Asian migration did not eventuate.[40]

As Grassby's use of the term 'multicultural' suggested, the Department of Immigration from 1973 was moving towards a more pluralistic view of Australian society. The reconceptualisation of Australian society, which was to be given official sanction in the 1980s in the form of a multicultural policy, encouraged Australians to view the obvious racial and cultural differences of Asian immigrants as just another part of the mosaic of ethnic diversity which had changed the pattern of Australian society since 1947. From then on, racism could no longer be disguised as the patriotic defence of an essentially British and homogeneous society. The purging of discriminatory legislation by 1975, essentially a response to the Australian government's desire to integrate European migrants, also facilitated the social absorption of non-Europeans and helped to prevent their economic marginalisation.

CHAPTER 11

The Department of Immigration under Labor 1972–75

THE election of the first Labor government for 22 years in December 1972 launched the Department of Immigration on a period of often turbulent cultural and administrative change which ended in its dismemberment in June 1974. Although the government strove to create the appearance that immigration had radically changed, the racial composition of the migration intake was not substantially altered during the short time it was in power.

The annual intake targets of migrants were immediately reduced under Labor 'due to the advent of the world recession'. Labor continued its predecessor's policy of reducing the numbers of assisted migrants, which steadily declined from almost 132 000 in 1969/70 to 82 000 in 1971/72, 57 000 in 1972/73 and 36 000 in 1974/75. While slightly more British were assisted than aliens, the numbers of independent British permanent and long-term arrivals greatly outnumbered independently arriving aliens under both Liberal and Labor governments between 1970 and 1975. The numbers of people coming to Australia for either permanent or long-term stay declined from an all-time high of over 253 000 in 1969/70 to 204 000 in 1973/74 and 173 000 in 1974/75. Despite the abolition of the 'white Australia policy', the number of non-Europeans admitted under Labor was small.[1]

The first Labor Minister for Immigration since Arthur

Calwell, A.J. (Al) Grassby, was a highly visible parliamentarian noted for his somewhat startling taste in clothes and strong links to the Italian community—particularly in southern NSW, where he had worked in the 1950s with non-English speaking farmers as an officer with the NSW Department of Agriculture's Irrigation Research and Extension Organisation. He visited Italy with the United Nations Food and Agricultural Organisation in 1956, and was elected to the NSW Parliament as member for Murrumbidgee in 1965. In 1970 he was made a Knight Commander by the Italian government, and represented the electorate of Riverina in the Commonwealth Parliament from 1969 to 1974.[2]

Cultural Change: Redefining Australian National Identity

The Labor government presented the Australian public with a new image of their national identity. The vision of Australian society put by Grassby to the Conference of Commonwealth and State Ministers for Immigration on 11 May 1973 was that of 'the family of the nation'. He stressed the need to give Australians in all their diversity a sense of pride in their national identity as Australians, without abandoning their pride in their own national origins. The following August this vision was disseminated by means of a publication entitled *A Multi-Cultural Society for the Future*. The term 'multicultural' was borrowed from Canada, which in 1973 was devoting considerable resources to developing an understanding of minority cultures among Canadians. This publication argued that, as 46 per cent of the Australian population was under 25, a generation had grown up having no knowledge of Australia without ethnically diverse mass migration and 'the dynamic process of social and cultural change it has brought about'. It attacked the 'conspiracy of silence' which denied the impact of this ethnic diversity, and which asserted that only Anglo-Saxon influences affected Australian national life. This was an aggressive attempt to acknowledge and celebrate the cultural pluralism brought to Australia by 30 years of immigration.[3]

The tone was new but the perception that Australian society had become more diverse was not. Australia had been more cautiously described as 'a nation of immigrants' by the former Secretary of the Department of Immigration, Sir Peter Heydon, in a booklet 'The evolution of a policy' in March 1971. Heydon's acknowledgement of diversity had been constrained by the image of Australia as an essentially British country prevailing in the Liberal government at this time. Grassby put it more boldly: in December 1973 he told Parliament that 'Australia is a nation of immigrants and the descendants of immigrants. Our national character has been determined by the interaction of the diverse elements of population who came here from the past from many countries and by their experience after they came here'.[4]

Legislative Change: Removing Discrimination

The image of Australia as a nation of essentially British culture and ethnicity had been sustained by a network of legislative discrimination on the grounds of ethnicity and race. The Labor government set about dismantling what remained of this. As well as declaring its intention to abandon all discrimination in the selection of migrants, in February 1973 it announced its decision to repeal the provisions of the *Migration Act*, which prevented the departure of Aborigines from Australia without the approval of the Minister for Immigration. In May 1973 it announced that the *Aliens Act 1947–66* would be amended to eliminate the requirement that aliens notify the authorities annually of changes in their address, occupation and marital status. The same month it amended the provisions of the *Crimes Act*, which allowed naturalised Australian citizens to be deported. In July 1973 Grassby announced the ending of pro-British discrimination. The treaty with Britain would be amended to allow the entry of all migrants—including for the first time British migrants—to be controlled by visas. The *Citizenship Act 1948–69* would be amended to make the requirements the same for all applicants for Australian citizenship. Like other applicants, British migrants would be required to have lived in Australia three years before they could apply for citizenship, and they would have to attend naturalisation ceremonies and take the oath of allegiance. An amendment to the *Electoral Act* was proposed to prevent British non-citizens from enrolling as voters.[5]

New benchmarks for the rights of all Australians were set by Labor's decision in 1973 to ratify the United Nations Covenant on Civil and Political Rights, the Convenant on Economic, Social and Cultural Rights, the Convention on the Political

Rights of Women and the Convention adopted by the International Labour Conference in 1958 abolishing discrimination in employment.[6]

ADMINISTRATIVE CHANGE: ENLISTING ETHNIC COMMUNITIES

The Labor government intensified the Department of Immigration's earlier efforts to involve ethnic communities in encouraging the social inclusion of their members. It recognised that past secrecy and administrative discrimination had created mistrust among migrants, particularly of the Department. As a new government in power it was able to assert without embarrassment that most service-providing institutions had failed adequately to communicate with or meet the needs of migrants.

The Department of Immigration was restructured in July 1973 and a new Division was created which combined its settlement and citizenship functions. It dealt with migrant education, information, welfare, accommodation, and action on integration, and included the Survey Section, which had collected information on migrants and their settlement problems. The government signalled its intention to involve ethnic communities in advising the Minister on migration policy by appointing four post-war migrants to the Immigration Advisory Council. It also established a community relations committee of the Council to examine discrimination against migrants, their exploitation, and the extent to which they used community services. Task forces were created to pinpoint settlement problems in all States and new roles were defined for Good Neighbour Councils, which were encouraged to work more closely with ethnic groups. Service delivery was to be improved by the appointment of 48 multilingual welfare officers, the introduction of the Emergency Telephone Interpreter Service and increased numbers of Grants-in-Aid. Prime Minister Gough Whitlam ordered the release of the valuable information on migrants accumulated by the Department of Immigration in its research reports, the distribution of which had previously been restricted.[7]

Ethnic radio and television

The relaxation of controls on the ethnic media, particularly radio and television, reflected government's new attitudes towards ethnic communities. When Labor came to power the Australian

Broadcasting Control Board restricted the use of foreign languages in both radio and television on the grounds that English should be the predominant language of Australia and migrants should be encouraged to learn it as quickly as possible. Radio programs in foreign languages were limited to not more than two and a half hours a week, and had to be accompanied by an English translation occupying at least one-quarter of the total time spoken in another language. In 1973 the Department of Immigration argued that these regulations were no longer relevant, as multilingual programs assisted the early settlement of migrants, provided opportunities to inform them of important services, and helped to make the community aware of the cultural backgrounds of various ethnic groups. On 12 November 1973 the regulations were amended to allow foreign language programs and advertisements, provided they were accompanied by an English explanation. A broadcasting subcommittee of the NSW Migrant Task Force was established to examine ways and means of raising foreign language broadcasting content. In June 1975 two ethnic radio stations were opened in Sydney and Melbourne for a trial period of twelve weeks, and the Department of the Media began to plan policy on ethnic broadcasting.[8]

Devolution of Migrant Services 1973–74

The new government's policy of multiculturalism defined Australia as 'a society in which equal opportunity is accompanied by cultural diversity in an atmosphere of acceptance and tolerance'. Its focus on equal opportunity placed new emphasis on the provision of services for migrants by departments other than the Department of Immigration, and on the provision of welfare services by ethnic organisations supported by Commonwealth funding rather than by mainstream welfare bodies. Grassby outlined his government's plans for reducing the role the Department had to play in the settlement process in his statement to Parliament on 6 December 1973:[9]

> Basic to the Department's citizenship and settlement activities should be the principle that separate services for migrants should not be established where appropriate community services exist. Where existing community services are not oriented towards meeting migrants' needs, the Department's task should be to seek the necessary adaptation, by demonstration of the need (through example, survey or research) followed by consultation, and where necessary, the

judicious application of temporary financial assistance during the adaptation stage.

Effect on other government departments—Social Security

Under Labor, the Department of Immigration became proactive in getting other government departments to participate in the government's new vision of the role of the bureaucracy in relation to migrants, and ultimately in inducing them to accept more responsibility for migrants. In 1973 migrants still tended to be invisible to other service-delivery departments, as the initial planning of the Department of Social Security's Australian Assistance Plan revealed. In April 1973, Cabinet approved the establishment of an eleven-member National Commission on Social Welfare (NCSW) under the chairmanship of Marie Coleman, to make recommendations to the government on the provision of social welfare to all Australians. The purpose of the Australian Assistance Plan was to ensure universal access to welfare services, income support, the removal of the stigma previously associated with the receipt of welfare benefits, and the involvement of the community as consumers and volunteers in the decentralised prevention of social breakdown. It was an attempt to coordinate the provision of social welfare by Commonwealth, State, local government and voluntary agencies by creating a network of regional Councils for Social Development, composed of nominees of various authorities and elected representatives in various regions. In July 1973 the Department of Immigration drew attention to the lack of anyone on the NCSW qualified to speak on the special social welfare needs of migrants. It argued for its own inclusion on the grounds that one in four of the population was now either a migrant or a child of a migrant, and much of the burden of meeting their needs fell on the Department. It was subsequently invited to help set the Commission's parameters.[10]

At a meeting with Coleman in August 1973, Secretary R.E. Armstrong outlined his Department's attitude towards migrant settlement. He emphasised that the Department of Immigration had been going through a learning process and was still developing new initiatives. It was to be hoped that after an initial education phase the migrant community would be able to draw on normal community resources. At the first meeting of the NCSW at which it was represented, the Department emphasised its intention to encourage migrants to use services available to the mainstream community. Shortly afterwards this message of devolution was reinforced at ministerial level, when Grassby indicated to the Minister for Social Security, W.G. Hayden, that his Department did not want to provide facilities for migrants beyond those necessary to help them overcome the special difficulties caused by the fact that they were migrants. It sought, he explained, to encourage them 'to avail themselves of the resources that are available to the community generally where these are appropriate'. The role played by the Department of Immigration in the Commission was subsequently ignored by academic analyses of the Australian Assistance Plan.[11]

The increased sensitivity of the Department of Social Security towards migrant clients was indicated by its plans by August 1973 to develop its own interpreter service with assistance from the Department of Immigration's Emergency Telephone Interpreter Service. In November 1973 Hayden, who during his earlier career as a policeman in Queensland from 1953 to 1961 had been a member of the Ipswich Migrant Advisory Council, indicated that he would appreciate the opportunity to meet a group of people informally to discuss issues related to migration and social welfare. The meeting, held on 18 December 1973 at the Greek Orthodox Community Centre in Melbourne, included Marie Coleman, representatives of the Health Commission, the Department of Immigration and of the Greek, Italian, Spanish, Turkish, Maltese, Jewish and Fijian communities, as well as the Ecumenical Migration Centre and the Good Neighbour Council. The meeting stressed the desirability of getting the conception of Australia as a multicultural and pluralist society widely accepted. The main point to emerge from this meeting was the need for financial support to be given to ethnic organisations to ensure that cultural pluralism was generally accepted and became a reality. The officials communicated clearly to the migrant representatives the government's intention to devolve much responsibility for service provision to migrants to their own community organisations. The migrant representatives received the idea with enthusiasm. The spokesman of the Orthodox Community of Melbourne and Victoria, Mr George Papadopoulos, remarked that 'apart from the Department of Immigration no-one else appears to have done much for migrants'.[12]

The formation of Ethnic Community Councils 1974

Although the Australian Assistance Plan was short-lived (it was dismantled by the Coalition government in 1976), it had at least one lasting effect. The consultations between the Department of Social Security and migrant groups which it initiated were the direct catalyst for the formation of the first combinations of ethnic groups as representatives of ethnic interests in public affairs. Ethnic Community Councils were established in Victoria and South Australia in 1974 and in New South Wales the following year. By 1979 Ethnic Community Councils had been set up in all States and the Federation of Ethnic Community Councils established.[13]

DISSEMINATING THE VISION TO AUSTRALIANS

Citizenship education

Throughout 1973, Grassby planned strategies to disseminate his government's new vision of Australian society and citizenship to the general community. He hoped to develop courses in citizenship for school children which would 'be related more closely to the present-day nature of Australian society'. He also intended to develop similar courses for migrants and for the Australian-born, to give them 'a greater awareness of our history, the preservation of objects of national interest and protection and respect for the environment'. By September 1973 he had discussed the issue with the Minister for Education, and proposed to submit it for examination by the Education Committee of the Immigration Advisory Council.[14]

An immigration history

Grassby believed that a history of immigration was essential to an understanding of the changes that had taken place in Australian society. Despite the importance of immigration to Australia's post-war development, no history of its social impact had been attempted by 1970. Nor was there a history of the Department of Immigration, although both Tasman Heyes and Peter Heydon had appreciated the importance of the records of their Department to the history of post-war migration. In November 1951 Heyes had delivered a lengthy paper to the Public Service Board's School of Instruction for Branch Officers on his Department's role and experience over the previous six years. In April

1951 he unsuccessfully sought approval from his Minister, Harold Holt, for funds to have this talk expanded into a history of his Department. He was, he explained, 'concerned that the story of the unique social experiment in which we are engaged so successfully is not being written except in the files of the Department'.[15]

In May 1953 the official historian of the 1914–18 war, C.E.W. Bean, approached the Prime Minister as chairman of the Commonwealth Archives Committee, requesting that a history of the Department of Immigration be written. A rather grandiose plan was subsequently prepared by the Department for a 32-chapter history of 3000 pages based on Departmental files and interviews with officers. It was anticipated that it would take six years to cover the period 1945–54. The National Librarian, H.L. White, offered the Library's assistance, and Arthur Calwell contributed his collection of 1947 press clippings. Not surprisingly, the Public Service Commission baulked at funding such a large project and it was eventually abandoned. In 1960 a much more modest ten-page chronicle of the Department's post-war activities was produced at the request of the Public Service Board, and another was prepared in March 1967 at the request of the Parliamentary Joint Committee on Public Accounts.[16]

The publication of a short history of Australia's immigration policy from 1945 was suggested again in March 1970 to Minister for Immigration Phillip Lynch by Labor parliamentarian and member of the Immigration Advisory Council L.H. Keogh. Lynch thought the suggestion an excellent one and promised to make inquiries. Peter Heydon, who was planning to write his own history of immigration during his retirement, believed the work should be done by an academic historian (preferably of some distinction). He discussed the project with a number of his academic friends in various States in 1970, but he had not drawn up a list of likely authors when he died in May the following year. Keogh again raised the issue in September 1972 with Lynch's successor, A.J. Forbes. He was told that staff constraints had caused planning to be postponed.[17]

When Keogh approached Grassby his suggestion of a short history of post-war migration was greeted with enthusiasm and expanded. The Minister envisaged a paperback history of 70–80 000 words extending from 1788 to the present, written by an academic historian of senior status, with research and other assistance provided by the Department. It would have a print run of 20 000 copies and was anticipated to cost $82 000 in salaries. In June 1973 the Department of Immigration asked the Public Service Board for a short list of history graduates from the recent graduate intake, and sought funds from the Treasury to establish a historical section within the Department. Treasury approved but no funds were allocated. The responsible officer, T.W. Eckersley, preferred Melbourne historian Geoffrey Blainey, whose style, he believed, suited a popular history and who would appreciate the economic significance of migration. Blainey was highly recommended by the Secretary in September 1973 when he submitted a list of sixteen 'eminent men' for the Minister to choose from. Grassby, however, preferred a 'narrative dealing directly with people'. The Department therefore recommended Melbourne social historian Michael Cannon, who was completing a trilogy on Australia during the late 19th century with a grant from the Commonwealth Literary Fund.[18]

In a news release, issued in November 1973, announcing the proposed Departmental history, Grassby described the proposed history as 'a tribute to this institution which has been such a fine catalyst in helping the building of the new nation we now are in 1973'. It was announced in Parliament on 4 December. Cannon was surprised by the Department's approach in April 1974, as immigration history had not been his particular area of interest. He was offered a contract based on those agreed to by official war historians. He asked for copyright and freedom from censorship, but the Department insisted that the copyright lay with the Commonwealth and would allow only Departmental research officers access to official documents less than 30 years old. The project was abandoned when Grassby lost office in the June 1974 elections and the Department of Immigration was dismembered. The new Department of Labor and Immigration forgot about it until January 1975, when it discovered that its Minister Clyde Cameron, Grassby, Keogh and Cannon had not been informed of the history's demise. In informing his Minister of the fate of the project, the Secretary commented that no single work existed on the popular history of migration and that Grassby had believed 'that a popular understanding of the role of immigration in Australia's development is fundamental to a sense of national identity'.[19]

A migration museum

Grassby's second and more ambitious attempt to expand the imagined community of Australian citizens was rather more fruitful. From 1970 Victorian Labor parliamentarian and medical practitioner Henry Alfred Jenkins had been attempting to arouse government interest in establishing a museum of immigration to preserve and display the documentary and photographic sources and 'relics' of migration history. He suggested as a model the museum established at the base of the Statue of Liberty in New York. In May 1973 he outlined the project to Grassby, who adopted it enthusiastically as 'a monument to migrants'.[20]

In July 1973 Grassby proposed to the Minister for the Capital Territory that a folklore museum be established in Canberra. He envisaged it as 'a compilation of documents and material recording the history of Australia's immigration and citizenship'. He imagined a building with exhibitions of arts and crafts, artifacts from the history of Australian communications and transport, as well as an open-air section where 'the environment of national life' would be represented by reconstructed and furnished dwellings, such as those of the Aborigines or of the first European settlers. Grassby argued that such a museum would complement the Australian War Memorial as, 'in addition to being attracted to Canberra to review Australia's record in war, the Australian citizen, both old and new, should also have the opportunity of appreciating, as an ensemble, the progress this country has made since it was first populated from Europe'. He suggested that when a new Parliament House was built on Capital Hill the old building could become the site of a museum on migration and citizenship.[21]

The concept of a migration museum became incorporated into a wider proposal for a national museum. In April 1974 Lionel Bowen, Special Minister for State, announced the government's decision to establish a committee of inquiry into the development and coordination of museums and collections. It was to plan the establishment of an institute to foster collections, research and displays of historical, cultural and scientific material of national significance. Chaired by P. Pigott, managing director of several companies concerned with conservation, its purpose was:

> not only to advance the cause of knowledge by preserving and developing the heritage of Australians for present and future generations but to provide a positive focus for our growing national feeling . . . At present Australia has no national institution which tells the story of Aboriginal man, early white settlement and discovery, the gold rushes and so on, through to modern times.

Rather than being a 'storehouse of things dead and past', this proposed museum was to be 'a living and dynamic institution which would educate Australians about their history and cultural heritage'. No mention was made of immigration.[22]

When approached by the Department of the Special Minister for State to make a submission to this inquiry, the Department's response indicated the awareness of cultural diversity which had resulted from its research into ethnic organisations, and which could be advocated officially by its representatives by 1974. The coordinator of the National Groups Survey reported:[23]

> I indicated that our Minister viewed migration material to be of great significance in the story of the nation, and the Australian cultural heritage to be particularly composed of strands drawn from ethnic cultures . . . The issue would seem to be one of great potential value in our longer-term community relations planning and would, I believe, be of interest to the Minister for Immigration, of whatever political affiliations.

The Department's submission stressed the desirability of including a substantial migration and ethnic component in the proposed national museum. As one in four of Australia's population was a migrant or a child of a migrant from 50 ethnic minorities, it argued, 'a major part of Australia's total population is linked directly by birth, or less directly, by family and marriage to the history, language, culture and traditions of an overseas country'. It described Australia as a 'multicultural' society in which 'each component is guaranteed the freedom to create its own communal life if it chooses, while at the same time being an integral part of the Australian nation'.[24]

In May 1974 Grassby announced the launching of an Australian Ethnic Heritage Program to preserve local ethnic collections of cultural and archival material, and to commission histories of various ethnic groups which would record their contributions to Australian life. A survey was conducted of holdings by groups such as the Latvian and Lithuanian communities in Adelaide, of cultural materials suitable for incorporation into a national museum. The Program would stage exhibitions using cultural, photographic and audiovisual material on the theme of 'the family of the nation'. The Department's concern that 'the unique contribution of ethnic groups to the life of the Australian nation be fully recognised and interpreted to the whole community' had been stimulated by projects initiated by the Canadian government. The Canadian National Museum of

Man, the Public Archives, the National Film Board, and the National Library since 1971, had held exhibitions aimed at 'sensitizing the majority groups in Canadian society to the cultural riches within the country'.[25]

THE DISMEMBERMENT OF THE DEPARTMENT OF IMMIGRATION 1974

When Grassby lost his seat in the 1974 Federal elections, Prime Minister Gough Whitlam took the opportunity of further devolving the responsibilities of the Department of Immigration by abolishing it. As he later explained:[26]

> It had become impossible for a department with only 2000 staff members to deal adequately with the needs of migrants in such diverse areas as immigration, emigration, settlement, citizenship and social policy. The decentralisation of responsibilities . . . improved the quality of migrant policy and services by tapping a wider range of human and financial resources within the bureaucracy.

There were other less rational motives. Somewhat unfairly, Whitlam never forgave the Department for its compliance with the request of its Minister, A.J. Forbes, that it supply him with summaries of Labor opinion on immigration in the period leading up to the 1972 election. It also contained an element of 'shooting the messenger'. 'Grassby found the Department of Immigration incurably racist', Whitlam later explained, citing as evidence a document prepared by the Department for the Liberal government in 1972. While many officers undoubtedly believed in the racially discriminatory policy they had been required to administer for almost 30 years, those who did not had had no choice but to make their decisions in accordance with a government policy which until the mid-1960s had the support of the Opposition and most Australians. Whitlam's abolition of the Department served dramatically to distance migration under his administration from the 'white Australia policy' of the past.[27]

A new Department of Labor and Immigration was created on 12 June 1974 under Clyde Cameron as Minister, comprising an Immigration Group operating from a central office in Canberra and a Labor Group with its headquarters in Melbourne. The Immigration Group retained the divisional structure of the former Department of Immigration and responsibility for migration planning, the selection, movement and reception of migrants, assisted migration, control and entry of visitors and citizenship. In February 1975, responsibility for migrant welfare and the administration of the *Immigration (Guardianship of Children) Act 1946* was transferred to the Department of Social Security, the Department of Education became responsible for migrant education and the Department of Housing and Construction for migrant accommodation. Although a number of experienced staff also transferred, the suddenness initially affected the quality of services offered to migrants.

Trust in the bureaucracy, in which voluntary compliance is necessarily rooted—and which the officers of the Department of Immigration involved in assimilation and integration activities had long striven to construct and sustain among the migrant community—was shaken. This was largely the result of the culture and history of the Department of Social Security, not of bureaucratic obstructionism. John Tarbath, the first officer of the Department of Immigration's Integration Branch to be transferred to Social Security, was greeted by Director General Laurie Daniels with: 'You blokes are going to be a breath of fresh air in this cheque factory'. Daniels' optimism was, however, unwarranted. As a director in the Department of Social Security explained to him in March 1975, the transfer of responsibilities for migrant settlement to a department that had been noted for its history of 'benign neglect' of migrants was greeted with suspicion and hostility by some migrants. It was important, he argued, that Social Security persuade migrants of its will and capacity to assume responsibility for their needs. He urged the provision of training for staff at all levels to sensitise them to the cultural and linguistic differences of migrants, the provision of pamphlets on social security in translation, and the creation of a pool of trained interpreters. A conference of senior assistant directors, officers in charge of Migrant Service Sections and senior social workers from all States, was held in May 1975 to achieve these ends.[28]

The Department of Social Security's staff establishment was inadequate to meet its new responsibilities for migrant welfare, and ethnic organisations were incapable of filling the gap. Only a few of the larger communities had their own service capacities by 1975, and even they were inadequate to meet all the needs of their communities. Many migrants still looked to government departments rather than to ethnic organisations for assistance, and the smaller groups would still be dependent on government-supplied services for many years. 'We do not really know the extent and depth of the needs of migrants beyond what we are confronted with on a day to day basis', complained a senior officer of the Department of Social Security. He felt his department was merely 'scratching the surface' in the provision of services, and perceived that pressure was building up from migrant communities for more appropriate and adequate services, and more readily accessible migrant welfare staff. The Department of Social Security in 1975 received far less correspondence from migrants than had the old Department of Immigration. This was attributed to its lack of focus on migrant issues. In the view of P.M. Rice, the dismemberment of the Department was a disaster. Social Security was not interested in migrant settlement, as its entire preoccupation was with the assessment and payment of pensions and benefits. John Tarbath described its culture as 'hide-bound by regulations'. He and his fellow officers were housed in a separate building from mainstream social security staff, and he experienced little sympathy and 'some antipathy' in working with them on migration issues. 'It was very much a we and them situation', he commented.[29]

The sudden transfer of settlement services by the Labor government in 1974 to other Commonwealth departments had been clearly premature and ill-prepared. The Department of Employment and Industrial Relations' migrant advisory service was particularly ineffective. On 22 December 1975, after the dismissal of the Labor government by the Governor-General, the Department of Labor and Immigration was abolished and its immigration responsibilities were transferred to a newly created Department of Immigration and Ethnic Affairs under Michael McKellar as Minister and with L.F. Bott as Secretary. Following the recommendations of the Bailly Task Force on Coordination in Welfare and Health in 1977, many but not all settlement functions were returned from the Department of Social Security to the Department of Immigration and Ethnic Affairs. The report, which obtained input from the Department of Immigration, recommended that the new Department of Immigration and Ethnic Affairs provide services to migrants within the first three to six months of arrival and that the long-term needs of migrants be met by relevant functional departments. It stressed, however, that other departments should, with the assistance of the Ethnic Affairs Office, review their services to ensure 'that they are geared to provide migrants, *as members of the general community*, with relevant services'. This recommendation was to develop into 'access and equity' policies in the next decade.

The report also recommended that where specific welfare services were needed for migrants over a long period these should be provided by funding welfare workers attached to ethnic and community groups. Administration of the *Immigration (Education Act) 1971* was taken back from the Department of Education (except that relating to the education of migrant children), and the Good Neighbour Movement was coordinated by the Department of Social Security until 1977.[30]

Conclusion

Labor's reduced immigration targets caused a significant decline in migrant intake during its less than three years in power. While most of the administrative restructuring it effected during its last year and a half in office was reversed by its successors, the effects of the cultural and legal changes it implemented were irreversible. Its movement towards a redefinition of Australia as a multicultural society was endorsed and promoted by all succeeding governments, both Labor and Liberal. Its efforts to involve other Commonwealth departments and ethnic communities in facilitating migrant settlement were also continued by future governments.

Even if it was not immediately implemented, Labor's clear commitment to an entry policy that would not discriminate on the grounds of race or ethnicity removed all barriers to the future migration of large numbers of Vietnamese and other non-European migrants. The elimination of this long-standing administrative discrimination opened Australia to another wave of demographic change, the cultural effects of which would be no less transforming than those begun by the European refugees from Europe 30 years earlier.

CHAPTER 12

Immigration, citizenship and settlement: goals, achievements and unintended consequences 1945–75

AUSTRALIA'S economic, social and cultural history during the period 1945–75 was shaped by large, interventionist, proactive governments. Government-assisted mass immigration was one of their most visible achievements. Responsibility for the successful social and economic absorption of the 2.6 million migrants who settled in Australia during this period lay with one Commonwealth department which managed immigration, citizenship and settlement. This centralisation of immigration-related functions, unique among migrant-receiving countries, permitted a considerable degree of coordination. However, within the Department of Immigration each of these areas had different goals, had by 1975 experienced different degrees of success, and had produced some unanticipated outcomes. They had also achieved very different public profiles and developed distinctly different bureaucratic cultures.

IMMIGRATION

The stated goals of the migration program, as outlined in the immediate post-war period, were to counteract the decline in population produced by an ageing population; to create full employment by diversifying the economy; and to improve Australia's defence capacity. The government's success in achieving these goals was very visible to the electorate by 1975. Labor's goal of an annual population growth of 1 per cent through immigration was largely realised by the Liberal governments that succeeded it. By the 1971 Census, immigrants (64 per cent of whom had arrived with government assistance), with their Australian-born children, had swelled the population by approximately 3.3 million in a total growth of 5.6 million over the period. In other words, directly and indirectly, immigration was responsible for about 59 per cent of Australia's population growth between 1947 and 1971, and one in three Australians was either a post-war migrant or the child of one. The intake was, however, more diverse than the one alien in eleven arrivals Calwell had hoped for in 1946—only just under 40 per cent of migrants over the 1947–74 period came from Britain.[1]

The contribution of immigration to the economic progress of Australia was also obvious by 1975. Secondary industry had flourished due to migration. Because of the high proportion of migrants in the working-age groups, migration boosted the growth in the labour force much more than it did that of the total population. Migrants comprised more than two-thirds of the net increase in the manufacturing workforce in the 1950s, and in the 1960s there was an absolute decline in the number of native-born workers in factories. The post-war lag in housing had been eliminated by the late 1950s, largely due to migrant labour, and great progress had been made in raising Australian standards of living. The demand created by immigration contributed to the low levels of unemployment that characterised this period and increased the production of additional social overhead capital such as housing, roads, transport, hospitals, schools and energy.[2]

Australia's increased population injected a new self-confidence into its defence policy, which by the 1960s gave priority to Australia's own regional interests and had abandoned many traditional links with Britain. Australia's entry into the American war in Vietnam in 1965, a war in which Britain did not participate, was made possible by the introduction of conscription, and many of the 63 735 conscripts who served in Vietnam were the Australian-born sons of migrants or naturalised Australians.[3]

By 1975 some unintended consequences of Australia's mass migration policy had become evident. In striving to maintain high annual intakes the government introduced an increasingly diverse range of cultures to Australia. The migration agreement with Turkey, concluded in October 1967, for the first time brought in significant numbers of non-Christian migrants. The 1966 reforms, which allowed the entry of skilled non-Europeans, effectively destroyed the 'white Australia policy'. Ironically, Australia's intervention in the war in Vietnam, promoted by the government as a defence against Asian invasion, resulted in the first large influx of Asian refugees. Like the refugees from Europe, who came as a result of Australia's obligations as a participant in the 1939–45 war, these Vietnamese refugees initiated a new phase of profound cultural transformation in Australia.

Citizenship

The government's goal was that all those granted permanent residence in Australia should become Australian citizens. In order to achieve that goal it introduced legislative and administrative changes which made citizenship easier to acquire, and removed legislative provisions which made citizenship by grant seem a second-class form of citizenship. It also removed incentives to acquire citizenship for what it believed to be the wrong reasons—most notably the requirement that applicants for age, invalid and widows' pensions be Australian citizens. By 1975 all applicants for Australian citizenship were treated equally, regardless of nationality; the discrimination that had long favoured British applicants had ended.

These achievements were less visible to the electorate than the lack of success experienced by the Department of Immigration in its attempts to encourage eligible migrants to accept Australian citizenship. British migrants were the least likely to apply, and the requirements that applicants for Australian citizenship renounce their former citizenship and take an oath of allegiance to the Queen remained a deterrent for some aliens.

The principal unintended consequence in the area of citizenship by 1975 was a reconceptualisation of the nature of Australian citizenship. This came about, in part, as a result of the interaction by the Department of Immigration over 30 years with an increasingly diverse migrant intake. By 1975 the earlier conception of citizenship as membership of a society essentially British in culture and ethnicity had been largely replaced by an understanding of citizenship based on the attainment of full social, civil and political rights. This was assisted by the philosophy of the Labor government which, in 1973, set new benchmarks for citizenship in Australia by deciding to ratify a number of United Nations covenants on civil, political, cultural and economic rights, and on the rights of women. This changed conception of citizenship attracted new criticism to the Department in the 1970s, particularly from some academics, who now condemned it for its past failure to protect the rights of migrant citizens and proto-citizens.

Settlement

Unlike most European countries during this period, the Australian government had no intention of attracting 'guest workers'; its goal was to achieve the full social and economic integration of those it accepted for permanent stay in Australia. Initially, many legislative and administrative obstacles prevented compliance with this expectation. Through the insight obtained by its social workers in particular, the Department of Immigration became aware of these obstacles and advocated with other agencies for their removal. In some cases, such as with the removal of the nationality bar to age, invalid and widows' pensions, they were successful; in other cases, particularly in the area of skills recognition, they were not. Where advocacy failed, or was inappropriate, the Department set up its own facilities for migrants, often in collaboration with other agencies. On-arrival accommodation for migrants was managed in collaboration with the Department of Labour and National Service. Through the Adult Migrant Education Scheme the Department of Immigration provided funding, management, and policy advice to Commonwealth and State Departments of Education on teaching English to adult migrants. They, in turn, contributed the professional and technical advice, organised the curriculum and supplied the teachers and classrooms. In 1968, when its attempts to advocate with bodies having the legislative power to register professionally qualified migrants failed, the Department set up its own agency to assist them—the Committee on Overseas Professional Qualifications.[4]

None of this activity by the Department of Immigration was visible to the Australian public. Even those functions which it managed entirely alone—such as Grants-in-Aid to enable organisations to provide welfare assistance to migrants, or the

Australia-wide network of telephone interpreting it provided from 1973—gained little public recognition, even from academic writers on migrant settlement in Australia.

The fears of the early opponents of migration were not realised: the social integration of over 3 million migrants and their children was achieved without ethnic violence, political subversion, the erosion of the wages and conditions of Australian workers, or the creation of ethnic ghettos. As the demographer W.D. Borrie commented in 1975, 'the integration of non-British settlers since 1947 has run remarkably smoothly given the diversity and size of the ethnic mix'. This could not have been achieved without considerable government intervention in a society such as Australia was in the 1940s and 1950s, in which discrimination on the grounds of nationality and ethnicity was entrenched in legislation and major institutions. It would be naive in the extreme to attribute the social harmony achieved by 1975, despite the influx of so many migrants from such a wide range of cultures, to the easy-going tolerance of the host community rather than to some degree of good management.[5]

The successful management of migrant settlement was, however, beyond the power of one government department. This was accepted by the government only in the 1970s, although the hasty devolution of the Department of Immigration's responsibilities to other departments by the Labor government in 1974 was ill-conceived and, in the case of its settlement services, largely counterproductive. The inadequacy of one government department to deal with the myriad problems of new arrivals in an unfamiliar society had long been recognised by Department of Immigration social workers, who constructed networks of individuals and organisations on whom they could rely to provide the interpreting and other practical assistance their clients needed. However, because of their conception of Australia as a homogeneous, British society and their lack of understanding of cultural diversity and of the difficulties involved in migration, senior bureaucrats and politicians were slow to recognise this. During the 1950s they placed their faith in the largely Anglo-Celtic Good Neighbour Movement as an agent of assimilation, and had unwarranted confidence in its ability to encourage migrants to take advantage of the English-language classes available to them.

The Department of Immigration's ability to work constructively with other bodies concerned with migrant welfare was patchy. While Departmental social workers enlisted the help of individual migrants and some ethnic groups, the National Groups Liaison Unit found most migrant organisations in the late 1960s and early 1970s to be largely social clubs, ill-equipped to provide services to needy members of their communities. Those with well-developed welfare services, notably two from the Italian and Jewish communities, became the first recipients of Grants-in-Aid. This funding helped to transform many migrant organisations into structured, competitive and politically astute lobbyists on behalf of their communities. The Department attempted to enlist the help of religious and other community bodies in migrant welfare through the Good Neighbour Movement. Most, however, developed their own independent services for migrants, such as the Roman Catholic Church, particularly for Italians; the Maronite Catholic and Antioch Orthodox Churches, which catered for Lebanese Christians; the Greek and Russian Orthodox Churches; the Lutheran Church, to which many German and Scandinavian migrants looked for assistance; and, towards the end of this period, Muslim associations and Mosques were established to cater for Muslim migrants, particularly Lebanese and Turks. The Department also had frequent contact with diplomatic representatives, who advocated on behalf of their citizens in Australia. Some, like the Italian, Yugoslav and Maltese diplomats, insisted on having guarantees of adequate settlement provisions incorporated into migration agreements.

After initial planning under Calwell, the Department of Immigration's settlement policy tended to be reactive rather than proactive until the late 1960s. Nevertheless, its responses were generally constructive, as demonstrated by the establishment of child-minding facilities in migrant accommodation centres in the early 1950s to enable migrant mothers to work. Minister for Immigration Alexander Downer deprived individual migrants of a valuable source of assistance, other agencies of a way of becoming involved in meeting the needs of migrants, and his own Department of an important source of policy advice, when he slashed the numbers of its social workers in 1959. Despite this, the Survey and Integration Sections in the 1960s still managed to draw on the work of the remaining social workers to collect and analyse information on the settlement experiences of migrants. This monitoring process produced two important Departmental innovations in the late 1960s and early 1970s—Grants-in-Aid and the Telephone Interpreter Service.

The experience gained by the Department of Immigration in

settling migrants led to an outcome never intended by Calwell and the early planners of migrant settlement. They had assumed that the social and economic assimilation of migrants would take place without changing mainstream culture. In fact, in order to absorb migrants, a whole raft of laws and regulations, which had sustained Australia as a country of essentially British culture and ethnicity, had to be changed—not least of which were the administrative arrangements by means of which the Department had preserved 'white Australia'. By 1973 the reconceptualisation of Australia as a multicultural society was first enunciated by the Minister for Immigration.

By 1974 the long period of economic growth that had enabled successive governments to complete the process of industrial diversification outlined by the Labor government in 1945 had ended. In Australia, as in other countries, the conditions so conducive to economic and social progress during the post-war period were replaced by stagflation. Australia entered a new, and still current, phase of economic restructuring. The role of the state was reduced, manufacturing was reshaped to make it more competitive, markets were deregulated and revitalised, and a much higher level of unemployment was regarded as acceptable, while new sources of employment growth were anxiously sought. Migrant settlement is now conducted in a very different economic climate than it was in the period 1945–75. Stephanie Charlesworth, now a family court lawyer, compares unfavourably the medical, dental, legal and other community facilities available today with those on which she could call to assist her clients in the late 1940s and early 1950s, when she began her career as a social worker with the Department of Immigration. She remarks with passion, 'it was infinitely better . . . it was heaven compared to now'.[6]

Appendix

Australian Archives records of post-war immigration

The Australian Archives holds a range of records documenting the Commonwealth government administration of post-war immigration. These are the records of Commonwealth departments, offices, and official inquiries, as well as the personal papers of Prime Ministers and Ministers for Immigration. The national office in Canberra holds the records of Cabinet and of the Department of Immigration, while each of the State offices hold files relating to migrants who settled in those states.

All members of the public have a general right of access to records over thirty years old. To help provide access to these records, the Archives documents the numbers and titles of particular files and also the groups or categories of records (known as series) to which they belong and the government agency which created them. This information about agencies and series is available on the Internet on the Australian Archives site at *http://www.aa.gov.au* while information about individual items is available on a database which can be accessed at any of the Archives' offices.

All this information can be searched by keywords, names and dates to locate records about a particular subject. Original records can be inspected in the reading room of the office which holds them. For some popular series such as passenger lists there are microfilm copies held at each office.

Information about post-war immigration covers the full range of government records from Cabinet papers and policy documents to files about individuals who migrated to Australia. Some of this material will only be available in future years when it is thirty years old.

Material held in Canberra includes:

- Correspondence files of the Department of Immigration including policy files and case files containing information about unassisted migrants, migrant education, individual migrant centres, and workers' hostels.
- Cabinet submissions and decisions of all ministries of the period.
- Migrant selection documents comprising intending migrants' applications for assisted passage to Australia. The Canberra office also holds the selection documents and personal files of displaced persons.
- Passenger lists (from 1924) and passenger cards for all ports in Australia.
- Naturalisation files and duplicate copies of naturalisation certificates. Reference staff can consult a microfiche version of the Department of Immigration Citizenship Index on behalf of researchers to help them identify the right files.
- Volumes of reports and committee papers of the Commonwealth Immigration Planning Council, 1949–66. The Council reported on progress in absorbing migrants into industry and development projects, reviewed accommodation and employment problems encountered by migrants, and made recommendations on ways immigration contributed to desirable patterns of development in Australia.
- Volumes of agenda, notes, minutes and reports of the Commonwealth Immigration Advisory Council, 1947–68. The Council (containing representatives from parliament, industry and social bodies) advised the Minister for Immigration on relevant administrative, legislative and sociological matters. Committees were established to research issues concerning citizenship, interpreter needs, social patterns, migrant women, the incidence of mental illness among migrants, and community relations.
- Correspondence, working papers, reports and transcripts of public hearings of the National Population Inquiry,

1970–78. A Commonwealth government initiative, the Inquiry was managed and jointly funded by the Department of Immigration and the Australian National University. The Inquiry was concerned with all aspects of population growth, both natural increase and immigration, with the aim of contributing to the formulation and application of national policies.

The Victorian office holds the minutes, agenda and reports of the Committee on Overseas Professional Qualifications, 1969–84. The Committee's major responsibilities were the collection and supply of information relevant to the recognition of overseas professional qualifications and the evaluation of their comparison to Australian standards.

The records of the Immigration Publicity Council, including the minutes and agenda 1969–70, are held by the South Australian office.

Personal archives

The Australian Archives holds the personal archives (including correspondence, speeches, and newspaper cuttings) of many of the Ministers for Immigration who held office between 1945 and 1975, including H.F. Holt (1949–56), A.R. Downer (1958–63), P.R. Lynch (1969–71), A.J. Forbes (1971–72), L.H. Barnard (1972), C.R. Cameron (1974–75), J.R. McClelland (1975) and A.A. Street (1975). Most of these records are only available to the public once they are thirty years old.

Personal archives of prime ministers for the period are also available after thirty years: J.B. Chifley (1945–49), H.E. Holt (1966–67), J.G. Gorton (1968–71) and E.G. Whitlam (1972–75).

The National Library of Australia holds the personal papers of A.J. Grassby (Minister for Immigration, 1972–74) and prime minister R.G. Menzies.

Overseas posts records

During the post-war period, the Immigration Department increased its overseas representation through Australian Migration Offices at embassies, consulates and high commissions throughout the world. The Canberra office holds general correspondence and migrant case files from overseas posts in many countries in Europe, Africa and Asia.

Immigration case files

Each State office holds Department of Immigration case files and migrant selection documents relating to migrants who first settled in the State. These are usually held in separate series according to country or continent of origin (e.g. British, Maltese, European), or whether migrants were assisted or unassisted. There are more specific series such as those relating to British Child Migrants (held in Victoria and Western Australia) and migrants arriving in Queensland under the Netherlands–Australia Migration Scheme Agreement.

Passenger lists

Inwards passenger lists for ports, listing all passengers by name, port of embarkation, occupation, age and nationality, arriving on a particular ship or aircraft on a particular date, are held by each State office. The Fremantle lists, a microfilm copy of which is held in all offices, are a particularly useful source because ships from Europe would arrive there before proceeding to the eastern States.

Migrant accommodation and services

- Correspondence files, case files, name index cards, photographs and plans of various migrant accommodation centres (including Benalla, Bonegilla, Rushworth, Greta, Kapooka, Stuart, Wacol and Somers) are held by the Canberra office.
- Department of Labour and National Service records (central office, Victorian office, and Migrant Workers Accommodation Division) are held by the Victorian office, together with records of the Somers Migrant Accommodation Centre, migrant applications for hostel transfer, and welfare case files.
- Department of Labour and National Service correspondence of the Migrant Workers Accommodation Division (including files relating to migrants at migrant accommodation centres in New South Wales and other States), migrant transitory flats scheme files, and records relating to the

telephone interpreter service are located in the New South Wales office.
- The Western Australian office holds migrant post-arrival assistance (welfare) case files and Department of Immigration and Department of Health correspondence files including monthly reports from the migrant accommodation centres at Northam and Cunderdin.
- Records from the migrant accommodation centres at Wacol and Enoggera and registers of migrants admitted for treatment of tuberculosis are held by the Queensland office.
- The South Australian office has migrant accommodation records for Woodside, approvals for migrant movement from hostels in South Australia, Victoria and New South Wales, together with Department of Labour and National Service records of the Migrant Workers Accommodation Division for South Australian hostels, and social work case files.

Good Neighbour Councils

Good Neighbour Councils were autonomous bodies financed through the Commonwealth government from 1950 whose purpose was to assist in the welcome, welfare and integration of migrants to Australia. Records include minutes, agendas, reports, correspondence and publications of the Good Neighbour Council of the Australian Capital Territory (Canberra office), records of the Good Neighbour Council of Victoria (Victorian office) and records of the Western Australian Branch of the Good Neighbour Council (Western Australian office).

Notes

Chapter 1 The Role of the Department of Immigration in Migrant Settlement

1. Jean I. Martin, *The Migrant Presence. Australian Responses 1947–1977*, Research Report for the National Population Inquiry, George Allen & Unwin, Sydney, 1978, p. 9, pp. 61–2.
2. T.H.E. Heyes, secretary Department of Immigration to Harold Holt, minister for immigration, 11.7.1951, Australian Archives (AA), Australian Capital Territory (ACT): A445/1, 142/4/2.
3. The concept of 'imagined community' is derived from Benedict Anderson, *Imagined Communities: Reflections on the Origin and Spread of Nationalism*, Verso, London, 1983 (1991 reprint); for a more detailed account of the formation and role of the Department of Immigration and of discrimination on the grounds of race, gender and disability in Australian citizenship legislation see Ann-Mari Jordens, *Redefining Australians: Immigration, Citizenship and National Identity*, Hale & Iremonger, Sydney, 1995, pp. 1–33.
4. Examples of Department of Immigration advocacy are detailed in this book, also in Jordens, *Redefining Australians* (see particularly chapter 4 on access by aliens to public and private sector housing, chapter 6 on social welfare benefits, and chapter 7 on skills recognition).
5. See also Jordens, *Redefining Australians*, chapter 9, for the political debate on the removal of pro-British discrimination.

6   Margaret Levi, *The Construction of Consent*, Administration, Compliance and Governability Program working paper no. 10, March 1993, p. 27.
7   Commonwealth Parliamentary Debates, House of Representatives (CPDHR) vol. 184, p. 4911–5; *Population and Australia: A Demographic Analysis* (chairman W.D. Borrie), vol. 1, Australian Government Publishing Service, Canberra, 1975, pp. 99–100; for a more detailed account of post-war manpower planning see Jordens, *Redefining Australians*, chapter 2.
8   *What Immigration Means to Australia*, report by minister for immigration the Rt. Hon. H.E. Holt, 30 August 1956, Parliament of the Commonwealth of Australia, p. 9; CPDHR, vol. 196, 16 April 1948 and vol. 211, p. 3787, 6 December 1950; for further information on community-based advisory bodies see Jordens, *Redefining Australians*, chapters 2 and 5.
9   CPDHR vol. 189, p. 508; *Population and Australia*, pp. 99–100; statistics from Department of Immigration, *Australian Immigration Quarterly Statistical Summary*, table of permanent and long-term arrivals 1945, p. 35, 1976; CPDHR, vol. 204, p. 144, 8 September 1949.
10 For details of the employment arrangements for IRO refugees and other assisted migrants see Jordens, *Redefining Australians*, pp. 28–31. The most comprehensive account of the post-war refugee resettlement programs is to be found in Louise W. Holborn, *The International Refugee Organisation, A Specialised Agency of the United Nations: Its History and Work 1946–1952*, Oxford University Press, London, 1956.
11 For details of the employment arrangements for German scientists see Jordens, *Redefining Australians*, pp. 115–16; information on the European refugee situation is derived from a paper by Sir Clifford E. Heathcote-Smith, 'Proposal for a new era of emigration. Europe's uprooted millions', 7 April 1949, and from extracts prepared from report no. 1841, 'Expellees and Refugees of German Ethnic Origin', by the Committee of Judiciary, US House of Representatives, 24 March 1950, AA(ACT): A445/1, 194/2/3.
12 For an account of the advocacy of the Department of Immigration in relation to trade and professional skills recognition see Jordens, *Redefining Australians*, chapter 7.
13 Barrie Dyster and David Meredith, *Australia in the International Economy in the Twentieth Century*, Cambridge University Press, Melbourne, 1990, pp. 100–201.
14 Information on the co-option of the RSSAILA is derived from a letter, R.G. Casey to Harold Holt, 16 August 1950, AA(ACT): A445/1, 194/2/3, and submission, Tasman Heyes to Minister, 31 August 1950, AA(ACT): A445/1, 142/5/2.
15 For further details of this PICMME scheme see Jordens, *Redefining Australians*, pp. 37–8; unpublished paper prepared on 10 April 1953

for Pierre Jacobsen, deputy director ICEM, Geneva, entitled 'Report on Berlin' was supplied to the author by Harold Grant.

16 For a more detailed account of the effect of the 1952 recession on alien workers see Jordens, *Redefining Australians*, pp. 38–40, and chapter 2 of this book.

17 *What Immigration Means to Australia*, report by minister for immigration the Rt. Hon. H.E. Holt, 30 August 1956, Parliament of the Commonwealth of Australia, p. 11; Dyster and Meredith, p. 208; statement by Alexander Downer, CPDHR, vol. 24, p. 968.

18 For a detailed account of the issue of Aboriginal Conscription during the 1960s see Ann-Mari Jordens, 'An Administrative Nightmare: Aboriginal Conscription 1965–72', *Aboriginal History*, vol. 13, nos 1–2, 1989, pp. 124–34; for a more detailed description of the citizenship status of Aborigines see Jordens, *Redefining Australians*, pp. 10–13; for an account of the pressure for the conscription of aliens in the 1960s see Jordens, *Redefining Australians*, pp. 142–9.

19 For more detail on this topic see chapter 10; information about Sydney University is derived from Dyster and Meredith, p. 212.

20 Dyster and Meredith, p. 234, pp. 236–8, p. 259.

21 Information on the economy is derived from Dyster and Meredith, pp. 261–3; migration target figures are from Charles A. Price and Jean I. Martin, *Australian Immigration: A Bibliography and Digest*, no. 3, 1995, part 1, p. A11; the migration statistics, which have been rounded to the nearest thousand, are from Department of Immigration, Australian Immigration Quarterly Statistical Summary, table of permanent and long-term arrivals 1945, p. 35, 1976, AGPS, Canberra, 1977, p. 35; see chapter 10 for a detailed account of the erosion of the 'white Australia policy'.

22 Dyster and Meredith, pp. 261–3, pp. 314–15.

23 *Arrivals and Departures*, p. 166.

24 *Decade of Migrant Settlement*, pp. 91–3, pp. 123–34.

25 *The Migrant Presence*, p. 28, p. 38, p. 50, pp. 61–2.

26 David Cox and Jean I. Martin (eds), *The Welfare of Migrants*, AGPS, Canberra, 1975, pp. 5–19.

27 *Australian Social Work*, vol. 36, no. 3, September 1983, pp. 10–17.

28 David R. Cox, *Migration and Welfare: An Australian Perspective*, Prentice Hall, New York, 1987, p. 213, p. 216, p. 222; for example *Welfare Practice in a Multicultural Society*, p. 185.

29 Janis Wilton and Richard Bosworth, *Old Worlds and New Australia: The Postwar Migrant Experience*, Penguin Books, Ringwood, 1984, the references and quotations in this paragraph are derived, in order, from p. 100, p. 187, p. 26, p. 178.

30 Jock Collins, *Migrant Hands in a Distant Land*, Pluto Press, Sydney, 1988, p. 167.

31 A. Jakubowicz, 'State and ethnicity: multiculturalism as ideology',

The Australian and New Zealand Journal of Sociology', vol. 17, no. 3, November 1981, p. 6, p. 10.
32 A. Jakubowicz, 'Welfare provision' in J. Jupp (ed.), *The Australian People,* Angus & Robertson, Sydney, 1988, pp. 963–7; for an analysis of the causes for the reduction in qualifying periods for non-British migrants seeking pensions and the removal of the nationality requirement for age, invalid and widows' pensions see Jordens, *Redefining Australians,* pp. 95–101; Andrew Jakubowicz, 'The state and the welfare of migrants in Australia', *Ethnic and Racial Studies,* vol. 12, no. 1, January 1989, pp. 1–35.
33 Stephen Castles et al., *Mistaken Identity: Multiculturalism and the Demise of Nationalism in Australia,* Pluto Press, Sydney, 1988, quotations from 3rd edn, 1992, pp. 43, 47, 53, 54.
34 Edited by Gary P. Freeman and James Jupp; quotations from pp. 138, 141, 142, 146–7.
35 Oleh Lukomskyj, *An Overview of Australian Government Settlement Policy 1945–1992,* Bureau of Immigration Research, 1992, pp. 1–10.
36 Mark Wooden et al., *Australian Immigration: A Survey of the Issues,* AGPS, Canberra, 1944, p. 26 ; pp. 322, 320, 312–13, 320.
37 Adam Jamrozik, Cathy Boland and Robert Urquhart, *Social Change and Cultural Transformation in Australia,* Cambridge University Press, Melbourne, 1995, pp. 68, 182, 70, 72–3, 182.
38 John Lack and Jacqueline Templeton, *Bold Experiment,* Oxford University Press, Melbourne, 1995, pp. 74–9 (quotation from p. 89).

CHAPTER 2 THE TWO FACES OF THE DEPARTMENT OF IMMIGRATION

1 Interview with P.M. Rice, 14 September 1996.
2 H. Dobson, report of the Social Welfare Section, Department of Immigration, Melbourne, 26.3.1952, AA(ACT): A445/1, 140/5/6; minute G.C. Watson to assistant secretary Encouraged Migration Division, 19.10.1948, AA(ACT): A434/1, 150/3/17477.
3 H. Dobson, report of the Social Welfare Section, Department of Immigration, Melbourne, 26.3.1952, AA(ACT): A445/1, 140/5/6; minute G.C. Watson to assistant secretary Encouraged Migration Division, 19.10.1948, AA(ACT): A434/1, 50/3/17477.
4 H. Dobson, report of the Social Welfare Section, Department of Immigration, Melbourne, 26.3.1952, AA(ACT): A445/1, 140/5/6; minute, G.C. Watson to assistant secretary Encouraged Migration Division, 19.10.1948. AA(ACT): A434/1, 150/3/17477.
5 Interviews with Pauline Griffin, 12 September 1996; Stephanie Charlesworth, 18 October 1996 and John Tarbath, 22 October 1996. Information on Dobson's relations with Heyes provided by Nancy

Anderson, a social worker who joined the Brisbane office of the Department in 1966, given to her by the late Florence Ferguson, a senior social worker in the Sydney office of the Department.

6 Report of the Social Welfare Section, Department of Immigration, Melbourne, 26.3.1952, AA(ACT): A445/1, 140/5/6; statement by the Social Welfare Section prepared for the first meeting, Committee of the Immigration Advisory Council on Social Welfare, 22.4.1952, AA(ACT): A445/1, 140/5/6.

7 Report of the Social Welfare Section, Department of Immigration, Melbourne, 26.3.1952, AA(ACT): A445/1, 140/5/6; for further information on the Good Neighbour Movement see Jordens, *Redefining Australians*, chapter 5.

8 Interviews with John Tarbath, 22 October 1996; Pauline Griffin, 12 September 1996, Stephanie Charlesworth (née Armstrong), 18 October 1996; and Nora Sebesfi (née Brack) and Sylvia Lyons, 30 October 1996.

9 Interviews with Stephanie Charlesworth, 18 October 1996; and Sylvia Lyons, 30 October 1996.

10 Interviews with Pauline Griffin, 12 September 1996; and Stephanie Charlesworth, 18 October 1996.

11 Annual report 1950–51 senior social worker NSW, AA(ACT): A445/1, 276/3/2; interview with Pauline Griffin, 12 September 1996; report of Social Welfare Section 1949–51, AA(ACT): A445/1, 140/5/6; interview with Stephanie Charlesworth, 18 October 1996.

12 S. Lyons, annual report 26.1.1951; annual report July 1949–June 1950, senior social worker Sydney, AA(ACT): A445/1, 276/3/2. For further information on discrimination on the grounds of nationality in the grant of social welfare benefits see Jordens, *Redefining Australians*, chapter 6.

13 G.N. Hunter, monthly report for February, 1950, 23.3.1950, AA(ACT): A445/1, 276/3/4; interview with Sylvia Lyons, 30 October 1996.

14 Reports 15/16.9.1949, AA(ACT): A445/1, 276/3/2.

15 Interview with Pauline Griffin, 12 September 1996.

16 Interview with Sylvia Lyons, 30 October 1996; report for period 1.10.1951–5.11.1952, G.N. Hunter, social worker SA, 6.11.1952, AA(ACT): A445/1, 276/3/4.

17 Interview with Pauline Griffin, 12 September 1996, and Stephanie Charlesworth, 18 October 1996.

18 Interview with Pauline Griffin, 12 September 1996, and Nora Brack, 30 September 1996.

19 B.C. Wall, CMO Sydney to Mr Armstrong, 11.11.1952, AA(ACT): A445/1, 276/3/2.

20 Report of action by the Department of Immigration and Good Neighbour Organisation to implement resolutions of the fourth Australian Citizenship Convention, Canberra, January 1953,

AA(ACT): A445/1, 146/8/14; letter by T.H.E. Heyes, n.d. (c. 13.6.1952), AA(ACT): A445/1, 194/2/3.
21 H.E. Holt, 'What Immigration Means to Australia', parliamentary paper printed 30.8.1956, p. 10; T.H.E. Heyes, secretary Department of Immigration to Colonel R.R. Ryan, chairman Commonwealth Advisory Council on Social Welfare, 24.12.51, AA(ACT): A445/1, 140/5/6.
22 Notes of meeting of Social Welfare Committee meeting 1.2.1952, and minute by M.F. Manning, 7.4.1952, AA(ACT): A445/1, 140/5/6.
23 Boyd Graham, VCSS, to Minister 15.11.1951, AA(ACT): A445/1, 276/1/9; secretary Department of Immigration to H.E. Best, secretary and director, Department of Tourist Activities and Immigration, Sydney, 19.6.1953; paper on the immigration program prepared by the Immigration Planning Council, 18.12.1953, AA(ACT): A445/1, 142/5/2.
24 Interview with Nora Brack, 30 September 1996; verbatim notes of Social Welfare Committee and reports of interested organisations at a meeting in Canberra 1.2.1952; notes required by Mr Heyes for interview with Professor Paton 3.4.1952, AA(ACT): A445/1, 140/5/6; Rosalie A. James, report, 7.1.1952–30.6.1952, AA(ACT): A445/1, 276/3/2; statistics of immigrants from Department of Immigration, Local Government and Ethnic Affairs, *Australia and Immigration 1788–1988*, AGPS, Canberra, 1988, p. 36.
25 Notes required by Mr Heyes for interview with Professor Paton 3.4.1952; statement on role of Social Welfare Section for the first meeting of the Advisory Council on Social Welfare 28.4.1952, AA(ACT): A445/1, 140/5/6.
26 Report of Social Welfare Section, 26.3.1952, section 2, p. 7, AA(ACT): A445/1, 140/5/6.
27 Social Welfare Section reports, 26.3, 22.4 and 20.5.1952; notes for the Secretary, 3.4.1952, AA(ACT): A445/1, 140/5/6.
28 Report of action by the Department of Immigration and the Good Neighbour Organisation to implement resolutions of the Fourth Australian Citizenship Convention held in Canberra, January 1953, p. 6, AA(ACT): A445/1, 156/8/14; interview with Stephanie Charlesworth, 18 October 1996.
29 Hazel Dobson, officer in charge Social Welfare Section, report dated 14.5.1952; minute, R.E. Armstrong to Secretary, n.d. AA(ACT): A445/1, 276/2/4.
30 Hazel Dobson in her report for financial year 1956/57 indicated that during 1955/57 one client in every seven reported employment as the major problem. The figures for 1956–57 were: NSW 1 in 4; Vic. 1 in 3; SA 1 in 7, AA(ACT): A445/1, 276/2/4.
31 Hazel Dobson, report for financial year 1956/7, AA(ACT): A445/1, 276/2/4.
32 See file entitled 'Social workers' reports on hostel visiting' (1953), AA(ACT): A445/1, 276/1/15; for further detail on government

accommodation for migrants see Jordens, *Redefining Australians,* chapter 3.
33 Letter 12.3.1952, AA(ACT): A445/1, 194/1/3.
34 Report on the 1951 Immigration Program, T.H.E. Heyes to Minister, p. 2, 31.8.1950, AA(ACT): A445/1, 142/5/2; memo by assistant secretary Department of Immigration A.L. Nutt, 4.3.1949, AA(ACT): A434/1, 49/3/5831; interview with Stephanie Charlesworth, 18 October 1996.
35 Secretary Department of Immigration to CMO Cologne, 21.3.1952, and attached Department of Labour and National Service note on conditions of domestic employment, AA(ACT): A445/1, 194/1/3; secretary Department of Immigration to CMO Cologne, 23.6.1952, principal terms and conditions of employment in Australia, AA(ACT): A445/1, 118/1/4.
36 Hazel Dobson, Social Welfare Section, Department of Immigration, report 1956/7, AA(ACT): A445/1, 276/2/4; Andrew Jakubowicz and Berenice Buckley, *Migrants and the Legal System,* Australian Government Commission of Inquiry into Poverty, AGPS, Canberra, 1975, p. 1, and Australian Government Commission of Inquiry into Poverty (Chairman R.F. Henderson), first main report, AGPS, Canberra, 1975, vol. 1, p. 270.
37 CPDHR, vol. 8, pp. 1305–6, 6.10.1955 (Coutts); vol. 13, pp. 1151–2, 4.10.1956 (Bruce); other references to the suitability of women for domestic work and/or marriage were made by Alexander Downer, vol. 7, pp. 1022, and Clyde Cameron, pp. 1024–6, 28.9.1955, and Downer, vol. 12, p. 269, 6.9.1956.
38 Department of Immigration paper 'Discrimination in entry policy', n.d. (c. 1973), AA(ACT): A445/T31, 175/78542.
39 Tom Stratton in *Angels and Arrogant Gods: Migration Officers and Migrants Reminisce 1945–85,* AGPS, Canberra, 1989, p. 92.
40 Charles Price (ed.), *Greeks in Australia,* ANU Press, Canberra, 1975, p. 24; E.C. Vrisakis to Allan Fraser MP, 18.10.1948, Calwell's reply, 15.12.1948; Christy Freeleagus, consul-general for Greece to W.P. Conelan MP, 11.2.1949 and Calwell's reply, 24.3.1949, AA(ACT): A445/1, 197/1/2.
41 Eugene Gorman, consul for Greece to the secretary of the Department of Immigration, 25.1.1951, AA(ACT): A445/1, 197/1/2; report by A.N. Boyle, immigration attaché, Rome, to secretary Department of Immigration, 21.2.1951; memorandum on the visit of a Greek delegation by CMO South Australia, to Secretary, 23.2.1951; Walter J. Cooper, minister of repatriation to minister for immigration H. Holt, forwarding cutting from the *Hellenic Herald* (Sydney), 14.5.1951, AA(ACT): A445/1, 197/1/2.
42 Secretary to Minister, notes on the Prospect of Greek Migration, 31.1.1952, AA(ACT): A445/1 197/1/2; E.C. Vrisakis, 7.1.1952, AA(ACT): A445/1, 197/1/2; paper on the Immigration Program prepared by the Immigration Planning Council, 18.12.1953,

AA(ACT): A445/1, 142/5/2; cablegram from the Australian consulate-general Geneva, to the acting minister Department of Immigration, AA(ACT): A445/1, 16.8.1952, 197/1/2; Hugh Gibson, ICEM, to secretary Department of Immigration, 6.11.1953, AA(ACT): A445/1, 118/1/9.
43 Minute, R.H. Rowbridge to assistant secretary, 2 12.1952, AA(ACT): A445/1, 197/1/5; minute B.M. Martyn to secretary, 30.11.1953, AA(ACT): A445/1, 197/1/9; minute, G.C. Watson to first assistant secretary, 9.12.1953; A.H. Bland, secretary Department of Labour and National Service (DLNS) to secretary Department of Immigration, 8.12.1953; secretary Department of Immigration to secretary Department of External Affairs, 15.12.1953, AA(ACT): A445/1, 197/1/9.
44 R.F. Harris, minute on Greek assisted migrants, 29.5.1953; resumé of address of welcome by Mr Lambros, 18.4.1952, AA(ACT): A445/1, 197/1/5; report, R.G. Dawson, director Bonegilla, 14.7.1953, AA(ACT): A445/1, 197/1/9.
45 Text of treaty, AA(ACT): A445/1, 197/1/2; G.C. Watson, minute to secretary, 4.12.1953; minute B.M. Martyn to secretary, 30.11.1953, AA(ACT): A445/1, 197/1/9.
46 T.H.E. Heyes to Minister, paper, '1951 Immigration Program', 31.8.1950, AA(ACT): A445/1, 142/5/2.
47 Minute, Heyes to Holt, 16.8.1950; paper, Heyes for Holt, 'Notes on . . . the general question of the migration of ex-enemy aliens', p. 7, 16.8.1950, AA(ACT): A445/1, 194/2/3.
48 T.H.E. Heyes to Minister, 27.3.1952, AA(ACT): A445/1, 140/5/14.
49 T.H.E. Heyes to Minister, 27.3.1952, AA(ACT): A445/1, 140/5/14.
50 T.H.E. Heyes to Minister, 27.3.1952, AA(ACT): A445/1, 140/5/14.
51 T.H.E. Heyes to Minister, 27.3.1952, AA(ACT): A445/1, 140/5/14.
52 Report for the IAC committee on control of alien immigration, 1.4.1952, AA(ACT): A445/1, 140/5/14.
53 Report for the IAC committee on control of alien immigration, 1.4.1952; note, Heyes to Holt, 29.4.1952, AA(ACT): A445/1, 140/5/14.
54 Report for the IAC committee on control of alien immigration, 1.4.1952; note, Heyes to Holt, 29.4.1952; AA(ACT): A445/1, 140/5/14; agenda item no. 5, IAC meeting, 24.5.1952; memorandum, Heyes to CMOs in all States, 7.10.1953, 1AA(ACT): A445/1, 40/5/14.
55 CPDHR, vol. 19, pp. 1505–6.
56 *Population and Australia: A Demographic Analysis and Projection.* First report of the National Population Inquiry (chairman C.D. Borrie), AGPS, Canberra, 1975, vol. 1, p. 124.
57 CPDHR, vol. 21, p. 1253, 16.9.1958 (Anderson); CPDHR, vol. 21, p. 1254, 16.9.1958 (Bruce).
58 CPDHR, vol. 21, p. 1270 (Coutts), p. 1281 (Hulme), p. 1263 (Snedden) 16.9.1958.

262   ALIEN TO CITIZEN

59   *Arrivals and Departures*, p. 141.
60   Charles A. Price, 'Australian Immigration: the Whitlam Government 1972–75' in Charles A. Price and Jean I. Martin, *Australian Immigration: A Bibliography and Digest*, part 1, no. 2, 1975, Department of Demography, Australian National University, Canberra, 1976, p. A3; Andrew Jakubowicz and Berenice Buckley, *Migrants and the Legal System*, Australian Government Commission of Inquiry into Poverty, AGPS, Canberra 1975, p. 46.

CHAPTER 3 NON-COMPLIANT WOMEN IN HOLDING CENTRES

1   Memorandum, 'The refugee and the demographic problem presented by Western Germany', appendix B.B.H. Robertson, headquarters, Control Commission for Germany (British Element) to Rt. Hon. Ernest Beven MP, Foreign Office, 26.2.1949, AA(ACT): A445/1, 194/2/1; paper, 'German refugees in Germany, 23.8.1950, AA(ACT): A445/1, 194/2/3; H.C.M. Bass, office of the High Commissioner for the United Kingdom to G.C. Watson, Department of Immigration, Canberra, 4.10.1949, and Control Commission for Germany (British Element) press releases 'Sudeten German women to work in UK', 11.4.1949, and 'German Girls in England', 26.8.1949, sent by F.G. Galleghan, head Australian Military Mission, Germany to secretary Department of Immigration, 26.8.1949, AA(ACT): A445/1, 194/2/1.
2   Statistics from Egon F. Kunz, *Displaced Persons: Calwell's New Australians*, Australian National University Press, Canberra, 1988, pp. 46–47. Details of different requirements and accommodation arrangements for British and alien workers are from report of meeting of the subcommittees of the Immigration Planning Council and the National Security Resources Board 7.8.1951, AA(ACT): A445/1, 142/5/2;. for further information on migrant accommodation see Jordens, *Redefining Australians*, chapter 3; interview with Stephanie Charlesworth, 18 October 1996.
3   G.C. Watson to assistant secretary Encouraged Migration Division, 19.10.1948, AA(ACT): A434/1, 50/3/17477; the respective roles of both departments, united under Harold Holt who held both portfolios from 19.12.1950, were not formally clarified until an interdepartmental meeting on 5.7.1951; secretary Department of Immigration to Minister, 11.7.1951, AA(ACT): A445/1, 142/4/2.
4   Memorandum S.J. Dempsey to assistant secretary Encouraged Migration Division, 25.10.1948, AA(ACT): A434/1, 50/3/17477; memorandum E. Morrison, CMO Sydney to Department of Immigration, Canberra, 30.8.1948, AA(ACT): A434/1, 50/3/17477; extract

from summary of proceedings of CMOs conference 23–25.8.1948, AA(ACT): A445/1, 50/3/17477.
5 J.R. Scott, senior social worker NSW, notes of interview with W. Funnell, secretary DLNS, 14.9.1949, AA(ACT): A445/1, 276/3/2.
6 Report of the joint meeting of the subcommittees of the Immigration Planning Council and the National Security Resources Board, Melbourne, 7.8.1951, AA(ACT): A445/1, 142/5/2; a number of women from Greta Holding Centre joined their husbands at the Chullora Railway Settlement Camp in July 1949, in 1950–51 wives 'squatted' at the ACT men's hostels at Riverside and Fairbairn, Jean R. Scott, NSW to Hazel Dobson, 22.7.1949, AA(ACT): A445/1, 276/3/2; ACT social worker's report for 1950–51, AA(ACT): A445/1, 276/2/6; quotation from Hilda Wilson, report dated 25.7.1949, AA(ACT): A445/1, 276/3/4.
7 South Australia's social worker's reports, 15.3.1950, 30.6.1950 and 15.3.1951, AA(ACT): A445/1, 276/3/4; report Hazel Dobson to Secretary, 13.4.1950, AA(ACT): A445/1, 276/3/1.
8 Social workers' reports are in AA(ACT): A445/1, 276/2/4–7; Boyd Graham, president VCSS to H. Holt, 7.3.1952, AA(ACT): A445/1, 276/1/9.
9 Victorian Council for Social Services to Hazel Dobson, officer in charge Social Welfare Section, Aliens Assimilation Division, 14.7.1948; reply by secretary T.H.E. Heyes, 27.7.1949, AA(ACT): A445/1, 276/1/9.
10 Jean R. Scott, reports of Sydney social workers July–November 1949, 8.12.1949, AA(ACT): A445/1, 276/3/2.
11 Report by Hilda Wilson, senior social worker, for 12 months to 30.6.1959, AA(ACT): A445/1, 276/3/4.
12 Hilda Wilson to Hazel Dobson, 12.4.1950, AA(ACT): A445/1, 276/3/4.
13 Maureen Dyson to CMO Perth, report of Social Welfare Section, Perth, 1.7.1950–31.7.1951, AA(ACT): A445/1, 276/3/1.
14 Linda V. Dickson, senior social worker, Victoria, annual report 1950–51, AA(ACT): A445/1, 276/3/1; report Hazel Dobson to Secretary, 9.3.1951, AA(ACT): A445/1, 276/2/10.
15 P.R. Heydon, secretary Department of Immigration to Minister, 31.1.1964, AA(ACT): A446/101, 63/45619; for an explanation of the social welfare benefits available to aliens see Jordens, *Redefining Australians*, chapter 6.
16 Report, Hazel Dobson to Secretary, 9.3.1951, AA(ACT): A445/1, 276/2/10.
17 Hazel Dobson to R.E. Armstrong, 15.11.1951, AA(ACT): A445/1, 276/1/9, and report, Hazel Dobson to Secretary, 9.3.1951, AA(ACT): A445/1, 276/2/10.
18 Report, H. Dobson to Secretary, 9.10.1951 and 6.11.1951, AA(ACT): A445/1, 276/2/10.
19 J.D. Schroder, controller Migrant Accommodation Centres to R.E.

Armstrong, n.d. (c. 13.3.1952), AA(ACT): A445/1, 146/2/1; report 30.7.1951, AA(ACT): A445/1, 146/2/1.
20 Commonwealth Immigration Advisory Council, sixteenth meeting 29.2.1952, minute no. 365 agenda item no. 14 'Provision of pre-school facilities for migrant children in Immigration Centres and Workers' Hostels'.
21 Response to resolutions 81–84 of the 1951 Citizenship Convention, n.d. (c. 5.8.1951), AA(ACT): A445/1, 146/2/1.
22 Commonwealth Immigration Advisory Council, sixteenth meeting 29.2.1952, minute no. 365 agenda item no. 14 'Provision of pre-school facilities for migrant children in Immigration Centres and Workers' Hostels'.
23 W.J. Weeden, a/g director Commonwealth Office of Education to secretary Department of Immigration, 5.8.1951, AA(ACT): A445/1, 146/2/1.
24 Report on Migrant Holding Centres and Hostels in Victoria by Linda V. Dickson, senior social worker, 25.9.1953, AA(ACT): A445/1, 276/3/1; extract from the minutes of the Commonwealth Hostels board meeting, Melbourne, 5.4.1954, AA(ACT): A445/1, 146/8/20.
25 Handwritten unsigned and undated note to Hazel Dobson (c. November 1952), AA(ACT): A445/1, 276/3/2.
26 Instruction by unnamed senior officer to Hazel Dobson, 14.1.1953; report Olga Leschen, 14.11.1952, AA(ACT): A445/1, 146/3/3 and 276/3/2.
27 Rosalie A. James to Hazel Dobson, 11.11.1952, 19.12.1952, report for year June 1952–June 1953, AA(ACT): A445/1, 276/3/2; report on Migrant Holding Centres and Hostels in Victoria by Linda V. Dickson, senior social worker, 25.9.1953, AA(ACT): A445/1, 276/3/1.
28 P.R. Heydon, secretary Department of Immigration to E.L. Sommerlad, Federation of Australian Commercial Broadcasting, 13.8.1969, AA(ACT): A446/T31, 75/79688; list of tariffs and charges in Migrant Hostels, September 1975; minutes of meeting 9.12.1975, p. 2, AA(ACT): A446/T31, 75/79664.

CHAPTER 4 MARGINALISED MIGRANTS

1 M. Keary, 'Report of psychiatric cases 1950–51', AA(ACT): A445/1, 276/2/5.
2 CPDHR, vol. 212, p. 691, 16.3.1951; vol. 218, pp. 1277–8, 12.9.1952; vol. 14, 3.4.1957, pp. 505–6.
3 M. Keary, 'Report of psychiatric cases 1950–51', AA(ACT): A445/1, 276/2/5 ; see Jordens, *Redefining Australians*, chapter 7, pp. 122–8, for attempts to have the qualifications of migrant doctors recognised in Australia.

4   M. Keary, 'Report of psychiatric cases 1950–51', AA(ACT): A445/1, 276/2/5.
5   Hazel Dobson, 'Report, Social Welfare Section (1949–51)', AA(ACT): A445/1, 140/5/6.
6   Interviews with Sylvia Lyons, 30 October 1996, Stephanie Charlesworth, 18 October 1996, John Tarbath, 22 October 1996; Hazel Dobson, 'Report, Social Welfare Section (1949–51)'. AA(ACT): A445/1, 140/5/6.
7   CPDHR, vol. 14, 3.4.1957, pp. 505–6.
8   CPDHR, vol. 21, pp. 1287–9, 16.9.1958; vol. 36, p. 1395, 10.10.1962.
9   CPDHR, vol. 28, pp. 170–2.
10 CPDHR, vol. 77, p 1768, 18.4.1972; paper, 'Polish-born workers in Australia by occupation as at census of 30 June 1966'; pp. 9–10; AA(ACT): A446/T31, 75/78842.
11 Paper prepared by Survey Section for a mental health seminar 14.8.1973, AA(ACT): A446/T31, 75/78909; interview with P.M. Rice, 14 September 1996.
12 See chapter 7 for information on the computerisation of information from social workers' reports.
13 P.M. Rice to G.C. Watson, 26.10.1972, AA(ACT): A446/T31, 75/78786.
14 P.M. Rice to G.C. Watson, 26.10.1972, AA(ACT): A446/T31, 75/78786.
15 Interview with John Tarbath, 22 October 1996.
16 Correspondence relating to this survey is on AA(ACT): A446/T31, 75/76693; CPDHR, vol. 77, p. 1768, 18.4.1972; P.R. Heydon to E.L. Sommerlad, 13.8.1969, AA(ACT): A446/T31, 75/79688.
17 H.A. Bland to T.H.E. Heyes, 9.5.1952, AA(ACT): A445/1, 146/3/3; see Jordens, *Redefining Australians*, chapter 5, for further information on the Good Neighbour Movement.
18 *What Immigration Means to Australia*, report by minister for immigration the Rt. Hon. H.E. Holt, 30.8.1956, Parliament of the Commonwealth of Australia, pp. 7–8; speech by Sir John Storey, chairman Immigration Planning Council to the 1954 Citizenship Convention, 28.1.1954, pp. 5, 14.
19 T.H.E. Heyes to CMO Cologne, 11.6.1953, AA(ACT): A445/1, 194/1/5; draft report of the 1954 Citizenship Convention, n.d., AA(ACT): A445/1, 146/8/20.
20 *Population and Australia: A Demographic Analysis and Projection*, First report of the National Population Enquiry (chairman C.D. Borrie), AGPS, Canberra, 1975, vol. 1, p. 124; response by the Department of Immigration to agenda items 75 and 153 of the 1951 Annual Congress of the RSSAILA, AA(ACT): A445/1, 145/7/3.
21 For example: CPDS, vol. 213, p. 1453, 12.8.1951; vol. 216, p. 315, 26.2.1952; CPDHR, vol. 216, p. 706, 4.3.1952; vol. 217, p. 225, 13.5.1952, pp. 813, 837, 855, 27.5.1952; vol. 218, p. 308, 14.8.1952,

p. 958, 4.9.1952. Senator Benn's quote is from CPDS, vol. 219, p. 2769, 9.10.1952.

22 Holt's address, 29.1.1952; letter, secretary Department of Immigration to the National Farmers' Union and other rural bodies, 7.5.1952; list of resolutions relating to rural migrants, R.E. Armstrong, assistant secretary Assimilation Division, to secretary Immigration Planning Council, April 1952, AA(ACT): A445/1, 146/3/3.
23 Resolution 76, AA(ACT): A445/1, 146/8/20.
24 Draft summary of comments on resolution 42 of 1954 Citizenship Convention, n.d. (c. 12.10.1954), AA(ACT): A445/1, 146/8/2; N.N. Drummond, acting secretary, Immigration Planning Council to assistant secretary Assimilation Division, 26.3.1952, AA(ACT): A445/1, 146/3/3; Joan Rydon, *A Biographical Register of the Commonwealth Parliament 1901–1972*, Australian National University Press, Canberra, 1975.
25 Queensland Dairymen's Organisation to A. Calwell, 28.4.1948 and Calwell's reply, 19.5.1948, AA(ACT): A434/1, 48/3/8061.
26 CPDHR, vol. 217, p. 225, 13.5.1952 and p. 813, 27.5.1952.
27 Beazley, CPDHR, vol. 218, p. 308, 14.8.1952, Keon, p. 560, 21.8.1952; Peters, CPDHR, vol. 1, p 855, 30.9.1953; Buttfield, CPDS, vol. 6, p. 717, 26.10.1955; New Settlers League of NSW, report on resolution 51 of the 1953 Citizenship Convention, 13.11.1953, AA(ACT): A445/1, 146/9/8.
28 Minute, G.C. Watson, assistant secretary Planning and Research Division to assistant secretary Assimilation Division, 9.12.1952, AA(ACT): A445/1, 146/3/3.
29 CPDHR, vol. 217, p. 225, 13.5.1952; minute, G.C. Watson, assistant secretary Planning and Research Division to assistant secretary Assimilation Division, 9.12.1952, AA(ACT): A445/1, 146/3/3; CPDHR, vol. 217, p. 226, 13.5.1952; speech by Sir John Storey, chairman Immigration Planning Council to the 1954 Citizenship Convention, 28.1.1954, p. 14.
30 CPDHR, vol. 221, p. 142, 19.2.1953.
31 CMO Sydney to Central Office, 24.4.1953, AA(ACT): A445/1, 146/9/8; Hazel Dobson to Secretary, 10.4.1953, AA(ACT): A445/1, 276/3/4.
32 Hilda Wilson, senior social worker South Australia to secretary Department of Immigration, 19.12.1949, 13.4.1950, 30.11.1950, 21.10.1952, AA(ACT): A445/1, 276/3/4; the social workers' reports quoted in this and subsequent paragraphs are from AA(ACT): A445/1, 276/3/4 and 276/2/13.
33 The description of the *Aliens Act* is from CPDHR, vol. 194, p. 2927, 26.11.1947.
34 Interview with John Tarbath, 22 October 1996.
35 T.H.E. Heyes to secretary Department of External Affairs, October 1950; Heyes to Minister, 15.3.1951, AA(ACT): A445/1, 194/2/4;

statistics of special process workers are from letter by Heyes, 2.9.1952, AA(ACT): A445/1, 194/1/3.
36 Report of visits to Port Pirie and Port Augusta 14–31.1.1952 and 4.3.1952, AA(ACT): A445/1, 276/3/4.
37 See correspondence October 1952–March 1953, AA(ACT): A445/1, 194/1/9. The sponsoring firms included the Snowy Mountains Authority, Railways of SA and Victoria, Commonwealth Railways, Tasmanian Hydro-Electric Authority, Le Corche Frères, Overseas Construction, Compagnie Industrielle, International Constructions, Jennings (Canberra), Wender & Duerholt, and Etudes et Enterprises.
38 Minute to Minister, 19.11.1952, AA(ACT): A445/1, 194/1/9; report of visit 8–14.10.1953, 24.4.1952, AA(ACT): A445/1, 276/2/13.
39 Statistics of migrants in urban and rural areas by State are in CPDHR, vol. 73, p. 1303, 14.9.1971.

Chapter 5 Communicating with Migrants

1 CPDHR, vol. 1, p. 815, 30.9.1953; CPDHR, vol. 181, pp. 161–2, 28.3.1945.
2 CPDHR, vol. 181, p. 472, 8.3.1945; CPDHR, vol. 18, p. 88, 27.2.1958. For a discussion of the origins of Australian monolingualism see Michael Clyne 'Monolingualism, Multilingualism and the Australian Nation' in *Australian National Identity*, Charles A. Price (ed.), Academy of the Social Sciences in Australia, 1991, pp. 83–98.
3 Department of Immigration, *Australian Immigration Quarterly Statistical Bulletin*, vol. 2, no 1, November 1961, p. 14, *Budget Papers*, Parliament of the Commonwealth of Australia; 'A history of adult migrant education', pp. 2–3, paper prepared by Miss J. Ennor, 1962, AA(ACT): A446/96, 64/45732.
4 N.W. Lamidey to T.H.E. Heyes, secretary Department of Immigration, minute 'Adult Migrant Education Scheme', 15.2.1957, AA(ACT): A445/1, 140/5/20; paper 'Citizenship and settlement', June 1973, p. 17, AA(ACT): A446/51, 74/75962.
5 N.W. Lamidey to T.H.E. Heyes, secretary Department of Immigration, minute 'Adult Migrant Education Scheme', 15.2.1957, AA(ACT): A445/1, 140/5/20; paper 'Citizenship and settlement', June 1973, p. 17, AA(ACT): A446/51, 74/75962.
6 CPDHR, vol. 1, p. 339, 12.3.1951; 'A history of adult migrant education', p. 10, paper prepared by Miss J. Ennor, 1962, AA(ACT): A446/96, 64/45732; Department of Immigration summary of comments on resolution 42 of the 1954 Citizenship Convention, AA(ACT): A445/1, 146/8/2.
7 N.W. Lamidey to T.H.E. Heyes, secretary Department of Immigration, minute 'Adult Migrant Education Scheme', 15.2.1957, AA(ACT): A445/1, 140/5/20.

8   N.W. Lamidey to T.H.E. Heyes, secretary Department of Immigration, minute 'Adult Migrant Education Scheme', 15.2.1957, AA(ACT): A445/1, 140/5/20; 'A history of adult migrant education', Section ii p. 3, paper prepared by Miss J. Ennor, 1962, AA(ACT): A446/96, 64/45732.

9   N.W. Lamidey to T.H.E. Heyes, secretary Department of Immigration, minute 'Adult Migrant Education Scheme', 15.2.1957, AA(ACT): A445/1, 140/5/20; 'A history of adult migrant education', section ii, p. 3, paper prepared by Miss J. Ennor, 1962, AA(ACT): A446/96, 64/45732; CPDHR, vol. 61, p. 3014, 19.11.1968; paper, 'Measures the government has taken of particular concern to women', prepared in response to a request from the Department of Prime Minister and Cabinet, 9.4.1974, AA(ACT): A446/51, 74/75801; CPDS, vol. 52, 31.8.1972; paper 'Citizenship and settlement', June 1973, pp. 23–4, AA(ACT): A446/51, 74/75962.

10   'A history of adult migrant education', Section ii, pp. 3–5, paper prepared by Miss J. Ennor, 1962, AA(ACT): A446/96, 64/45732; interview with Pauline Griffin, 12 September 1996.

11   N.W. Lamidey to T.H.E. Heyes, secretary Department of Immigration, minute 'Adult Migrant Education Scheme', 15.2.1957, AA(ACT): A445/1, 140/5/20 and 'A history of adult migrant education', section ii, pp. 5–6, paper prepared by Miss J. Ennor, 1962, AA(ACT): A446/96, 64/45732; paper, 'Migrant Education Program progress report: July 1971' p. 3, AA(ACT): A446/T31, 75/79691; paper 'Citizenship and settlement', June 1973, p. 19, AA(ACT): A446/52, 174/75962.

12   'A history of adult migrant education', pp. 3–5 and section ii, pp. 1–3, paper prepared by Miss J. Ennor, 1962, AA(ACT): A446/96, 64/45732; ministerial statement on Migrant Education and Welfare Services; CPDS, vol. 52, p. 614, 31.8.1972; paper 'Citizenship and settlement', June 1973, p. 19, AA(ACT): A446/51, 74/75962; *Budget Papers 1969–73*.

13   CPDHR, vol. 96, p. 1720, 2.10.1975; paper 'Citizenship and settlement', June 1973, p. 19, AA(ACT): A446/51, 74/75962; Galbally (1978) vol. 2, pp. 91–2.

14   Agenda note for the Commonwealth Immigration Advisory Council (IAC) meeting 7.7.1953, AA(ACT): A445/1, 140/5/20; *Who's Who in Australia 1955*.

15   Report to the Commonwealth Immigration Advisory Council of committee appointed to consider the necessity for an advanced course in English under the Adult Migrant Education Scheme, meeting 16/17.4.1953, AA(ACT): A445/1, 140/5/20; Department of Immigration, *Statistical Bulletin*, January 1954, p. 13, *Budget Papers*.

16   Department of Immigration, *Australian Immigration Quarterly Statistical Bulletin*, vol. 2, no. 1, November 1961, p. 14; N.W. Lamidey to T.H.E. Heyes, secretary Department of Immigration,

minute 'Adult Migrant Education Scheme', 15.2.1957, AA(ACT): A445/1, 140/5/20; A.L. Nutt, acting secretary Department of Immigration to Minister, 29.5.1957, AA(ACT): A445/1, 140/5/20; although £434 000 was the estimated cost in 1956/57 only £414 592 was actually spent, *Budget Papers*, H. Holt, 11.4.1956, CPDHR, vol. 9, p. 118; H.A. Bruce, 30.4.1957, vol. 15, p. 856; Alexander Downer, 28.9.1955, CPDHR, vol. 7, p. 1022; quotation by Howard Beale (Liberal NSW) CPDHR, vol. 7, p. 1023.

17 Minutes of meeting of the IAC 25/26.10.1956, AA(ACT): A445/1, 140/5/20. Members of the Committee were: Mr Gordon Freeth MP, J.R. Darling O.B.E, Senator N. Buttfield, Hon. P. J. Clarey MP, Air Marshall Sir Richard Williams, KBE, CB, DSO, L. Withall, OBE.

18 Report of the Committee of Experts 27.3.1957, AA(ACT): A445/1, 140/5/20; note 'Committee on Migrant Education Service' by J.R. Darling 26.4.57, A.L. Nutt, acting secretary Department of Immigration to Minister, 29.5.1957 with annotation by Minister, AA(ACT): A445/1, 140/5/20.

19 CPDS, vol. 22, p. 1531, 28.11.1962.

20 CPDHR, vol. 18, p. 88, 27.2.1958.

21 CPDHR, vol. 24, p. 326, 19.8.1958 and vol. 27, p. 2242, 2.6.1960.

22 CPDHR, vol. 22, p. 132, 19.2.1959.

23 CPDHR, vol. 28, pp. 1136–8, 20.9.1960; CPDS, vol. 22, pp. 1126–7, 24.10.1962 and vol. 50, p. 2046, 24.11.1971.

24 CPDS, vol. 22, p. 1130, 24.10.1962; CPDHR, vol. 38, p. 49, 26.3.1963; CPDS, vol. 42, p. 1074, 18.9.1969; Galbally (1978) vol. 2, pp. 83–4.

25 *Auditor-General's Report 1969–70*, p. 146; and 1970–71, p. 155; CPDHR, vol. 61, p. 3014, 19.11.1968, p. 3099, 21.11.1968; paper, 'Migrant Education Program progress report: July 1971' p. 1, pp. 5–6, AA(ACT): A446/T31; paper 'Citizenship and settlement', June 1973, p. 21, AA(ACT): A446/51, 74/75962; Galbally (1978) vol. 2, pp. 78–9.

26 Paper 'Migrant Education Program progress report: July 1971', p. 3, AA(ACT): A446/T31, 75/79691; CPDHR, vol. 71, 10.3.1971, p. 825; Galbally (1978) vol. 2, p. 78.

27 Paper 'Citizenship and settlement', June 1973, p. 20, AA(ACT): A446/51, 74/75962; Galbally (1979) vol. 2, p. 78.

28 Paper 'Citizenship and settlement', June 1973, p. 20, AA(ACT): A446/51, 74/75962; Galbally (1979) vol. 2, p. 88.

29 Interviews with Pauline Griffin, 12 September 1996, and Arthur Marshman, 30 September 1996; summary of comments on resolution 42 (migrant education), n.d. (c. 12.10.1954), AA(ACT): A445/1, 146/8/2; *Auditor General's Report 1965–66*, p. 62; CPDHR, vol. 61, p. 3013, 19.11.1968; paper 'Migrant Education Program progress report: July 1971', p. 4, AA(ACT): A446/T31, 75/79691.

30 Paper 'Citizenship and settlement', June 1973, p. 19, AA(ACT): A446/51, 74/75962; CPDHR, vol. 92, p. 4826, 5.12.1974.

31 CPDHR, vol. 86, pp. 1719-20, 2.10.1975; Professor Ronald Sackville, Commissioner: Law and Poverty, *Second Main Report October 1975*, AGPS, Canberra, 1975, p. 235; Galbally (1978) vol. 2, p. 78, pp. 89-90.
32 CPDS, vol. 42, pp. 1068-70, 1073-74, 18.9.1969; *Auditor-General's Report, 1971-72*, p. 50.
33 Ronald F. Henderson, Alison Harcourt, R.J.A. Harper, *People in Poverty: A Melbourne Survey*, University of Melbourne, 1970, chapter 8, 'Migrants' by Jean McCaughey, pp. 119-45; minute Program Development subsection to the assistant secretary Planning and Development Branch, 12.1.1972, AA(ACT): A446/T31, 75/78903.
34 Report of the Immigration Advisory Council, 29.11.1971, AA(ACT): A446/T31, 75/80969; paper for IAC committee on survey of migrant employment problems, 29.11.1971, AA(ACT): A446/T31, 75/80866; Jean Martin (chairman), *A Decade of Migrant Settlement: Report on the 1973 Immigration Survey*, pp. 85-93; the Galbally Report (1978) listed its reservations concerning the findings of this report in relation to fluency, vol. 2, p. 93.
35 Jean Martin (chairman), *A Decade of Migrant Settlement: Report on the 1973 Immigration Survey*, p. 84; for statistics of costs and enrolments see table.
36 Galbally (1978) vol. 2, p. 95; Department of Immigration summary of comments on resolution 42 of the 1954 Citizenship Convention, AA(ACT): 146/8/2, A445/1; CPDS, vol. 42, p. 1077.
37 Paper dated 29.11.1971, AA(ACT): A446/T31, 75/80866; *Australian Immigration, Quarterly Statistics*, December 1973; *Auditor-General's Report 1973-74*, p. 69; Professor Ronald Sackville, commissioner Law and Poverty, *Second Main Report October 1975*, AGPS, Canberra, 1975, p. 235.
38 CPDHR, vol. 9, p. 1189, 11.4.1956.
39 CPDHR, vol. 38, p. 48, 26.3.1963; CPDHR, vol. 51, p. 936, 19.4.1966.
40 CPDHR, vol. 56, p. 1928, 19.9.1967 and vol. 57, pp. 2614-15.
41 CPDHR, vol. 61, pp. 2298-9, 24.10.1968 and p. 2576, 7.11.1968.
42 CPDHR, vol. 65, p. 1004, 9.9.1969; CPDS, vol. 42, pp. 1072-3, p. 1077, 18.9.1969.
43 R.E. Armstrong to Minister, 28.3.1972, AA(ACT): A446/T31, 75/78903.
44 CPDS, vol. 52, p. 615, 31.8.1972; *Auditor-General's Report, 1970-71*; draft report of the Survey of Child Migrant Education in Schools of High Migrant Density, 16.11.1972, AA(ACT): A446/T31, 75/78905.
45 Ronald F. Henderson, Alison Harcourt, R.J.A. Harper, *People in Poverty: A Melbourne Survey*, University of Melbourne, 1970, chapter 8, 'Migrants' by Jean McCaughey, p. 145; report is included in AA(ACT): A446/T31, 75/78903; minute, Program Development

Subsection to the assistant secretary Planning and Development Branch, 12.1.1972, AA(ACT): A446/T31, 75/78903.
46 G.C. Watson, first assistant secretary, to E.L. Charles, assistant secretary, 25.1.1972; R.E. Armstrong to Minister, 28.3.1972, AA(ACT): A446/T31, 75/78903.
47 File note by E.L. Charles, 29.2.1973, Charles to Watson, 29.2.1972; Watson to Secretary, 2.3.1972; M. Fraser to Alexander Forbes, 4.4.1972; Forbes to Fraser, 10.5.1972, AA(ACT): A446/T31, 75/78903; CPDHR, vol. 52, p. 615, 27.4.1972.
48 See various drafts of Survey of Child Migrant Education in Schools of High Migrant Density and Department of Immigration minutes 1972–73, AA(ACT): A446/T31, 75/78905; CPDHR, vol. 87, p. 3510, 20.11.1973; paper 'Citizenship and settlement', June 1973, p. 19, AA(ACT): A446/51, 74/75962.
49 CPDHR, vol. 96, p. 1720, 20.10.1975; see chapter 8 for further information on the *Immigration (Education) Act*.
50 Marian Sawer, 'Reclaiming social liberalism: the women's movement and the State' in *Women and the State Australian Perspectives* (ed. Renate Howe), special edition of the *Journal of Australian Studies*, Latrobe University Press, 1993, pp. 1–21.
51 For example, see Michael Morrissey et al., *Immigration and Industry Restructuring in the Illawarra*, Bureau of Immigration Research, AGPS, Canberra, 1992.

CHAPTER 6 TOWARDS ACCESS AND EQUITY

1 Comment on resolution no. 8, c. 10.3.1952, AA(ACT): A445/1, 146/3/3.
2 Hon. H.W. Leggatt to Holt, 12.5.1950, reply 1.6.1950; Heyes to Hon. K. Dodgshun, 4.8.1950, AA(ACT): A446/T31, 75/79151.
3 T.W. Mitchell to Holt, 25.6.1951; Heyes to the acting secretary Department of Labour and National Service, 31.7.1951, AA(ACT): A446/T31, 75/79151.
4 A.H. Prest to Secretary, 2.10.1951, AA(ACT): A446/T31, 75/79151; minute, R.E. Armstrong, assistant secretary Assimilation Division to Secretary, 24.6 and 24.7.1951; medical superintendent Kenmore to welfare officer Department of Immigration, Canberra, 18.7.1951, reply by Secretary 24.7.1951, AA(ACT): A446/T31, 75/79151.
5 Senator Henty, CPDHR, vol. 24, p. 900, 26.3.1963.
6 Report by John D. Tarbath, Department of Immigration social worker, Tasmania, 1951, AA(ACT): A445/1, 276/3/1; copy of draft booklet, 31.7.1951, AA(ACT): A445/1, 146/2/1; article, 'Unfair tests for migrant drivers' by Ian D. Elliott, senior lecturer in law, University of Melbourne, *The Age*, 17.5.1973.
7 Article dated 6.9.1953; Heyes to CMO Melbourne, c. 19.11.1953, AA(ACT): A446/T31, 75/79151.

8   Minute, S. Lindsay Thompson to the officer in charge Assimilation, 4.4.1963, AA(ACT): A446/T31, 75/78908.
9   See correspondence dated 21.2, 28.4, 4.5, 2.6.1964, AA(ACT): A446/T31, 75/79151.
10 Minute, W. Cawood, Integration and Education Section to C.H. Smith, Citizenship Branch, 16.2.1968, G.E. Hitchins to Secretary, 27.5.1968, AA(ACT): A446/T31, 75/78908.
11 Notes on Finland and Finnish migration to Australia, April 1969; minute, P.R. Heydon, secretary, on discussions with Finnish Ambassador, 11.4.1969, L.A. Taylor, acting director Establishment Section to Commonwealth directors of migration in all States, 23.4.1969, AA(ACT): A446/T31, 75/78908; minute, P.R. Heydon, secretary, on discussions with Finnish Ambassador, 11.4.1969, AA(ACT): A446/T31, 75/78908; State responses are in AA(ACT): A446/T31, 75/78908; interview with George Pridannikoff, 30 November 1996.
12 F. Ferguson to the senior migration officer Citizenship Branch, 3.5.1968, AA(ACT): A446/T31, 75/78908.
13 F.H. Jago, minister for health to Mr Justice R. Else-Mitchell, 8.1.1968, AA(ACT): A446/T31, 75/78869.
14 Carl Wood to B.M. Snedden, 20.2.1968, AA(ACT): A446/T31, 75/78869.
15 CPDS, vol. 40, p. 267, 4.3.1969, p. 436, 16.3.1969, pp. 436–7, 1064–9, 18.3.1969; vol. 54, p. 2065, 16.10.1972 and vol. 55, p. 295, 8.3.1973.
16 The organisations represented by ACOSS in 1969 were the Australian Association of Social Workers, Australian Council of Churches, Australian Psychological Association, Catholic Immigration Committee, European/Australian Christian Fellowship, Federation of Australian Jewish Welfare Societies, Federal Inter-Church Migrant Committee, Methodist Church of Australia, International Social Service, Lutheran World Federation, National Youth Council of Australia, Salvation Army, United Nations Association of Australia, Young Men's Christian Association, Young Women's Christian Association, report of the ACOSS/ACFOA Joint Committee on Migrant Welfare, May 1969; AA(ACT): A446/T31, 75/79169, terms of reference of ACOSS/ACFOA Joint Migrant Welfare Committee, report 20.6.1972, AA(ACT): A446/T31, 75/79738; report on interpreters by subcommittee of ACOSS/ACFOA joint migrant welfare committee, n.d., AA(ACT): A446/T31, 75/79156.
17 Agenda item for Commonwealth/State Conference of Ministers for Immigration, 24.9.1970, AA(ACT): A446/T31, 75/78908; minutes of 34th ACOSS council meeting, 6.8.1970; ACOSS council meeting 6/7.8.1970; G.C. Watson, first assistant secretary to Mr Charles, 14.8.1971, AA(ACT): A446/T31, 75/79169.
18 IAC, draft chairman's notes, 'Migrant integration—interpreters in hospitals', 23.11.1970, AA(ACT): A446/T31, 75/78908.
19 Paper 'Interpreters in hospitals', 24.9.1970 and P.R. Heydon, secre-

tary Department of Immigration to Minister, 10.3.1971, AA(ACT): A446/T31, 75/78908.
20 Chairman's notes, 'Migrant integration—interpreters in hospitals', 23.11.1970, a/g assistant secretary, S.J. Rooth to Mr Rice, 22.12.1970, N.J. Attwood, a/g Commonwealth Public Service inspector to Department of Immigration, 23.1.1970, J.J. Smith, Commonwealth director of migration for Victoria to secretary Department of Immigration, 2.12.1970, AA(ACT): A446/T31, 75/78908.
21 P.R. Heydon, secretary Department of Immigration to Minister, 10.3.1971, parliamentary question 9.3.1971, AA(ACT): A446/T31, 75/78908.
22 CPDS, vol. 54, p. 1551, 12.10.1972.
23 Report on the survey of interpreting and translating needs in the community, October 1973, pp. 1–110.
24 Interview with P.M. Rice, 14 September 1996, and information supplied by Nancy Anderson.
25 CPDS, vol. 52, p. 1362, 27.4.1972 (Greenwood again referred to the planned telephone interpreting service in the Senate on 12 October 1972, p. 1551); Budget speech, CPDS, vol. 53, pp. 614–15, 31 August 1972.
26 Interview with P.M. Rice, 14 September 1996. The distinction between 'keepers' and 'getters' in the Department of Immigration is his.
27 Information on reasons for delay in establishing ETIS provided by P.M. Rice; Jean Martin in *The Migrant Presence* (1978), p. 50 claims ETIS was merely 'foreshadowed' by the Liberal government; *Debrett's Handbook of Australia*, Sydney, 1987; interview with P.M. Rice, 14 September 1996.
28 Paper on ETIS prepared for the meeting of the IAC 9.3.1973, AA(ACT): A446/T31, 75/79156; *SMH* 6.1.1976; P.M. Rice recalls that the Department's request for eight interpreters in each office was halved by the Public Service Board.
29 Minutes of meeting 26.1/19.3.1973; agenda of IAC meetings 19.3.1973 and 16.7.1973; report on interpreters by subcommittee of ACOSS/ACFOA joint migrant welfare committee, n.d., AA(ACT): A446/T31, 75/79156.
30 Note on interpreter services, 26.9.1973; AA(ACT): A446/T31, 75/79156.
31 Minutes of meeting 1.8.1973, AA(ACT): A446/T31, 75/79156; report of ACOSS/ACFOA migrant welfare committee subcommittee on interpreter facilities, September 1972, AA(ACT): A446/T31, 75/79738; extracts from ACOSS annual report 1972/73, AA(ACT): A446/T31, 75/79291.
32 Information on the selective release of this report is from Secretary's note to Minister on interpreter services, 26.9.1973, p. 2; agenda of IAC meeting 16.7.1973, AA(ACT): A446/T31, 75/79156;

CPDS, vol. 52, p. 1362, 27.4.1972, pp. 614–15, ministerial statement 31.8.1972; CPDS, vol. 54, p. 1551, 12.10.1972; CPDHR, vol. 84, pp. 2923, 30.5.1973; *Australian*, 2.10.1973; CPDHR, vol. 85, p. 1417, 25.9.1973.

33 Grassby to Myers, 26.11.1973, AA(ACT): A446/T31, 75/78598; minute of IAC meeting 22.11.1973; secretary P.N. Shaw to G.C. Watson, synopsis of consultation conducted by the committee on interpreter needs, Sydney, 22.11.1973, AA(ACT): A446/T31, 75/79153; Ian G. Sharp, secretary Department of Labour and Immigration to the administrator Royal Adelaide Hospital, 4.10.1974, AA(ACT): A446/T31, 75/78598; R.E. Armstrong to minister A.J. Grassby, 26.9.1973, attached statistics showed that from July to September the Department had translated a total of 1336 items for 28 government departments which dealt with the public and 21 departments which did not, attached notes for the Minister on interpreter services, AA(ACT): A446/T31, 75/79156; CPDHR, vol. 86, p. 2981, 8.11.1973.

34 Clyde R. Cameron to Senator J.A. Mulvihill, 20.12.1974, AA(ACT): A446/T31, 75/78598.

35 P.M. Rice to G. Kiddle, 9.8.1973, AA(ACT): A446/T31, 75/79167; CPDHR, vol. 86, p. 2576–7, 24.10.1973.

36 R.L. Hooper, administrator Royal Adelaide Hospital to regional director Department of Labor and Immigration, South Australia, 16.8.1974, AA(ACT): A446/T31, 75/78598; *Sydney Morning Herald*, 13.11.1974; information on Department of Immigration advocacy from P.M. Rice.

37 Minute, J.R. Blackie, regional director Melbourne, 28.2.1974, *Medical Journal of Australia*, 25.2.1974, AA(ACT): A446/51, 77/76561.

38 CPDHR, vol. 96, pp. 1719–29, 2.10.1975.

39 *Poverty in Australia*, First Main Report, April 1975, Australian Government Commission of Inquiry into Poverty (chairman Ronald F. Henderson, AGPS, Canberra, 1975, p. viii and p. 269–81; Andrew Jakubowicz and Berenice Buckley, *Migrants and the Legal System*, Australian Government Commission of Inquiry into Poverty, AGPS, Canberra, 1975.

40 Circular, D.R. Scott, assistant director general Department of Social Security to branch assistant directors general, 7.5.1975, responses from Adelaide 3.7.1975 and Hobart 12.6.1975, AA(ACT): A446/T31, 75/78616.

41 Interview with George Pridannikoff, 30 November 1996.

42 R. Dowell, director DSS Migrant Services Sydney to director general DSS, 6.10.1975, AA(ACT): A446/T31, 75/78616; John Bennett, Victorian Council of Civil Liberties to Minister for Labour and Immigration, 7.5.1975, Bernard Freedman, director Immigration Information Branch, Australian Information Service to W.G. Kiddle, assistant director-general, Migrant Community Services DSS, 14.3.1975, AA(ACT): A446/T31, 75/79729.

CHAPTER 7 FROM ASSIMILATION TO INTEGRATION

1 Commonwealth of Australia, Department of Immigration, *Statistical Bulletin*, no. 1, January 1952, table A3.
2 Departmental report on resolution no. 59 of the 1951 Citizenship Convention, n.d. (c. 22.8.1951); AA(ACT): A445/1, 146/2/1; report of action by the Department of Immigration and Good Neighbour Organisation to implement resolutions of the fourth Australian Citizenship Convention, Canberra, January 1953, p. 167, p. 18, AA(ACT): A445/1, 146/8/14. For the origins of the term 'New Australian' see Colm Kiernan, *Calwell: A Personal and Political Biography*, Nelson, Melbourne, 1978, pp. 129–30.
3 A.L. Nutt a/g secretary Department of Immigration to Immigration Publicity Officer, 9.12.1954, AA(ACT): A445/1, 146/8/20; memorandum by J.D. Shroder, 22.1.1952, AA(ACT): A445/1, 146/2/1; A. Brown, comment on resolution 54 of the 1954 Citizenship Convention, n.d., AA(ACT): A445/1, 146/8/20; instruction 184, 20.8.1951, AA(ACT): A445/1, 229/1/2.
4 Report of action by the Department of Immigration and Good Neighbour Organisation to implement resolutions of the fourth Australian Citizenship Convention, Canberra, January 1953, p. 167, p. 18, AA(ACT): A445/1, 146/8/14.
5 Holt's address to the 1952 Citizenship Convention, 30.1.1952, AA(ACT): A445/1, 146/3/3; *Migration Today*, vol. 14, Spring 1970, p. 62; the degree to which the British component was outnumbered by the alien by 1956 was the subject of considerable attention in Parliament, see CPDHR, vol. 13, p. 1146, p. 1181, p. 1182, p. 1184, p. 1187, p. 1190–1, p. 1198, 4.10.1956.
6 CPDHR, vol. 25, p. 1756, 1.10.1959.
7 Annual report (1950–51), Information Project, Margaret Ramsay, NSW, AA(ACT): A445/1, 276/3/2; report of Social Welfare Section 1949–51, AA(ACT): A445/1, 140/5/6.
8 Annual report (1950–51), Information Project, Margaret Ramsay, NSW, AA(ACT): A445/1, 276/3/2.
9 CPDHR, vol. 24, p. 968; interview with John Tarbath, 22 October 1996.
10 George Kiddle (assistant secretary Integration Branch), 'Post arrival services for migrants 1947–81', unpublished manuscript written December 1995, held in the library of the Department of Immigration and Multicultural Affairs, Canberra, p. 18.
11 Paper 'Citizenship and settlement', June 1973, AA(ACT): A446/51, 74/75962; interview with P.M. Rice, 14 September 1996; W.G. Kiddle, 'The Grant-in-Aid scheme: an appreciation', August 1981, para. 6, copy supplied to the author by Conor Bradley DIMA, March 1994.
12 Report 'Survey of Yugoslav migrants', 27.3.1968, AA(ACT): A446/T31, 75/79686.

13 Department of Immigration, 'Submission to the Senate Select Committee on civil rights of migrant Australians,' July 1973, p. 10; minute S.J. Rooth to S.J. Dempsey, 29.9 and 5.10.1967, AA(ACT): A446/T31, 75/79205; interview with P.M. Rice, 14 September 1996.
14 P.M. Rice to G.C. Watson, 26.10.1972, AA(ACT): A446/T31, 75/78786; minute S.J. Rooth to assistant secretary Management Services Division, June 1969; minute E.L. Charles, assistant secretary Integration Branch, April 1971, AA(ACT): A446T31, 75/79201; the case recording system was introduced in Townsville in December 1972, see AA(ACT): A446/T31, 75/79199.
15 CPDHR, vol. 70, 1.10.1970, p. 1995; minute K. Kern to S.J. Rooth and E.L. Charles, 20.4.1971, AA(ACT): A446/T31, 75/79201; notes on specific comments, K.R. Batterham to P.M. Rice, May 1971, AA(ACT): A446/T31, 75/79203; interview with P.M. Rice, 14 September 1996.
16 List of unpublished Integration Branch reports 1962–72, AA(ACT): A446/T31, 75/78895.
17 Interview with P.M. Rice, 14 September 1996.
18 Interview with Nancy Anderson, 16 September 1996.
19 Interview with P.M. Rice, 14 September 1996.
20 List of unpublished Integration Branch reports 1962–72, AA(ACT): A446/T31, 75/78895; interview with P.M. Rice, 14 September 1996.
21 Parliament of the Commonwealth of Australia, *Budget Papers*, 1945–75, Commonwealth Government Printer, Canberra; report on Grant-in-Aid to the Public Accounts Committee, July 1969, AA(ACT): A446/78, 67/71761; CPDHR, vol. 73, p. 1303; CPDHR, vol. 73, p. 130, 14.9.1971.
22 Interim report from social worker statistics, Melbourne 1968–69, AA(ACT): A446/T31, 75/79197; CPDHR, vol. 73, p. 1303, 14.9.197; report on employment difficulties 1970–72, AA(ACT): A446/T31, 75/72904.
23 Department of Immigration, 'Submission to the Senate Select Committee on civil rights of migrant Australians', July 1973, p. 6; W.G. Kiddle, 'The Grant-in-Aid scheme: an appreciation', August 1981, paras 14, 24 and 44, copy supplied to the author by Conor Bradley, DIMA, March 1994.
24 Undated report on GIA compliance monitoring (c. 1970) AA(ACT): A446/T31, 75/78721; W.G. Kiddle, paras 15–6, 43, 44; interview with P.M. Rice, 14 September 1996.
25 Interview with George Pridannikoff, 20 September 1996.
26 Interviews with P.M. Rice, 14 September 1996 and John Tarbath, 22 October 1996.
27 P.M. Rice to Dr Fabian Bryant, 29.2.1970, AA(ACT): A446/T31, 75/79201.
28 Report on the integration case recording system 1970–71, 28.3.1973, AA(ACT): A446/T31, 75/79204; interview with P.M. Rice, 14 September 1996.

29 CPDHR, vol. 74, 28–29.10.1971, p. 2799. Table, Source of referral of Department of Immigration welfare cases by period of residence, 1971–72, report on employment difficulties 1970–72, AA(ACT): A446/T31, 75/7904.
30 Department of Immigration 'Submission to the Senate Select Committee on civil rights of migrant Australians', July 1973, p. 6; CPDHR, vol. 84, p. 2923, 30.5.1973; Kiddle, 'Post arrival services for migrants 1947–81', p. 21.
31 Kiddle, paras 9, 35; Australian Institute of Multicultural Affairs, *Evaluation of Post-Arrival Programs*, 1982, pp. 199–205.
32 List of unpublished Integration Branch reports 1962–72, AA(ACT): A446/T31, 75/78895; interview with P.M. Rice, 14 September 1996; brief for Departmental representative . . . for 37th council meeting of ACOSS, 18.2.1972; minute P.M. Rice to G. Kiddle, 26.9.1973, AA(ACT): A446/T31, 75/79738; Department of Immigration, 'Submission to the Senate Select Committee on civil rights of migrant Australians', July 1973, p. 9; Immigration Advisory Council agenda item no. 6, 12.9.1971, pp 4/1–2.
33 A copy of the pro-forma and a statistical analysis of responses dated 12.11.1972 is in AA(ACT): A446/T31, 75/79209; list of questions asked in survey of national group organisations, n.d. (c. 30.6.1973), AA(ACT): A446/T31, 75/79208; Departmental paper 'Citizenship and settlement', p. 11, AA(ACT): A446/51, 74/75962; interview with P.M. Rice, 14 September 1996.
34 Houston's request of March 1970 and a number of replies are in AA(ACT): A446/51, 71/75443.
35 J.H. Houston, national groups liaison officer to Dr Rogers, president Comitato Dante Alighieri di Hobart, 18.11.1971, AA(ACT): A446/T31, 75/79223; see also AA(ACT): A446/T31, 75/79222.
36 Minutes of first meeting of the Immigration Planning Council's Migrant Studies Committee, 1.3.1971, AA(ACT): A446/T31, 75/79201.
37 K.R. Batterham to P.M. Rice, 31.5.1971; P.M. Rice to Lippmann, 31.12.1971, Walter Lippmann, chairman ACOSS to J. Houston, 22.11.1971, brief for Departmental representative attending 37th council meeting of ACOSS 18.2.1972, minutes of meeting of Migrant Welfare Committee 20.6.1972, minute J.H. Houston, senior migration officer National Groups Unit to Mr Macleod, 7.12.1972, file note by J.H. Houston, 5.2.1973, minute P.M. Rice to G. Kiddle, 26.9.1973, AA(ACT): A446/T31, 75/79738.
38 File note, J.H. Houston, 5.2.1973, AA(ACT): A446/T31, 75/79738; minute T.P. Graham to G. Kiddle, 13.6.1975, AA(ACT): A446/T31, 75/78609.
39 CPDHR, vol. 70, p. 1923, 30.9.1970.
40 For an account of the Good Neighbour Movement to 1970 see Jordens, *Redefining Australians*, chapter 5.
41 Malcolm Blight to Bernard Freedman, director Information Branch,

12.1 and 18.4.1974, other correspondence in AA(ACT): A446/51, 73/77800, report on Migrant Social Welfare Conference, 23/24.6.1975, AA(ACT): A446/T31, 75/79627.
42 Departmental paper 'Citizenship and settlement', pp. 14–15, AA(ACT): A446/51, 74/75962; the 1973 charter was published in Galbally (1978), appendix 52, p. 131.
43 Department of Immigration, *Committee on Community Relations Final Report*, AGPS, Canberra 1975, p. 58; A.D. Taylor to director general DSS, 9.4.1975, report of Migrant Social Welfare Conference, 23–24.6.1975, AA(ACT): A446/T31, 75/79627.
44 Task force on coordination in welfare and health, *First Report: Proposals for Change in the Administration and Delivery of Programs and Services*, December 1976, AGPS, Canberra, 1977, p. 156.
45 Galbally (1978), vol. 2, appendix 50, p. 129 (summary of development 1950–75); appendix 51 (functional statement), p. 130; quotation from vol. 1, pp. 78–9.
46 Interviews with George Pridannikoff and Arthur Marshman (former director of the State Migration Office, Queensland), 30 September 1996.

CHAPTER 8 PROMOTING AUSTRALIAN CITIZENSHIP

1 Submission to Cabinet n.d. (c. October 1945), AA(ACT): A446/91, 65/45884.
2 Australia's citizenship legislation did not recognise that many British subjects were not Anglo-Celtic. At this time, Britain admitted all British subjects regardless of race (i.e. granted them full rights of movement). Australia, unable to discriminate overtly through legislation against British subjects from the British Commonwealth, excluded those who were not Anglo-Celtic by administrative means. See chapter 10 and Jordens, *Redefining Australians*, p. 2; the *Nationality and Citizenship Act 1948–50* defined 'protected person' as 'a person who is included in such prescribed classes of persons as are under the protection of the Government of any part of His Majesty's dominions'. This was interpreted by the Department of Immigration as referring to inhabitants of the Australian UN Trust Territories of Nauru and New Guinea.
3 CPDHR, vol. 189, pp, 508–9, 22.11.1946.
4 Biographical details are from Mary Elizabeth Calwell's unpublished speech to the Australian Jewish Historical Society of Victoria, 2.4.1990; for a more detailed discussion of Australian citizenship and national identity see Jordens, *Redefining Australians*, chapter 1.
5 T.H.E. Heyes to Harold Holt, 31.5.1953, AA(ACT): A446/119, 56/66624.
6 See correspondence on a Charter of Australian Citizenship, AA(ACT): A446/119, 56/66624. For a more detailed account of the

proposed Citizenship Charter see Jordens, *Redefining Australians*, pp. 6–7; Snedden, CPDHR, vol. 21, p. 1263, 16.9.1958.
7   CPDHR, vol. 51, p. 995, 20.4.1966.
8   T.H.E. Heyes to CMOs, 23.5.1953, AA(ACT): A446/101, 63/45378.
9   H. McGinness to Secretary, 27.4.1953, AA(ACT): A446/101, 63/45378.
10 G.A.M. Edson to Secretary, 26.6.1953, W.P. Devlin, Melbourne to T.M. Nulty, secretary CMO Brisbane, 14.7.1953, AA(ACT): A446/101, 63/45378; G. McNamara, director Cowra Holding Centre, 18.8.1954, T.H.E. Heyes to Minister, 31.8.1953, AA(ACT): A445/1, 146/8/20.
11 Tables 29.8.1954 and 1.10.1954, AA(ACT): A446/115, 58/65701.
12 Pamphlet, 'This is how you can help someone to become an Australian Citizen', n.d. (c. 1952), AA(ACT): A446/101, 63/45378; McGinness to Secretary, 23.10.1953, AA(ACT): A445/1, 146/8/20; minister for immigration A.R. Downer to Senator Wardlaw, 13.4.1959, AA(ACT): A446/92, 65/45065; CPDHR, vol. 4, p. 384, 18.8.1954 and p. 1218, 14.9.1954; CPDHR, vol. 6, pp. 102–3, 21.4.1955.
13 CPDHR, vol. 197, p. 4948, 15.6.1948; vol. 4, p. 383, 18.8.1954, p. 532, 24.8.1954; p. 1218, 14.9.1954 (quotation); CPDHR, vol. 5, p. 2356, 27.10.1954 (fee); vol. 6, pp. 104–5, 21.4.1955; vol. 37, p. 1874, 24.10.1962.
14 CPDS, vol. 22, p. 639, 3.10.1962 (Fitzgerald); p. 1127, 24.10.1962; secretary P.R. Heydon to Australian High Commissioner, Ottawa, 2.4.1962, AA(ACT): A446/109, 60/67616.
15 CPDHR, vol. 51, pp. 999–1001, p. 1019, 20.4.1966.
16 CPDHR, vol. 51, p 992, 20.4.1966; CPDS, vol. 182, p. 2904, 13.6.1945.
17 CPDHR, vol. 206, p. 399, 7.3.1950.
18 CPDS, vol. 19, p. 203, 15.3.1961 & vol. 25, p. 441, 7.4.1964 (Buttfield); vol. 21, p. 406, 7.3.1962 (Davidson); vol. 22, p. 767, 11.10.1962 & vol. 24, p. 1577, 30.10.1963 (Henty); CPDS, vol. 29, p. 1088, 20.10.1965 & vol. 30, p. 1113, 21.10.1965 (O'Byrne); p. 1111, 21.10.1965 (Fitzgerald); CPDHR, vol. 48. pp. 2187–9; vol. 51, p. 993 (Daly), p. 1061 (Jones), 20.4.1966; CPDS, vol. 57, p. 418, 11.9.1973 (IAC resolutions); CPDHR, vol. 51, p. 993, 20.4.1966 (Citizenship Convention);
19 CPDHR, vol. 50, p. 833, 31.3.1966; vol. 51, p. 991–2, 20.4.1966, pp. 1063–4, 21.4.1966; vol. 85, pp. 362–3, 23.8.1973, pp. 866–9, 12.9.1973; CPDS, vol. 57, p. 417, 11.9.1973. For a more detailed account of the political debate on the oath of allegiance in particular and citizenship in general in this period see chapters 9 and 10 of Jordens, *Redefining Australians*.
20 H. McGinness to Secretary, 18.11.1952, AA(ACT): A446/101, 63/45378; for an account of the promotion of Australian citizenship in the ethnic press see Miriam Gilson and Jerzy Zubrzycki, *The*

Foreign-Language Press in Australia 1848–1964, Australian National University Press, Canberra, 1967, pp. 103–6.

21 H. McGinness to assistant secretary, 'Notes on recent developments in passports and citizenship matters', 29.7.1953; pamphlet, 'This is how you can help someone to become an Australian citizen', n.d. (c. 1952); H. McGinness to Secretary, 27.4.1953; S.J. Dempsey, CMO Melbourne to H. McGinness, 26.5.1954, reply 27.5.1954, AA(ACT): A446/101, 63/45378. For a more detailed account of discrimination on the grounds of nationality in the grant of social welfare benefits and of the effects of residency requirements on migrants see Jordens, *Redefining Australians*, chapter 6.

22 Draft notes on naturalisation for Minister's speech, 7.11.1956, AA(ACT): A446/109, 60/67616.

23 Statistics of certificates of naturalisation issued 1945–57 are in CPDHR, vol. 19, pp. 1503–4, 6.5.1958; AA(ACT): A446/109, 60/67616; CPDHR, vol. 4, p. 59, 5.8.1953 & p. 151, 11.8.1954; *Truth*, 20.11.1955; *Daily Telegraph* 21.11.1955; S.R. Lewis to Secretary, 11.9 and 20.11.1956.

24 CPDS, vol. 14, p. 283, 10.3.1959 (Robertson); CPDS, vol. 16, p. 1357, 11.11.1959 (Branson),

25 Translation from *The Torch*, 12.6.1959, AA(ACT): A446/115, 58/66807.

26 Minute, S.R. Lewis to assistant secretary (General Division), 13.7.1956; S.J. Dempsey to Secretary n.d. (c. 16.8.1956), AA(ACT): A446/92, 65/45065.

27 Secretary to CMOs all States, 7.2.1958, AA(ACT): A446/92, 65/45065.

28 Annual naturalisation figures were 1954: 16 366; 1955: 32 527; 1956: 40 399; 1957: 36 825; Secretary to CMOs all States, 7.2.1958, AA(ACT): A446/92, 65/45065; press statement by A.R. Downer, 2.10.1959, AA(ACT): A446/109, 60/67616.

29 Secretary to Minister, 21.10.1965, AA(ACT): A446/71, 68/71260; press statement by A.R. Downer, 2.10.1959; the formula arrived at is described in minute G.H. Spicer to assistant secretary, 14.3.1960, AA(ACT): A446/109, 60/67616; the numbers who had, and had not, applied for citizenship by nationality are given in CPDHR, vol. 32, pp. 855–6, 5.9.1961 and the numbers and percentages naturalised by nationality in vol. 37, pp. 1789–90, 23.10.1962; CPDHR, vol. 40, p. 1754, 10/11.10.1963.

30 Strategies adopted were outlined in CPDHR, vol. 37, p. 2297, 8.9.1962, vol. 40, p. 1570, 8.10.1963; vol. 47, p. 640, 31.8.1965; CPDS, vol. 24, p. 849–50, 26.9.1963; CPDHR, vol. 47, p. 640, 31.8.1965, p. 644, 1.9.1965.

31 Commonwealth of Australia, *Commonwealth Parliamentary Directory*, 1962; minute P.R. Heydon, secretary to Minister, 21.10.1065, AA(ACT): A445/71, 68/71260.

32 W. Eric Stinton, Rotary International to T.H.E. Heyes, 4.3.1957; extracts from minutes of quarterly council meeting, Good Neigh-

bour Council of Victoria, 2.2.1957; reports on lunch-hour addresses, 24.10.1957 and 31.3.1958, minutes of meetings of naturalisation officers, 29.11.1957; report E. Otzen, Passports and Nationality Division to CMO, 20.2.1958; Secretary to State CMOs, 31.3.1958 and related correspondence, AA(ACT): A446/101, 63/45379.

33 S.J. Dempsey, CMO Melbourne to Secretary, 12.4.1957; CMO Sydney to Secretary, 9.1.1959, AA(ACT): A446/92, 65/45065; for details of this campaign see Jordens, *Promoting Australian Citizenship*, ACGP working paper no. 22, 1994, pp. 24–5; correspondence 11.1.1963 to 30.7.1965, AA(ACT): A446/101, 63/45369; interview with George Pridannikoff, 30 September 1996.

34 Secretary to Minister, 21.10.1965, AA(ACT): A446/71, 68/71260; CPDHR, vol. 45, pp. 761–2, 8.4.1965 and pp. 1025–39, 29.4.1965; CPDHR, vol. 48, p. 1300, 28.9.1965; vol. 51, p. 986, 20.4.1966.

35 CPDS, vol. 29, p. 1088, 20.10.1965 & p. 1101, 21.10.1965; *Sun*, 2.8.1966; Anderson quotation from CPDS, vol. 29, p. 1040, 20.10.1965; at June 1965 there were 255 000 eligible aliens of whom 32 324 were naturalised, in 1968 a pool of 276 000 produced 35 047, and in 1969 a pool of 262 000 produced 26 845 naturalisations, Secretary to Minister, October 1970, AA(ACT): A446/71, 68/71260; CPDHR, vol. 47, p. 640, 31.8.1965.

36 For further information on the removal of the nationality requirements for pensions see Jordens, *Redefining Australians*, chapter 6; reports from CMOs to Secretary, Melbourne, 10.8.1966, Sydney, 24.10.1966, and Perth 7.11.1966; report 8.5.1970; AA(ACT): A446/71, 68/71260; CMO Adelaide to Secretary, 3.5.1972, AA(ACT): A446/77, 67/72904; report, Research and Coordination Branch, March 1972, AA(ACT): A446/109, 60/67616; statistics of naturalisations 1963–68 are in CPDS, vol. 39, p. 1712, 6.11.1968; statistics of naturalisations by country 1945–1972 are in CPDHR, vol. 84, pp. 3031–5, 31.5.1973.

37 Reports of Survey Section, 1966 and 1971, AA(ACT): A446/115, 58/66807; report T.P. Evans to Assistant Secretary, 19.12.1966, AA(ACT): A445/78, 67/72349.

38 Section 4, *Immigration (Education) Act 1971*; CPDHR, vol. 71, p. 138, 17.2.1971.

Chapter 9 Towards a More Equal Citizenship Bargain

1 CPDS, vol. 9, p. 943, 25.10.1956. Similar statements were made by Liberal Senator J.F. Hanan, CPDS, vol. 9, p. 950, 25.10.1956 and Labor MHR F.M. Daly, CPDHR, vol. 40, p. 1999, 17.10.1963.

2 The notion of a 'policy bargain' is derived from the work of Margaret Levi, particularly *The Construction of Consent*, adminis-

tration, compliance and governability working paper no. 10, March 1993, Administration, Compliance and Governability Program, Research School of Social Sciences, Australian National University, pp. 16–27.
3 K.J. Smith, CMO Victoria, to public service inspector Victoria, 29.11.1971, AA(ACT): A446/T31, 75/79686.
4 Quoted by F. Daly, CPDHR, vol. 51, pp. 990–1, 20.4.1966.
5 Press statement by A.R. Downer, 2.10.1959, AA(ACT): A446/109, 60/67616; see also CPDHR, vol. 21, p. 1123, 11.9.1958 for Downer on British migrants and citizenship; for Labor criticisms of citizenship promotion see J. Cairns, CPDHR, vol. 13, p. 1191, 13.4.1956; Leslie Haylen, CPDHR, vol. 13. pp. 1147–8, 4.10.1956.
6 Memorandum to Secretary 14.8.1946, AA(ACT): A446/101, 63/45379; CPDS, vol. 29. p. 117, 21.10.1965, gives statistics of grants of citizenship to British migrants as 3344 in 1962/63; 3315 in 1963/64; and 4002 in 1964/65; CPDS, vol. 29 pp. 1229–30, p. 1232, 22.10.1964; vol. 29, p. 1100, pp. 1113–14, 21.10.1965 (Murphy); see also CPDHR, vol. 42, pp. 2212–13, 20.5.1964.
7 CPDHR, vol. 51, p. 832, 31.3.1966.
8 *Australian Financial Review*, 24.4.1973; *The Age*, Melbourne, 16.7.1973.
9 Minute, T.P. Evans to Assistant Secretary, 19.12.1966, AA(ACT): A445/78, 67/72349; address by Minister to the Newman Society, Canberra, 15.2.1973; David Page to director Information Branch, 1.6.1973, AA(ACT): A446/52, 73/75832; note by G.C. Watson, first assistant secretary Department of Immigration, of conversation with Frank Ley, chief electoral officer, 19.2.1973, AA(ACT): A446/52, 73/75324; information on voting rights of British from A. Kyburz, DIMA, Citizenship Section, January 1994; table, 'Aliens granted Australian Citizenship (January 1945–December 1975), Department of Immigration, *Australian Immigration, Quarterly Statistical Summary*, 1976, p. 32; annual statistics of those granted and refused citizenship 1950–69 and the reasons for their rejection are given in CPDS, vol. 42, pp. 1009–10, 18.9.1969.
10 CMO Hobart to Secretary, 16.5.1950, reply 7.6.1950; Heyes to CMO London, 31.7.1950, AA(ACT): A445/1, 124/6/35.
11 E.M. Hanlon, premier Queensland, to Menzies, 3.4.1951; Heyes to secretary Prime Minister's department, 30.4.1951, Hanlon to Prime Minister, 21.6.1951, Heyes to secretary Prime Minister's department, 11.7.1951, AA(ACT): A445/1, 124/6/35; CPDS, vol. 1, pp. 793–4, 21–22.10.1953; CPDHR, vol. 14, pp. 505–6, 3.4.1957.
12 CPDHR, vol. 2, p. 789, 2.12.1953.
13 R.D. Lumb and K.W. Ryan, *The Constitution of the Commonwealth of Australia Annotated*, 1981, s. 51(XX), 298 and (xxvii) 336; Jean Martin, *The Migrant Presence*, 1978, p. 17; Snedden quotation from CPDHR, vol. 21, p. 1288, 16.11.1958.
14 R.D. Lumb and K.W. Ryan, *The Constitution of the Commonwealth*

of Australia Annotated, 1981, s. 51 (xxvii) 336; interview with John Tarbath, 22 October 1996; see the section on mentally ill migrants in chapter 4 of this book for further information on the deportation of the mentally ill.

15 CPDHR, vol. 21, p. 1290, 16.11.1958; statistics of deportations by year and grounds are in CPDHR, vol. 36, p. 1395, 10.10.1962 and for 1966–70, vol. 71, pp. 822–3, 10.3.1971.
16 P.M. Rice to G.C. Watson, 26.10.1972, AA(ACT): A446/T31, 75/78786.
17 CPDHR, vol. 83, p. 1637, 1.5.1973; report by Helen Eisen 'The problems of migrants in Australia', 17.12.1968, AA(ACT): A446/T31, 75/79206.
18 Minute P.M. Rice to S.J. Rooth, 'Repatriation of Italians and Sicilians', 20.11.1969, AA(ACT): A446/T31, 75/79668.
19 See correspondence between the Departments of Health and Immigration from 2.6.1969, Quotation from report 'Repatriation of Migrants', 24.11.1970, AA(ACT): A446/T31, 75/78793.
20 CPDHR, vol. 15, pp. 1444–6, 12.5.1957; vol. 25, p. 1768, 6.10.1959 (Cairns); CPDS, vol. 22, p. 626, 2.10.1962, vol. 24, p. 1101, 15.10.1963, vol. 26, p. 596–8, 17.9.1964 (McClelland); CPDS, vol. 22, pp. 1167–8, 25.10.1962; vol. 28, pp. 722–4, 11.5.1965, vol. 29, p. 655, 28.9.1965 (Cavanagh); CPDS, vol. 22, p. 1375, 14.11.1962 (Henty), CPDS, vol. 29, p. 1089, 20.10.1965 (Fitzgerald).
21 Statistics of applications refused or deferred between 1945 and 1962 are in CPDS, vol. 22, p. 626, 2.10.1962; statistics of rejections 1949–58 are in CPDHR, vol. 21, p. 1293, 16.9.1958 and those for 1961–66 are in CPDS, vol. 36, p. 1241, 18.10.1967; statistics of aliens naturalised and refused naturalisation security and other grounds by country 1953–57 are in CPDHR, vol. 18, p. 894, 15.4.1958 and vol. 36, pp. 1292–3, 10.10.1962; statistics of rejected or deferred naturalisation applications (without detailed reasons) for 1950–57 are in CPDHR, vol. 19, p. 1503, 6.5.1958; statistics of refusals on security grounds 1950–65 by nationality are in vol. 53, p. 2365, 27 & 28.10.1966.
22 CPDHR, vol. 17, p. 2087, 12.11.1957 and vol. 18, p. 667, 26.3.1958; vol. 19, p. 1196, 23.4.1958; vol. 25, p. 2171, 21.10.1959 and vol. 36, p. 1054, 2.10.1962; vol. 37, p. 2827, 20 & 30.11.1963.
23 CPDHR, vol. 37, pp. 2820, 29.11.1962.
24 CPDHR, vol. 37, pp. 2818–20, 29.11.1962.
25 CPDHR, vol. 38, p. 48, 26.3.1963; CPDS, vol. 24, p. 1101, 15.10.1963.
26 CPDS, vol. 30, p. 1239, 27.10.1965; CPDS, vol. 36, p. 1599–1600, 20.10.1967; vol. 37, p. 993, 15.5.1968.
27 CPDS, vol. 42, pp. 1009–10, 18.9.1969, pp. 1081–8; CPDHR, vol. 65, p. 1666, 19.9.1969; CPDS, vol. 49, pp. 7387–8, 15.9.1971, CPDS, vol. 56, p. 1802, 22.5.1973.
28 Statistics of rejections on the grounds of character are in CPDS,

vol. 37, p. 993, 15.5.1968; Senator McManus's complaints are in CPDS, vol. 29, p. 1111, 21.10.1965.
29 Paper 'Citizenship, Passports and Aliens Registration Section— elimination of discriminatory practices', 22.12.1972, AA(ACT): A446/T31, 75/78542.
30 CPDHR, vol. 20, pp. 711-2, 26.8.1958.
31 CPDHR, vol. 84, p. 2508, 23.5.1973.
32 CPDHR, vol. 84, pp. 2506-8, 23.5.1973.
33 For example speech by R.M. Holten (CP VIC) CPDHR, vol. 37, pp. 1797-8, 23.10.1962; Clyde Cameron, vol. 60, pp. 223-7, 15.8.1968; report on first meeting of the Interdepartmental Committee on Social Security Agreements with other countries, 5.3.1970, AA(ACT): A446/64, 69/72584.
34 CPDHR, vol. 48, p. 2207, 26.10.1965; see chapter 2 for further information on discrimination against southern Europeans.
35 CPDHR, vol. 67, 24.3.1970; W.D. Borrie (chairman), *Population and Australia: A Demographic Analysis and Projection,* First Report of the National Population Inquiry, vol. 1, AGPS, Canberra, 1974, p. 15; in 1973 it was estimated that of the 72 160 Maltese who had arrived between 1947 and 1973, 11 240 (30 per cent) had left, W.D. Borrie, p. 124; see also Constance Lever-Tracy, 'Return migration to Malta: neither failed immigrants nor successful guest workers', *Australian and New Zealand Journal of Sociology,* vol. 25, no. 3, November 1989, pp, 428-50; migration and settlement agreement between the government of the Commonwealth of Australia and the government of Malta, June 1970, AA(ACT): A446/T31, 75/79674.
36 CPDHR, vol. 25, p. 2171, 21.10.1959; statistics of arrivals and departures by year from 1946 to June 1962 are in CPDHR, vol. 36, pp. 1396-7, 10.10.1962; statistics of departure by three categories for 1959-62 are in CPDHR, vol. 40, p. 2450, 29 & 30.10.1963.
37 CPDHR, vol. 7, p. 203, 31.8.1955 and CPDS, vol. 22, p. 1130, 24.10.1962.
38 CPDHR, vol. 13, p. 1187, 4.10.1956.
39 CPDHR, vol. 48, p. 2196, 26.10.1965; vol. 57, pp. 1604-5; vol. 74, p. 2752, 28.10.1971.
40 See Jordens, *Redefining Australians,* chapter 6, pp. 101-8 for further details of portable pensions; report by Immigration Advisory Council Committee on social patterns, 'Inquiry into the departures of settlers from Australia', 29.11.1971, AA(ACT): A446/T31, 75/80869; J. Zubrzycki to L.S. Reed, president All Nations Club, October 1971 and other correspondence, AA(ACT): A446/T31, 76/80838; Oleh Lukomskyj and Peter Richards, 'Return migration from Australia: a case study', *International Migration,* 24 (1986), 3, pp. 603-7; see also National Population Council, population report no. 9, *Emigration,* AGPS, Canberra, May 1990, p. 23.

Chapter 10 The Role of the Department of Immigration in Eroding the 'White Australia Policy'

1 T.H.E. Heyes, secretary Department of Immigration to Minister, 3.2.1956 & 19.11.1959, AA(ACT): A446/86, 66/45342.
2 P.R. Heydon, secretary Department of Immigration to governor general Lord Casey, 1.7.1966, AA(ACT): A446/86, 66/45348.
3 Heyes to Minister, 19.11.1959, AA(ACT): A446/86, 66/45342.
4 Heyes to Minister, 19.11.1959, AA(ACT): A446/86, 66/45342.
5 By March 1958 there were 4851 private non-European students in Australia and 809 sponsored by the Australian government; this grew to 11 158 private and 1159 sponsored by March 1963 and to 11 000 private and 1700 sponsored by the end of 1966, notes on non-European policy, n.d. (c. 17.2.1964), AA(ACT): A446/86, 66/45348, and speech by B.M. Snedden to the Constitution Club, 7.8.1967, AA(ACT): A446/78, 67/71960; for example, resolutions from the Australian Student Christian Movement, 24.5.1956, national union of Australian university students, 25.6.1956; G.C. Watson to H. McGinness, 15.10.1957, AA(ACT): A446/64, 70/75457; Harvey L. Perkins, secretary World Council of Churches to the Prime Minister, 8.3.1960, this file also contains resolutions supporting Asian immigration from the conference of the Churches of Christ in Victoria and Tasmania, 11.5.1960, and the president of the Kilburn Blair Athol Methodist Men's Fellowship, 15.5.1960, AA(ACT): A446/86, 66/45342; see also correspondence files, AA(ACT): A446/86, 66/45343, 66/45344 & 66/45345, and AA(ACT): A446/71, 68/71864.
6 Minute, Secretary to all posts, on changes approved by Cabinet, 10.10.1956, AA(ACT): A446/86, 66/45342; notes for the Minister, 'Developments on entry policy', Martyn to Assistant Secretary, n.d. (c. 10.5.1966); P.R. Heydon, secretary Department of Immigration to governor general Lord Casey, 1.7.1966, AA(ACT): A446/86, 66/45348; Department of Immigration paper 'Discrimination in entry policy' n.d. (c. 1972), AA(ACT): A446/T31, 75/78542; quotation from memorandum 'Entry of Asians for permanent residence in Australia', Heyes to Minister, 19.11.1959, AA(ACT): A446/86, 66/45342.
7 Heyes to Trevor Pyman, DLNS, 4.11.1959, AA(ACT): A446/86, 66/45342.
8 Alan Gregory, hon. secretary Melbourne University, Students Representative Council, 20.4.1960, AA(ACT): A446/86, 6/45342; *The Age*, 23.7.1960.
9 L.F. Crisp (ed.), *Peter Richard Heydon 1913–1971: A Tribute From His Friends*, Privately Published, Canberra, 1972, pp. 15–8, p. 20,

pp. 40–41; *The Age*, 27.12.1972, epitaph of Sir Peter Heydon by Bruce Grant.
10 Secretary to Mr Drury, 24.7.1963, AA(ACT): A446/101, 63/45379; *Sun-Herald*, 13.5.1971; E.L. Charles, Assistant Secretary, instructions on distribution, 6.5.1965, and A.L. Nutt, acting secretary Department of Immigration to the secretary Department of External Affairs, 12.5.1965, AA(ACT): A446/65, 69/70953.
11 'Brief notes on Australia's established immigration policy', 27.3.1963; letter K.J. Smith to T.H. Chou, 29.3.1963 (with annotations by the Secretary and Assistant Secretary); AA(ACT): A446/101, 63/45695.
12 Crisp, p. 29 & p. 41; *Sun-Herald*, 13.5.1971.
13 Notes on non-European policy, n.d. (c. 17.2.1964), AA(ACT): A446/86, 66/45348; P.R. Heydon, secretary Department of Immigration to governor general, Lord Casey, 1.7.1966, AA(ACT): A446/86, 66/45348.
14 Draft speech for Minister, 'The evolution of a policy', 24.8.1970, AA(ACT): A446/63, 70/78495; quotation from A.J. Forbes to R.N. Sachs (stock response), 21.7.1972, AA(ACT): A446/55, 72/77602.
15 T.H. Halsey, 'Non-Europeans in Australia: 1961 Census results,' 18.11.1964, AA(ACT): A446/65, 69/70953; notes on non-European policy, c. 17.2.1964, AA(ACT): A446/86, 66/45348.
16 Revised 'Brief notes on Australia's established immigration policy', 1.5.1965; A.L. Nutt, acting secretary Department of Immigration to the secretary Department of External Affairs, 13.5.1965, AA(ACT): A446/65, 69/70953; Maximillian Walsh, *Sun-Herald*, 13.5.1971, and Kenneth Rivett, *Sydney Morning Herald*, 18.5.1971.
17 Notes for the Minister, developments on entry policy, Martyn to assistant secretary, n.d. (c. 10.5.1966), AA(ACT): A446/86, 66/45348; Department of Immigration paper 'Discrimination in entry policy' n.d. (c. 1972), AA(ACT): A446/T31, 75/78542; Quotations from Crisp, pp. 41–2.
18 *Sun-Herald*, 13.5.1971.
19 Statement 'Review of immigration policy', 8.3.1966, AA(ACT): A446/65, 69/70953.
20 P.R. Heydon, secretary Department of Immigration to governor general Lord Casey, 1.7.1966, AA(ACT): A446/86, 66/45348.
21 Ministerial responses 1.8.1966 and 22.8.1966, AA(ACT): A446/86, 66/46369.
22 A.C. Treloar to Assistant Secretary, 15.3.1966, AA(ACT): A446/86, 66/45481; speech, 'Non-European migration' delivered by minister for immigration B.M. Snedden to the Constitution Club, 7.8.1967, AA(ACT): A446/78, 67/71960; Department of Immigration, 'Australia's Immigration Policy', July 1970, AA(ACT): A446/33, 70/77176; draft speech for Minister 'The evolution of a policy', 24.8.1970, AA(ACT): A446/63, 70/78495.
23 T.P. Evans to CMO, 31.3.1971, AA(ACT): A446/55, 71/76150.

24 H. McGinness, first assistant secretary, to Mr Dempsey and G.C. Watson, 22.7.1970, AA(ACT): A446/65, 69/70953.
25 H. McGinness, first assistant secretary, to Mr Dempsey and G.C. Watson, 22.7.1970, AA(ACT): A446/65, 69/70953.
26 P.R. Heydon, secretary to minister P.R. Lynch, 1.10.1970, AA(ACT): A446/64, 69/72415 (this series of files contains numerous press clippings reacting to the policy change introduced in March 1966).
27 Heydon to R.R. Gordon, chairman Australian Council for Social Services, 27.5.1968, AA(ACT): A446/71, 68/71661, AA; minister for immigration B.M. Snedden to senior research officer B.G. Hartcher, Liberal Party of Australia, 17.5.1968, 12.6.1968, AA(ACT): A446/71, 68/71602; E.L. Charles to First Assistant Secretary, 'Brief to inform State Ministers on non-European migration', 19.7.1968, AA(ACT): A446/71, 68/71963.
28 Heydon to Minister, 29.10.1970; H. McGinness, 2.11.1970, AA(ACT): A446/63, 70/78495; quotation from Heydon to Minister, 20.1.1971, AA(ACT): A446/63, 70/78615.
29 Copy at AA(ACT): A446/55, 71/75621.
30 Quotation from ALP Federal platform from P.R. Heydon to Minister, 4.2.1971, summary of public comments on non-European migration by Labor Party members requested in January 1971, AA(ACT): A446/54, 71/77025; CPDHR, vol. 53, p. 1320, 27.9.1966.
31 P.R. Heydon to Minister, 4.2.1971, summarising ALP opinion; press clippings April–July 1971, AA(ACT): A446/54, 71/77025.
32 Telex H. McGinness to Minister, 21.6.1971, AA(ACT): A446/54, 71/77025.
33 R.E. Armstrong to A.J. Forbes, 29.6.1971; H. McGinness to R.E. Armstrong, 12.8.1971, AA(ACT): A446/54, 71/77025.
34 *Sydney Morning Herald*, 15.10.1971; transcription of Whitlam's statements on *This Day Tonight*, 14.10.1971, AA(ACT): A446/55, 71/75761; W.G. Kiddle to First Assistant Secretary, 19.10.1971, AA(ACT): A446/54, 71/77633.
35 Speech, 'Labor's approach to immigration', 24.10.1971, AA(ACT): A446/52, 72/78683.
36 See statement tabled in the House of Representatives by A.J. Grassby, 'Objectives of citizenship and settlement policy', 6.12.1973, AA(ACT): A446/51, 74/75962.
37 R.E. Armstrong 'Procedures under revised rules for entry for residence and eligibility for assisted passages', 25.5.1973, AA(ACT): A446/52, 73/75503.
38 R.E. Armstrong to Minister, confidential working paper, 'Immigration under a Labor government', 20.12.1972, AA(ACT): A446/52, 72/95574; K. Waller to H. McGinness, a/g secretary Department of Immigration, 11.7.1973; memorandum, 'Procedures under revised rules of entry', Waller to Heads of Mission, 25.5.1973; Armstrong to Waller, 17.7.1973; Armstrong to Grassby, 19.7.1975, AA(ACT): A446/52, 73/76724; the increase in the migrant contribution to

assisted passages had been proposed by the previous government, see R.E. Armstrong to secretary Department of Prime Minister and Cabinet, 18.4.1972, AA(ACT): A446/55, 71/76308; *Financial Review*, 6.6.1973; information on assisted passages 1974 from AA(ACT): A446/52, 72/95574 and *Glen Innes Examiner*, 18.6.1973; for Cameron's reform see Charles A. Price, 'Australian Immigration: the Whitlam government 1972–75' in Charles A. Price and Jean I. Martin (eds), *Australian Immigration: A Bibliography and Digest*, part 1, no. 2, 1975, Department of Demography, Australian National University, Canberra, 1976, p. A7.

39 The Whitlam quotation is from Clyde Cameron, *The Cameron Diaries*, Allen & Unwin, Sydney, 1990, p. 801; a more detailed (and colourful) account of Whitlam's initial attitude to the migration of Vietnamese refugees was given by Cameron in his book *China, Communism and Coca-Cola*, Hill of Content, Melbourne, 1980, pp. 228–33; statistics from undated paper by Department of Social Security (c. June 1975) 'Social welfare provisions available to refugees and other persons from South Vietnam', AA(ACT): A446/T31, 75/78855.

40 Statistics of Asian immigration from *Population and Australia: A Demographic Analysis* (chairman W.D. Borrie) vol. 1, AGPS, Canberra, 1975, p. 117.

Chapter 11 The Department of Immigration Under Labor

1 Quote from Gough Whitlam, *The Whitlam Government 1972–75*, Viking, New York, 1985, p. 502. Labor reduced the annual intake target from 140 000 to 110 000 in December 1972 to 80 000 in late 1974 and to 50 000 in late 1975 (migration target figures are from Charles A. Price and Jean I. Martin, *Australian Immigration: A Bibliography and Digest*, no. 3, 1995, part 1, p. A11); the statistics of migrant intake quoted have been rounded to the nearest thousand and are derived from Department of Immigration and Ethnic Affairs, *Australian Immigration. Quarterly Statistical Summary*, vol. 3, no. 33, December 1975, AGPS, Canberra, 1977, p. 35.

2 *Debrett's Handbook of Australia*, Sydney, 1987, p. 387.

3 Submission by the Department of Immigration to the Senate Select Committee on the Civil Rights of Migrants, July 1973, section 3, integration.

4 Statement tabled in the House of Representatives by M.H.R. minister for immigration, the Hon. A.J. Grassby, 6.12.1973, AA(ACT): A446/51, 74/75962. See chapter 10 for an account of the construction of a departmental history of non-European migration in 1971.

5 List of achievements 1973, AA(ACT): A446/51, 74/75925; *Daily*

Telegraph, 17.7.1973; CPDHR, vol. 83, pp. 1312–4, 11.4.1973; pp. 1998–2019, 9/10.5.1973; vol. 84, pp. 2505–8, 23.5.1973.
6 List of achievements 1973, AA(ACT): A446/51, 74/75925.
7 News release, 15.7.1973; paper 'Policies in action', n.d. (c. 26.11.1973), AA(ACT): A446/T31, 75/78546; minute L. H. Mead to branch head, 12.12.1972, AA(ACT): A446/T31, 75/78895.
8 Commonwealth of Australia, Immigration Advisory Council Committee on Community Relations, *Interim Report*, August 1974, pp. 35–7, *Final Report*, 1975, pp. 42–3.
9 Submission J.A. Battanta to director general Department of Social Services, 7.10.1973, AA(ACT): A446/T31, 75/79286; statement by minister for immigration A.J. Grassby, 'Objectives—citizenship and settlement policy', tabled in the House of Representatives, 6.12.1973, AA(ACT): A446/51, 74/75962.
10 Press statement by minister for social security W.G. Hayden, 3.4.1973; prime minister E.G. Whitlam to deputy prime minister L.H. Barnard, 24.1.1974, undated statement of NCSW interim committee philosophy, AA(ACT): A446/T31, 75/79167; report on NCSW seminar, 25.3.1974, AA(ACT): A446/T31, 75/79290; CPDHR, vol. 84, 30.5.1973, p. 2923; minute, G.C. Watson to C.H. McGinness, 4.7.1971, C.H. McGinness, a/g secretary Department of Immigration to Marie Coleman, chairman NCSW, 5.7.1973, AA(ACT): A446/T31, 75/79167; W.G. Hayden, minister for social security to A.J. Grassby, 5.6.1974, AA(ACT): A446/T31, 75/79294.
11 File note by G.C. Watson 11.8.1973, file note of meeting 24/25.8.1973; Grassby to Hayden, 31.8.1973, AA(ACT): A446/T31, 75/79167;For example by Jean I. Martin, *The Migrant Presence*, George Allen & Unwin, Sydney, 1978, pp. 50–2.
12 P.M. Rice to G. Kiddle, 9.8.1973, AA(ACT): A446/T31, 75/79167; file note of meeting between the Minister for Social Security and migrant groups, 2.1.1974, AA(ACT): A446/T31, 75/79286.
13 Jean I. Martin, *The Migrant Presence Australian Responses 1947–77*, research report for the National Population Inquiry Studies in Society 2, Sydney, 1978, pp. 50–2; James Jupp and Marie Kabala, *The Politics of Australian Immigration*, AGPS, Canberra, 1993, p. 204.
14 CPDHR, vol. 83, p. 1537, 1.5.1973; p. 1626, 2.5.73; vol. 86, p. 2310, 17.10.1973.
15 Notes prepared for talk to be delivered to the school of administration for branch officers, 28.11.1949; Heyes to Holt, 9.3.1951, AA(ACT): A446/55, 71/75347.
16 C.E.W. Bean to the Prime Minister's department, 25.5.1953; paper for Secretary 'History of the Department and post-war migration', 18.6.1954; minute F. Robson to G.C. Watson, 14.7.1954; Arthur Calwell to T.H.E. Heyes, 12.1.1955, W.E. Dunk, chairman Public Service Board to Heyes, 3.12.1959, reply 18.1.1960; draft of history for Public Service Board, B.L. Murray to Assistant Secretary,

25.3.1960, history of the Department of Immigration, March 1967, AA(ACT): A446/55, 71/75347.
17 CPDHR, vol. 66, p. 1025, 9/10.4.1970; A.J. Forbes to Keogh, 3.11.1972; W.R. Clark, assistant secretary Population Planning and Research to Mr Dempsey, 8.6.1973, AA(ACT): A446/51, 73/77724.
18 W.R. Clark, assistant secretary Population Planning and Research to Mr Dempsey, 8.6.1973; T.W. Eckersley to first assistant secretary Planning and Research Branch, 14.6.1973, 31.7.1973, 10.1973; F.H. Wheeler, secretary to the Treasury to R.E. Armstrong, secretary Department of Immigration, 24.9.1973, Armstrong to Minister, W.R. Clark, assistant secretary Planning and Research to Mr Dempsey, 26.11.1973, Dempsey's reply 28.2.1974, AA(ACT): A446/51, 73/77724.
19 News Release 82/73, p. 3; CPDHR, vol. 87, p. 4185, 4.12.1973; Grassby to Michael Cannon, 1.4.1974; record of conversation with Michael Cannon, 8.5.1974; Cannon to Peter Gregson, 15.6.1974; W.R. Clark, assistant secretary Planning and Research Branch, Department of Labor and Immigration to First Assistant Secretary, 16.1.1975; Ian G. Sharp secretary to Minister, 29.1.1975, AA(ACT): A446/51, 73/77724.
20 CPDHR, vol. 69, p. 1911, 30.9.1970; vol. 84, p. 2170, 16.5.1973; Jenkins to Grassby, 16.5.1973, AA(ACT): A446/51, 73/77724.
21 Grassby to K.E. Enderby, minister for the Capital Territory, 6.7.1973, AA(ACT): A446/51, 73/77724; CPDHR, vol. 85, p. 279, 23.8.1973.
22 Statement by Lionel Bowen, 10.4.1974, AA(ACT): A446/51, 73/77724. Other members of the committee were Professor Geoffrey Blainey, R.W. Boswell of the Atomic Energy Commission, Professor J. Mulvaney, Australian National University, Dr F.H. Talbert, director of the Australian Museum, Sydney, Dr D.F. Waterhouse, CSIRO, Andrew Clayton, National Parks and Wildlife Foundation, and Frank Waters, former president of the Australian Public Workers' Union.
23 J.H. Houston, senior migration officer National Groups, to G. Kiddle, 2.5.74, AA(ACT): A446/51, 73/77724.
24 I.G. Sharp, secretary, to chairman of the Committee of Inquiry on Museums and National Collections, AA(ACT): A446/51, 73/77724.
25 Submission by the Department of Labour and Immigration to the Committee of Inquiry on Museums and National Collections, 23.7.1974, AA(ACT): A446/51, 73/77724.
26 Gough Whitlam, *The Whitlam Government 1972–75*, Viking, 1985, pp. 503–4.
27 *ibid.*, p. 494, pp. 503–4.
28 Interview with John Tarbath, 22 October 1996; A.D. Taylor, director, to director-general Department of Social Security, AA(ACT): A446/T31, 75/79627.
29 A.J. Battanta, first assistant secretary Management, to director-

general DSS, paper 'The future of migrant services', 22.12.1976; T.P Graham to G. Kiddle, September 1975, AA(ACT): A446/T31, 75/78609; interviews with P.M. Rice, 14 September 1996 and John Tarbath, 22 October 1996.
30 *Government Gazette*, no. 262, 22 December 1975; task force on co-ordination in welfare and health, *First Report, Proposals for Change in the Administration and Delivery of Programs and Services*, December 1976, (chairman P.H. Bailey), AGPS, Canberra, 1977, pp. 150-9.

CHAPTER 12 IMMIGRATION, CITIZENSHIP AND SETTLEMENT

1 The annual increase by migration 1945-72 was 0.89 per cent, see Charles A. Price, 'Australian immigration: the Whitlam government 1972-75' in Charles A. Price and Jean I. Martin (eds), *Australian Immigration: A Bibliography and Digest*, part 1, no. 2, 1975, Department of Demography, Australian National University, Canberra, 1976, p. A3, p. A14; *Population and Australia: A Demographic Analysis* (chairman W.D. Borrie), vol. 1, AGPS, Canberra, 1975, pp. 101-2.
2 *Population and Australia*, p. 110; Barrie Dyster and David Meredith, *Australia in the International Economy in the Twentieth Century*, Cambridge University Press, Melbourne, 1990, p. 236, p. 259, p. 314; for information on housing see Jordens, *Redefining Australians*, chapter 4.
3 Ann-Mari Jordens, 'Conscription and dissent: the genesis of anti-war protest' in Gregory Pemberton (ed.), *Vietnam Remembered*, Weldon Publishing, Sydney, 1990, p. 70.
4 For further information on this Committee see Jordens, *Redefining Australians*, pp. 133-4.
5 The quotation by Borrie is from *Population and Australia*, p. 118.
6 Dyster and Meredith, *Australia in the International Economy*, pp. 314-5; interview with Stephanie Charlesworth, 18 October 1996.

Bibliography

PUBLISHED SOURCES

Books

Anderson, Benedict *Imagined Communities Reflections on the Origin and Spread of Nationalism*, Verso, London, 1983 (reprint 1991)
Australian Institute of Multicultural Affairs *Evaluation of Post-Arrival Programs and Services*, The Institute, Melbourne, 1982
Barbalet, J.M. *Citizenship. Rights, Struggle and Class Inequality*, Open University Press, Milton Keynes, 1988
Cameron, Clyde *China, Communism and Coca-Cola*, Hill of Content, Melbourne, 1980
——*The Cameron Diaries*, Allen & Unwin, Sydney, 1990
Castles, Stephen et al. *Mistaken Identity. Multiculturalism and the Demise of Nationalism in Australia*, Pluto Press, Sydney, 1994
Collins, Jock *Migrant Hands in a Distant Land: Australia's Post-War Immigration*, Pluto Press, Sydney, 1988
Cox, David R. *Migration and Welfare: An Australian Perspective*, Prentice Hall, New York, 1987
Debrett's Handbook of Australia, Collins, Sydney, 1987
Dyster, Barrie and Meredith, David *Australia in the International Economy in the Twentieth Century*, Cambridge University Press, Melbourne, 1990
Freeman, Gary P. and Jupp, James (eds) *Nations of Immigrants: Australia, the United States, and International Migration*, Oxford University Press, Melbourne, 1992
Gilson, Miriam and Zubrzycki, Jerzy *The Foreign-Language Press in*

Australia 1848-1964, Australian National University Press, Canberra, 1967

Henderson, Ronald F. et al. *People in Poverty: A Melbourne Survey*, Cheshire, for the Institute of Applied Economic Research, University of Melbourne, 1970

Holbern, Louise *International Refugee Organisation, a Specialised Agency of the United Nations: Its History and Work, 1946-52*, Oxford University Press, London, 1956

Howe, Renate *Women and the State: Australian Perspectives*, special edition of the *Journal of Australian Studies*, Latrobe University Press, Melbourne, 1993

Jamrozik, Adam et al. *Social Change and Cultural Transformation in Australia*, Cambridge University Press, Melbourne, 1995

Jupp, James *Arrivals and Departures*, Cheshire-Lansdowne, Melbourne, 1966

Jupp, James (ed.) *The Australian People*, Angus & Robertson, Sydney, 1988

Jordens, Ann-Mari *Redefining Australians: Immigration, Citizenship and National Identity*, Hale & Iremonger, Sydney, 1995

Kewley, T.H. *Social Security in Australia 1900-72*, Sydney, University Press, 1973

Kiernan, Colm *Calwell: A Personal and Political Biography*, Nelson, Melbourne, 1978

Kunz, Egon F. *Displaced Persons, Calwell's New Australians*, ANU Press, Canberra, 1988

Lack, John and Templeton, Jacqueline *Bold Experiment: A Documentary History of Australian Immigration since 1945*, Oxford University Press, Melbourne, 1995

Lane, P.H. *The Australian Federal System*, 2nd edn, Law Book Company, Sydney, 1979

Levi, Margaret *Of Rule and Revenue*, University of California Press, Berkeley, 1988

Lumb, R.D. and Ryan, K.W. *The Constitution of the Commonwealth of Australia*, 3rd edn, Butterworths, Sydney, 1981

Marshall, T.H. *Sociology at the Crossroads and Other Essays*, Heinemann, London, 1963

Martin, Jean I. *The Migrant Presence: Australian Responses 1947-77*, Research Report for the Australian Population Inquiry, George Allen & Unwin, Sydney, 1978

Pemberton, Gregory *All the Way: Australia's Road to Vietnam*, Allen & Unwin, Sydney, 1987

—— (ed.) *Vietnam Remembered*, Weldon Publishing, Sydney, 1990

Price, Charles (ed.) *Greeks in Australia*, ANU Press, Canberra, 1975

—— *Australian National Identity*, Academy of the Social Sciences in Australia, Canberra, 1991

Price, Charles and Martin, Jean I. (eds) *Australian Immigration: A Bibliography and Digest*, part 1, nos 2 and 3, Department of Demography, Australian National University, Canberra, 1976

Riordan, John A. *The Laws of Australia*, Law Book Company, Melbourne, 1993

Rydon, Joan *A Biographical Register of the Commonwealth Parliament 1901–1972*, ANU Press, Canberra, 1975
Turner, Brian S. *Citizenship and Capitalism: The Debate Over Reformism*, Allen & Unwin, London, 1986
Wilton, Janis and Bosworth, Richard *Old Worlds and New Australia: The Post-War Migrant Experience*, Penguin Books, Ringwood, Vic, 1984
Whitlam, Gough *The Whitlam Government 1972–75*, Viking, Ringwood, Vic, 1985
Who's Who in Australia, Herald and Weekly Times, Melbourne, 1955, 1962

Articles and Monographs

Braithwaite, John and Makkai, Toni 'Trust and Compliance', compliance and governability working paper no. 9, Administration, Compliance and Governability Program, Research School of Social Sciences, Australian National University, Canberra, February 1993
Clyne, Michael 'Monolingualism, multilingualism and the Australian nation' in *Australian National Identity* (ed. Charles A. Price), Academy of the Social Sciences in Australia, Canberra, 1991
Cox, David 'Welfare services in a multicultural society', *Australian Social Work*, vol. 36, no. 3, September 1983
Crisp, L.F. *Peter Richard Heydon 1913–1971: A Tribute from his Friends*, Privately printed, Canberra, 1972
Edwards, Graham A. 'Psychiatric treatment and services in Australia, 1914–1994', *Medical Journal of Australia*, vol. 161, 4 July 1994
Evans M.D.R. 'Choosing to be a citizen: the time path of citizenship in Australia', *International Migration Review*, vol. xxii, no. 2, pp. 43–64
Jakubowicz, A. 'State and ethnicity: multiculturalism as ideology', *Australian & New Zealand Journal of Sociology*, vol. 17, no. 3, November 1981
——'Welfare provision' in Jupp, James (ed.), *The Australian People*, Angus & Robertson, Sydney, 1988
——'The state and the welfare of immigrants in Australia', *Ethnic and Racial Studies*, vol. 12, no. 1, January 1989
Jordens, Ann-Mari 'An administrative nightmare: Aboriginal conscription 1965–72', *Aboriginal History*, vol. 13, nos 1–2, 1989, pp. 124–34
——'Conscription and dissent: The genesis of anti-war protest' in G.J. Pemberton (ed.), *Vietnam Remembered*, Weldon Publications, Sydney, 1990
——'Redefining Australians: immigrant non-compliance and the extension of citizenship rights in Australia since 1945', working papers in Australian studies no. 79, Sir Robert Menzies Centre for Australian Studies, Institute of Commonwealth Studies, University of London, 1992
——'Alien integration: the development of administrative policy and practice within the Department of Immigration since 1945', administration, compliance and governability working paper no. 6, Administration, Compliance and Governability Program, Research

School of Social Sciences, Australian National University, Canberra, August 1992
—— 'Redefining "Australian Citizen" 1945–75', administration, compliance and governability working paper no. 8, Administration, Compliance and Governability Program, Research School of Social Sciences, Australian National University, Canberra, January 1993
—— 'Communicating with migrants: the development of language teaching and of translating and interpreting services in Australia 1945–75', administration, compliance and governability working paper no. 12, Administration, Compliance and Governability Program, Research School of Social Sciences, Australian National University, Canberra, May 1993
—— 'From discrimination to equality: social welfare benefits and non-British migrants', administration, compliance and governability working paper no. 14, Administration, Compliance and Governability Program, Research School of Social Sciences, Australian National University, Canberra, September 1993
—— 'Migrant supporting mothers and the state' in Howe, Renate (ed.), *Women and the state*, Latrobe University Press, Melbourne, 1993
—— 'Accommodating migrants', administration, compliance and governability working paper no. 19, Administration, Compliance and Governability Program, Research School of Social Sciences, Australian National University, Canberra, January 1994
Jupp, James 'Immigration and settlement policy in Australia' in *Immigration and the Politics of Ethnicity and Race in Australia and Britain* (ed. Nile, Richard), Bureau of Immigration Research, Sir Robert Menzies Centre for Australian Studies, University of London, 1991, pp. 53–69
—— 'The ethnic lobby and immigration policy', in Jupp, James and Kabala, Marie (eds), *The Politics of Australian Immigration*, Bureau of Immigration Research, AGPS, Canberra, 1993
Kelly, J. and McAllister, I. 'The decision to become an Australian citizen', *Australian and New Zealand Journal of Sociology*, vol. 18, no. 3, pp. 428–40
Lever-Tracy, Constance 'Return migration to Malta: neither failed immigrants nor successful guest workers', *Australian and New Zealand Journal of Sociology*, vol. 25, no. 3, November 1989
Levi, Margaret 'The construction of consent', administration, compliance and governability working paper no. 10, Administration, Compliance and Governability Program, Research School of Social Sciences, Australian National University, Canberra, March 1993
Lewins, F. 'Assimilation and integration' in Jupp, James (ed.), *The Australian People*, Angus & Robertson, Sydney, 1988
Lukomskyj, Oleh and Richards, Peter 'Return migration from Australia: a case study', *International Migration (Geneva)*, vol. 24, no. 3, 1986.
McCaughey, Jean 'Migrants' in Henderson R.F. et al. (eds), *People in Poverty: A Melbourne Survey*, University of Melbourne, 1970
Martin, Jean I. 'Migration and social pluralism' in *How Many Australians*, Australian Institute of Political Science, 37th summer school, Angus & Robertson, Sydney, 1971
Ongley, Patrick and Pearson, David 'Post-1945 international migration:

New Zealand, Australia and Canada compared', *International Migration Review*, vol. xxix, no. 3, Fall 1995.
Price, Charles A. 'Australian immigration: the Whitlam government 1972-75' in Price, Charles and Martin, Jean I. (eds), *Australian Immigration: A Bibliography and Digest*, no. 3, part 1, Department of Demography, Australian National University, Canberra, 1975
——'Environment, Aborigines, nationalism, ethnic origins and intermixture' in *Australian National Identity* (ed. Price, Charles A.), Academy of the Social Sciences in Australia, Canberra, 1991
Sawer, Marian 'Reclaiming social liberalism: the women's movement and the state' in Howe Renate (ed.), *Women and The State*, Latrobe University Press, Melbourne, 1993
Tsounis, M.P. 'Greek communities in Australia' in Price, Charles (ed.) *Greeks in Australia*, ANU Press, Canberra, 1975

Official Publications

Acts of the Australian Parliament 1901-1973, Australian Government Publishing Service (AGPS), Canberra, 1974
'Australia: review of post arrival programs and services to migrants', *Migrant Services and Programs*, chairman F. Galbally (Galbally Report), report and appendixes, vols. 1 and 2, AGPS, Canberra, 1978
Australian Government Commission of Inquiry into Poverty, first main report, April 1975, *Poverty in Australia April 1975*, vol. 1, Professor Ronald F. Henderson, chairman, AGPS, Canberra, 1975
——second main report, October 1975, *Poverty in Australia October 1975*, vol. 2, Professor Ronald Sackville, chairman, AGPS, Canberra, 1975
Australian Council on Population and Immigration Council, *A Decade of Migrant Settlement: Report on the 1973 Immigration Survey*, AGPS, Canberra, 1976
Bureau of Immigration Research, statistics section, *Australian Citizenship*, statistical report 1, AGPS, Canberra, 1990
Commonwealth Gazette, no. 138, Government Printer, Canberra, 13 July 1945
Commonwealth of Australia, Auditor-General, *Audit Reports*, Government Printer, Canberra, 1949-75
——*Budget Papers*, Government Printer, Canberra, 1945-75
——*Commonwealth Parliamentary Debates* (Hansard), House of Representatives and Senate, AGPS, Canberra, 1945-75
——*Commonwealth Parliamentary Directory*, Government Printer, Canberra, 1962
——*Full Employment in Australia*, Government Printer, Canberra, tabled in Parliament, 30 May 1945
——Immigration Advisory Council Committee on Community Relations, *Interim Report August 1974, Final Report, 1975* (chairman W.M. Lippmann), AGPS, Canberra
——*Population and Australia: A Demographic Analysis and Projection*, report of the National Population Inquiry (chairman W.D. Borrie), 2 vols, AGPS, Canberra, 1975

——Department of Immigration, *Statistical Bulletin*, Canberra, no. 1 January 1952–no. 39 July 1961
Cox, David 'The role of ethnic groups in migrant welfare' in *Welfare of Migrants*, Commission of Inquiry into Poverty, AGPS, Canberra, 1975
Department of Immigration, *Australian Immigration Quarterly Statistical Bulletin*, vol. 2, Canberra, no. 1, November 1961–no. 20 1966
——*Australian Immigration Quarterly Statistical Summary*, AGPS, Canberra, vol. 3, no. 1, September 1966–vol. 3, no. 35, December 1976
——'Submission to the Senate Select Committee on civil rights of migrant Australians', July 1973
——Survey Section, *Report on the Survey of Interpreting and Translating Needs in the Community*, October 1973
——*Committee on Community Relations Final Report*, AGPS, Canberra, 1975
Department of Immigration and Ethnic Affairs, *National Consultations on Multiculturalism and Citizenship* (chairman J. Zubrzycki), AGPS, Canberra, 1982
Department of Immigration, Local Government and Ethnic Affairs, *Australia and Immigration 1788–1988*, AGPS, Canberra, 1988
——*Angels and Arrogant Gods: Migration Officers and Migrants Reminisce 1945–85*, AGPS, Canberra, 1989
Department of Labor and Immigration, Committee on Community Relations, *Final Report*, AGPS, Canberra, September 1976
Department of Prime Minister and Cabinet, Office of Multicultural Affairs, *National Agenda for a Multicultural Australia*, AGPS, Canberra, July 1989
Grassby, A.J. *A Multi-Cultural Society for the Future*, AGPS, Canberra, 1973
Hasluck, Paul *The Government and the People 1942–45*, Australian War Memorial, Canberra, 1970
Holt, H.E. *What Immigration Means to Australia*, report tabled 30. 8. 1956, Government Printer, Canberra, 1956
Immigration Advisory Council Committee on Social Patterns, *Inquiry into the Departure of Settlers from Australia*, (chairman J. Zubrzycki), final report, AGPS, Canberra, July 1973
Jakubowicz, Andrew and Buckley, Berenice *Migrants and the Legal System*, Australian Government Commission of Inquiry into Poverty, Law and Poverty Series, AGPS, Canberra, 1975
Jupp, James and Kabala, Marie (eds) *The Politics of Australian Immigration*, Bureau of Immigration Research, AGPS, Canberra, 1993
Lukomskyj, Oleh *An Overview of Australian Government Settlement Policy 1945–92*, Bureau of Immigration Research, Commonwealth of Australia, Melbourne, 1992
Marshall, Anthony, Williams Lynne S. *Discrimination Against Immigrant Workers in Australia*, report prepared by the Bureau of Immigration Research for the International Labor Office, AGPS, Canberra, 1991
Martin, Jean I. 'The economic condition of migrants' in *Welfare of*

Migrants, Australian Government Commission of Inquiry into Poverty, AGPS, Canberra, 1975, pp. 151–80
Morrissey, Michael et al. *Immigration and Industry Restructuring in the Illawarra*, Bureau of Immigration Research, AGPS, Canberra, 1992
National Population Council, population report no. 9, *Emigration*, Commonwealth of Australia, AGPS, Canberra, 1990
Price, C.A. 'Australian migration: settler gain and loss' in *Inquiry into the Departure of Settlers to and from Australia*, final report, Immigration Advisory Council's Committee on Social Patterns, AGPS, Canberra, July 1973
Task Force on Coordination in Welfare and Health, *First Report Proposals for Change in the Administration and Delivery of Programs and Services*, December 1976 (chairman P.H. Bailey), AGPS, Canberra, 1977
Wooden, Mark et al. *Australian Immigration: A Survey of the Issues*, AGPS, Canberra, 1994

Newspapers

Age (Melbourne) 11.1.1972; 27.12.1972; 17.5.1973; 16.7.1973; 31.12.1973.
Australian 2.10.1973.
Australian Financial Review 24.4.1973, 6.6.1973.
Daily Telegraph 21.11.1955; 17.7.1973.
Glen Innes Examiner 18.6.1973.
Sun (Sydney) 2.8.1966.
Sun-Herald 13.5.1971.
Sydney Morning Herald 18.5.1971, 13.11.1974; 6.1.1976.
Truth (Brisbane) 16.5.1971.

UNPUBLISHED SOURCES

Department of Immigration and Ethnic Affairs Library, Canberra

Commonwealth Immigration Advisory Council, *Minutes*

Australian Archives, Canberra

CA 51 (Department of Immigration)
A434/1   48/3/8061; 49/3/5831; 50/3/17477
A445/1   118/1/4; 118/1/9; 124/6/35; 140/5/6; 140/5/14; 140/5/20; 142/4/2; 142/5/2; 145/7/3; 146/1/1; 146/2/1; 146/3/3; 146/8/2; 146/8/14; 146/8/20; 146/9/8; 156/8/14; 185/12/12; 194/1/3; 194/1/5; 194/1/9; 194/2/1; 194/2/2; 194/2/3; 194/2/4; 197/1/2; 197/1/5; 197/1/9; 229/1/3; 276/1/9; 276/1/15; 276/2/4–7; 276/2/10; 276/2/13; 276/3/1; 276/3/2; 276/3/4.

A446/1   62/67118
A446/33   70/77176
A446/51   73/77724; 73/77800; 74/75801; 74/75925; 74/75962;
            77/76561
A446/52   72/95574; 73/75324; 73/75503; 73/75832; 72/78683;
            73/76724
A446/53   72/77371
A446/54   71/77025; 71/77633
A446/55   71/75347; 71/75443; 71/75621; 71/75761; 71/76150;
            71/76308; 72/77602
A446/63   70/78495; 70/78615
A446/64   69/72584; 70/75457
A446/65   69/70953; 69/72415; 71/75347
A446/71   68/71260; 68/71602; 68/71661; 68/71864; 68/71963
A446/77   67/72904
A446/78   67/71761; 67/71960; 67/72349
A446/85   66/46369
A446/86   66/45342–5; 66/45348
A446/91   65/45884; 65/46984; 66/45481
A446/92   65/45065
A446/96   64/45732
A446/101   63/45368; 63/45378; 63/45379; 63/45397; 63/45619;
            63/46695
A446/109   60/67616; 65/45065
A446/115   58/65701; 58/66807
A446/119   56/66624
A446/T31   75/76693; 75/78542; 75/78543; 75/78546; 75/78598;
            75/78609; 75/78616; 75/78721; 75/78785; 75/78786;
            75/78793; 75/78837; 75/78842; 75/78855; 75/78869;
            75/78895; 75/78903; 75/7904; 75/78905; 75/78908;
            75/78909; 75/79151; 75/79153; 75/79156; 75/79167;
            75/79169; 75/79197; 75/79198; 75/79199; 75/79201;
            75/79203; 75/79204; 75/79205; 75/79206; 75/79208;
            75/79209; 75/79222; 75/79223; 75/79286; 75/79291;
            75/79294; 75/79624; 75/79627; 75/79664; 75/79668;
            75/79669; 75/79674; 75/79675; 75/79686; 75/79688;
            75/79690; 75/79691; 75/79692; 75/79729; 75/79738;
            75/80866; 75/80969; 76/80838

Unpublished Papers

Calwell, Mary Elizabeth, Speech to the Australian Jewish Historical
    Society of Victoria, given to the author by Harold Grant, Canberra
Kiddle, W.G. 'The Grant-in-Aid scheme: an appreciation', draft paper,
    August 1981, given to the author by Conor Bradley, DIMA
Kiddle, George 'Post arrival services for migrants 1947–81' (copy available in DIMA library, Canberra)

Levi, Margaret and Sherman, Richard 'Designing institutions for economic development: what bureaucracies can do to promote cooperation and productivity', paper delivered at the compliance workshop, Urban Research Program, Research School of Social Sciences, July 1993

Zubrzycki, Jerzy 'The questing years', paper prepared at the invitation of the Minister for Immigration for the 1968 Citizenship Convention

Oral Sources

Anderson, Nancy, 1996 (Brisbane)
Charlesworth, Stephanie (née Armstrong), 1996 (Melbourne)
Flaherty, Stanley, 1996 (Canberra)
Griffin, Pauline, 1996 (ANU Canberra)
Houston, James, 1996 (Melbourne)
Kyburz, Andrew, 1993–94 (DIMA Canberra)
Lyons, Sylvia, 1996 (Sydney)
Marshman, Arthur, 1996 (ECC Brisbane)
Price, Charles, 1992 (ANU Canberra)
Pridannikoff, George, 1996 (DIMA Brisbane)
Rice, Peter, 1996 (Eden, NSW)
Sebesfi, Nora (née Brack), 1996 (Sydney)
Tarbath, John, 1996 (Canberra)
Watson, G.C., 1992 (Canberra)

INDEX

Aborigines, 3, 15–16, 228, 236
Aliens Act 1947, 89, 184–5, 228
Anderson, C.G., 57
Anderson, K.M., 192
Anderson, Nancy, 136, 156–7
ANZ Bank, migrant services, 129, 130, 154
Armstrong, R.E., 119, 222, 231
assimilation, 3, 34, 149–50, 152–3, 174, 248; *see also* integration
Australian Assistance Plan, 231–3
Australian Broadcasting Commission, 100–1, 230
Australian Citizenship Act 1984, 194; *see also* Nationality and Citizenship Act 1948
Australian Council for Overseas Aid, 131
Australian Council of Social Services, 131, 140–1, 142, 150, 164
Australian Council of Trade Unions, 53
Australian Institute of Multicultural Affairs, 162

Bach, Robert, 27
Bailly Report, 167, 240

Bean, C.E.W., 234
Beazley, Kim, 120
Benn, A.M., 81
Blainey, Geoffrey, 235
Bland, H.A., 80
Boland, Cathy, 28
Borrie, W.D., 1, 164, 246
Bosworth, Richard, 24
Bott, L.F., 240
Bowen, Lionel, 236
Bowen, N.H., 203
Brack, Nora, 35, 37, 41, 43
Branson, G.H., 181
British migrants
   discrimination favouring, 7, 10, 56, 81, 160, 188, 191–3, 194–5, 198, 228
   intake of, 10, 150, 243
   rural workers, 81
Bruce, H.A., 48, 57
Bryant, Gordon, 117, 199, 200
Bureau of Immigration and Population Research, 28
Burnside Homes, 64
Buttfield, Dame Nancy, 83, 105, 179, 199, 201

Cairns, Jim, 56, 116, 198

Calwell, Arthur, 2, 8, 34, 98, 172, 210, 221, 227, 234, 243, 247, 248
Cameron, Clyde, 224, 235, 238
Cannon, Michael, 235
Castles, Stephen, 26–7
Cavenagh, J.L., 198, 201
Charles, Ted, 136, 214
Charlesworth, Stephanie (Armstrong), 34, 35, 36, 37, 40, 45, 47, 248
Chifley, J.B., 9,
Child Welfare Department, 65
Chou, T.H., 214
citizenship
   Aborigines, 3, 15
   advertisements by intending applicants, 177
   applications for, 107, 175–6, 180–1, 182–3, 186, 193–4
   'bargain', 189–208
   Declaration of Intention to Apply for, 177
   deprivation of, 201–3
   education on, 233
   ethnic press on, 180
   fees for, 177
   incentives to apply, 186, 244
   invitation letters, 182–3
   legislation, 2, 171
   meaning of, 171–3, 192–4, 244–5
   non-Europeans, 3
   oath of allegiance, 179–80, 244
   promotion of, 170–88
   refusal of, 107
      on character grounds, 201
      on language grounds, 199
      on political grounds, 198–201
   renunciation of former allegiance, 178–80, 244
Citizenship Conventions, 10, 18, 44, 68, 82, 99, 103, 110, 123, 133, 149, 152, 153, 172, 177, 179, 185
Cleaver, Richard, 178
Coleman, Marie, 231, 232
Collins, Jock, 25
Colombo Plan, 16
Committee on Overseas Professional Qualifications, 142, 245
Commonwealth Bank, migrant services, 128, 129, 130, 154
Commonwealth Employment Service, 36, 38, 46, 61–2, 65, 90–1, 113
Commonwealth Hostels Ltd, 43, 45, 69
compliance
   non-compliant migrants, 6–8, 60–72, 89, 143–4, 184–5
   theory, 5
conscription, 15, 175, 185, 224, 243; see also Vietnam
Constitution, Australian
   on Aborigines, 3, 15
   on citizenship, 2
   on immigration, 2
Costa, Dominic, 97, 106
Costanzo, Dr, 184
Country Women's Association, 87, 102
Coutts, W. C., 48, 57
Cox, David, 23–4, 28
Crimes Act, 195, 202, 203, 228
Cuddihy, G.T., 85–7, 90, 92
Curtin, John, 9

Daly, F.M., 179, 185, 221, 222, 296
Daniels, Laurie, 239
Darling, J.R., 103, 104, 183–4
Davidson, G. S., 179
De Lemos, M., 118–19
Dempsey, John, 157
departures, 205–7
deportation, 77, 91, 196; see also repatriation
Dickson, Linda, 70–1
dictation test, 195, 209
Dobson, Hazel, 33, 34, 35, 38, 60, 66, 67, 76, 85, 150, 151
Downer, Alexander, 14, 56, 77,

151–2, 181, 183, 192, 199, 202, 210, 247
Drury, E.N., 206
Dunin-Karwicki, J., 184
Dunstan, Don, 221, 222
Duthie, D.W., 206

Eckersley, T.W., 235
Education, Commonwealth Department of, 69, 98–9, 100, 119, 245
Education, State Departments of, 99, 103, 105, 111, 115, 245
Edvi-Illes, S., 127
Electoral Act, 228
Else-Mitchell, Ray, 131
Encel, Sol, 162
Enderby, K., 203, 221
Ethnic Community Councils, 233
ethnic radio and television, 229–30
European Economic Community, 7, 15, 190–1, 201–4, 207

Fitzgerald, J.F., 178, 179, 185, 198–9
Forbes, A.J., 75, 119, 221, 222, 234, 238
Francis, Sir Josiah, 191
Fraser, Allan, 50
Fraser, Malcolm, 119
Full Employment in Australia, White Paper, 9
Funnell, W., 62

Galbally Report, 30, 114, 159, 162, 167–8
Georges, George, 201
Germans, 80
　assisted, 56
　ICEM-sponsored, 13
　refugees, 11, 12,
　scientists, 10–11,
　Special Project Workers, 12–13, 91–3
Good Neighbour Movement (Councils), 10, 18, 35, 40, 66, 80, 85, 87, 90, 91, 102, 114, 130, 132, 145, 153, 156, 158, 159, 160, 177, 180, 184, 186, 198, 229, 232, 241, 246, 247
　cost of, 158, 167
　decline of, 165–70
Grant, Bruce, 212–13
Grant, Harold, 13
Grants-in-Aid, 17
Grassby, A.J., 19, 83, 138, 141–2, 193, 203, 221, 223, 224, 227, 228, 230, 233, 235–7, 238
Greeks, 20, 49–52, 56, 201
Greenwood, Gordon, 135, 137
Griffin, Pauline, 34, 35, 36, 37, 38, 39, 40, 41, 101, 110
Grimblat, Dr, 143–4

Harrison, Sir Eric, 191
Hayden, W.G., 232
Haylen, Leslie, 78, 97, 150, 192
Henderson, Ronald, 112, 118
Henty, N.H., 179
Heydon, Peter, 17, 209, 212–13, 214, 215, 216, 217, 218, 220, 221, 227–8, 233, 234
Heyes, Tasman, 34, 53–6, 68, 80, 104, 172, 175, 194, 195, 209, 212, 233
Holt, Harold, 12, 14, 51, 54, 55–6, 65, 82, 85, 99, 115, 117, 124, 172, 181, 196, 210, 215, 217, 234
Hospital Employees Association, 39
Houston, James, 162–3
Hulme, A.S., 57
Hunter, G.N., 38, 39, 40

Immigration, Commonwealth Department of
　Adult Migrant Education Scheme, 96–115, 116
　accelerated classes, 109
　advanced English, 110
　classes, 99–100, 104
　continuation classes, 107–8

correspondence lessons, 100, 103, 105, 114, 194
home tutors, 102
intensive classes, 108–9
pre-embarkation and shipboard lessons, 101–2
radio broadcasts 100–1
television programs, 101
workplace English, 110–12
Aliens Assimilation Division, 34
Child migrant language training, intervention in, 115–121
Commonwealth Migration Officers, 34, 62, 176
culture of, 4, 8, 17, 31–2, 165, 168–9, 171, 173, 193, 237, 246
dismemberment of, 19–20, 145, 238
establishment of, 2
ethnic groups directory, 150–1, 164–5
functions of, 2, 4, 6, 230
Grants-in-Aid, 153, 156–60, 161, 245–6, 247
history planned, 233–235
Holding Centres, 10, 37, 43, 44, 47, 60–72, 93
 Benalla, 65, 67, 70
 child minding centres in, 65, 68, 69–71
 Cowra, 64, 176
 Cunderin, 66, 67–8
 Greta, 43, 71
 Scheyville, 149
Integration and Education Section, 153, 155–6
Integration Branch, 197
interpreting services, 35–6, 90, 124–6, 135, 153
'national groups', attitude to, 148–50
National Groups Liaison Unit, 18, 162–4, 246
Public Relations Section, 42
Reception Centres, 13
 Bathurst, 43, 150
 Bonegilla, 13, 41, 43, 51, 52, 64, 65, 66, 106
refugees, response to, 11–12, 98
Social Welfare Section, 11, 31–48, 74–80, 141–2, 160–2
Survey Section, 135, 154–5, 186–7
Telephone Interpreting Service, 30, 136–9, 143, 145, 153, 247
translating service, 128–30, 134, 135, 145, 153
work contract, 13
Immigration Advisory Council, 9, 42, 53, 54, 56, 68, 77, 78, 98, 99, 102, 103, 104, 105, 112, 113, 121, 139–40, 141, 144, 166, 172, 179, 197, 206, 229
Immigration and Ethnic Affairs, Commonwealth Department of, 240
Immigration (Education) Act 1971, 118–19, 187–8, 241
Immigration (Guardianship of Children) Act 1956, 239
Immigration Planning Council, 9, 53, 62–3, 84, 133, 164
Immigration Publicity Council, 183–4
integration, 152–4
Intergovernmental Committee for European Migration, 13, 47, 51, 84, 101, 102
International Refugee Organisation, 10, 89, 101
Italians, 52–58, 83, 97, 197–8, 201, 204

Jago, F.H., 131, 132
Jakubowicz, Andrew, 25–6, 28
Jamrozik, Adam, 28
Japanese, 210
Jenkins, H.A., 236
Jewish refugees, 10
Jones, Keith, 179
Jupp, James, 21, 26, 27, 28, 57, 152, 156

INDEX 305

Keary, Madeline, 74, 75–6
Kennelly, Patrick, 190
Keogh, L.H., 234, 235
Kiddle, George, 30, 152, 153, 162, 222
Klugman, R.E., 187, 203
Korean War, 13
Krumm, F.G., 42
Kunz, Egon, 29

Labor and Immigration, Commonwealth Department of, 145, 238–9
Labour and National Service, Commonwealth Department of
  migrant hostels, 32, 43, 45, 47, 61, 62, 80, 84, 245
    child-minding centres in, 68–9
    Gawler, 63
    Woodside, 63, 64–5
  migration role defined, 3
Lack, John, 29–30
Lambros, Dimitri, 52
Lawrence, William, 96, 179
Leschen, Olga, 42, 68, 70
Levi, Margaret, 8
Lewins, Frank, 26
Lindsay Thompson, Stephanie, 127–8
Lippmann, Walter, 133
Lukomskyj, Oleh, 28
Lynch, Phillip, 165, 234
Lyons, Sylvia, 34, 36, 37, 38, 39, 43

McClelland, James, 107, 198
McEwan, Sir John, 191, 215
McGinness, H., 177, 220, 314
McKellar, Michael, 240
McMahon, William, 112
McManus, F.P., 201
Maltese, 49, 205, 207
Marshman, Arthur, 111
Martin, Jean, 1, 2, 21–3, 28, 164
Matherson, Alan, 137

Mental Health of Migrants Committee, 130–1
mental hospitals, 74
  Broughton Hall, 76
  Callan Park, 74, 75
  Gladesville, 75
  Parramatta, 75
Menzies, R.G., 214, 215, 216, 217
migrants
  assisted, 19, 226
  health and character checking of, 77, 194–5, 198
  mentally ill, 73–80, 91, 132–3, 196, 197, 198
  rural, 80–94
  women, 46–8, 60–72, 101, 102, 106, 109, 112
Migration Act 1958, 2, 6, 77, 195, 196, 228
Monk, Albert, 53, 54
Moore, Mr Justice, 142–3
multicultural Australia, 225, 227, 248
Mulvihill, J.A., 131–2, 137
Murphy, L.K., 192, 203
museum of migration, proposed, 235–8
Myers, D.M., 142

National Accreditation Authority for Translators and Interpreters, 142
National Commission on Social Welfare, 231–2
National Council of Women, 42
National Health and Medical Research Council, 8
National Population Inquiry, 1
Nationality and Citizenship Act 1948, 2, 6, 171, 172, 180, 191–3, 202; see also Australian Citizenship Act
National Service Act, 15–16, 18
Neagle, J.C., 53, 54
Norris, Ada, 42, 54, 55, 103

O'Byrne, J.H., 179